Great Moments
In
Army Football

From the beginning of Football all the way to Army's 2017 team

This book is written for those of us who love the West Point Academy and especially Army's Black Knights Football Team. You'll like all the stories from the Academy's founding in 1820 just under 200 years ago, to the beginning of American football to the beginning of the Army football program in 1890... and all through the great Army teams of the mid-20th century to today with a revitalized Army Football Team under coach Jeff Monken.

You will learn that like no other football team, the US Army Cadets are fierce and passionate competitors. From the stadium to the classroom to the research lab, the US Army Black Knights always play to win.

You will learn that Army's first official football game was in 1890 even before American football had been completely defined. They lost against Navy, 0-24 and never forgot it. Army made up for that game many times over the years.

You'll also learn why the immortal Dennis Michie can easily be captioned as the father of Army Football and it is not just because he did such a great job positioning the team for future greatness. He not only coached the first team in 1890, he was the team captain. Today the Stadium's name is in his honor.

From here, the book moves you one Army coach at time through the immortals—Charles Daly, Biff Jones, Ralph Sasse, and Earl "Red" Blaik. And then, on the way to today, we stop for other fine coaches such as Bob Sutton and Jim Young. Army has had many great seasons, great coaches, and a ton of great players.

The history of Army Football as told here is just fascinating. This book captures the many great moments and the contributions of each of the 37coaches and standout players such as Army's three Heisman winners, the immortal Felix "Doc" Blanchard, Pete Dawkins, and of course Glenn Davis. In this book, we look at every game in every season and we take the reader through great chapters about all the Army teams with great stories and accounts of 127 seasons worth of great games (1222 games) with many great moments.

This book is your finest source for a great read on your favorite service academy college football team. (Cadets / Black Knights). It is the closest thing to an all-encompassing, full-blown encyclopedia of Army Football—a blow by blow history—with tales of the great moments. We capture all the action and all the memorable moments of Army football. This book is for your reading pleasure but it also can be a great reference tool for when you want to see how a particular Army game in any year happened to turn out.

If you are an Army Football fan. you will not want to put this book down.

Brian Kelly

LETS GO PUBLISH

Copyright © August 2017, Brian W. Kelly
Title: Great Moments in Army Football

Editor: Brian P. Kelly
Author Brian W. Kelly

All rights reserved: No part of this book may be reproduced or transmitted in any form, or by any means, electronic or mechanical, including photocopying, recording, scanning, faxing, or by any information storage and retrieval system, without permission from the publisher, LETS GO PUBLISH, in writing.

Disclaimer: Though judicious care was taken throughout the writing and the publication of this work that the information contained herein is accurate, there is no expressed or implied warranty that all information in this book is 100% correct. Therefore, neither LETS GO PUBLISH, nor the author accepts liability for any use of this work.

Trademarks: A number of products and names referenced in this book are trade names and trademarks of their respective companies.

Referenced Material: *Standard Disclaimer: The information in this book has been obtained through personal and third-party observations, interviews, and copious research. Where unique information has been provided, or extracted from other sources, those sources are acknowledged within the text of the book itself or in the References area in the front matter. Thus, there are no formal footnotes nor is there a bibliography section. Any picture that does not have a source was taken from various sites on the Internet with no credit attached. If resource owners would like credit in the next printing, please email publisher.*

Published by: ....LETS GO PUBLISH!
Editor in Chief ....Brian P. Kelly
Email: ....info@letsgopublish.com
Web site ....www.letsgopublish.com

Library of Congress Copyright Information Pending
Book Cover Design by Michele Thomas
Editor—Brian P. Kelly

ISBN Information: The International Standard Book Number (ISBN) is a unique machine-readable identification number, which marks any book unmistakably. The ISBN is the clear standard in the book industry. 159 countries and territories are officially ISBN members. The Official ISBN for this book is

978-1-947402-04-1

The price for this work is:.......... $ 19.95 USD

10   9   8   7   6   5   4   3   2   1

Army Football seasons by Year/Coach.

Army Coach	Year	Wins	Losses	Ties
Dennis Michie & he was captain	1890	0	1	0
Henry Williams (4-1-1)	1891	4	1	1
Dennis Michie (3-1-1)	1892	3	1	1
Laurie Bliss (4-5)	1893	4	5	0
Harmon Graves (3-2)	1894	3	2	0
Harmon Graves (5-2)	1895	5	2	0
George Dyer (3-2-1)	1896	3	2	1
Herman Koehler (6-1-1)	1897	6	1	1
Herman Koehler (3-2-1)	1898	3	2	1
Herman Koehler (4-5)	1899	4	5	0
Herman Koehler (7-3-1)	1900	7	3	1
Leon Kromer (5-1-2)	1901	5	1	2
Dennis Nolan (6-1-1)	1902	6	1	1
Edward King (6-2-1)	1903	6	2	1
Robert Boyers (7-2)	1904	7	2	0
Robert Boyers (4-4-1)	1905	4	4	1
Ernest Graves (2-5-1), Henry Smither (1-0)	1906	3	5	1
Henry Smither (6-2-1)	1907	6	2	1
Harry Nelly (6-1-2)	1908	6	1	2
Harry Nelly (3-2)	1909	3	2	0
Harry Nelly (6-2)	1910	6	2	0
Joseph Beacham (6-1-1)	1911	6	1	1
Ernest Graves (5-3)	1912	5	3	0
Charles Daly (8-1)	1913	8	1	0
Charles Daly (9-0)	1914	9	0	0
Charles Daly (5-3-1)	1915	5	3	1
Charles Daly (9-0)	1916	9	0	0
Geoffrey Keyes (7-1)	1917	7	1	0
Hugh Mitchell (1-0-0)	1918	1	0	0
Charles Daly (6-3)	1919	6	3	0
Charles Daly (7-2-0)	1920	7	2	0
Charles Daly (6-4-0)	1921	6	4	0
Charles Daly (8-0-2)	1922	8	0	2

Coach (Record)	Year	W	L	T
John McEwan (6-2-1)	1923	6	2	1
John McEwan (5-1-2)	1924	5	1	2
John McEwan (7-2)	1925	7	2	0
Biff Jones (7-1-1)	1926	7	1	1
Biff Jones (9-1)	1927	9	1	0
Biff Jones (8-2)	1928	8	2	0
Biff Jones (6-4-1)	1929	6	4	1
Ralph Sasse (9-1-1)	1930	9	1	1
Ralph Sasse (8-2-1)	1931	8	2	1
Ralph Sasse (8-2-0)	1932	8	2	0
Gar Davidson (9-1)	1933	9	1	0
Gar Davidson (7-3)	1934	7	3	0
Gar Davidson (6-2-1)	1935	6	2	1
Gar Davidson (6-3)	1936	6	3	0
Gar Davidson (7-2)	1937	7	2	0
William Wood (8-2)	1938	8	2	0
William Wood (3-4-2)	1939	3	4	2
William Wood (1-7-1)	1940	1	7	1
Red Blaik (5-3-1)	1941	5	3	1
Red Blaik (6-3)	1942	6	3	0
Red Blaik (7-2-1)	1943	7	2	1
Red Blaik (9-0)	1944	9	0	0
Red Blaik (9-0)	1945	9	0	0
Red Blaik (9-0-1)	1946	9	0	1
Red Blaik (5-2-2)	1947	5	2	2
Red Blaik (8-0-1)	1948	8	0	1
Red Blaik (9-0)	1949	9	0	0
Red Blaik (8-1)	1950	8	1	0
Red Blaik (2-7)	1951	2	7	0
Red Blaik (4-4-1)	1952	4	4	1
Red Blaik (7-1-1)	1953	7	1	1
Red Blaik (7-2)	1954	7	2	0
Red Blaik (6-3)	1955	6	3	0
Red Blaik (5-3-1)	1956	5	3	1
Red Blaik (7-2)	1957	7	2	0
Red Blaik (8-0-1)	1958	8	0	1
Dale Hall (4-4-1)	1959	4	4	1
Dale Hall (6-3-1)	1960	6	3	1
Dale Hall (6-4)	1961	6	4	0
Paul Dietzel (6-4)	1962	6	4	0

Coach (Record)	Year	W	L	T
Paul Dietzel (7-3)	1963	7	3	0
Paul Dietzel (4-6)	1964	4	6	0
Paul Dietzel (4-5-1)	1965	4	5	1
Thomas Cahill (8-2)	1966	8	2	0
Thomas Cahill (8-2)	1967	8	2	0
Thomas Cahill (7-3)	1968	7	3	0
Thomas Cahill (4-5-1)	1969	4	5	1
Thomas Cahill (1-9-1)	1970	1	9	1
Thomas Cahill (6-4)	1971	6	4	0
Thomas Cahill (6-4)	1972	6	4	0
Thomas Cahill (0-10)	1973	0	10	0
Homer Smith (3-8)	1974	3	8	0
Homer Smith (2-9)	1975	2	9	0
Homer Smith (5-6)	1976	5	6	0
Homer Smith (7-4)	1977	7	4	0
Homer Smith (4-6-1)	1978	4	6	1
Lou Saban (2-8-1)	1979	2	8	1
Ed Cavanaugh (3-7-1)	1980	3	7	1
Ed Cavanaugh (3-7-1)	1981	3	7	1
Ed Cavanaugh (4-7)	1982	4	7	0
Jim Young (2-9)	1983	2	9	0
Jim Young (8-3-1)	1984	8	3	1
Jim Young (9-3)	1985	9	3	0
Jim Young (6-5)	1986	6	5	0
Jim Young (5-6)	1987	5	6	0
Jim Young (9-3)	1988	9	3	0
Jim Young (6-5)	1989	6	5	0
Jim Young (6-5)	1990	6	5	0
Bob Sutton (4-7)	1991	4	7	0
Bob Sutton (5-6)	1992	5	6	0
Bob Sutton (6-5)	1993	6	5	0
Bob Sutton (4-7)	1994	4	7	0
Bob Sutton (5-5-1)	1995	5	5	1
Bob Sutton (10-2)	1996	10	2	0
Bob Sutton (4-7)	1997	4	7	0
Bob Sutton (3-8)	1998	3	8	0
Bob Sutton (3-8)	1999	3	8	0
Todd Berry (1-10)	2000	1	10	0
Todd Berry (3-8)	2001	3	8	0
Todd Berry (1-11)	2002	1	11	0

Coach (Record)	Year	W	L	T
John Mumford (0-7), Todd Berry (0-6)	2003	0	13	0
Bobby Ross (2-9)	2004	2	9	0
Bobby Ross (4-7)	2005	4	7	0
Bobby Ross (3-9)	2006	3	9	0
Stan Brock (3-9)	2007	3	9	0
Stan Brock (3-9)	2008	3	9	0
Rich Ellerson (5-7)	2009	5	7	0
Rich Ellerson (7-6)	2010	7	6	0
Rich Ellerson (3-9)	2011	3	9	0
Rich Ellerson (2-10)	2012	2	10	0
Rich Ellerson (3-9)	2013	3	9	0
Jeff Monken (4-8)	2014	4	8	0
Jeff Monken (2-10)	2015	2	10	0
Jeff Monken (8-5)	2016	8	5	0
Jeff Monken (8-5)	2017	0	0	0

Army almost always played as an independent Team. However, from 1998 to 2004, the team competed in a fledgling conference known as Conference USA, the Black Knights went back to Independent Status in 2005.

Total Games 1,222
Seasons 127
Total Wins 663
Total Losses 508
Total Ties 51   * Prior to Overtime Rules
Stats from 1890 Through August 2017

Acknowledgments:

I appreciate all the help that I received in putting this book together, along with the 121 other books from the past.

My printed acknowledgments were once so large that book readers needed to navigate too many pages to get to page one of the text. To permit me more flexibility, I put my acknowledgment list online at www.letsgopublish.com. The list of acknowledgments continues to grow. Believe it or not, it once cost about a dollar more to print each book.

Thank you all on the big list in the sky and God bless you all for your help.

Please check out www.letsgopublish.com to read the latest version of my heartfelt acknowledgments updated for this book. Thank you all!

In this book, I received some extra special help from many avid football friends including Dennis Grimes, Gerry Rodski, Wily Ky Eyely, Angel Brent Evans, Angel Irene McKeown Kelly, Angel Edward Joseph Kelly Sr., Angel Edward Joseph Kelly Jr., Ann Flannery, Angel James Flannery Sr., Mary Daniels, Bill Daniels, Robert Garry Daniels, Angel Sarah Janice Daniels, Angel Punkie Daniels, Joe Kelly and Diane Kelly.

References

I learned how to write creatively in Grade School at St. Boniface. I even enjoyed reading some of my own stuff as a toddler.

At Meyers High School and King's College and Wilkes-University, I learned how to research, write bibliographies and footnote every non-original thought I might have had. I learned to hate ibid, and op. cit., and I hated assuring that I had all citations written down in the proper sequence. Having to pay attention to details took my desire to write creatively and diminished it with busy work.

I know it is necessary for the world to stop plagiarism so authors and publishers can get paid properly, but for an honest writer, it sure is annoying. I wrote many proposals while with IBM and whenever I needed to cite something, I cited it in place, because my readers, IT Managers, could care less about tracing the vagaries of citations and their varied formats.

I always hated to use stilted footnotes, or produce a lengthy, perfectly formatted bibliography. I bet most bibliographies are flawed because even the experts on such drivel do not like the tedium.

I wrote 120 books before this book and several hundred articles published by many magazines and newspapers and I only cite when an idea is not mine or when I am quoting, and again, I choose to cite in place, and the reader does not have to trace strange numbers through strange footnotes and back to bibliography elements that may not be readily accessible or available. Academicians knowing all the rules of citation are not my audience. In this book, if you are a lover of Army West Point football, you are my intended group of readers

Yet, I would be kidding you, if in a book about the Great Moments in Army Football, I tried to bluff my way into trying to make you think that I knew everything before I began to write anything in this book. I spent as much time researching as writing. I might even call myself an expert of sorts now about the Army West Point Black Knights. This team literally is America's team. Everybody in America has at one time watched and enjoyed Army football, especially when Army is having winning seasons, and more especially when Army is beating Navy.

Without any pain on your part you can read this book from cover to cover to enjoy the stories about the many Great Moments in Army Football.

It took me about two months to write this book. If I were to have made sure that a thought of mine was not a thought somebody else ever had, this book never would have been completed or the citations pages would more than likely exceed the prose. Everybody takes credit for everything in sports writing—at least that's what I have found.

I used Army Cadet and Black Night Season summaries and recaps from whatever source I could to get the scores of all the games. I verified facts when possible. There are many web sites that have great information and facts. Ironically most internet stories are the same exact stories. Who's got the original? While I was writing the book, I wrote down a bunch of Internet references and at one time, I listed them right here en masse in this article. They were the least read pages. No more. Unless I am citing a reference in a section of the book, you will not see the URL.

I have no favorite source for information to put in my books. However, I continually hunt for articles written by students to amplify the text I present.

While I was writing this book, because I was not sure that my citations within the text would be enough, and I was not producing a bibliography, I copied URLs into some of the book text in those cases in which I had read articles or had downloaded material and had brought articles or pieces of articles into this book. Hopefully, this will satisfy any request for additional citations. If there is anything which needs a specific citation, I would be pleased to change the text. Just contact me. Your stuff is your stuff.

Many of the facts in this book are also put forth in the Army Football Media Guide, freely available on the Internet. Our thanks for the use of this material for the accurate production of this book.

There is a great site about Army football where you can explore great pictures and great stories about the greatest. It is called "For what they gave on Saturday Afternoon."--
https://forwhattheygave.com
Here is one of the whole links describing the beginning of Army football: https://forwhattheygave.com/2013/08/17/1890-1908-army-navy-football/ Enjoy

Preface:

This book is all about the great moments in Army football over the years. Whether the team was playing as the Cadets, the Black Knights on the Hudson, or Army West Point, it never seemed to matter to the fans or the players. We have the football history right as we begin this book.

Since 1899, in the tenth year of Army football. Army's mascot has officially been a mule because of the animal's historical importance in military operations. For many years, Army's teams were known as the "Cadets." The academy's football team was nicknamed "The Black Knights of the Hudson" due to the black color of its uniforms. In 1999, Army adopted "Black Knights" as its official nickname in all sports. Based on the purpose, they may also use "Cadets" in certain circumstances.

The U.S. sports media like to use "Army" as a synonym for the academy, while in 2015, the academy itself declared their name to be "Army West Point." How this all sorts out over time, we'll all see. For this book, we use all the names.

Along the way to today, we study the founding of West Point Academy; then the preliminaries before Army football officially began, and then we delve right into the storied Army Football Program--its struggles; its greatness; and its long-lasting impact on American life. This takes us to the football careers of many great college football coaches and players from the Army team as it engaged tough competition over the years.

As a Pennsylvanian, I admit I wrote a similar book about Penn State Football but only after I had fulfilled the family Irish wish and had written about Notre Dame Football. But, I still recall as a kid with our Admiral Black and White TV, my dad calling us to order for the annual Army-Navy-Game, which was always enjoyable.

I picked Army as my next book because the Cadets have a long and bold tradition of playing great football. With many immortal coaches such as the great Red Blaik, and immortal players, especially the three Heisman winners, Doc Blanchard (1945), Glenn Davis (1946), and Pete Dawkins (1958). Army has four National Championships, 1914, 1944, 1945, 1946 and eight undefeated seasons. I have an honorable discharge from the Army and I am proud to write this book about such a storied institution and a great football program.

Supporters who love Army Football as played by Army West Point will read this book and get an immediate burst of emotions such as warmth and love for their favorite team. You will love this book because it has it all – every great season and every great game. Go Army West Point!

This book walks you through the whole Army football journey. We examine players, coaches, and successes from the early teams to today. This period began in 1890 with the first Army Navy Game. Like all new teams, you can imagine the struggle of playing on a college football team when getting the right equipment was one of the biggest issues.

The 37 great Army coaches are listed within the football seasons in which they coached--from season 1 in 1890 to season 127. In other words, the seasons are examined chronologically and the coaches and certain games and certain players are highlighted within the seasons in which the games were played. I sure hope you enjoy this unique approach.

Before Red Blaik put in an eighteen-year stint starting in 1941, few of Army's 24 coaches to that point took the team for more than a couple years. Yet, they still produced some powerful teams with powerful players. Of the 37 coaches in the Black Knights history, most had winning seasons as Army's overall record has 150 more wins than losses. That's a lot of winning for any football program.

Army is a long-time football power

One hundred twenty-eight years is a long time to be playing football. Army has a history of being recognized as one of the finest teams in the nation. For many years, the teams were ready to win a national championship at the drop of the next hat. Though it has been over seventy years since the last championship, Army is still tough and nobody can deny that. With a new coach who brought in a great team in 2016, would it not be great for Army, the major defenders of our Nation to bring home another football championship soon

Your author would like you to know that when football season closes in the second week of January each year, there is now a great football item—this book—that is available all 52 weeks of the year and in fact all 365 days each year. It does not rely on the stadium gates being open for you to get a great dose of Army Football. Just begin reading right here.

It is now available for you to add to your Army Football experience. and your book collection. Once you get this book, it is yours forever unless, of course you give it away to one of the many who will be in awe, and who will accept it gladly. For those who love to use gadgets to read, this book is also available on Kindle.

We open the book with the first story set shortly after the beginning of college football as a sport in America. It then moves on to the first official game with the first official coach and all the way to Coach Jeff Monken's great 2016 record. It tells a story about all the football seasons and the great coaches and great players and great moments from the first coached game in 1890 to today.

You are going to love this book because it is the perfect read for anybody who loves Army West Point's storied football program and wants to know more about the most revered athletes to have competed in one of the finest football programs of all time.

Few sports books are a must-read but Brian Kelly's <u>Great Moments in Army Football</u> will quickly appear at the top of Americas most enjoyable must-read books about sports. Enjoy!

Who is Brian W. Kelly?

Brian W. Kelly is one of the leading authors in America with this, his 122nd published book. Brian is an outspoken and eloquent expert on a variety of topics and he has also written several hundred articles on topics of interest to Americans.

Most of his early works involved high technology. Later, Brian wrote a number of patriotic books and most recently he has been writing human interest books such as <u>The Wine Diet</u> and <u>Thank you, IBM</u>. His books are always well received.

Brian's books are highlighted at <u>www.letsgopublish.com</u>. Quantities from 20 to 1000 can be made available from <u>www.letsgopublish.com.</u> You may see most of Brian's works by taking the following link <u>www.amazon.com/author/brianwkelly</u>.

The Best!

Sincerely,

Brian W. Kelly, Author
Brian P. Kelly, Editor in Chief
I am Brian Kelly's eldest son.

Table of Contents

Chapter 1   Introduction to Army West Point Football 1
Chapter 2   The Founding of the United States Military Academy 15
Chapter 3   The West Point Mission 29
Chapter 4   Historic Army West Point Fields & Stadiums 31
Chapter 5   The Evolution of Modern American Football 45
Chapter 6   Army Launches First Football Team 63
Chapter 7   Army Football Seasons from 1897-1907 77
Chapter 8   Coaches Nelly, Beacham, & Graves 1908-1912 113
Chapter 9   Coaches Daly, Keyes, Mitchell & Daly 1913-22 123
Chapter 10 Coaches McEwan, Jones, & Sasse 1923-1932 155
Chapter 11 Coaches Garrison Davidson & William Wood, 1933-40 .. 187
Chapter 12 Coach Red Blaik 1941 - 1958 205
Chapter 13 Coaches Hall & Dietzel 1959-1965 257
Chapter 14 Coaches Tom Cahill & Homer Smith 1966-1978 273
Chapter 15 Coaches Saban, Cavanaugh & Young 1979 - 1989 297
Chapter 16 Coaches Bob Sutton & Todd Berry 1991-2002 321
Chapter 17 Coaches Mumford, Ross, Brock, & Ellerson 2003 – 13 .. 341
Chapter 18 Coach Jeff Monken 2014-2016 363
Chapter 19 Coach Jeff Monken 2017- 381
Chapter 20 The Army, Notre Dame Football Rivalry Part I of II 385
Chapter 21 Army-Notre Dame Rivalry Part II of II 399
Chapter 22 History of the Army-Navy Game by Mandy Howard etc.. 417
LETS GO PUBLISH! Books by Brian Kelly 426

About the Author

Brian Kelly retired as an Assistant Professor in the Business Information Technology (BIT) Program at Marywood University, where he also served as the IBM i and Midrange Systems Technical Advisor to the IT Faculty. Kelly designed, developed, and taught many college and professional courses. He continues as a contributing technical editor to a number of technical industry magazines, including "The Four Hundred" and "Four Hundred Guru," published by IT Jungle.

Kelly is a former IBM Senior Systems Engineer. His specialty was problem solving for customers as well as implementing advanced operating systems and software on his client's machines. Brian was a certified Army Instructor before retiring. He is the author of 122 books and hundreds of magazine articles. He has been a frequent speaker at technical conferences throughout the United States.

Brian was a candidate for the US Congress from Pennsylvania in 2010 and he ran for Mayor in his home town in 2015. He loves Army Football and can't wait to see the Black Nights top last year's fine record. God bless the Army West Point Cadets!!

Chapter 1 Introduction to Army West Point Football

Army's 128th Year in 2017!

Coach Monken With the Army Team Ready for the Game

The Army West Point Black Knights football team represents the United States Military Academy in college football. Army is currently a Division I Football Bowl Subdivision (FBS) member of the NCAA. The Black Knights currently play their home games in West Point, New York at Michie Stadium, with a capacity of 38,000. Army is currently coached by Jeff Monken, who is in his 4th season as head coach. Army is a four-time national champion, winning the title in 1914, 1944, 1945, and 1946. You'll hear that a lot in this book. Army has also has a total of eight undefeated seasons.

With the exception of seven seasons (1998–2004) where the team was a member of Conference USA, the Army team has competed as an independent. That means that, like Notre Dame, they have no affiliation with any conference. Currently, Army is one of four schools in the FBS that does not belong to any conference; the other three being BYU, Notre Dame, and UMass. However, all four of these schools belong to conferences for all other sports. Army is primarily a member of the Patriot League, BYU is a member of the West Coast Conference, Notre Dame belongs to the Atlantic Coast Conference, and UMass belongs to the Atlantic 10 Conference.

The Army West Point Black Knights have fielded a team every season since the inaugural 1890 season. That's a lot of football games. To be exact, it's 1,222 games in its 127 seasons, with 2017 as # 128… and the Black Knights have a fine all-time record of 663 wins, 508 losses, and 51 ties. That's a lot of great Army football folks.

Officially the Army West Point Cadets recognize a long and great football history that dates back to 1890. If you are from Navy or Air Force or some other rival school, you have to be kind. Such rivals know that Army was born great and then got greater when the immortal Earl "Red" Blaik coached from 1941 – 1958, Before Blaik, out of fifty-one prior years, Army had just four losing seasons. None of the four were worse than one more loss than win.

As noted, Red Blaik did not make Army a great team. They were already great. But, Blaik made the team even greater finishing with seventeen great winning seasons and just one losing season in 1951. He compiled a career college football record of 166–48–14. His Army football teams won three consecutive national championships in 1944, 1945 and 1946, and he was always near the top when not at the top. As good a Blaik was, as noted Army had always been good even before he came to coach. The Cadets had a great record of 293—107—28 pre-Blaik

After Blaik, the Army squad was never quite as crisp but it was not until about 1970 when for an unexplained reason, the team was expected to lose more than win. From Blaik to 1969, the team record was not so bad but not as good percentage wise. The record for this period was 64-41-4. Something happened to the team after 1970. Nobody can explain it well. From 1970 through 2016, Army had just ten winning seasons with an overall record of 195-332-7.

In 1996 Coach Bob Sutton broke out of the mold and coached the Cadets to a fantastic 10-2 record. It was tough going after Sutton was fired for unexplained reasons. He is held in high regard by most and with the trouble Army has had over the recent years in winning, there have been many calls for his return.

I do not mean to suggest that Bob Sutton did not have his critics because Army alums, like most, are a fickle bunch. But Sutton did two things that none of the three permanent coaches following him has been able to do: He beat Navy on a regular basis, going 6-3 with five straight wins over the Midshipmen. And he gave Army a chance almost every single game of his career regardless of the opponent. That is a lot to say. From Sutton on, life really got tough for Army

So, now with just one winning season in between Sutton and four-year coach Jeff Monken's 8-5 winning season in 2016, we all hope for big things from Army. My analysis is Army is moving forward. The Army West Point Black Knights are ready to win again and losing is no longer an option.

Some are joking after the fantastic 2016 Army victory over Navy that the new Army goal is to out-Navy, Navy. For the moment, that mission has been accomplished.

It's been long coming with just one winning season and one bowl run from 1997 to 2015, and a huge losing streak to Navy along the way, 2016 was the season that the Jeff Monken coaching era needed to kick in. It needed to come when there was a sign that Army football could potentially be decent, and it came up with something even worthy of deep praise. Is Army back? Let's say "yes," to that.

As an independent all of its years, the schedule had been set up to be relatively favorable – with a slew of lightweights and two FCSers mixed in along with some real tough games such as Notre Dame, Air Force, and low-end Power Fivers Duke and Wake Forest.

In his prior years with Army, the ground game always worked under Monken. The 2014 Army team finished fifth in the nation in rushing, and the 2015 team was 12th – both teams, however overall were awful and they posted awful records.

In 2016, something different was in the air. The players had been in place awhile and they did not just average 340 yards per game and finish second in the country, but they actually took over games and went on long, sustained marches. They began to win. There is something contagious about the glorious feeling of winning football games.

It took Monken a few years to find the right pieces on defense and to build up the depth. It all came together. The linebacking corps was inspired and performed stellar. The pass rush was better than it's been in for long, long time, and the young talent in the secondary got beyond their experience and rose up for the nation's sixth-best pass defense. Not too shabby!

Oh yeah, did I mention that Army was invited and went to a bowl game, and they won it.

And the Black Knights came up with an alumni-pleasing big victory over Navy in 2016.

For a program that's been known for trying hard and gaining little more than "try-hard misery" for years and years and years, this season was very important. This coach and this group of football players needed to prove that it is possible to keep winning football games at Army. They did exactly that in 2016.

The rushing team is back again and that is good news for Army and Army fans. Everyone who gained a meaningful rushing yard is back in 2017 behind a fine line that returns four starters. The quarterback situation is deep, experienced and talented, and the receiving corps has some experience but with a leading rushing unit, pressure won't be on the receivers. Their bar is set at just catching an occasional pass, which they ought to do quite handily.

Not everything is perfect as the defense has to replace irreplaceable linebackers Jeremy Timpf and Andrew King, but 11 of the top 14 tacklers return with – and this was what was missing in the past – enough depth to rotate in and keep everyone fresh. If the pass rush is almost as strong, and the young defensive backs that were so good early on can shine again, at the very least, there won't be a massive drop-off. Army is ready for a repeat and even a better performance than 2016. It is a great thought.

2016 cannot go down as a *one-of* or as they like to say in today's parlance, <u>a one-off</u>. Monken is too good for that. The team is too good for that. There are too many strong pieces in place, and – Ohio State game aside – a schedule that most Power Fivers would groove into a nine-win campaign. The message to fans is "Go ahead and get excited for what Army football is becoming."

And of course, it goes without saying that if Army really wants to become the new Navy (at least in terms of its record), that takes just one thing – Go ahead army and beat Navy! Yeah!

This book that you are reading celebrates The United States Military Academy USMA; its founding; its struggles; its greatness; and its long-lasting impact on freedom and American life. People like me, who love Army, will love this book. Army haters, such as those from the Naval Academy will want their own copy just for additional ammo. Yet, it won't help them! Hah!

We begin the rest of the Army football story in Chapter 2 with the founding of USMA West Point over 214 years ago and we continue in subsequent chapters, right into the founding of the full Army West Point football program in 1890 after the Cadets had been begging the argument by exercising playing American football on the campus in an intramural fashion.

The first nighttime football game was played in Mansfield, Pennsylvania on September 28, 1892 between Mansfield State Normal and Wyoming Seminary and ended at halftime in a 0–0 tie. The Army-Navy game of 1893 saw the first documented use of a football helmet by a player in a game. Joseph M. Reeves had a crude leather helmet made by a shoemaker in Annapolis and wore it in the game after being warned by his doctor that he risked death if he continued to play football after suffering an earlier kick to the head.

Football is a great contagion. Rather than not play, Reeves figured out a way to protect his head. Over the years, more injury-preventive devices were created and used by players and teams. Improvements are made every day.

In defining the format of the book, we chose to use a timetable that is based on a historical chronology. Within this framework, we discuss the great moments in Army football history, and there are many great moments. No book can claim to be able to capture them all, as it would be a never-ending story, but we sure do try.

The U. S. Military Academy has produced 3 Heisman Trophy winners

We have already discussed Army's new rise to national football prominence with a great showing in 2016. While the United States Military Academy has slipped from its one-time lofty status as one of college football's top programs, there's no denying the successful past of Army football that produced national championship football teams and players that were recognized as college football's best.

Throughout the college football landscape there is traditionally a long list of programs that have produced waves of great teams and All-Americans. While many might hesitate to put Army in that category, only four schools, Notre Dame, Ohio State, Oklahoma and USC, have produced more Heisman Trophy winners than the Black Knights.

The lethal rushing combination of Felix "Doc" Blanchard and Glenn Davis first brought Heisman glory to West Point following the 1945 and 1946 seasons. Not only did the backfield duo both gain the nation's top individual award and earn All-American status three years; they helped lead the Cadets to three consecutive (1944-46) national championship claims. Let's take some time to look at these three Army stalwarts:

USMA Heisman Winners—DOC BLANCHARD 1945, GLENN DAVIS 1946, PETE DAWKINS 1958.

USMA Statue Featuring Heisman Trophy Winners & Coach Blaik

Doc Blanchard

Blanchard became the first junior to win the award. He was known as "Mr. Inside" because of his punishing running style delivered by his six-foot, 200-pound plus frame. Oddly enough Blanchard only entered West Point after being rejected from the Navy's V-12 program because he was considered overweight and because he had a vision problem.

Whatever vision problems Blanchard had, Army Legendary Coach Earl Red Blaik never lost sight of how the South Carolina native struck fear into Army opponents.

"Doc Blanchard was the best built athlete I ever saw: 6 feet and 208 pounds at his peak, not a suspicion of fat on him, with slim waist, atlas shoulders, colossal legs," Blaik wrote in his book "You Have to Pay the Price."

For a big man, 'Doc' was the quickest starter I ever saw, and in the open he ran with the niftiness as well as the speed of a great halfback...."

Glenn Davis

The dynamic duo of Glenn Davis and Doc Blanchard Time Magazine.

The perfect complement to Doc Blanchard's power running style was Glenn Davis who was dubbed "Mr. Outside" for his ability to shed tacklers with his blazing speed. In his first year as a varsity regular, the California native led the nation in scoring in 1944 while averaging an amazing 11.1 yards-per-carry.

"He was emphatically the greatest halfback I ever knew," Coach Blaik wrote. "He was not so much a dodger and side-stepper as a blazing runner who had a fourth, even fifth gear in reserve, could change direction at top speed and fly away from tacklers as if jet-propelled."

When the dust had settled after their final year at Army in 1946, both players had combined to score an NCAA record of 97 touchdowns and 585 points while leading the Black Knights to a 27-0-1 record.

When considering their Heisman impact, Blanchard and Davis still rank as the most dominating backfield tandem of all time. The pair ranked an amazing 2-3 in 1944, 1-2 in 1945 and 1-4 in the 1946 Heisman balloting.

While Davis had much in common with his running mate Blanchard, it paled in comparison to a bond he would later develop with another Heisman winner. Davis married Yvonne Ameche, the widow of Wisconsin's Alan Ameche who won the award in 1954. Another love interest of Glen Davis was Hollywood starlet Elizabeth Taylor, who he dated prior to marrying actress Terry Moore.

Another similar comparison to Blanchard is the fact that both Heisman winners donated their trophies to their high schools. Davis' resides at Bonita High in Laverne, CA., while Blanchard's spent many years at St. Stanislaus High School in Bay St. Louis, Miss. The trophy resided at Davis' high school until it was washed away by Hurricane Katrina. Davis is buried at West Point near his former Army head coach, Red Blaik.

Pete Dawkins Army's 3rd Heisman winner in 1958.

Pete Dawkins

Not only did the 1958 season produce Army Heisman winner Pete Dawkins, but it was also the Black Knights last undefeated season. Dawkins totaled 12 touchdowns during the season as he combined his rushing, receiving and kick returning skills to account for 1,216 total yards. Dawkins' tackling of the Heisman Trophy was just one of his many accomplishments as the rambling Cadet ranked 10th in his 1959 graduating class of 499.

Following his career at West Point, Dawkins snubbed the NFL's Baltimore Colts and studied at Oxford University as a Rhodes Scholar instead. Displaying the same leadership that he did on the field and in the classroom, Dawkins became the youngest Brigadier

General on active duty in the U.S. Army at the age of 43. Pete Dawkins was a Rhodes scholar at Oxford and later earned a PhD. from Princeton. He was awarded two bronze stars for valor in Vietnam and retired as a Brigadier general. He finished his "business" career as a high-ranking executive with Citibank in New York.

It may not be the Coolest Pep Rally in College Football...but...

The Army West point Black Knights may not have the coolest pre-game tradition in College Football. When you go to an Army Home game, you might miss it but if you get to go, it should be a lot of fun.

In 2007 for example, the Dave Matthews Band played for Army football — at two free shows. It was a victory before the game was even played. The U.S. Military Academy beat out Air Force, Navy and more than 100 other colleges that participated in the World's Loudest Pep Rally contest to win a visit from the rock star. Matthews played for Cadets Nov. 14 and 15, 2007

Cadet 2nd Class Garrison Haning [right] asks Dave Matthews a question during the meet-and-greet before the Wednesday night concert at West Point. Cadet 2nd Class Roderic O'Connor listens. (Photo Credit: Eric Bartelt)

12 Great Moments in Army Football

"Congratulations! We'll see you in November," Matthews, 40, said in a videotape that was to be shown to Cadets at West Point's mess hall before the event. The videotape itself was exciting.

Cadets at the storied Hudson Valley academy won the contest by submitting invitations by text messages or postings at attblueroom.com. AT&T sponsored the contest. What a neat idea.

Cadets showed off their hip-hop moves in one posted video, while others made direct pleas to Matthews, such as "West Point NEEDS someone to ROCK our stonewalled campus."

WEST POINT, N.Y. (Army News Service, Nov. 19, 2007) -- The U.S. Military Academy was rocking Wednesday and Thursday nights as Cadets, faculty and other local community members packed Eisenhower Hall for two nights of free concerts by the Dave Mathews Band.

The concerts, billed as "The World's Loudest Pep Rally," were the result of a competition by colleges and universities across the country. AT&T sponsored the contest, which encouraged students from participating schools to each send up to 50 online invitations per day, via a Web site, asking Dave and the band to perform at their school.

West Point -- a service academy with a student body of just over 4,000 -- competed with powerhouses like Iowa State University, the University of Maryland, the University of Nebraska and countless others. Lucky for the Cadets, the contest was based on the number of votes submitted relative to student population, and the USMA student population was up to the challenge.

Matthews performs at free Cadets Concert

The initial voting began with only a few Cadets. Cadet 2nd Class Jeff Caslon, a "Dave" fan who found the contest, recruited his classmate Luke Gebhart to start sending text messages and set out to spread the word through the Corps of Cadets.

During the second week of the contest, Cadets Caslen and Gebhart approached the director of Cadet Activities, Lt. Col. Craig Flowers, about what would happen if the cadet corps was successful in winning the contest. Once the DCA was on board, the rest of the corps got heavily involved. The DCA and the USCC Chief of Staff's office began sending e-mails out to the brigade reminding everyone to vote and West Point jumped from 12th place to 2nd place overnight.

"I think we were pumped to win this competition because West Point isn't a big college like the other ones,"

Cadet Caslen said. "We've gotten looked over on things before, and this fired the Corps up even more."

Thanks to the sheer tenacity and competitive nature of the Cadets and the Long Gray Line, West Point was in first place within two days of the first brigade-wide e-mail.

When the other service academies saw Army's success, they jumped on the bandwagon. The Air Force Academy even managed to edge into first place for three days, mid-contest. But by the close of voting Oct. 15, West Point was solidly in first place and Air Force and Navy were 2nd and 3rd, respectively. And while the Cadets are excited about their victory, they aren't the only ones with high hopes for the "World's Loudest Pep Rally."

"To be invited by a school in this sort of way is unusual, and I think all of us are just really excited about it," Dave Matthews said during an exclusive interview. "I think it was the Cadets who are the ones who brought us here and the reason we're coming is because it was the Cadets who made it happen.

"When the audience is responsible for you being there, it's different than just having tickets available," he added. "Everyone shares the same humility and awe and eagerness to put on a hell of a [show], well, as good a show as we can."

In 2003, Dave Matthews gave an acoustic performance at West Point, but this was his first Ike Hall performance with the entire band.

"The whole experience last time, from top to bottom [was great]. [I was so impressed with] just how gracious everyone was," Dave Matthews said. "It was just unusual how respectfully we were treated. "It was really inspiring to us," he added.

Army's Black Knights were 3-5 when Dave Matthews got the concert gig. Things are changing every year for Army football. A few recorded words from Red Blaik would be the next best thing to Dave Matthews?

Chapter 2 The Founding of the United States Military Academy

One of the Beautiful Sites on USMA Campus

The West Point short story: Courtesy of USMA

Founded in 1802, West Point is our nation's oldest service academy. Graduates of West Point "serve this nation honorably, sharing a strong sense of purpose, pride, and satisfaction that comes from meaningful service to others."

Attending the United States Military Academy is a wonderfully unique and challenging experience. West Point is a four-year college with a mission to develop leaders of character for our army—leaders who are inspired to careers as commissioned officers and lifetime service to the nation. The students of West Point (called Cadets) are selected from the most talented, energetic, and well-rounded young people in the country. Located on 16,000 acres in the scenic Hudson Valley region of New York State, West Point is conveniently situated just fifty miles north of New York City. The year-round pageantry and tradition make the Military Academy a national treasure and a popular tourist spot. People come from all over the world to see Cadets in action, and there is so much to see.

Notes from USMA graduate:

> "What do I remember most about West Point? It would be impossible for me to choose just one event. Perhaps it was marching with my class onto the parade field at the end of the very first day and taking the oath as my family and friends watched anxiously from the stands. Or maybe it was the exhilarating feeling of parachuting from an airplane 1,250 feet in the sky and the shock of seeing my parents waiting for me on the drop zone! Or it may very well have been the day I found out I passed physics. Or perhaps the day we beat Navy in football for the fifth straight year. Or the day I scored two goals in our Army-Navy lacrosse game and we won by one goal in the last second. Or it could have been when I was a squad leader and my squad successfully completed squad stakes competition and found our way home. Or perhaps the day I became platoon leader at CTLT (cadet troop leader training) at Fort Campbell, Kentucky. Or it might have been when I shook the hand of the President of the United States after receiving my diploma. Now that was a day to remember...."

Choosing West Point opens the door to countless opportunities. Cadets receive a topnotch education, training in leader development, and numerous professional opportunities. They learn first how to be a follower, and then to be a leader—skills that will carry them in all of their life endeavors. Not to mention the fact that they are guaranteed a five-year job in the military.

So, what makes West Point such a special place? West Point is more than a school; it is a tightly knit community. The officers and noncommissioned officers who serve as instructors at West Point share a special bond with the Cadets. The students and their instructors at West Point are members of the same profession and are dedicated to the same principles of "duty, honor, and country."

Cadets at West Point live under an Honor Code that states that "a cadet will not lie, cheat, or steal, or tolerate those who do." The penalty for those who violate this code is serious. The Honor Code is meant to develop Cadets into true leaders of character. Cadets internalize the importance of living honorably and carry this value with them into the army.

West Point is indeed a special place. Where else can you eat virtually every meal in less than twenty minutes with the entire student body? Where else can you march into a stadium on national television and be a part of the Army-Navy rivalry? Where else can you stop on the way to class and pose for a picture with tourists?

Where else can you make so many friends for a lifetime? At no other school does the word classmate mean so much. The bonds that are formed at West Point are unparalleled. On the very first day Cadets are advised to "cooperate and graduate." This mantra follows them through victories and defeats, through successes and failures, from reception day until graduation day. The West Point Experience prepares Cadets for all that life has to offer. When they throw their hats in the air, they are truly ready to be all that they can be.

Academics: The Core Curriculum

Academics at West Point are tough, but with the amount of assistance available, Cadets are set up for success. The overall curriculum contains classes in both science and the arts. Unlike most colleges and universities, the core curriculum is very extensive. In other words, during the first two years, there is not much flexibility in course selection.

The core curriculum consists of thirty-six courses that the academy considers essential to the broad base of knowledge necessary for all graduates: a course in Information Technology for all but engineering majors; and a three-course core engineering sequence for those who do not major in engineering. This core curriculum, when combined with physical education training and military science, constitutes the Military Academy's "professional major."

This broad base of classes serves several purposes. Cadets not only get a solid foundation before specializing in one area, but have also studied in all of the academic departments and have a sound basis for selecting one of ninety-nine majors. Besides their major or field of study, all students take what is called a five-course engineering sequence. This sequence strengthens the cadet's engineering background and in a sense, gives him or her a second major. The engineering sequences include electrical engineering, environmental engineering, civil engineering, mechanical engineering, nuclear engineering, systems engineering, and computer science. All graduates receive a Bachelor of Science degree.

The United States Military Academy introduced a "major with honors," which contains a minimum of twelve courses, an individual research requirement, and requires a minimum academic program score cumulative (APSC) of 3.0 in the core curriculum and a 3.5 in the major.

I'll never forget my first day of classes as a plebe (freshman). I was astonished to see that each of my classes had only about fifteen Cadets in it, about half the size of my high school classes. The first thing each professor did was write his or her home phone number on the blackboard. 'Call me at home anytime, day or night,' each one said. The classroom experience at West Point is unlike any other. There simply are no crowded lecture halls or graduate assistants.

Each class is taught by an instructor whose primary responsibility is to teach Cadets. Each class has a maximum number of eighteen students. You just can't get that kind of personal interaction at other universities—many of my friends at other schools had as many graduate assistants as they did professors. My professors taught every lesson, were available for additional help at all hours of the day or night, and even came out to support me at my athletic matches!

Resources

The resources available to Cadets are very impressive. The library contains over 600,000 volumes of resources and 2,000 academic journals and newspapers. All Cadets have desk-top computers in their room and full access to the Internet. In addition, the Center for

Enhanced Performance assists Cadets in achieving their potential in all aspects of academy life, offering classes, open to all students, in reading efficiency and student success.

One-on-one additional instruction is available to Cadets from their instructors and is what sets the military academy apart from other schools.

Physical Education and Military Development

Part of the overall curriculum includes physical education and military development. The physical education curriculum spans the four years. Physical education classes are incorporated into the grade point average, which highlights the importance of physical fitness in the army. Cadets receive grades in each physical education class as well as the Army Physical Fitness Test and the Indoor Obstacle Course Test. The physical program is quite challenging, but rewarding and fun as well.

Military development is also part of the curriculum. Cadets are graded based on military performance within their cadet companies as well as their performance during summer training and military intersession. The heart of the military training takes place during the summer. During their first summer, new Cadets are introduced to the academy through the rigors of Cadet Basic Training, a six-week experience that transforms the new class from civilians to Cadets, and gives the upper two classes the opportunity to practice small unit leadership. During Cadet Basic Training—also called "Beast Barracks"—new Cadets learn what it means to be a cadet as well as what it means to be a soldier.

The summer after plebe or freshman year, Cadets participate in Cadet Field Training. At Camp Buckner, sophomores or "yearlings" complete seven weeks of advanced military training including weapons, tank, and aviation training. During this time, Cadets are also introduced to the different branches of the army and how their focus contributes to its overall mission. They apply the skills they learned in the classroom as they practice tactical exercises in small units. Like Cadet Basic Training, upper-class Cadets serve as the cadre for this training.

Camp Buckner is also a time for recreation and class bonding. During the summers before junior ("cow") and senior ("firs tie") year, opportunities for Cadets broaden significantly. During these summers, Cadets must participate in either Cadet Troop Leader Training or Drill Cadet Leader Training. This involves being assigned to an active army unit for six weeks and acting as either platoon leaders or drill sergeants. For most Cadets, it is their first experience in the regular army and it is both exciting and rewarding. A cadet must also serve as a leader or cadre member for either Cadet Basic Training or Cadet Field Training during one of these summers.

This leaves two periods open for Cadets to participate in Individual Advanced Development (IADs). Some military IADs include Airborne School (parachuting), Air Assault School (rappelling out of helicopters), Combat Engineer Sapper School, Mountain Warfare School, and Special Forces Scuba School. There are also physical IADs such as training at the U.S. Olympic Center and Outward Bound. Very popular among Cadets are academic IADs.

These are similar to internships students at civilian colleges might participate in. Some academic IAD Cadets participate, including duty with the Supreme Court, Crossroads to Africa, the Foreign Academy Exchange Program, NASA, and the National Laboratories.

Perhaps this is a curriculum unlike any you've ever seen. A cadet's total QPA (quality point average) is based on fifty-five percent academics, thirty percent military, and fifteen percent physical. Cadets must be well rounded. The curriculum is meant to develop "enlightened military leaders of strong moral courage whose minds are creative, critical, and resourceful." It was Thucydides who said, "The Nation that makes a great distinction between its scholars and its warriors will have its thinking done by cowards and its fighting done by fools."

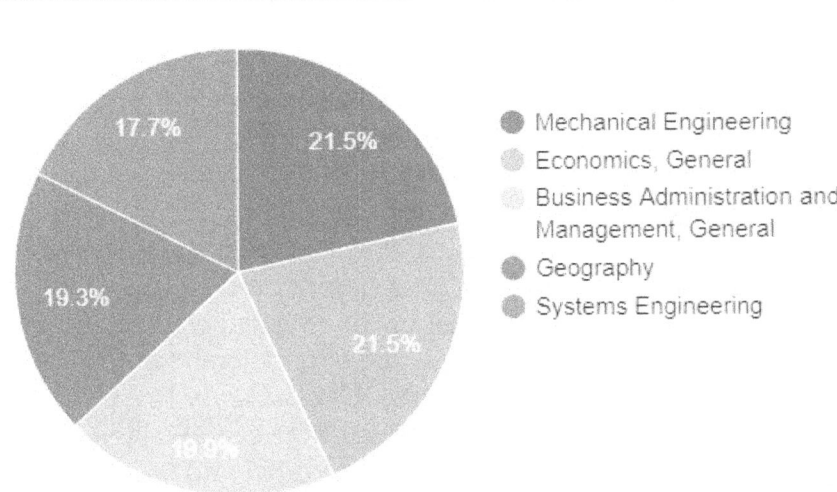

Admissions

Admission to West Point is highly competitive, and the application process is much more involved than that of a civilian school. Of the approximate 12,000 candidates who start files each year, only about 1,500 are offered admission. While most colleges and universities look primarily at a student's academic background, West Point is interested in the whole package. Not only must candidates be of high academic caliber, they must qualify physically and medically as well. Candidates must also earn a nomination from a U.S. representative, senator, the president, vice president, or from the Department of the Army (these nominations are service-related).

The admissions committee seeks students who are bright, athletic, and have "demonstrated leadership potential" throughout their high school years. To determine the academic strength and potential of a candidate, the admissions committee examines both the high school transcript and the SAT/ACT scores. To determine the physical fitness and potential of a candidate, the committee looks at the athletic activities in which the candidate participated during high school. In addition, candidates are required to take a physical aptitude examination (PAE), which consists of several events such as a 300-meter run, pull-ups, and a broad jump, designed to determine athletic ability and potential. Leadership Potential

Because West Point strives to be the premier leader development institute in the world, it is important that the academy admit Cadets who have leadership potential that can be built upon. With that in mind, the admissions committee looks for students who were part of the student government in their school, primarily student body or class president. Other indications of exceptional leadership potential might include participation in boys/girls state, scouting, debate, school publications, and varsity athletics. In a typical class of about 1,200 new Cadets, more than 1,000 earned varsity letters in high school and about 750 were team captains. Over seventy-five percent of the class graduated in the top fifth of their high school class. The mean SAT I score for a recent class was 630 Verbal and 647 Math, 28 on the ACT, and some 237 earned National Merit Scholarship Recognition.

Candidates must also be at least seventeen and not older than twenty-three years of age on July first of the year they enter the academy. They must also be U.S. citizens, be unmarried, and not be pregnant or have a legal obligation for child support.

Steps in Applying

There are several steps in applying to West Point.

Make a self-assessment. Determine if you qualify for West Point and if this is something that you would be interested in doing.
Start a candidate file. This is done by contacting the USMA Admissions Office.

Seek a nomination from the representative in your district and your senators.

You must complete all of your SAT and ACT testing, as well as your physical and medical examinations.
You then have the option of visiting West Point and spending the day with a cadet on a candidate orientation visit. This is optional, but

highly recommended. An orientation visit is the best way to get a feel for academy life and if it's for you.

If you complete all of these steps and are admitted into the incoming class, your final step is to enroll in the academy on Reception Day. For those candidates who consider USMA to be their top college choice and are interested in applying early, West Point offers an Early Action plan. Under this plan, applicants are informed of their admissions status by January 15. Persistence is "key," as about thirty percent of each incoming class are second-time applicants.

Financial Aid

All Cadets at West Point are active-duty soldiers in the regular army. As such, they receive approximately $10,000 a year in pay. They are provided medical and dental care, and room and board. For this, Cadets perform assigned duties and agree to serve as commissioned officers for a minimum of five years following graduation. From the cadet salary, deductions are made in order to pay for uniforms, textbooks, a desk-top computer, laundry, grooming, and similar necessities. Upon acceptance of the appointment, Cadets are asked to make a one-time, nonrefundable deposit of about $2,900. The total cost of a cadet's full education is about $275,000. This is quite an impressive national investment!

Notes from USMA graduate:

> Because there is no tuition cost associated with attending the United States Military Academy, all students have an equal chance of attending. This creates a diverse population within the corps of Cadets. Because we wore the same uniforms and none of us paid tuition, we really didn't know how well-off our fellow Cadets were, nor was it our concern. We accepted one another for who we were, not for our family's background.

Students

One of the toughest things about being a cadet is deciding what activities to become involved in. From sports to dramatics to religious activities, West Point truly has it all.

A few years ago, a couple of seniors painted 'West Point is a party school!' on the side of their R.V. in an attempt to rouse spirit among the corps. The irony of this statement roused more than a few chuckles, because Cadets know that nothing could be further from the truth, but, while the rowdy fraternity party scene is not alive and well at West Point, don't be fooled into thinking that being a cadet isn't fun. With the number of available activities, it can be an absolute blast!

Clubs

In addition to sports, there are countless other activities for Cadets to enjoy. For instance, there are over 100 recreational clubs for Cadets to participate in:

There are clubs that support the corps such as the cadet band and the cadet radio station.

There are clubs that are academic in nature such as the debate club. There are clubs that are geared toward the arts such as the Theatre Arts Guild. *There are numerous religious groups and activities. Religion plays a large part in the lives of many Cadets and Cadets are the backbone of the churches on post. From singing in the choir, to teaching Sunday school, Cadets find plenty of time to grow in their spirituality both personally and as a member of the larger community. Almost all religious denominations have services on post for Cadets to attend.

There are also many social activities for Cadets to attend. There is an on-post movie theater, frequent dances, a golf course, a ski slope, a bowling alley, boat rides, and tailgates. You'll very rarely ever hear a cadet say that he or she is bored!

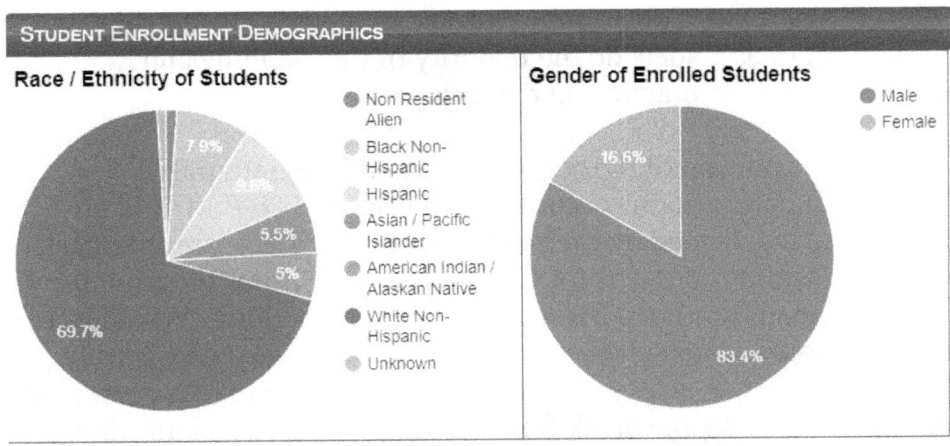

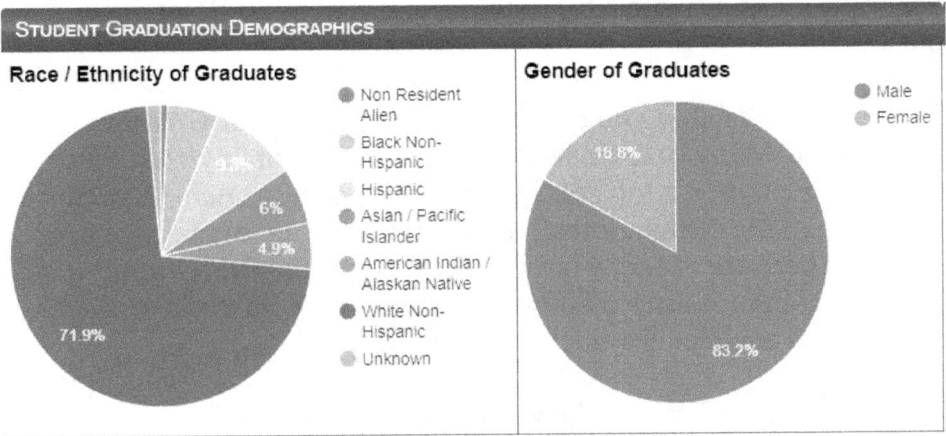

Athletics

Because "every cadet is an athlete, and every athlete will be challenged," all Cadets must participate in sporting activities throughout the year. West Point has a highly competitive varsity program, with sixteen men's varsity sports and eight women's, each competing at the Division I level. More than twenty-five percent of the corps participates at this level. Some examples of varsity sports are football, basketball, baseball, softball, soccer, track, lacrosse, and swimming.

For those Cadets not involved in varsity athletics, there are twenty - nine competitive club sports. Some examples of club sports are crew, equestrian, fencing, mountaineering, rugby, sport parachute, marathon, martial arts, skiing, team handball, water polo, and women's lacrosse. Competitive club sports are great leadership opportunities as Cadets do the majority of the planning and executing of team practices and events.

Yet another portion of the corps is involved in intramurals. Intramural competitions occur twice a week at 4:00 P.M. and are between teams fielded by each cadet company. There are seventeen different intramural sports for Cadets to choose from. Intramurals foster company spirit, sportsmanship, and competition. Whichever level of sports a cadet chooses to participate in, each cadet is truly challenged. Sports at West Point are highly competitive, a great deal of fun, and a welcome break from the rigors of the academic day. School spirit and support for sporting teams at West Point are outstanding.

Every athletic facility you can think of is available for your use at West Point. Many of these facilities compare favorably with those found in the nation's top colleges and universities. Michie Stadium is the home of the Army football team with a seating capacity of over 39,000. There are capacity crowds throughout the fall season. Holleder Center houses 5,000-seat Christi Arena for basketball and 2,400-seat Tate Rink for hockey competition.

The Arvin Cadet Physical Development Center, which features five gymnasiums and three swimming pools, begins a major renovation soon. It features Crandall Pool, an Olympic-size 50-meter pool. There are numerous special purpose rooms for squash, handball, racquetball, wrestling, and weight training. Gillis Field House is used for varsity and intramural indoor track competition. There is an all-weather outdoor track oval and football field at the renovated Shea Stadium complex that is used for daylight and evening competitive events. Lichtenstein Indoor Tennis Complex is the newest of the athletic facilities at West Point. There are also pistol and rifle ranges, numerous outdoor tennis courts, a ski slope, and an 18-hole golf course, which has also been redesigned.

Alumni

Graduates of West Point tend to be very proud of their alma mater; it seems that the older they get, the prouder they become. Alumni weekends are always very inspiring and very crowded. Grads come decked out from head to toe in paraphernalia that indicates their year of graduation. The alumni are known as "old grads" and the funny thing is, one is referred to as an "old grad" the second he or she tosses that hat in the air on graduation day. The common joke is that "old grads" are always complaining that the structure and discipline at West Point is simply not as rigid as when they were Cadets. But most agree, it is the values and traditions that make West Point an enduring national treasure.

Some of my fondest memories of West Point involve marching in the alumni parades. Marching along an endless line of distinguished alumni and trying our hardest not to let them down was just an awesome experience. I recall one time when I was moved to tears as an 'old grad' in a wheelchair struggled to his feet as my company marched by. We were his old company, and he was not going to sit in his wheelchair as we passed his position. As he applauded and cheered, 'Looking good H-4! Go Hogs!' I could not help but get choked up. I was so proud to be even the smallest part of this amazing place. I was part of a tradition, part of history, and someday I too would be standing there facing the corps, recalling my days as a cadet, and cheering them on.

West Point has had more than a handful of distinguished graduates. Much of the U.S. Army leadership since the Civil War were members of the Long Gray Line—and the tradition continues. West Point graduates have, and will continue to make wonderful contributions to our nation. More than 100 graduates have competed on various U.S. Olympic teams. West Pointers have served as everything from presidents of corporations to presidents of the United States. Service is what West Point is all about, and our graduates serve our nation well.

Prominent Graduates

Most of you will recognize most of these names as they are truly famous historical figures in many ways:

Robert E. Lee, 1829
Ulysses S. Grant, 1843

George Goethals, 1880
John J. Pershing, 1886
Douglas MacArthur, '03
George Patton, '09
Omar Bradley, '15
Dwight D. Eisenhower, '15
Matthew Ridgway, '17
Leslie Groves, '18
Maxwell Taylor, '22
Creighton Abrams, '36
Doc Blanchard, '47
Glenn Davis, '47
Alexander Haig, Jr., '47
Brent Scowcroft, '47
Frank Borman, '50
Fidel Ramos, '50
Edward White, '52
H. Norman Schwarzkopf, '56
Peter Dawkins, '59
Mike Krzyzewski, '69

Read more: United States Military Academy (USMA, West Point) Introduction and Academics - West Point, NY

http://www.stateuniversity.com/universities/NY/United_States_Military_Academy.html#ixzz4lhDlUoTP

Chapter 3 The West Point Mission

United States Military Academy West Point

The mission is simple:

"To educate, train, and inspire the Corps of Cadets so that each graduate is a commissioned leader of character committed to the values of Duty, Honor, Country and prepared for a career of professional excellence and service to the Nation as an officer in the United States Army."

Chapter 4 Historic Army West Point Fields & Stadiums

The Plain is not in Spain It is in West Point

The 1912 West Point football team--Dwight Eisenhower is third from left; Louis Merillat is eighth from the left, in the A sweater; Omar Bradley on the far right

When you check out the history of the USMA and its West Point facility, you learn a lot more than you bargain for. For example, if you read anything about Army Football today, you know they play at Michie Stadium and have played there for over 90 years. But, what about the other years? It is not so easy to find a lot of information about those years as the scribes and the student writers are mostly long gone.

Digging a little deeper, however, and checking out the site of the first Army Navy game, one can discern that there is another field upon which Army had played before Michie. It played the first football game, and the first Army-Navy game at the Plain. One would think West Point would write a lot about the spot where they played football for over thirty years. It sure would have made my job easier.

I like to report on the stadiums and/or fields upon which teams play as it better tells the story of the team. Just because Army played on the plain, does not mean when they had a big game, that they would not shift it to a big park such as Yankee Stadium—like when Notre Dame came to town.

The Plain today is the parade field at the United States Military Academy at West Point, New York. It has its own fascinating story which we will tell as it had a major role in American victories in wars back to the revolution.

The flat terrain of the Plain contrasts with the varied and hilly terrain of the remainder of the campus. The Plain rises approximately 150 feet (46 m) above the Hudson River and has been the site of the longest continually occupied US Army garrison in America since 1778. In its early years, the entire academy was located on the Plain and it was used for varying activities ranging from drill and mounted cavalry maneuvers to an encampment site for summer training. Currently, the Plain refers to just the parade field where Cadets perform ceremonial parades.

Geography

The Plain in the early days of the academy comprised approximately 40 acres of relatively flat ground rising approximately 150 feet above the Hudson River. It was not always level and manicured as the parade ground that is seen today.

History

The Plain in 1828. All structures in the painting are now gone and Wood's Monument is moved to the cemetery.

Before the development of the modern academy, the term "The Plain" referred to the relatively flat geographic area that the current academy occupies. It included the area where Fort Clinton was constructed. The term now specifically applies to the parade field.

Football on the Plain Circa 1906

The Connecticut militia that first occupied West Point on 27 January 1778 encamped there during that particularly harsh winter. That summer, construction began on Fort Arnold, later to be renamed Fort Clinton, which stood at the far eastern edge of the Plain and overlooked the sharp westerly turn in the Hudson River.

The land was owned by a private citizen, a Mr. Stephen Moore of North Carolina. Secretary of the Treasury Alexander Hamilton authorized the army's purchase of the land for $11,085 in 1790.

Football on the Plain, c1900.

Execution Hollow is clearly visible just above the diagonal walkway in the mid-right of this picture. Battle Monument is on the back-right side of it.

In the early days of the academy, the Plain was used for many purposes beyond its current use for ceremonial parades. From its earliest days until just after World War I, the Corps of Cadets spent their summers encamped on the Plain as part of their tactical field training.

Semi-permanent tents were erected, hard-floor planking, and furniture and books were moved out to the campsite as the Cadets moved out of the barracks for the summer. Cadets practiced military drill and cavalry maneuvers on the Plain's open areas.

However, after the superintendency of Douglas MacArthur from 1919 to 1922, summer camp was no longer held on the Plain. Before the construction of Michie Stadium, the Army football team played their home games upon the Plain.

For the first 100 years of the academy, there was a large depression on the northern edge of the plain near trophy point. This area was known locally as Execution Hollow as reportedly military executions occurred there during the Revolutionary War period. The hollow remained until 1912, when it was filled in with soil excavated from the construction of Bartlett Hall.

The area now is a small grassy field between the Superintendent's review stands, Clinton Field, and Battle Monument on Trophy point. The field contains a small putting green used by the Department of Physical Education for golf instruction and a spruce tree planted in 2009 as a post-Christmas tree.

The Plain – Modern Day Look

The Plain in present-day is used primarily for ceremonial parades, known at the academy as "reviews". Because of the cold weather common at the academy, cadet reviews are usually held between April and November. Cadets also use the Plain for recreational activities or as a place to retreat from the barracks during the late spring or early fall.

The general-public is asked not to walk on the grass Plain. Visitors can access and view the Plain up-close from Diagonal Walk, a walkway which bisects the Plain running north-south from Eisenhower statue to MacArthur statue.

The Plain is also the location of the Corps of Cadets' Tap Vigils when a member of the corps passes away. Shortly before 2330 hours, the entire corps assembles in silence on the large paved southern edge of the plain, known as the Apron. The traditional military hymn "Taps" is played, followed by a singing of the "Alma Mater" by the corps, followed by the playing of "Amazing Grace" by the Pipes and Drums. The Cadets then disperse in silence back to their rooms.

Cadet Review on the Plain

The periphery of the Plain is home to several monuments to past American military leaders. A horse-mounted George Washington is depicted atop Washington Monument on the western edge looking out over the Plain. World War II Generals of the Army are remembered with Eisenhower Monument and MacArthur Monument, which sit at opposite ends of Diagonal Walk.

In the far north-west corner, Thayer Monument commemorates the "Father of the Military Academy", and stands watch over the Plain. On the far eastern edge of the Plain, just beyond Clinton field, Polish General Tadeusz Kosciuszko looks out over the Hudson River at Kosciuszko's Monument.

"Ike" statue at south end of the Plain

Thayer statue at northwest corner of the Plain

Washington Statue

Michie Stadium

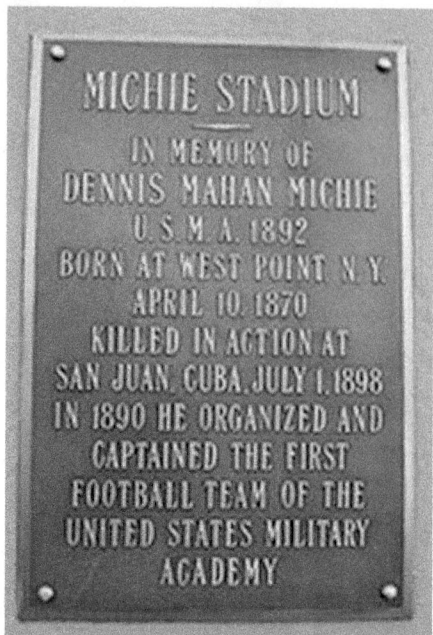

Dennis Michie

Michie Stadium is dedicated to the memory of Dennis Michie (1870–1898), who was instrumental in starting the football program while a cadet at the Academy. A member of the Class of 1892, Michie organized, managed, and coached the first football team at West Point in 1890.

Six years after graduation, he was killed in Cuba during the Spanish–American War. There have been several renovations since the stadium's first game in October 1924, when Army defeated Saint Louis, 17–0.

Blaik Field at Michie Stadium West Point NY

Michie Stadium is an outdoor football stadium on the campus of the U.S. Military Academy in West Point, New York. The home field for the Army Black Knights, it opened 94 years ago in 1924 and has a current seating capacity of 38,000.

The stadium sits at the upper portion of campus, directly west of Lusk Reservoir. The field is at an elevation of 335 feet (102 m) above sea level and runs in the traditional north-south configuration, with the press box above the west sideline. Due to the view offered by its location overlooking the Hudson River and the Neo-Gothic architecture of the campus below, it was rated as Sports Illustrated's #3 sports venue of the 20th century.

Michie Stadium, splendid in its scenic beauty and long recognized as one of the most popular stadiums in the nation, will celebrate its 94th season as the home of Army football during the 2017 campaign.

Over the years, the venerable stadium has received its share of plaudits as one of the most desired locations in which to watch a college football game. Recently, noted football analyst Mel Kiper Jr. of ESPN.com hailed the Academy's game day atmosphere as among the most inspirational in the country.

In addition, renowned sports periodicals Sports Illustrated and The Sporting News have heaped lofty praise upon the historic arena by listing it among their top all-time venues.

A new FieldTurf playing surface was installed during the summer of 2008, along with plans to complete a state-of-the-art video board before the start of the 2008 campaign. These enhancements ensure that the venerable facility will maintain its lofty status for years to come.

Construction of the $7 million Hoffman Press Box was completed in the spring of 2003. The new press box houses a full-service media operations center with state-of-the-art radio and television broadcast booths.

Work on the $40 million Kimsey Athletic Center, just outside the south end zone, was also concluded in the spring of 2003. The facility houses state-of-the-art locker rooms, coaches' offices, athletic training facilities, equipment rooms, meeting rooms and the Kenna Hall of Army Sports, a large display area that will chronicle Army's vast athletics history. Construction of Randall Hall, the project's second phase, was completed this past summer.

The entire stadium annex is the jewel of an aggressive athletic facilities renovation plan that has seen recent major improvements to Gillis Field House, Shea Stadium, Johnson Stadium at Doubleday Field, Clinton Field and Malek Courts. The acclaimed Lichtenberg Tennis Center just completed its fifth full academic year. In the spring of 2002, Army dedicated the Gross Sports Center, which provides the Army gymnastics team with a state-of-the-art home while also lending extra indoor space for the Black Knights' basketball programs.

Realizing the need for a permanent athletic field as Army's football program continued to assert itself nationally, West Point officials selected a patch of meadow land adjacent to Lusk Reservoir and within the shadow of historic Fort Putnam. Construction of Michie Stadium was completed in 1924, just in time for Army's 35th football campaign.

In 91 previous campaigns in Michie Stadium, the Black Knights have compiled a remarkable record of 326-156-7.

The Black Knights posted more home wins than any previous Army team while forging a perfect 6-0 mark at Michie in 1996, the 28th undefeated home campaign in Academy grid annals. In addition to 28 unblemished seasons, there have been two undefeated but tied campaigns at Michie. Following a 14-14 tie in the "Dedication Game" in the home finale of 1924, the Cadets won 39 straight contests in Michie Stadium, spanning more than six seasons.

Only 15 Division I-A stadiums, and just six located east of the Mississippi River, are older than fabled Michie Stadium. The original stadium structure was formally dedicated to the memory of Dennis Mahan Michie, who was instrumental in starting the game of football at the U.S. Military Academy in 1890. It was Michie who organized, managed and coached the first football team in history at West Point.

There have been several facelifts since that first game in 1924 when Army defeated Saint Louis University 17-0.

Temporary East stands and upper stands were added before construction of permanent East stands was completed in 1962. In the summer of 1969 an upper deck on the West side was added, boosting the seating capacity to 41,684. Capacity has since been adjusted to 38,000. Army's most prolific attendance came in 1972 when the Black Knights averaged a record 41,123 fans. Army ranked among the nation's attendance leaders in 2000, averaging 38,516 per game, or 96.5 percent of Michie Stadium's capacity.

A major change occurred on the playing field in 1977 when AstroTurf replaced the natural grass surface. The artificial turf greatly reduced maintenance costs and guaranteed the Army team an excellent practice facility for use all fall while providing for multiple uses. SuperTurf replaced the AstroTurf in 1984, which was in turn replaced by AstroTurf 8 in 1992. Since 2008, the playing surface has been FieldTurf. This replaced AstroPlay, which had been used since 2001. The stadium's playing field was natural grass until AstroTurf was installed in 1977.

Blaik Field

In honor of legendary mentor Earl "Red" Blaik, Army christened the Michie Stadium playing surface "Blaik Field" in 1999. Blaik, a gridiron innovator, compiled an 18-year Army record of 121-33-10 and brought Army its only three national championships (1944, 1945, 1946). The winningest coach in Army annals, Blaik is enshrined in the College Football Foundation Hall of Fame.

In the spring of 2002, Army dedicated the Gross Sports Center, which honored the dedication in grand style, trouncing Ball State 41-21

Army–Navy Game

Michie Stadium has hosted the Army–Navy Game only once, in 1943 during World War II, after it was played at Thompson Stadium at Annapolis the year before. Neither Army nor Navy have played at an on-campus facility since very early in the rivalry, since teams' home stadiums are not nearly large enough to accommodate the crowds and media that usually attend the rivalry games. Their rivalry game is normally played at a neutral site between the campuses on the East Coast, usually in Philadelphia in early December.

Chapter 5 The Evolution of Modern American Football

Yale vs. Columbia

Lots of playing before playing became official

The official agreed upon date for the first American-style college football game is November 6, 1869. If you can find a replay of this game someplace in the heavens, however, you would find it would not look much like football as we know it. But, it was not completely soccer or rugby either.

Before this game, teams were playing a rugby style similar to that played in Britain in the mid-19th century. At the time in the US, a derivative known as association football was also played. In both games, a football is kicked at a goal or run over a line. These styles were based on the varieties of English public-school football games. Over time, as noted, the style of "football" play in America continued to evolve.

On November 6, 1869, the first football game in America featured Rutgers and Princeton. Before the teams were even on the field it was being plugged as the first college football game of all time. Penn State did not get a Rugby team until the early 1960's. Nobody at Penn State in 1869, from what I could find, was even thinking about the game of football.

The first game of intercollegiate football was a sporting battle between two neighboring schools on a plot of ground where the present-day Rutgers gymnasium now stands in New Brunswick, N.J. Rutgers won that first game, 6-4.

There were two teams of 25 men each and the rules were rugby-like, but different enough to make it very interesting and enjoyable.

Like today's football, there were many surprises; strategies needed to be employed; determination exhibited, and of course the players required physical prowess.

1st Game Rutgers 6 Princeton 4 College Field, New Brunswick, NJ

At 3 p.m. the 50 combatants as well as 100 spectators gathered on the field. Most sat on a low wooden fence and watched the athletes discard their hats, coats and vests. The players used their suspenders as belts. To give a unique look, Rutgers wore scarlet-colored scarfs, which they converted into turbans. This contrasted them with the bareheaded boys from Princeton.

Two members of each team remained more or less stationary near the opponent's goal in the hopes of being able to slip over and score from unguarded positions. Thus, the present day "sleeper" was conceived. The remaining 23 players were divided into groups of 11 and 12. While the 11 "fielders" lined up in their own territory as defenders, the 12 "bulldogs" carried the battle.

Each score counted as a "game" and 10 games completed the contest. Following each score, the teams changed direction. The ball could be advanced only by kicking or batting it with the feet, hands, heads or sides.

Rutgers put a challenge forward that three games were to be played that year. The first was played at New Brunswick and won by Rutgers. Princeton won the second game, but cries of "overemphasis" prevented the third game in football's first year when faculties of both institutions protested on the grounds that the games were interfering with student studies.

This is an excerpt of the Rutgers account of the game on its web site. A person named Herbert gave this detailed account of the play in the first game:

"Though smaller on the average, the Rutgers players, as it developed, had ample speed and fine football sense. Receiving the ball, our men formed a perfect interference around it and with short, skillful kicks and dribbles drove it down the field. Taken by surprise, the Princeton men fought valiantly, but in five minutes we had gotten the ball through to our captains on the enemy's goal and S.G. Gano, '71 and G.R. Dixon, '73, neatly kicked it over. None thought of it, so far as I know, but we had without previous plan or thought evolved the play that became famous a few years later as 'the flying wedge'."

"Next period Rutgers bucked, or received the ball, hoping to repeat the flying wedge," Herbert's account continues. "But the first time we formed it Big Mike came charging full upon us. It was our turn for surprise. The Princeton battering ram made no attempt to reach the ball but, forerunner of the interference-breaking ends of today, threw himself into our mass play, bursting us apart, and bowing us over. Time and again Rutgers formed the wedge and charged; as often Big Mike broke it up. And finally, on one of these incredible break-ups a

Princeton bulldog with a long accurate, perhaps lucky kick, sent the ball between the posts for the second score.

It was at this point that a Rutgers professor could stand it no longer. Waving his umbrella at the participants, he shrieked, "You will come to no Christian end!"

Herbert's account of the game continues: "The fifth and sixth goals went to Rutgers. The stars of the latter period of play, in the memory of the players after the lapse of many years, were "Big

Mike" and Large (former State Senator George H. Large of Flemington, another Princeton player) ...

The University of Notre Dame did not get into the football act until the late 1880's. At this time, the rules of rugby kept changing to accommodate the infatuation for the Americanized style of "football" play that would ultimately become the American game of football.

Walter Camp: the father of American football?

Walter Camp was a very well-known rugby player from Yale. In today's world, he would have been characterized as a rugby hero. It was his love of the game, his knowledge of the game as it was played, and his innovative mind that caused him to take the evolution of football even further. He pioneered the changes to the rules of rugby that slowly transformed the sport into the new game of American Football.

The rule changes that were introduced to the rugby and

association style (like soccer) of play were mostly those authored by Camp, who was also a Hopkins School graduate. For his original efforts, Walter Camp today is considered to be the "Father of American Football". Among the important changes brought to the game were the introduction of a line of scrimmage; down-and-distance rules; and the legalization of interference (blocking).

There was no such thing in those days as a forward pass and so the legalization of interference in 1880 football permitted blocking for runners. The forward pass would add another dimension to the game that made it much different than rugby or association football.

Soon after the early football changes, in the late nineteenth and into the early twentieth centuries, more game-play type developments were introduced by college coaches. The list is like a who's who of early American College Football. Coaches, such as Eddie Cochems, Amos Alonzo Stagg, Parke H. Davis, Knute Rockne, John Heisman, and Glenn "Pop" Warner helped introduce and then take advantage of the newly introduced forward pass. College football as well as professional football, were introduced prior to the 20th century. Fans were lured into watching again and again once they saw the game played.

College football especially grew in popularity despite the existence of pro-football. It became the dominant version of the sport of football in the United States. It was this way for the entire first half of the 20th century. Bowl games made the idea of football even more exciting in the college ranks. Rivalries grew and continued and the fans loved it! This great football tradition brought a national audience to college football games that still dominates the sports world today.

This book has little to do with pro-football or any other sport. However, there is no denying that the greatest college football players more often than not eventually found their fortunes in professional football. Pro football can be traced back to the season that Notre Dame brought forth a real football team after a two-year lapse from its last half-Rugby season in 1889. It was 1892 when William "Pudge" Heffelfinger signed a $500 contract to play for the Allegheny Athletic Association against the Pittsburgh Athletic Club.

Twenty-eight years later, the American Professional Football Association was formed. This league changed its name to the National Football League (NFL) just two years later. Eventually, the NFL became the major league of American football. Originally, just a sport played in Midwestern industrial towns in the United States, professional football eventually became a national phenomenon. We all know this because from August to February, in America, many of us are glued to our TV sets or chained to our seats in some of the most intriguing pro-football stadiums in America.

Rules and Penalties

The big problem players from different teams and different geographies had when playing early American-style football in college was that the style of play was not standardized. The rulebooks were not yet written or were at best incomplete and disputable.

A rule over here, for example, would be a penalty over there. And, so in the 1870's there was a lot of work to try to make all games to be played by the same rules. There were minor rule changes such as team size was reduced from 25 to 20 but of course over the years, this and all other rules continued to evolve. For years, there was no such thing as a running touchdown. The only means of scoring was to bat or kick the ball through the opposing team's goal.

Early rugby rules were the default. The field size was rugby style at 140 yards by 70 yards v 120 X 53 1/3 (including end zones) in today's football game. There was plenty of room to huff and puff and almost get lost. There were no breaks per se for long periods. Instead of fifteen-minute quarters, the game was more like Rugby and Soccer with 45-minute halves played continuously.

In 1873 to put some order to the game, Columbia, Princeton. Rutgers, and Yale got together in a hotel in New York City and wrote down the first set of intercollegiate football rules. They changed a few things along the way but the end-product was a much more standard way of playing football games. Rather than use the home team's rules, all teams then were able to play by the same rules

Harvard did not to comply with American rules

For its own reasons, Harvard chose not to attend the rules conference. Instead, it played all of its games using the Harvard code of rules. Harvard therefore had a difficult time scheduling games. In 1874, to get a game, Harvard agreed to play McGill University from Montreal Canada. They had rules that even Harvard had never seen. For example, any player could pick up the ball and run with it, anytime he wished.

Another McGill rule was that they would count tries (the act of grounding the football past the opponent's goal line. Since there was no end zone, which technically makes a football field of today 120 yards long, a touchdown gave no points. Instead, it provided the chance to kick a free goal from the field. If the kick were missed, the touchdown did not count.

In 1874 McGill and Harvard played a two-game series. Each team could play 11 men per side. This was in deep contrast to the even earlier days of college football before standard rules when games were played with 25, 20, 15, or 11 men on a side.

The first game was played with a round ball using what were known as the "Boston" rules (Harvard). The next day, the teams played using the McGill rules, which included McGill's oval ball which was much like an American football, and it featured the ability to pick up the ball and run with it. Harvard enjoyed this experience especially the idea of "the try" which had not been used in American football. Eventually, the try evolved into the American idea of a touchdown and points were given when a try was successful.

Not all the rules lasted the duration and some were very strange by today's standards. One of the most perplexing rules was that a man could run with the ball only while an opponent chose to pursue him. When a tackler abandoned the ball-carrier, the latter had to stop, and was forced to kick, pass or even throw away what was called "his burden."

McGill has a great account of this match on their web site. Type *McGill web site football against Harvard* into your search engine.

Their players wore no protective pads. Woolen jerseys covered the torso, while white trousers encased the players' legs. Some trousers were short and some were long. It did not seem to matter for the game. A number of the men wore what they called black "football turbans" which were the ancestors of the modern helmet; others chose to wear white canvas hats.

The Harvard players wore undershirts made of gauze. Think about that for a while. They also wore what were called *full length gymnasium costumes*. They also wore light baseball shoes. Most of the team wore handkerchiefs, which were knotted about their heads.

The gauze undershirts were a trick. There was strategy in this choice of top uniform. When a player was first tackled, the gauze would be demolished and the next opponent would have nothing to grab other than "slippery human flesh." Harvard won this game by a score of 3-0

The next go at playing by the rules was when Harvard took on Tufts University on June 4, 1875. This was the first American college football game played using rules similar to the McGill/Harvard contest. Tufts won this game. Despite the loss, Harvard continued pushing McGill style football and challenged Yale.

The Bulldog team accepted under a compromise rule set that included some Yale soccer rules and Harvard rugby rules. They used 15 players per team. It was November 13, 1875 for this first meeting of Harvard v Yale. Harvard won 4-0. Walter Camp attended the game and the following year he played in the game as a Yale Bulldog.

Camp was determined to avenge Yale's defeat. Onlookers from Princeton, who saw this Harvard / Yale game loved it so much, they brought it back to Princeton where it was quickly adopted as the preferred version of football.

Once Walter Camp caught onto the rugby-style rules, history says he became a fixture at the Massasoit House conventions. Here the rules of the game were debated and changed appropriately. From these meetings, Camp's rule changes as well as others were adopted.

Having eleven players instead of fifteen aided in opening the game and it emphasized speed over strength. When Camp attended in 1878, this motion was rejected but it passed in the 1880 meeting. The line of scrimmage and the snap from center to the quarterback also passed in 1880. Originally the snap occurred by a kick from the center, but this was later modified so the ball would be snapped with the hands either as a pass back (long snap) or a direct snap from the center.

It was Camp's new scrimmage rules, however, which according to many, revolutionized the game, though it was not always to increase speed. In fact, Princeton was known to use line of scrimmage plays to slow the game, making incremental progress towards the end zone much like today during each down.

Camp's original idea was to increase scoring, but in fact the rule was often misused to maintain control of the ball for the entire game. The negative effect was that there were many slow and unexciting contests. This too would be fixed with the idea of the first down coming into play.

In 1982, at the rules meeting, Camp proposed that a team be given three downs to advance the ball five yards. These rules were called the down and distance rules. Along with the notion of the line of scrimmage, these rules transformed the game of rugby into the distinct sport of American football.

Among other significant rule changes, in 1881, the field size was reduced to its modern dimensions of 120 by 53 1/3 yards (109.7 by 48.8 meters). Camp was central to these significant rule changes that ultimately defined American football. Camp's next quest was to address scoring anomalies. His first cut was to give four points for a touchdown and two points for kicks after touchdowns; two points for safeties, and five points for field goals. The notion of the foot in football /rugby explains Camp's rationale.

In 1887, game time was fixed at two halves of 45 minutes each. Additionally, college games would have two paid officials known as a referee and an umpire, for each game. In 1888, the rules permitted tackling below the waist and then in 1889, the officials were given whistles and stopwatches to better control the game.

An innovation that many list as most significant to making American football uniquely American was the legalization of blocking opponents, which back then was called "interference." This tactic had been highly illegal under the rugby-style rules and in rugby today, it continues to be illegal.

The more those who know soccer and football find rugby to be more like soccer.

Though *offsides* is a penalty infraction today, *offsides* in the 1880's in rugby was very much the same as *offsides* in soccer. The prohibition of blocking in a rugby game is in fact because of the game's strict enforcement of its *offsides* rule. Similar to soccer, this rule prohibits any player on the team with possession of the ball to loiter between the ball and the goal. Blocking continues as a basic element of modern American football, with many complex schemes having been developed and implemented over the years, including zone blocking and pass blocking.

Camp stayed active in rule making for most of his life. He had the honor of personally selecting an annual All-American team every year from 1889 through 1924. Camp passed away in 1925. The Walter Camp Football Foundation continues to select All-American teams in his honor.

With many rule changes as noted, as American style rugby became more defined as American football, more and more colleges adopted football as part of their sports programs. Most of the schools were from the Eastern US. It was not until 1879 that the University of Michigan became the first school west of Pennsylvania to establish a bona-fide American-style college football team.

Back then, football teams played whenever they could in the fall or the spring. For example, Michigan's first game was in late spring, near the end of what we would call the academic year. On May 30, 1879 Michigan beat Racine College 1–0 in a game played in Chicago. In 1887, Michigan and Notre Dame played their first football game, which did not benefit from Camp's rules.

The first night time game

It was not until September 28, 1892 that the first nighttime football game was played. Mansfield State Normal played Wyoming Seminary in Mansfield, Pennsylvania. These schools are close to where I live. The game ended at a "declared" half-time in a 0–0 tie. It had become too dark to play.

Wyoming Seminary was not a college and to this day it is not a college. I live about five miles from the school. It is a private college preparatory school located in the Wyoming Valley of Northeastern Pennsylvania. During the time period in which the game was played, it was common for a college and high school to play each other in football—a practice that of course has long since been discontinued.

The reason that it got too dark to play, ironically was not because the game began at dusk. Mansfield had brought in a lighting system that was far too inadequate for game play. This historical game lasted only 20 minutes and there were only 10 plays. Both sides agreed to end at half-time with the score at 0-0. Though it may seem humorous today, for safety reasons, the game was declared ended in a 0-0 tie after several players had an unfortunate run-in with a light pole.

Mansfield and Wyoming Seminary are thus enshrined in football history as having played in the first night game ever in "college football." History and football buffs get together once a year to celebrate the game in what they call "Fabulous 1890's Weekend." This historic game is reenacted exactly as it occurred play by play just as the actual game is recorded in history. Fans who watch the game are sometimes known to correct players (actually actors) when they deviate from the original scripted plays. Now, that shows both a love of the game and a love of history.

Mansfield and Wyoming Seminary's game added additional fame to both schools when the 100th anniversary of the game just happened to occur on Monday, September 28, 1992. Monday Night Football celebrated "100 years of night football" with its regularly scheduled game between the Los Angeles Raiders and the Kansas City Chiefs at Arrowhead Stadium. The Chiefs won 27–7 in front of 77,486 fans. How about that?

More football history was recorded when Army played Navy in 1893. In this game, we have the first documented use of a football helmet by a player in a game. Joseph M. Reeves had been kicked in the head in a prior football game. He was warned by his doctor that he risked death if he continued to play football. We all know how tough the Midshipmen and Black Nights (Cadets) are regardless of who they may be playing. Rather than end his football playing days prematurely. Reeves discussed his need with a shoemaker in Annapolis who crafted a leather helmet for the player to wear for the rest of the season.

Football conferences

Things were happening very quickly in the new sport of football. Organization and rules became the mantra for this fledgling sport. It was being defined while it was being played. Formal college football conferences were just around the corner. In fact, the Southeastern Conference and the Atlantic Coast Conference both got started in 1894.

The forward pass

None of Camp's rules for American Football included the most innovative notion of them all – the forward pass. Many believe that the first forward pass in football occurred on October 26, 1895 in a game between Georgia and North Carolina. Out of desperation, the ball was thrown by the North Carolina back Joel Whitaker instead of having been punted. George Stephens, a teammate caught the ball.

Despite what most may think or surmise, it was Camp again when he was a player at Yale, who executed the first game-time forward pass for a touchdown. During the Yale-Princeton game, while Camp was being tackled, he threw a football forward to Yale's Oliver Thompson, who sprinted to a touchdown. The Princeton Tigers naturally protested and there appeared to be no precedent for a referee decision. Like many things in football including a game-beginning coin-toss, the referee in this instance tossed a coin, and then he made his decision to allow the touchdown.

Hidden ball trick

Dome one-time tricks have not survived football. For example, on November 9, 1895 Auburn Coach John Heisman executed a hidden ball trick. Quarterback Reynolds Tichenor was able to gain Auburn's only touchdown in a 6 to 9 loss to Vanderbilt. This also was the first game in the south that was decided by a field goal.

The trick was simple but would be illegal today. When the ball was snapped, it went to a halfback. The play was closely masked and well screened. The halfback then thrust the ball under the back of the quarterback's (Tichenor) jersey. Then the halfback would crash into the line. After the play, Tichenor "simply trotted away to a touchdown."

The end of college football?

Football was never a game for the light of heart. You had to be tough physically and tough mentally to compete. Way back in 1906, for example complaints were many about the violence in American Football. It got so bad that universities on the West Coast, led by California and Stanford, replaced the sport with rugby union. At the time, the future of American college football, a very popular sport enjoyed by fans nationwide was in doubt. The schools that eliminated football and replaced it with rugby union believed football would be gone and rugby union would eventually be adopted nationwide.

Soon other schools followed this travesty and made the switch. Eventually, due to the perception that West Coast football was an inferior game played by inferior men when compared to the rough and tumble East Coast, manhood prevailed in the West over the inclination to make the game mild. The many tough East Coast and Midwest teams had shrugged off the loss of the few teams out West and they had continued to play American style football.

And, so the available pool of rugby union "football" teams to play remained small. The Western colleges therefore had to schedule games against local club teams and they reached out to rugby union powers in Australia, New Zealand, and especially, due to its proximity, Canada.

The famous Stanford and California game continued as rugby. To make it seem important. The winner was invited by the British Columbia Rugby Union to a tournament in Vancouver over the Christmas holidays. The winner of that tournament was rewarded with the Cooper Keith Trophy. Nobody in America cared. Eventually the West Coast came back to football.

Nonetheless the situation of injury and death in football persisted and though there was a lot of pushback, it came to a head in 1905 when there were 19 fatalities nationwide. President Theodore Roosevelt, a tough guy himself, is reported as having threatened to shut down the game nationwide if drastic changes were not made. Sports historians however, dispute that Roosevelt ever intervened.

What is certified, however, is that on October 9, 1905, the President held a meeting of football representatives from Harvard, Yale, and Princeton. The topic was eliminating and reducing injuries and the President according to the record, never threatened to ban football. The fact is that Roosevelt lacked the authority to abolish football but more importantly, he was a big fan and wanted the game to continue. The little Roosevelts also loved the sport and were playing football at the college and secondary levels at the time.

Meanwhile, there were more rule changes such as the notion of reducing the number of scrimmage plays to earn a first down from four to three in an attempt to reduce injuries. The LA Times reported an increase in punts in an experimental game and thus considered the game much safer than regular play. Football lovers did not accept the new rule because it was not "conducive to the sport."

Because nobody wanted players injured or killed in a game, on December 28, 1905, 62 schools met in New York City to discuss major rule changes to make the game safer. From this meeting, the Intercollegiate Athletic Association of the United States, later named the National Collegiate Athletic Association (NCAA), was formed.

The forward pass is legalized

One rule change that was introduced in 1906 was devised to open up the game and thus reduce injury. This new rule introduced the legal forward pass. Though it was underutilized for years, this proved to be one of the most important rule changes in the establishment of the modern game.

Because of these 1905-1906 reforms, mass formation plays in which many players joined together became illegal when forward passes became legal. Bradbury Robinson, playing for visionary coach Eddie Cochems at St. Louis University, is recorded as throwing the first legal pass in a September 5, 1906, game against Carroll College at Waukesha.

Later changes were in the minutia category but they added discipline and safety to the game without destroying its rugged character. For example, in 1910, came the new requirement that at least seven offensive players be on the line of scrimmage at the time of the snap, that there be no pushing or pulling, and that interlocking interference (arms linked or hands on belts and uniforms) was not allowed. These changes accomplished their intended purpose of greatly reducing the potential for collision injuries.

As noted previously, great coaches emerged in the ranks who took advantage of these sweeping changes. Amos Alonzo Stagg, for example, introduced such innovations as the huddle, the tackling dummy, and the pre-snap shift. Other coaches, such as Pop Warner and Notre Dame's Knute Rockne, introduced new strategies that still remain part of the game.

Many other rules changes and coaching innovations came about before 1940. They all had a profound impact on the game, mostly in opening up the passing game, but also in making the game safer to play without diminishing its quality.

For example, in 1914, the first roughing-the-passer penalty was implemented. In 1918, the rules on eligible receivers were loosened to allow eligible players to catch the ball anywhere on the field. The previously more restrictive rules allowed passes only in certain areas of the field.

Scoring rules also changed which brought the scoring into the modern era. For example, field goals were lowered from five to three points in 1909 and touchdowns were raised from four to six points in 1912.

Jim Thorpe, Circa 1915

Star Players:

Star players emerged in both the collegiate and professional ranks including Jim Thorpe, Red Grange, and Bronko Nagurski were other stars. These three in particular, were able to move from college to the fledgling NFL and they helped turn it into a successful league.

Notable sportswriter Grantland Rice helped popularize the sport of football with his poetic descriptions of games and colorful nicknames for the game's biggest players, including Notre Dame's "Four Horsemen" backfield and Fordham University's linemen, known as the "Seven Blocks of Granite".

Legends existed all during the formation of football. There was Stagg, Halas, Warner, Thorpe, Heisman, Grange, Rockne and The Four Horsemen.

The Heisman

In 1935, New York City's Downtown Athletic Club awarded its first Heisman Trophy to University of Chicago halfback Jay Berwanger. He was also the first ever NFL Draft pick in 1936. The trophy continues to this day to recognize the nation's "most outstanding" college football player. It has become one of the most coveted awards in all of American sports.

Jay Berwanger, 1st Heisman Winner

New formations and play sets continued to be developed by innovative coaches and their staffs. Emory Bellard from the University of Texas, developed a three-back option style offense known as the wishbone. Bear Bryant of Alabama became a preacher of the wishbone.

The strategic opposite of the wishbone is called the spread offense. Some teams have managed to adapt with the times to keep winning consistently. In the rankings of the most victorious programs, Michigan, Texas, and Notre Dame are ranked first, second, and third in total wins.

And so that is as far as we will take it in this chapter about the early evolution of football. With so many conferences and sports associations as well as pro, college, high school, and mini sports, something tells me we have not yet seen our last rule change.

Chapter 6 Army Launches First Football Team

Michie,   Coach #1
Williams   Coach #2
Bliss   Coach #3
Graves   Coach #4
Dyer   Coach #5

Year	Coach	Record	Conf	Record
1890	Dennis Michie	0-1-0	Indep	0-1-0
1891	Henry Williams	4-1-1	Indep	4-1-1
1892	Dennis Michie	3-1-1	Indep	3-1-1
1893	Laurie Bliss	4-5-0	Indep	4-5-0
1894	Harmon Graves	3-2-0	Indep	3-2-0
1895	Harmon Graves	5-2-0	Indep	5-2-0
1896	George Dyer	3-2-1	Indep	3-2-1

1890 First Army Navy Game (Only game this season) Notice no protective gear

The 1890 season was unique in many ways. First of all, it was Army's first football season. Second, it is the only season that Army played just one game, and Third, it was the season in which the inaugural Army-Navy game was played – the only game.

Army's football program began on November 29, 1890, when Navy challenged the Cadets to a game of the relatively new sport. Navy defeated Army at West Point that year, but Army avenged the loss in Annapolis the following year.

The academies still clash every December in what is traditionally the last regular-season Division I college-football game. The 2016 Army–Navy Game marked Army's overcoming its fourteenth consecutive loss to Navy, defeating the Midshipmen in a great game W (21-17).

From 1944 to 1950, the Cadets had a phenomenal run which included all wins against Navy--57 wins, 3 losses and 4 ties. During this time span, Army won three national championships.

Army's football team reached its pinnacle of success during the Second World War under coach Earl Blaik when Army won three consecutive national championships in 1944, 1945 and 1946, and produced three Heisman trophy winners: Doc Blanchard (1945), Glenn Davis (1946) and Pete Dawkins (1958). Past NFL coaching greats—Vince Lombardi (Packers) and Bill Parcells (Giants et al) were Army assistant coaches early in their careers.

The football team plays its home games at Michie Stadium, where the playing field is named after Earl Blaik. Cadets' attendance is mandatory at football games and the Corps stands for the duration of the game. At all home games, one of the four regiments marches onto the field in formation before the team takes the field and leads the crowd in traditional Army cheers.

For many years, Army teams were known as the "Cadets." In the 1940s, several papers called the football team "the Black Knights of the Hudson." From then on, "Cadets" and "Black Knights" were used interchangeably until 1999, when the team was officially nicknamed the Black Knights.

Between the 1998 and 2004 seasons, Army's football program was a member of Conference USA, but starting with the 2005 season Army reverted to its former independent status. Army competes with Navy and Air Force for the Commander-in-Chief's Trophy.

On November 29th, 1890, over 125 years ago, Army hosted Navy at West Point on the Plain in their very first football game. Navy beat Army 24-0 that day.

Army did not take too long to learn how to win. The Cadets came back the next year with a 32-to-16 win.

Before it had lived for five years, the classic rivalry almost died an early death in 1894, when, for mostly stupid reasons, both academies were forbidden to play anything but HOME games.

One of the greatest football fans of the ages was Teddy Roosevelt. At the time, TR was Assistant Secretary of the Navy. After an appeal to bring back the games that was made to Theodore Roosevelt, the game was re-instated in 1899. Some bureaucrat in Washington had taken four good years away from the rivalry.

Since 1899, with just a few interruptions that should not have been scheduled, it's been "game on" ever since.

Few may know this but in the pre-Super Bowl era, Army-Navy was widely considered to be THE game. I can remember cozy up on the couch with my dad in his favorite chair watching the Army Navy game in the 1950's on our 1956 B/W Admiral Console TV.

Usually played on neutral ground in Philadelphia, the game quickly became a magnet for Presidents. Harry Truman was a frequent fan, and John F. Kennedy attended in 1962.

In the period of mourning following his assassination the very next year, it was Jacqueline Kennedy who urged that the game go on, as her late husband was a great fan.

Navy won 21-to-15, in a game also remembered for featuring the very first instant replay ... a CBS Sports innovation, as it happens. Sadly enough, that game cannot be replayed now as it was erased long ago.

After 117 games in the series, Navy currently leads the series with 60 wins to Army's 50, with seven ties. In the 2016 game, another president was in attendance. This was president elect Donald Trump. He was in the crowd for the 117th match

President-elect Donald Trump waved to the crowd and pumped his fist as he arrived in the first quarter of the Saturday December 10, 2016 edition of The Army-Navy game

Navy had won 14 straight contests in the rivalry, but Army's underdog Black Knights prevailed 21-17, in a fourth-quarter comeback that came weeks after Trump's stunning victory over Hillary Clinton.

Trump spent the first half of the game in the box of David Urban, a West Point graduate and one of his Republican advisers in battleground Pennsylvania, and the second half in the box of retired Marine Lt. Col. Oliver North, a graduate of Annapolis.

The 1890 Army-Navy-Game was the first game and the first Army Navy Game

This game which, since 1890, comes almost like clockwork in late November or early December, does not have the same national championship implications it once did during some of the 127 seasons of Army football. Some think that the rise of the National Football League has a lot to do with that, as elite young athletes now are choosing major colleges as a path to the professional game rather than one of the service academies as a path to serving their country. And there is nothing wrong with that.

The U.S. Armed Forces have fought for centuries to allow all Americans the right to choose whatever profession they desire. So, most of the players in the 118th version of the rivalry to be played in 2017 are more likely to end up at Fort Bragg than with the 49ers—a choice they've proudly made.

Still, the contest has produced its share of extremely talented players, including Heisman Trophy winners Roger Staubach (Navy, 1963), Joe Bellino (Navy, 1960), Pete Dawkins (Army, 1958), Glenn Davis (Army, 1946) and Felix "Doc" Blanchard (Army, 1945).

Entering this afternoon's matchup at FedEx Field in Landover, Md., the Midshipmen led the series 60-50-7 and lost the most recent contest.

As we go through each season we will pick ten in which we amplify the abbreviated coverage of arguably the 10 greatest games in the history of this historic rivalry featuring players who all eventually will end up on the same team.

1890 West Point Cadets 1st Football Coach & Player Dennis Michie

In their inaugural season, the Army Cadets football team represented the United States Military Academy in the 1890 college football season. In its first season fielding a team in intercollegiate football, the Cadets compiled a 0–1-0 record with just one game played.

Football had begun being played on campus at the Academy in 1889, but only one inter-class match game was played that year. During the 1890 season, the Cadets played only one official football game, on the West Point grounds. In this historical game, the Army team lost to the Navy team, L (0-24). Navy's Midshipmen were the only players to score in the kickoff game to a long-time series of great Army–Navy Games.

Even though it was a first for Army, there was a lot of pre-game publicity. A week before the game, the New York Times reported that the planned match "is beginning to assume almost national proportions."

During the game, Army's quarterback Kirby Walker was knocked out of the game four times, the last time being carried off the field and to the hospital in an unconscious state. As you can see, in those days there was no protective headgear.

After the victory, Navy Cadets in Annapolis "fired twenty-four great guns, and then paraded the streets with horns." If the score were reversed, Army would have been doing some powerful celebrating also. As it is, the Cadets would have to wait just one more year in order to get back at Navy for the loss.

A 20-year-old Army player, Dennis Michie, was the coach and the captain of the 1890 Army football team. Michie is often listed as the team's head coach because he served the purpose for the team. He actually put in a year as head coach in 1892. Dennis Michie was the lightest player on the team at 142 pounds. He had a wonderful career at the Academy but his life ended too soon.

Lieutenant Michie was killed in 1898 during the Spanish–American War. It is a stark reminder of the Army's mission of preserving liberty and democracy. Army's home football stadium, Michie Stadium, was dedicated in his honor when it opened in 1924. With just one game played, no Army Cadets were honored on the 1890 College Football All-America Team.

LIEUTENANT DENNIS M. MICHIE.

Dennis Michie – Army's 1st functioning Head Football Coach

1891 Army West Point Cadets Football Coach Henry Williams

The Army Cadets football team represented the United States Military Academy in the 1891 college football season. It was their second season of intercollegiate football. They were coached by Henry Williams in his first of just one year. The team played as an independent (no conference) and had a nice record of 4-1-1.

USMA Army Cadets 1891 Football Team

This was technically Army's first season fielding a team in intercollegiate football, the Cadets had compiled a 0-1-0 record with just one game played in 1890. And, so, in this, the first full season of Army football, the Cadets compiled a highly respectable 4–1–1 record.

<<< **Coach Williams**

Army outscored its opponents by a combined total of 80 to 73. The Cadets opened the season with a 10–6 victory over Fordham– the first win in Army football history. In the final game of the season, the Cadets defeated the Navy Midshipmen by a 32 to 16 score in the second annual Army–Navy Game.

Army's head coach in 1891 was 22-year-old Henry L. Williams, who had played football at Yale. Williams remained at the Academy only one year. He later served as head coach at Minnesota for 22 years and was inducted into the College Football Hall of Fame.

Not having been playing long enough to get noticed, no Army Cadets were honored on the 1891 College Football All-America list.

Games of the 1891 Season

In its first full length season, Army began its season at home at the Plain, its more or less makeshift football field at West Point NY. Fordham was the first official opponents in 1891 and the Cadets prevailed W (10-6. On Oct 31, having tasted victory and liking it, the Cadets played another home game against was tea known as the Princeton "B" team and though the team played well, all It could manage was a tie T (12-12). At home again on Nov 7, with a 1-0-1 record, Army beat Stevens Tech in a nail -biter W (14-12).

Playing home at the Plain again against Rutgers on Nov 14, the Cadets lost their first game of the season as they were overpowered by the Scarlet Knights, L (6-27). Next up at home on Nov 21 was the Schuylkill Navy AC and Army won W (6-0). Then, on Nov 28, in the final game of the season, the Cadets played their first away game at Worden Field in Annapolis MD. Against the Navy Midshipmen. Army made up for last year's disappointing loss with a big win W (32-16) to finish with a nice 4-1-1 record.

1892 Army West Point Cadets Football Coach Dennis Michie

The Army Cadets football team represented the United States Military Academy in the 1892 college football season. It was their third season of intercollegiate football. They were coached for the second time in their short span of playing intercollegiate football by Coach Dennis Michie. Playing as an independent, the team had another nice record of 3-1-1.

<< Coach Dennis Michie

Michie Led the team well with just one loss, shutting out three of their five opponents, and they outscored all opponents by a combined total of 90 to 18. In the third annual Army–Navy Game, the Cadets lost to the Midshipmen by a 12 to 4 score.

No Army Cadets were honored on the 1892 College Football All-America Team. It is worthy to note that Dennis Michie, who was captain of the Army football team in 1890 and 1891, and who technically was the coach in 1890, was the bona fide head coach of the 1892 team. Michie, as noted previously, was killed in 1898 during the Spanish–American War. Army's home football stadium, Michie Stadium, was dedicated in his honor when it opened in 1924.

Games of the season

The season opened at the Plain, on the campus of the US Military Academy in West Point NY on October 8 at home against Wesleyan. The Cadets and Wesleyan tied in this game T (6-6). At home on Oct 22, the Cadets shut-out Stevens Tech in a big game W (42-0). On Oct 29 at home, Army shut out Trinity W (24-0).

On Nov 19, at home, the Cadets defeated the Princeton "B" team W (14–0). In the final game of a short season, at home, the Cadets failed in an attempt to gain a repeat win from Navy and lost to the Midshipmen L (4–12) before an attendance of 3,000.

1893 Army West Point Cadets Football Coach Laurie Bliss

The Army Cadets football team represented the United States Military Academy in the 1893 college football season. It was their fourth season of intercollegiate football. They were coached by Laurie Bliss, shown in a picture from his Yale playing days. As an independent football entity, the team had a losing record of 4-5-0

<< Coach Laurie Bliss

In their first and only season under head coach Laurie Bliss, the Cadets compiled a 4–5-0 record and were outscored by their opponents by a combined total of 109 to 84. In the annual Army–Navy Game, the Cadets lost to the Midshipmen by a 6 to 4 score. No Army Cadets were honored on the 1893 College Football All-America Team.

Games of the season

The season opened with a close loss at the Plain, on the campus of the US Military Academy in West Point NY on Sept 30 at home against the Volunteer AC L (4-6). On Oct 7 at home, the Cadets defeated Lafayette in a shutout W (36-0). On Oct 14 again at home, Army lost to Lehigh L (0-18). On Oct 21, the Cadets beat Amherst W (12-4). Yale was a tough team in the 1890's as Walter Camp was so adept at football, he was building the rule book. On Oct 28, at home, the Cadets were beaten by Yale in a shutout L (0-28).

All games were played at the Plain until Dec 2 when Army would travel to Worden Field in Annapolis MD for the Army Navy Game, won by Navy again L (406). On Nov 4, the Cadets beat Union, W (6-0). Then, on Nov 11, Army defeated Trinity. The Cadets finished the season with two losses. The first loss was a blowout on Nov 18 v L (4-36) against Princeton. The next was the Army-Navy Game.

1894 Army West Point Cadets Football Coach Harmon Graves

The Army Cadets football team represented the United States Military Academy in the 1894 college football season. It was their fifth season of intercollegiate football. They were coached by Harmon Graves in his first of two seasons as head coach of Army. Harmon Graves, is shown in the below picture. As an independent football entity, the team had a winning record of 3-2-0.

<< Coach Harmon Graves

In their first season under head coach Harmon Graves, the Cadets compiled a 3-2 record and outscored their opponents by a combined total of 95 to 22. 1 The Army was not played in 1894 because of the rule about no away games. No Army Cadets were honored on the 1894 College Football All-America Team. All 1896 games were played at home.

The season opened on Oct 6 with a shutout win W (18-0) at the Plain, on the campus of the US Military Academy in West Point NY at home against Amherst W (18-0). In this short five-game season, the Cadets won every other game. On Oct 13, their first loss was a shutout against Brown L (0-10) On Oct 20, the Cadets picked up a shutout win v MIT W (42-0).

On Oct 27, the Cadets were defeated in a close game against Yale L (5-12). On Nov 3, the Army Cadets shut out Union for a nice win W (30-0). No Army-Navy game was held in 1894.

Chapter 6 Army Lunches First Football Team   75

1896 Army West Point Cadets Football Coach Harmon Graves

The Army Cadets football team represented the United States Military Academy in the 1894 college football season. It was their sixth season of intercollegiate football. They were coached by Harmon Graves in his first of two seasons as head coach of Army. As an independent football entity, the team had a winning record of 5-2-0.

In their second season under head coach Harmon Graves, the Cadets compiled a 5-2 record, shut out five of their seven opponents by a combined total of 141 to 32. It was a good year.

Because of away game restrictions, the Army-Navy Game was not played in 1895. On November 2, 1895, Army lost to Yale by a 28 to 8 score in what one press account called the greatest and most exciting game of football ever played on the West Point grounds."
No Army Cadets were honored on the 1895 College Football All-America Team.

Almost all games were played at home. The season opened on Oct 6 with a big shutout win W (50-0) at the Plain, on the campus of the US Military Academy in West Point NY at home against Trinity W (50-0). After a loss to Harvard L (0-4) on Oct 12, the Cadets won two shutouts in a row.

Oct19, Tufts W (35-0); On Oct 26, Dartmouth, W (6-0). On Nov 2, in a closer game than the score, Yale beat the Cadets L (8-28). Army finished with two more shutout wins. The first on Nov 16 v Union W (16-0) The next was an exception away game against Brown in Newburgh NY W (26-0) on Nov 23.

1896 Army West Point Cadets Football Coach George Dyer

The Army Cadets football team represented the United States Military Academy in the 1895 college football season. It was their seventh season of intercollegiate football. They were coached by George Dyer in his first and last season as head coach of Army. George Dyer is shown in the below picture. As an independent football entity, the team had a winning record of 3-2-1.

The Cadets compiled a 3-2-1 record, shut out five of their seven opponents by a combined total of 93 to 45 to 32. It was a so-so year.

Because of away game restrictions, the Army–Navy Game was not played in 1896. No Army Cadets were honored on the 1896 College Football All-America Team.

All games were played at home. The season opened on Oct 3 with a big shutout win W (50-0) at the Plain, on the campus of the US Military Academy in West Point NY at home against Tufts W (27-0). After a loss to Princeton, L (0-11) on Oct 17, the Cadets won a game, lost one, then tied one and then won again to close the season.

Oct24, Union, W (44-0); On Oct 31, Yale, Dartmouth, W (6-0). On Nov 2, in a closer game than the score, Yale beat the Cadets L (2-16). Then Wesleyan on Nov 7, T (12-12), finishing up with Brown, W (8-6) on Nov. 21.

Chapter 7 Army Football Seasons from 1897-1907

Koehler   Coach # 6
Kromer   Coach # 7
Nolan   Coach # 8
King   Coach # 9
Boyers   Coach #10
Smither   Coach #11
Graves   Coach #12

Year	Coach	Record	Conf	Record
1897	Herman Koehler	6-1-1	Indep	6-1-1)
1898	Herman Koehler	3-2-1	Indep	3-2-1)
1899	Herman Koehler	4-5-0	Indep	4-5-0
1900	Herman Koehler	7-3-1	Indep	7-3-1
1901	Leon Kromer	5-1-2	Indep	5-1-2
1902	Dennis Nolan	6-1-1	Indep	6-1-1
1903	Edward King	6-2-1	Indep	6-2-1
1904	Robert Boyers	7-2-0	Indep	7-2-0
1905	Robert Boyers	4-4-1	Indep	4-4-1
1906	Henry Smither	1-0-0	Indep	1-0-0
1906	Ernest Graves	2-5-1	Indep	2-5-1
1907	Henry Smither	6-2-1	Indep	6-2-1

1897 Army Team Picture Coach Herman Koehler

1897 Army West Point Cadets Football Coach Herman Koehler

The Army Cadets football team represented the United States Military Academy in the 1897 college football season. It was their eighth season of intercollegiate football. They were coached by Herman Koehler in his first of four seasons as head coach of Army. Herman Koehler is shown in the below picture. As an independent football entity, the team had an excellent record of 6-1-1.

<<Coach Herman Koehler

The Cadets compiled a 6-1-1 record, shut out five of their seven opponents by a combined total of 194 to 41. It was a fine year.

Because of away game restrictions, the Army-Navy Game was not played in 1897. The Cadets suffered their only loss against Harvard by a 10 to 0 score and played Yale to a 6–6 tie. The Army–Navy Game was not played in 1897.

Three Army Cadets were honored on the 1897 College Football All-America Team. Halfback William Nesbitt received second-team honors from Walter Camp. Quarterback Leon Kromer received second-team honors from the New York Sun. Tackle Wallace Scales received second-team honors from Walter Camp and The New York Sun.

All games were played at home. The season opened on Oct 3 with a big shutout win W (38-6) at the Plain, on the campus of the US Military Academy in West Point NY at home against Trinity. On Oct 9, the Cadets defeated Wesleyan W 12-9). After a loss to Harvard L (0-10) on Oct 16, the Cadets shut-out Tufts W (30-0)

On Oct30, the Cadets tied Yale T (6-6) and were more than ready when they walloped Lehigh on Nov 6 W (48-6). On Nov 13, the Cadets beat Stevens Tech W (18-4) and then Army finished the season against Brown with a nice W (42-0) shutout on Nov 20.\

1898 Army West Point Cadets Football Coach Herman Koehler

The Army Cadets football team represented the United States Military Academy in the 1898 college football season. It was their ninth season of intercollegiate football.

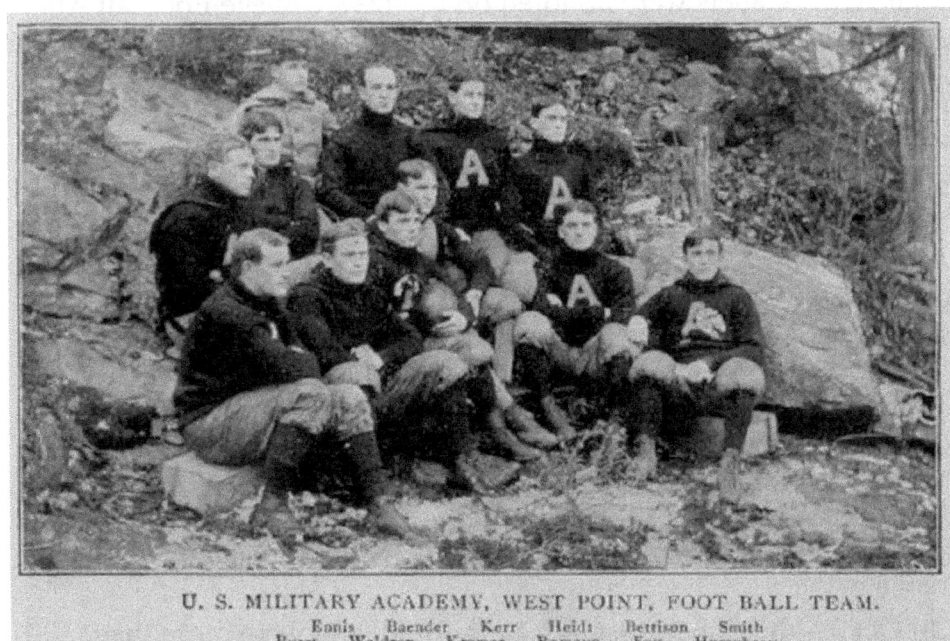

1898 Army Cadets Football team

They were coached by Herman Koehler in his second of four seasons as head coach of Army. As an independent football entity, the team had a winning record of 3-2-1.

The Cadets compiled a 3-2-1 record, shut out five of their seven opponents by a combined total of 90-51. It was an OK year.

Because of away game restrictions, the Army–Navy Game was not played in 1897. The Cadets' two losses came against undefeated co-national champion Harvard and Yale. The Army–Navy Game was not played in 1898.

The Cadets really played tough football against tough opponents. They suffered their only loss against National Champion Harvard by a 10 to 0 score and played co-champion Yale to a 6–6 tie. The Army–Navy Game stupidly was not played in 1898.

Army was no longer an also-ran. Army players were from this point on always contenders for national honors. The Army teams got strong early and stayed that way for many years.

Four Army Cadets were honored on the 1898 College Football All-America Team. Fullback Charles Romeyn was a consensus first-team All-American, receiving first-team honors from Caspar Whitney and the New York Sun. Quarterback Leon Kromer, tackle Robert Foy, and end Walter Smith were recognized as third-team All-Americans by Walter Camp.

All Army games again, because of unreasonable demands on opponents were played at home. Thus, there were fewer games as should have been on the Army schedule.

The 1898 season opened on Oct 3 with a big shutout win W (40-0) at the Plain, on the campus of the US Military Academy in West Point NY at home against Tufts. On Oct 8, the Cadets defeated Wesleyan W (27-8). After a loss to Harvard L (0-28) on Oct 15, the Cadets shut-out Lehigh W (18-0)

On Oct 29, the Cadets lost to Yale L (0-10) and were more than ready on Nov 5 when they put a run attack together to keep a tough Princeton squad at bay in a tie T (5-5).

1898 Player Highlights Charles Romeyn, Fullback

Fullback Charles Annesley Romeyn was a consensus first-team All-American, receiving first-team honors from Caspar Whitney and the New York Sun. Born December 14, 1874, he was a fine American football player and an accomplished United States Army officer. He played for the Army Cadets football team and was selected as a consensus first-team fullback on the 1898 College Football All-America Team.

Romeyn comes from a military family. He was born in Indian Territory, in what is now the state of Oklahoma. The son of Major Romeyn, West Point. He attended the United States Military Academy at West Point, New York. While at the Academy, he played at the fullback position for Army.

Shortly before the 1898 football season got underway, Romeyn was stripped of his captain's stripes due to an "unmilitary order" that he had given to Cadets under his command. He reportedly told Cadets, "Keep your faces to the front. Turn your eyes if you want to see things, but remain quiet and face front."

Romeyn graduated from the Military Academy in 1899 and spent his entire career in the Army. He was initially commissioned as a second lieutenant in the 10th Cavalry in February 1899 and stationed at Bayamo, Cuba until December 1899. In August 1905, Romeyn was promoted to captain while stationed at Fort Myer, Virginia. He next served at Fort Riley, Kansas, where he was a member of the Army Cavalry Rifle Team, entering national competitions in 1905, 1906 and 1907.

He also served as coach of the Army Cavalry Rifle Team in 1909. From December 1909 to May 1912, Romeyn served his third tour in the Philippines. He participated in action against "Moro bandits" in 1911 in the Cagayan Valley.
Romeyn returned to the United States in June 1912 and was assigned to Fort Bliss in Texas and then Fort Leavenworth in Kansas.

He was promoted to major of the cavalry in May 1917, adjutant-general in July 1917 and lieutenant-colonel in August 1917. In July 1918, he was promoted to colonel of the infantry and became a member of the Army General Staff in Washington, D.C. Romeyn retired from the military in December 1938 at age 64.

1899 Army West Point Cadets Football Coach Herman Koehler

The Army Cadets football team represented the United States Military Academy in the 1899 college football season. It was their tenth season of intercollegiate football. They were coached by Herman Koehler in his third of four seasons as head coach of Army. As an independent football entity, the team had a losing record of 4-5-0.

The Cadets compiled a 4-5-0 record, were outscored by their opponents by a combined total of 100 to 57. It was a negative year overall.

Because the away game restrictions were lifted, the Army–Navy Game was played again as a matter of course from 1899 onward. In this version of the annual Army–Navy Game, the Cadets defeated the Navy by a 17 to 5 score. Army had become a powerful player on the national stage.

As noted, Army was no longer an also-ran. Army players were from several years prior to 1899, always contenders for national honors. The Army teams got strong early and stayed that way for many years.

Because 1899 was a weak year overall for Army, like the olden days, there were no Army Cadets honored on the 1899 College Football All-America Team.

Even though restrictions were lifted, scheduling of games is not an instantaneous art and so all Army games again, because of prior unreasonable demands on opponents, were played at home. Thus, there were still fewer games as should have been on the Army schedule.

The 1899 season opened on Oct 2 with a big shutout win W (22-0) at the Plain, on the campus of the US Military Academy in West Point NY at home against Tufts. On Oct 7, the Cadets lost to Penn State L (0-6) After a loss to Harvard L (0-18) on Oct 14, the Cadets were shut-out by Princeton L (0-23).

On Oct 28, the Cadets defeated Dartmouth W (6-2) and then Army lost to Yale L (0-24). Then, the Cadets lost to Columbia L (0-16) and came back against Syracuse W (12-6) The season finale against Navy was on Dec 2 at a neutral site because of the anticipated crowd – Franklin Field in Philadelphia. Army beat Navy W (17-5) and so in 1899, the bus ride home was much more pleasant for the Cadets and fans than the Midshipmen and their fans.

1900 Army West Point Cadets Football Coach Herman Koehler

The Army Cadets football team represented the United States Military Academy in the 1900 college football season. It was their eleventh season of intercollegiate football. The 1900 team is shown below:

1—Phillips; 2—Kromer; 3—Sterling, Mgr.; 4—Davis; 5—Koehler; 6—Williams; 7—Clark; 8—Farnsworth; 9—Phipps; 10—Casad; 11—Boyers; 12—Hackett; 13—Zehl; 14—Nichols; 15—Burnett; 16—Bettison; 17—Smith, Capt.; 18—Bunker; 19—Goodspeed; 20—Finn.
Photo by Pach Bros.
WEST POINT MILITARY ACADEMY FOOT BALL TEAM.

The team was again coached by Herman Koehler in his fourth and final year of four seasons as head coach of Army. As an independent football entity, the team had a winning record of 7-3-1.

The Cadets compiled a 7-3-1 record, shut out seven opponents (including a scoreless tie with Penn State), and outscored all opponents by a combined total of 109 to 68.

Army end Walter Smith was recognized by the NCAA as a consensus first-team player on the 1900 College Football All-America Team, having received first-team honors from Caspar Whitney and third-team honors from Walter Camp. Tackle Edward Farnsworth also received third-team honors from Camp.

The Army–Navy Game was played again as a matter of course. In this version of the annual Army–Navy Game, played at Franklin Field in Philadelphia, Navy defeated the Cadets L (7-11).

Even though away-games were permitted, scheduling of games did not yet catch up to the waiving of the restrictions. Consequently, other than the Navy game at Franklin Field, all Army contests were played at home at the Plain. Army played eleven games in 1900.

The 1900 season opened on Sept 29 with a low scoring shutout win W (5-0) at the Plain, on the campus of the US Military Academy in West Point NY at home against Tufts. On Oct 6, the Cadets tied Penn State in a scoreless game T (0-0). Next, the Cadets shut out Trinity W (28-0) before facing Lasalle on Oct 17 W (11-) and then Harvard. L (0-29) on Oct 20. After the expected loss to this very strong Harvard team, Army shut out Williams on Oct 27 in a low-scoring game W (6-0).

On Nov 3, the Cadets were beaten by a tough Yale Squad L (0-18) Then on Nov 7, the Cadets shut out Rutgers W (23-0). Three days later, against Hamilton, Army won another close shutout W (11-0). On Nov 17, the Cadets beat Bucknell in a close match W (18-0)

The season finale against Navy was on Dec 1 at a neutral site because of the anticipated crowd – Franklin Field in Philadelphia. The Cadets lost to the Midshipmen L (7-11) at Franklin Field. At the time, Franklin Field was comparatively huge with a capacity for 30,000.

1900 Player Highlights Walter Smith, End

Walter Driscol Smith (November 16, 1875 – September 20, 1955) was a fine American football player and an accomplished military officer. He was a consensus All-American football player in 1900 while enrolled at the United States Military Academy. He served in the United States Army until 1946. He retired then as a Brigadier-General.

Smit grew up in Maryland and attended the United States Military Academy at West Point, New York. He played college football as an END for the Army Cadets football team from 1898 to 1900 and was the captain of the 1899 and 1900 teams. He was a consensus All-American in 1900. He was also selected by Walter Camp as a third-team All-American in 1898.

Smith graduated from the U.S. Military Academy in 1901. He then remained assigned to the U.S. Military Academy. He served as an instructor of mathematics from 1905 to 1906 and assistant to the quartermaster from 1906 to 1909. He was stationed in Panama as the Constructing Quartermaster with the Panama Canal Commission from 1909 to 1913. He returned to the U.S. Military Academy from 1915 to 1917 as an instructor in tactics, assistant adjutant, post exchange officer, treasurer, and assistant quartermaster.

In 1916, during the World War I effort, Smith was promoted to the rank of captain in the cavalry. In December 1917, he sailed for France and served as an observer with the British Army. In January 1918, he was assigned to the General Headquarters of the American Expeditionary Forces at Chaumont, France, serving as the Chief of Organization and Equipment Division. He was promoted to the rank of colonel of the field artillery in June 1918.

Smith participated in major engagements at Champagne-Marne, Aisne-Marne, Somme Offensive, Oise-Aisne, St. Michael, and Argonne-Mueuse. He was awarded the Order of St. Maurice and St. Lazarus and was cited by the commanding general of the American Expeditionary Force "for exceptional meritorious and conspicuous services in Organization and Equipment, General Staff, France."

After World War I, Smith attended the Army War College, the General Service Schools, and the Naval War College.

He retired in 1939 and was recalled during World War II with an assignment to the War Department from 1941 to 1946. He reached the rank of Brigadier-General.

1901 Army West Point Cadets Football Coach Leon Kromer

The Army Cadets football team represented the United States Military Academy in the 1901 college football season. It was their twelfth season of intercollegiate football.

1901 Army Cadets Football Team

The team was coached by Leon Kromer in his first and only year as head coach of Army. As an independent football entity, the team had a winning record of 5-1-2.

The Cadets compiled a 5-1-2 record, shut out four opponents, and outscored all opponents by a combined total of 98 to 22. The team's only loss was by a 6 to 0 score against an undefeated Harvard team that has been recognized as a co-national champion for the 1901 season. The Cadets also tied with Yale (5–5) and Princeton (6–6). In the annual Army–Navy Game, the Cadets defeated the Midshipmen by an 11 to 5 score.

Two members of the 1901 Army team have been inducted into the College Football Hall of Fame: quarterback Charles Dudley Daly and tackle Paul Bunker. Both are also recognized by the NCAA as consensus first-team players on the 1901 College Football All-America Team. Daly received first-team honors from Walter Camp, Caspar Whitney, the New York Post and The Philadelphia Inquirer. Bunker received first-team honors from Camp and the New York Post and second-team honors from Whitney.

Even though away-game limitations were called off, scheduling of games still had not yet caught up to the waiving of the restrictions. Consequently, other than the Navy game at Franklin Field, all Army contests were played at home at the Plain. Army played just eight games in 1901.

The 1901 season opened on Oct 5 with a shutout win W (22-0) at the Plain, on the campus of the US Military Academy in West Point NY at home against Franklin & Marshall. On Oct 12, the Cadets defeated Trinity (CT) W (17–0). Then, on Oct 19, #1 Harvard came in and the Cadets almost pulled it off but were defeated L (0-6). The Cadets then beat Williams on Oct 26 W (15-0). In another tough battle against one of the toughest teams in the nation, Army tied Yale on Nov 2 T (5-5).

Another tough team, Princeton came to West Point on Nov 9 and worked for a tie against the Cadets T (6-6). On Nov 23, the Cadets then shut out the always tough Penn Quakers W (24-0)

The season finale against Navy was on Nov 30 at a neutral site because of the anticipated crowd which approached 30,000. Franklin Field in Philadelphia was the venue. In this contest, the Cadets beat the Midshipmen W (11-5) in a tough but convincing battle. Harvard was the only loss for the entire season.

Best Army Navy Game #5

The 1901 game marked the first time a U.S. President attended the annual Army-Navy gridiron battle.

Less than three months after taking office following the assassination of then-President William McKinley, Theodore Roosevelt traveled to Philadelphia to watch the Cadets top the Midshipmen, 11-5.

Army's Charles Daly was the day's biggest standout.

He kicked a field goal, and, with his team down 5-3, returned a kickoff 95 yards to open the second half. The defenses took over from there, and the Cadets won for the second time in three seasons.

President Roosevelt ar 1901 Army Navy Game (Roosevelt loved Football)

1901 Player Highlights Charles Daly, QB

Charles Dudley "Charlie" Daly was born October 31, 1880. He was a great American football player and coach. He was also an author and he served in the United States Army during World War I. He played college football first as quarterback at Harvard University and then for the United States Military Academy. He served as the head football coach at West Point from 1913 to 1916 and again from 919 to 1922. His Army coaching record is 58–13–3. Daly was inducted into the College Football Hall of Fame as a player in 1951. He also served as Fire Commissioner in Boston during the 1910s.

After earning football letters at West Point in 1901 and 1902, Charles Daly returned to the Academy for two separate coaching stints, guiding the Black Knight gridders from 1913 to 1916 and again from 1919 through 1922. During his eight campaigns along the Army sideline, the Black Knights amassed a sparkling .804 winning percentage.

Daly directed the Black Knights to undefeated seasons in 1914, 1916 and 1922. Army's perfect 9-0 mark in 1914 was the first in the program's history. Daly's Army teams defeated Navy five times in eight meetings. And, it was Daly roaming the sideline for the Black Knights in 1913 when the Academy initiated its series with Notre Dame, beginning what would evolve into one of college football's most storied rivalries.

In 1951, Daly became the first player or coach from West Point to be enshrined in the College Football Hall of Fame, accepting his honor as part of the Hall's inaugural induction class. Daly was a founding member of the American Football Coaches Association and served as that organization's first president in 1922.

During his undergraduate playing days, which included stints as a quarterback at both Harvard and Army, Daly was named a first-team All-American four times (1898-1900 with the Crimson and 1901 at Army) before earning third-team plaudits at West Point in 1902.

In addition to the legacy Daly created on the gridiron, he also initiated a long-time family association with West Point that saw three of his sons, two grandsons and one great-grandson earn degrees from the Academy.

1902 Army West Point Cadets Football Coach Dennis Nolan

The Army Cadets football team represented the United States Military Academy in the 1902 college football season. It was their thirteenth season of intercollegiate football. They were coached by Dennis Nolan in his first and only year as head coach of Army. As an independent football entity, the team had a winning record of 6-1-1.

<< Coach Nolan

The Cadets compiled a 6-1-1 record, shut out five of eight opponents, and outscored all opponents by a combined total of 180 to 28. The team's only loss was by a 14 to 6 score against Harvard. The Cadets also defeated Syracuse by a 46 to 0 score and tied with an undefeated Yale team that has been recognized as a national co-champion. In the annual Army–Navy Game, the Cadets defeated the Midshipmen by a 22 to 8 score.

Two members of the 1902 Army team were inducted into the College Football Hall of Fame: quarterback Charles Dudley Daly and tackle Paul Bunker. During the 1892 college football season, the selectors were Caspar Whitney (CW) Harper's Weekly (HW) and the Walter Camp Football Foundation (WC). Whitney began publishing his All-America Team in 1889, and his list, which was considered the official All-America Team, was published in Harper's Weekly from 1891 to 1896

And, so, in addition to the two inductees, five members of the squad were honored by one or both of Walter Camp (WC) and Caspar Whitney (CW) on the 1902 College Football All-America Team. They are: Bunker (WC-1, CW-1); Daly (WC-3); center Robert Boyers (WC-2, CW-1); tackle Edward Farnsworth (CW-2); and fullback Henry Torney (WC-3

Even though away-game limitations were called off, scheduling of games still had not yet caught up to the waiving of the restrictions. Consequently, other than the Navy game at Franklin Field, all Army contests were played at home at the Plain. Army played just eight games in 1902.

The 1902 season opened on Oct 4 with a shutout low-score win W (5-0) at the Plain, on the campus of the US Military Academy in West Point NY at home against Tufts. On Oct 11, the Cadets shut out Dickinson W (17–0). Then, on Oct 18, #1 Harvard came in and the Cadets played well but Harvard played a bit better L (6-14). The Cadets then shut-out Williams on Oct 25 W (28-0). In another tough battle against one of the toughest teams in the nation, Army tied Yale on Nov 1 T (6-6).

The Union Team came to West Point on Nov 8 and were shut out and walloped good by the Cadets W (56-0. Then, on Nov 15, the Cadets shut out the Syracuse Orangemen in a great offensive display W (46-0).

The season finale against Navy was on Nov 29 at a neutral site because of the anticipated crowd which approached 30,000. Franklin Field in Philadelphia was the venue again. In this contest, the Cadets beat the Midshipmen W (22-8) in a tough but convincing match. Harvard again was the only loss for the entire season.

1902 Player Highlights Robert Boyers, L

Robert Emlen Boyers was born on Christmas Day, December 25, 1876. He was a United States Army officer and a great American football player and coach. He was an all-American center at Army in 1902., playing the position from 1899 through 1902.

He served as the head football coach at the United States Military Academy from 1904 to 1905, compiling a record of 11–6–1. Boyers graduated from West Point in 1903. He served during World War I with the 3rd Infantry Division in France and with the 332nd Infantry Regiment in Italy. He lost his foot as the result of wounds and retired in 1919 with the rank of captain.

1902 Player Highlights Robert Anderson, RB

Robert Paul Anderson
Class of 1960
Football (1957-59)

Bob Anderson was born in New Jersey on March 31, 1938. In High school, this great athlete won 15 letters in four sports at Cocoa, Florida H.S. Unlike most West Point football players, he was a widely sought after blue chip player who nearly went to powerhouse Georgia Tech. Instead he chose USMA at West Point.

In his plebe year, he played football and basketball and was the leading hitter for the baseball team. When he joined the Army football varsity in 1957 the Black Knights were coming off a 5-3-1 season and Coach Blaik was concerned about his defense, depth (a perennial problem) and an inexperienced line. The quarterback position, a thorn in the Cadets' side since Pete Vann's graduation, at least had an experienced operative in Dave Bourland but the plan was to avoid passing. The Cadets ran out of a tight "T" and their game was speed.

During spring training, Coach Blaik and his staff immediately saw the potential in two untried halfbacks. One of them was Bob Anderson from New Jersey. Blaik wrote an introduction of Anderson in his autobiography in 1960: "Anderson, 19, six feet 2, 205, from

Cocoa, Florida, was the best all-around football player at the Academy since Blanchard and Davis. While his classic naturalness in every phase of play delighted the connoisseur, Anderson was most exciting as a runner. He had power that blasted through and over tacklers, speed that could outstay pursuit, and a flavor of king-size niftiness... He did everything well, running, blocking, tackling, passing, catching passes, defending against them, punting. He was also one of the most self-effacing and selfless team players I ever encountered."

Bob Anderson was a two-time first-team All-America selection as a running back. He led Army in rushing during each of his three varsity seasons, and helped the Cadets forge a 19-6-2 (.741) record over his career. Anderson teamed with Heisman Trophy winner Pete Dawkins to give the Black Knights a potent backfield combination in 1958 as Army captured its most recent Lambert Cup.

With Anderson compiling 564 yards as a junior, the Black Knights rolled to an 8-0-1 record in 1958. Anderson, who saw his senior season hampered severely due to an injury, graduated with 1,887 career ground markers and 21 rushing touchdowns.

His yardage total listed second only to legendary Glenn Davis on Army's career rushing chart at the conclusion of his career, while that mark ranks 11th on the all-time ladder presently.

As a sophomore in 1957, Anderson burst onto the collegiate scene, amassing an eye-popping 987 rushing yards and 12 touchdowns, nearly becoming only the second Army player to reach 1,000 yards in a season. Anderson averaged 109.7 rushing yards per game that year, including an Academy-record 214 ground yards against Utah.

Anderson's performance versus the Utes remains the sixth-highest single-game rushing effort in Army grid annals. Anderson recorded five 100-yard rushing outings in his career.

A staunch two-way player, Anderson also led the Black Knights in interceptions in both 1957 and 1958. Additionally, Anderson lettered twice in baseball and in 1960 was presented the Army Athletic

Association Trophy as the top athlete in his graduating class. He was inducted into the College Football Hall of Fame in 2004.

1901 Player Highlights Paul Bunker, L

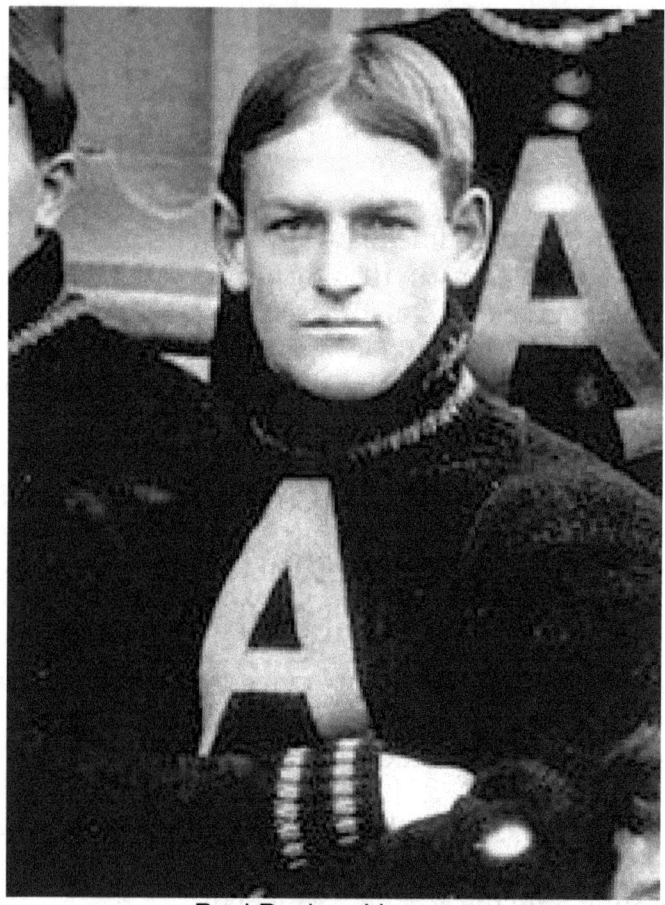

Paul Bunker, Lineman

Paul Delmont Bunker was born on May 7, 1881. He was a soldier and a great football player. Bunker attended the U.S. Military Academy and became the first football player at West Point to be selected as a first-team All-American by Walter Camp. Bunker was chosen as an All-American at the tackle position in 1901 and repeated as an All-American in 1902, but as a halfback.

He served in the U.S. Army for 40 years and was in command of the coastal artillery forces in the Battle of Corregidor. On the fall of

Corregidor, Bunker became a prisoner of war. He died of starvation and disease in a Japanese prison camp in 1943 after losing 70 pounds. His posthumously published journal, Paul Bunker's Diary, became a best-seller. He was elected to the College Football Hall of Fame in 1969. He was an American hero in football and in life.

He was born in Alpena, Michigan, and when the time came, Bunker enrolled at the U.S. Military Academy at West Point, New York. At West Point, Bunker played at the tackle and halfback positions on the academy's football team from 1899-1902. One writer summarized Bunker's football career at West Point as follows:

"A steel-chested, tow-haired, rugged tackle tipping the scales well over 215 pounds, Bunker made the cadet varsity as a plebe in 1899 and played without relief throughout the 1900, '01 and '02 grid campaigns. ... He was not the colorful elusive runner so prominent in football today, but depended on bull strength and a pair of piston-like legs that consistently sent him through the center of the line for three, four and five yards at a clip."

At West Point, Bunker was a classmate of Gen. Douglas MacArthur. MacArthur also served as the manager of the Army football team in 1902 when Bunker was at his peak. Bunker was selected by Walter Camp as a member of the 1901 and 1902 College Football All-America Teams. Bunker is one of a handful of athletes to win All-America honors at two different positions. He was selected as an All-American tackle in 1901 and as a halfback in 1902.

In 2008, Sports Illustrated sought to identify the college football players who would have likely won the Heisman Trophy as the best player in the sport during each of the years before the award's inception in 1935. Sports Illustrated selected Bunker as the retroactive Heisman Trophy winner for 1902.

Bunker went on to a 40-year career in the military specializing in coastal defense artillery. In 1940, Bunker, then a colonel, returned to the Philippines and assumed command of the 59th Coast Artillery Regiment (United States) at Fort Hughes in Manila Bay. There, Bunker was reunited with his college roommate, Gen. Douglas MacArthur.

Surrender of U.S. forces at Corregidor.

Following the Japanese military offensive against the Philippines, President Roosevelt ordered MacArthur to evacuate the islands. MacArthur reluctantly left, promising to send reinforcements that never came. In his autobiography, MacArthur recalled one of his last memories on leaving the Philippines was of Bunker:

"On the dock, I could see the men staring at me. I had lost 25 pounds living on the same diet as the soldiers, and I must have looked gaunt and ghastly standing there in my old war-stained clothes - no bemedaled commander of inspiring presence. ... Through the shattered ruins, my eyes sought 'Topside,' where the deep roar of heavy guns still growled defiance, with their red blasts tearing the growing darkness asunder. Up there, in command, was my classmate, Paul Bunker.

Forty years had passed since Bunker had twice been selected by Walter Camp for the All-American team. I could shut my eyes and see again that blond head racing, tearing, plunging - 210 pounds of irresistible power. I could almost hear Quarterback Charley Daly's shrill voice barking, 'Bunker back.' He and many others up there were old, old friends, bound by ties of deepest friendship."

In May 1942, when Gen. Wainwright decided to surrender at Corregidor, he ordered Bunker to lower the U.S. flag and burn it to prevent its falling into the hands of the Japanese forces. Wainwright later recalled, "Promptly at noon this May 6, 1942, I ordered the white flag run up and our firing ceased. It was with the sickest of feelings that I gave the white-flag-raising order to Colonel Paul D. Bunker."

Instead of burning the entire flag, Bunker cut off a piece and concealed it under a patch on his shirt. Before he died in the Japanese prison camp, Bunker sent for Colonel Delbert Ausmus, cut the flag remnant into two pieces and gave one of the pieces to Ausmus. He told Colonel Ausmus he did not expect to survive the prison camp and that it was Ausmus' duty to take his piece of the flag to the Secretary of War. Ausmus concealed the remnant in his shirt cuff, and shortly after the war ended, Ausmus delivered it to Secretary Patterson. In November 1945, Ausmus described the circumstances under which he received the remnant from Bunker:

"He was taken to Billibid prison in Manila and came down with pneumonia. While he was in the hospital Col. Paul D. Bunker of Taunton, Mass., was brought in suffering from seriously infected blisters on his feet and blood poisoning in one leg. On June 10, Bunker watching carefully 'to see that there were no Japs near,' swore him to secrecy, Ausmus continued, and 'said he wanted to turn something over to me to deliver to the Secretary of War.' From beneath a false patch set into the left pocket of his shirt Bunker took a bit of red cloth. Solemnly he gave Ausmus part of it and put the rest back."

While giving one piece of the flag to Ausmus, he held onto another piece until the time of his death. Gen. Wainwright later recalled the circumstances of Bunker's death in the prison camp, still holding onto the remnant: "He must have suffered ... constant pain of hunger ... I sat with him for a part of the last two hours of his life ... cremated in the rags in which he had carefully sewn a bit of the American flag he had pulled down in Corregidor."

Ausmus did deliver it to the Secretary of War who unveiled it during a speech on the event of Flag Day in June 1946. The remnant of the U.S. flag from Corregidor saved by Bunker and Ausmus is on display in the West Point museum.

In 1944, Bunker was posthumously awarded the Distinguished Service Medal for exceptionally meritorious service at Corregidor. The citation read:

"His courageous and incessent [sic] devotion to duty in directing the activities of his batteries and in supervising the immediate repair of damage inflicted by Enemy bombardment was outstanding. Colonel Bunker's outstanding leadership maintained superior morale and efficiency in his command through the campaign."

Bunker's 190-page diary of his time on Corregidor was published posthumously under the title Paul Bunker's War and became a best-seller.

Bunker was honored with burial in the cemetery at West Point. In June 1946, one of the U.S. Army's coastal artillery batteries located at Fort MacArthur was renamed the Battery Paul D. Bunker, BCN-127 to honor Bunker's memory.

He was posthumously inducted into the College Football Hall of Fame in 1969.

We all live freely because of great men such as Paul Bunker. War is hell but it is the cost of peace.

1902 Player Highlights Henry Torney, B

Henry Walter Torney was born on November 12, 1884. He became an American football player and an industrial engineer. He was an All-American slot at both the halfback and the fullback positions in 1904 and 1905 while he was attending the United States Military Academy. He later became an industrial engineer.

Torney was the son of George H. Torney, the Surgeon General of the United States Army. Torney played college football and was a member of the crew at Cornell from 1901 to 1902. He was later admitted to the United States Military Academy at West Point, New York, in June 1902.

He then played football for the Army football team. When selected as an All-American, he gained a first-team All-American slot in 1904 (as a halfback) and then in 1905 (as a fullback). In 1904, one of his big accomplishments was running 105 yards in one game against Yale. Torney's final game for Army was the 1905 Army-Navy game, played at Princeton, New Jersey, in front of President Theodore Roosevelt, former President Grover Cleveland, and future President Woodrow Wilson. Torney scored Army's only touchdown in a 6-6 tie.

Torney graduated from West Point in June 1906 and served in the artillery corps. He was stationed at Fort Totten, New York, from 1906 to 1907 and at Fort Hancock, New Jersey, from 1908 to 1909. He was transferred to the recruiting service in New York City in December 1910.

In January 1910, Torney, then a first lieutenant in the U.S. Army, was arrested in New York City as part of a protest with the Shirtwaist Strikers. Torney was dating Inez Milholland, the noted suffragette who was then a law student at New York University, and had attended the protest with her. The charges against Torney and Milholland were later dropped, but the arrests of Milholland and Torney drew extensive press coverage that raised questions about the role of the police in labor disputes.

New York Mayor William Jay Gaynor subsequently rebuked the "police dictators" for their conduct in making the arrests and instructed the police that they were not to take sides in labor disputes.

Torney married Bertha Benedict, the daughter of Seelye Benedict, on December 27, 1913, the same day that his father died. He went on to become a successful industrial engineer with a "palatial summer residence" at Southampton, Long Island.

In 1932, Torney, described in the press as a "millionaire industrial engineer," was the target of a blackmail plot by the former gardener at his Southampton estate. The Federal Bureau of Investigation arrested the blackmailer, and the story was featured in a lengthy feature article promoting the investigative prowess of the FBI's "G-Men." Torney died young in October 1942.

1903 Army West Point Cadets Football Coach Edward King

<< Coach Edward King

The Army Cadets football team represented the United States Military Academy in the 1903 college football season. It was their fourteenth season of intercollegiate football. They were coached by Edward King in his first and only year as head coach of Army. As an independent football entity, the team had a winning record of 6-2-1.

The Cadets compiled a 6-2-1 record, shut out five of their nine opponents, (including a scoreless tie with Colgate), and outscored all opponents by a combined total of 164 to 33. The team's only losses were to Harvard (5–0) and Yale (17–5). These two teams typically competed year after year for the mythical National Championship.

In an intersectional game, the Cadets defeated Chicago by a 10 to 6 score. In the annual Army–Navy Game, the Cadets, behind quarterback Horatio B. Hackett, defeated the Midshipmen by a huge 40 to 5 score.

Three members of the squad were honored by one or both of Walter Camp (WC) and Caspar Whitney (CW) on the 1903 College Football All-America Team. They are: guard Napoleon Riley (WC-

2); halfback Edward Farnsworth (CW-2); and fullback Frederick Prince (CW-2).

The 1903 season opened on Sept 26 with a scoreless tie T (0-0) at the Plain, on the campus of the US Military Academy in West Point NY at home against Colgate. On Oct 3, the Cadets shut out Tufts W (17–0). On Oct 10, the Cadets shut out Dickinson W (12-0). Then, on Oct 17, the always-tough Harvard squad came in to the Plain and the Cadets played well but Harvard played just a bit better, shutting out the Cadets L (0-5). The Cadets then faced another tough team, Yale and played well in defeat L (5-17).

On Oct 31, the Cadets shut out Vermont W (32-0). This was a warm-up game for Manhattan on Nov 7, in this game the Cadets walloped the Manhattan squad in a big shutout W (48-0). The Cadets did well in an intersectional game on Nov 14 v Chicago, pulling out a nail-biter win W (10-6).

The season finale against Navy was on Nov 28 again at a neutral site because of the anticipated crowd which always approached 30,000. Franklin Field in Philadelphia was the venue again because of proximity and size of stadium. In this match, the Cadets overwhelmed the Midshipmen W (40-5) in a one-sided match. Harvard and Yale were the only losses for the entire season. Army kept getting closer to beating these two great teams of the 1900's.

Having studied the history of many teams from their first game to their last, I always seemed to find the teams having sluggish seasons in the beginning and it was not until they hired a long-term coach that the team began to settle into winning.

Army is an enigma regarding this theory. The Cadets longest term coach at this point was Herman Koehler at just four years. Here we are in just the fourteenth season and the Army Cadets were on their third one-year coach in a row and yet they were not only winning games, they are almost knocking off perennial champs such as Harvard, Yale, Princeton, and Penn.

Before all the trickery and sophisticated play-calling that came from years of coaching, Army was whipping its opponents with first-year coaches. Why? Maybe there is something in a soldier's blood that makes them, all things being equal, fight lots harder for the victory. That's what I think. How about you?

1904 Army West Point Cadets Football Coach Robert Boyers

The Army Cadets football team represented the United States Military Academy in the 1904 college football season. It was their fifteenth season of intercollegiate football. They were coached by Robert Boyers in his first of two years as head coach of Army. As an independent football entity, the team had a winning record of 7-2-0.

The Cadets compiled a 7-2-0 record, shut out five of their nine opponents, (including a scoreless tie with Colgate), and outscored all opponents by a combined total of 136 to 27. The team's only losses were to Harvard (4–0) and Princeton (17–5). In the annual Army–Navy Game, the Cadets defeated the Midshipmen by an 11 to 0 score.

Five members of the squad were honored by one or both of Walter Camp (WC) and Caspar Whitney (CW) on the 1904 College Football All-America Team. They are: center Arthur Tipton (WC-1, CW-1); back Henry Torney (CW-1); end Alexander Garfield Gillespie (WC-2); halfback Frederick Prince (CW-2); and tackle Thomas Doe (WC-3)

Other than the Army-Navy Game, all games were played at The Plain on the Campus of the US Military Academy in West Point, NY.

The 1904 season opened on Oct 1 with a shutout against Tufts W (12-0). The next game on Oct 8 was another shutout against Dickinson, W (18-0) Then, on Oct 17, the always-tough Harvard squad came in to the Plain and the Cadets played well but Harvard played just a bit better, shutting out the Cadets L (0-5). The Cadets then faced another tough team, Yale and played well just like in the past but this time their efforts resulted in the Cadets' first win ever against Yale W (11-6).

On Oct 29, the Cadets shut out Williams W (16-0). This was a warm-up game for Princeton on Nov 5, but good fortune left the Cadets at the Williams game as Princeton beat Army L (6-12) in a nail-biter on Nov. 5. On Nov 12, the Cadets got back all their moxie and thumped NYU in a big shutout W (41-0). On Nov 19, the Cadets squared off against the Syracuse Orangemen, and brought home the W (21-5).

The season finale against Navy was on Nov 26 again at a neutral site because of the anticipated crowd which always approached 30,000. Franklin Field in Philadelphia was the venue again because of proximity and size of stadium. In this match, the Cadets held the Midshipmen scoreless while scrounging up 11 points to salt away the game W (11-0).at Franklin Field in Philadelphia, PA.

1904 Player Highlights Arthur Tipton

His name is Arthur Charles Tipton. However, like many in sports, Arthur had a nickname. He was affectionately known as "Bull." The "Bull" was born in Las Vegas, New Mexico where he attended public schools while growing up in the city. He also attended Sacred Heart College in Denver, Colorado, and Braden's Preparatory School before he entered the Military Academy in June 1901.

"Bull" was prominent in athletics as a cadet and was outstanding in football. He was designated a consensus first-team All-American Center in 1904. Upon graduation, he was assigned to the 5th Infantry and accompanied that regiment to Cuba in 1906. He resigned his commission September 20, 1909 but he reentered the service in 1917 to participate in WW I.

As a football player for the Army Cadets / Black Knights from 1903 to 1904, he had a great career. During the 1904 game against Navy, Tipton made history by kicking a loose ball down the field and he then fell on the ball for a touchdown after it crossed the goal line. The Rules Committee did not like this maneuver, and subsequently amended the rules to disallow such a play.

In the 1904 Army-Navy Game, this play was a real big deal. Midway through the first half, Navy lined up to accept Army's punt at the 50-

yard line. The ball apparently touched Navy's Homer Norton, and the Cadets' Art "Bull" Tipton, raced down the field, kicking the ball ahead of him.

The scuttle was that this game had suddenly transformed into a modern-day soccer match, with Tipton kicking the ball once again toward the Navy goal line. When the ball reached the end zone, Tipton fell on top of it for Army's first touchdown. Despite the controversy surrounding this incident, it was ruled a touchdown and set the tone for Army's 11-0 triumph. This was the Cadets' fourth win in a row over Navy and Army's first shutout in series history.

After his first hitch in the military, he became engaged in fruit and dairy farming in Sparta Township, New Jersey.
After reentering the service in May 1917, he had a successful career. He was promoted to the rank of lieutenant-colonel, adjutant general in May 1919 and major of the infantry in July 1920.

After World War I, "Bull" continued to serve as G-3, 78th Division, under General J. H. McRae. Tipton retired from the military due to service-related disability in September 1934, holding the rank of lieutenant colonel.

Tipton was married at Newark, New Jersey, in September 1907 to Theodora Coe Tipton. They had two daughters. He later moved to Gainesville, Florida, where he lived until he passed away in January 1942 at age 59.

1905 Army West Point Cadets Football Coach Robert Boyers

The Army Cadets football team represented the United States Military Academy in the 1905 college football season. It was their sixteenth season of intercollegiate football. They were coached by Robert Boyers in his second and last of two years as head coach of Army. As an independent football entity, the team had a break-even record of 4-4-1. In 1905, Coach Boyer and the many Army fans unhappily learned that Army could be beaten more than a few times in a season. It was a lesson well-learned. The next year, would find another head coach manning the squad.

The Cadets compiled a 4-4-1 record, shut out three opponents, and outscored all opponents by a combined total of 104 to 60. The team's big losses were to Virginia Tech, Harvard, Yale, and the Carlisle Indians. In the annual Army–Navy Game, the Cadets and the Midshipmen played to a 6-6 tie.

Halfback Henry Torney was honored as a consensus first-team player on the 1905 College Football All-America Team.

Other than the Army-Navy Game, all games were played at The Plain on the Campus of the USMA in West Point, NY.

The 1905 season opened on Sept 30 with a shutout against Tufts W (18-0). The next game on Oct 7 was another win against Colgate, W (1860) Then, on Oct 14, VPI defeated the Cadets L (6-16). Following this unexpected loss, the always-tough Harvard squad came in to the Plain and the Cadets played well again but Harvard played just a bit better again, shutting out the Cadets L (0-6). The Cadets then faced another tough team, Yale and played well just like in the past but this time their efforts were not good enough as the Yalees defeated the Cadets L (0-20) in a well-played game by Yale.

On Nov 11, the Cadets lost to the Carlisle Indians in a very close match L (5-6). After recovering from this loss, the Cadets took it out by shutting out Trinity W (34-0). On Nov 25, the Cadets squared off against the Syracuse Orangemen, and brought home another Win a shutout W (17-0).

The season finale against Navy was on Nov 26 again at a neutral site because of the anticipated crowd which always approached 30,000. University Field in Princeton NJ was the venue for the first time because of proximity and size of stadium. In its heyday, this stadium's maximum capacity was 20, 000. In this match, the Cadets held the Midshipmen to six points but the Midshipmen also held the Cadets to 6 points as the game ended in a tie T (6-6)

1906 Army West Point Cadets Football Coach Ernest Graves

The Army Cadets football team represented the United States Military Academy in the 1906 college football season. It was their

seventeenth season of intercollegiate football. The 1906 team is shown below:

1—Phillips; 2—Kromer; 3—Sterling, Mgr.; 4—Davis; 5—Koehler; 6—Williams; 7—Clark; 8—Farnsworth; 9—Phipps; 10—Casad; 11—Boyers; 12—Hackett; 13—Zehl; 14—Nichols; 15—Burnett; 16—Bettison; 17—Smith, Capt.; 18—Bunker; 19—Goodspeed; 20—Finn.
Photo by Pach Bros.

WEST POINT MILITARY ACADEMY FOOT BALL TEAM.

They were coached by Henry Smither and Ernest Graves. For both, it was their time being head coach of Army. Both would be back to coach in other years. As an independent football entity, the team had a record of 3-5-1. In 1906, Coaches Smither and Graves' combined record was worse than their predecessor, though technically Smither was 1-0. Army fans unhappily learned again that the Cadets could be beaten more than a few times in a season. It was a lesson well-learned. The next year, Army would rehire Smither to take over the squad. He had a fine year in 1907.

Coaches Graves & Smither

The Cadets compiled a 3-5-1 record, shut out four opponents, and outscored all opponents by a combined total of 59 to 37. Henry Smither was the coach in just the first game of the 1906 season, and Ernest Graves, Sr., was the coach in games two through nine. Smither was relieved from duty following a 12–0 victory over Tufts in the season opener. Ernest Graves, Sr. served as head coach for the remaining eight games of the season, leading Army to a record of 2–5–1. Graves came back to coach again in the 1912 season.

The team's setbacks included losses to Harvard, Yale, and Princeton. In the annual Army-Navy Game, the Cadets lost to the 1906 Midshipmen by a 10 to 0 score.

Two Army players were honored by either Walter Camp (WC) or Caspar Whitney (CW) on the 1906 College Football All-America Team. They are tackle Henry Weeks (WC-3, CW-2) and guard William Christy (WC-3).

Other than the Army-Navy Game, which was played at Franklin Field in Philadelphia, all games were played at The Plain on the Campus of the US Military Academy in West Point, NY.

The 1906 season opened on Sept 29 with a shutout against Tufts W (12-0). The next game on Oct 6, was another shutout—this one against Trinity W (24-0) The next game on Oct 13, Colgate played the Cadets to a scoreless tie T (0-0). Then, on Oct 20, Army shut out

Williams W (17-0). The Cadets looked like the season was under control with a 3-1 record after four games. The Williams' match would be the last win of the 1906 season as the Cadets went on a five-game losing streak to finish the season. The five losses were as follows:

On Oct 27, Harvard shut out the Cadets L (0-5). On Nov 3, Yale defeated the Cadets L (6-10) On Nov 10, Princeton turned a shutout against Army L (0-8).

On Nov 24, the Cadets squared off against the Syracuse Orangemen, and lost the match by an unusual score of L (0-4). The season finale against Navy was on Dec 1 at a neutral site because of the anticipated crowd which always approached 30,000. Franklin Field in Philadelphia PA was the venue. In this match, the Cadets held the Midshipmen to ten points but failed to score and were thus shut-out by Navy L (0-10).

1907 Army West Point Cadets Football Coach Henry Smither

The Army Cadets football team represented the United States Military Academy in the 1907 college football season. It was their eighteenth season of intercollegiate football. They were coached by Henry Smither in his first and only full year as head coach of the Cadets. As an independent football entity, the team had a record of 6-2-1. In 1907 Coach Smither got his act together and had a nice season.

The Cadets compiled a 6-2-1 record, shut out six of their nine opponents, and outscored all opponents by a combined total of 125 to 24. The team's only two losses were to Cornell and to Navy in the annual Army–Navy Game.

1907 Army Cadets Football Team Coach Henry Smithers

Two Army players were honored by either Walter Camp (WC) or Caspar Whitney (CW) on the 1907 College Football All-America Team. They are guard William Erwin (WC-1, CW-1) and tackle Henry Weeks (WC-3, CW-2).

Other than the Army-Navy Game, which was played at Franklin Field in Philadelphia, all games were played at The Plain on the Campus of the US Military Academy in West Point, NY.

The 1907 season opened on Sept 29 with a shutout against Franklin & Marshall W (23-0). The next game on Oct 12, was another shutout—this one against Trinity W (12-0). On Oct 19, Yale and Army played to a scoreless tie T (0-0). The Cadets then shut out Rochester W (30-0) on Oct 26.

In the next game on Nov 2, the Cadets shut out Colgate W (6-0) Then, on Nov 9, the Cadets picked up their first loss of the season v Cornell in a close match L (10-14).

1907 Army Cadets in Action on the Plain

On Nov 23, the Cadets squared off against Syracuse, and defeated the Orangemen W (23-4) The season finale against Navy was on Nov 30 at a neutral site because of the anticipated crowd which always approached 30,000. Franklin Field in Philadelphia PA was the venue. In this match, the Midshipmen shut out the Cadets L (0-6)

1907 Player Highlights Walter Irwin, L

William Walter Erwin was born April 6, 1884. He was a great American football player and an accomplished United States Army officer. He played for the Army Cadets football team and was selected as a consensus first-team guard on the 1907 College Football All-America Team.

Erwin was born in Kansas. He attended the United States Military Academy at West Point, New York. While at the Academy, he played at the guard position for the Army Black Knights football team and was a consensus first-team selection for the 1907 College Football All-America Team.

Erwin graduated from the Military Academy in 1908 and spent his entire career in the Army. He began as a second lieutenant in the 9th Cavalry in February 1908 and stationed in the Philippines from May 1908 to May 1909.

In May 1917, with the United States entry into World War I, Erwin was promoted to the rank of captain and placed in command of training camps at Fort Snelling in Minnesota.
In October 1918, Erwin sailed for France as a machine gun officer with the 31st Division.

The war ended in November 1918, and Erwin was assigned to the School for Care of Animals in France. He returned to the United States in August 1919 and was returned to the rank of captain in September 1919. Erwin died in 1953 and was buried at Saint Patrick's Cemetery in Chapman, Kansas.

Chapter 8 Coaches Nelly, Beacham, & Graves 1908-1912

Nelly   Coach #13
Beacham   Coach #14
Graves   Coach #12 (also coached in 1906)

Year	Coach	Record	Conference	Record
1908	Harry Nelly	6-1-2	Indep	6-1-2
1909	Harry Nelly	3-2-0	Indep	3-2-0
1910	Harry Nelly	6-2-0	Indep	6-2-0
1911	Joseph Beacham	6-1-1	Indep	6-1-1
1912	Ernest Graves	5-3-0	Indep	5-3-0

1908 Army West Point Cadets Football Coach Harry Nelly

<<< Coach Harry Nelly

The Army Cadets football team represented the United States Military Academy in the 1908 college football season. It was their nineteenth season of intercollegiate football. They were coached by Harry Nelly in his first of three seasons as head coach of the Cadets. As an independent football entity, the team had a record of 6-1-2. In 1908 Coach Nelly had a nice season.

The Cadets compiled a 6-1-2 record, shut out five of their nine opponents (including a scoreless tie with Princeton), and outscored all opponents by a combined total of 87 to 21. The team's only loss was to Yale. In the annual Army–Navy Game, the Cadets defeated the Midshipmen by a 6 to 4 score

1, Hines, Asst. Mgr.; 2, Moss; 3, Dean; 4, Devore; 5, Kelly, Mgr.; 6, Baehr; 7, Johnson; 8, Hyatt; 9, Besson; 10, Chamberlain; 11, Nix; 12, Carberry; 13, Walmsley; 14, Byrne; 15, Weir; 16, Philoon, Capt.; 17, Greble; 18, Stearns; 19, Pullen.

UNITED STATES MILITARY ACADEMY, WEST POINT, N. Y.

1908 Army Cadets Football Team Coach Harry Nelly

Two Army players were honored by Walter Camp (WC) on his 1908 College Football All-America Team. They were center Wallace Philcon (second team) and end Johnson Philcon (third team). Philcon also received first-team honors from the Washington Herald, Chicago Inter Ocean, and Fred Crolius. In addition, tackle Daniel Pullen was selected as a first-team All-American by the New York World, Fielding H. Yost, T. A. Dwight Jones, and the Kansas City Journal.

Other than the Army-Navy Game, which was played at Franklin Field in Philadelphia, all games were played at The Plain on the Campus of the US Military Academy in West Point, NY.

The 1908 season opened on Oct 3 with a shutout against Tufts W (5-0). The next game on Oct 10, was another shutout—this one against Trinity W (33-0). On Oct 17, Yale defeated Army L (0-6). The Cadets then shut out Colgate W (6-0) on Oct 24.

In the next game on Nov 7, the Cadets defeated Springfield (MA) W (6-5). Then, on Nov 14, the Cadets tied their second game of the season T (6-6) against Washington & Jefferson. On Nov 21, the Cadets beat shut out Villanova W (25-0). Then on Nov 28, at franklin

Field, in the annual Army-Navy Game, in a real nail-biter, the Army defeated the Navy W (6-4).

1909 Army West Point Cadets Football Coach Harry Nelly

The Army Cadets football team represented the United States Military Academy in the 1909 college football season. It was their twentieth season of intercollegiate football. They were coached by Harry Nelly in his second of three seasons as head coach of the Cadets. As an independent football entity, the team had a record of 3-2-0.

1909 Army Football Offense

The Cadets compiled a 3-2-0 record, shut out two of their five opponents, and outscored all opponents by a combined total of 57 to 32. The team's only losses were to Yale and Harvard. The Army–Navy Game was not played in 1909.

Tackle Daniel Pullen was selected by The New York Times as a second-team player on its 1909 College Football All-America Team. All games were played at The Plain on the Campus of the US Military Academy in West Point, NY.

The 1909 season opened on Oct 2 with a shutout against Tufts W (22-0). In the next game on Oct 9, the Cadets defeated Trinity W 17-6) On Oct 16, Yale shut-out Army L (0-17). The Cadets then shut out Lehigh W (18-0) on Oct 23. In the next game on Oct 30, Harvard shut-out the Cadets L (0-9). The Cadets played just five games and turned in a respectable 3-2 record, losing the big games to Yale and Harvard.

1910 Army West Point Cadets Football Coach Harry Nelly

The Army Cadets football team represented the United States Military Academy in the 1910 college football season. It was their twenty-first season of intercollegiate football. They were coached by Harry Nelly in his third and last of three seasons as head coach of the Cadets. As an independent football entity, the team had a record of 6-2-0. In 1910 Coach Nelly had a nice season.

The Cadets compiled a 6-2-0 record, shut out five of their eight opponents, and outscored all opponents by a combined total of 96 to 12 – an average of 12.0 points scored and 1.5 points allowed. The Cadets' two losses came against 1910 national champion Harvard by a 6 to 0 score and to the Navy Midshipmen by a 3 to 0 score in the annual Army–Navy Game.

Other than the Army-Navy Game, which was played at Franklin Field in Philadelphia, all games were played at The Plain on the Campus of the US Military Academy in West Point, NY.

The 1910 season opened on Oct 8 with a shutout against Tufts W (24-0) In the second game of the season, on Oct 15, the Cadets pulled out all the stops and defeated a fine Yale team W (9-3). The next game on Oct 21, was another shutout—this one against Lehigh, W (28-0). On Oct 29, Harvard, defending National Champions came to the Plain and barely shut out the Cadets W (6-0)

In the next game on Nov 5, the Cadets shut out Springfield (MA) W (5-0). Then, on Nov 12, the Cadets defeated Villanova in a shutout W (13-0). tied their second game of the season T (6-6) against On Nov 19, the Cadets beat shut out Trinity W (17-0). Then on Nov 28, at Franklin Field, in the annual Army-Navy Game, in a real nail-biter, the Navy defeated the Army L (0-3)

1911 Army West Point Cadets Football Coach Joseph Beacham

The Army Cadets football team represented the United States Military Academy in the 1911 college football season. It was their twenty-second season of intercollegiate football. They were coached by Joseph Beacham in his first and only season as head coach of the Cadets. As an independent football entity, the team had a record of 6-1-1. In 1911 Coach Beacham had a nice season.

The Cadets compiled a 6-1-1 record, shut out five of their eight opponents (including a scoreless tie with Georgetown), and outscored all opponents by a combined total of 88 to 11 – an average of 11.0 points scored and 1.4 points allowed. The Cadets' only loss came against the Navy Midshipmen by a 3 to 0 score in the annual Army–Navy Game.

Tackle Leland Devore was a consensus first-team player on the 1911 College Football All-America Team. Other notable players on the 1911 Army team include center Franklin C. Sibert, guard Archibald Arnold, and tackle Robert Littlejohn.

Other than the Army-Navy Game, which was played at Franklin Field in Philadelphia, all games were played at The Plain on the Campus of the US Military Academy in West Point, NY.

The season opener for 1911 was on Oct 7 with a Cadet shutout against Vermont W (12-0) In the second game of the season, on Oct 14, the Cadets shut out Rutgers by a score of W (18-0). The next game on Oct 21, was a great shutout against powerhouse Yale W (6-0). The next shutout was on Oct 28, against Lehigh W (20-0) Then, on Nov 4, the Cadets and Georgetown played to a scoreless tie T (0-0).

From here, working on an undefeated season, the Cadets took on Bucknell and defeated the Bisons, W (20-2). The, on Nov 18, keeping the season clean of losses, Army beat Colgate W (12-6). The heartbreaker came on November 25. Going into the annual Army-Navy Game undefeated, the Cadets got their first big blemish in the last game of the season in a nail biter at Franklin Field. They lost to Navy's Midshipmen L (0-3).

1911 Player Highlights Leland Devore, L

Leland Swarts Devore was born in 1889. He was a great American football tackle and a fine military officer. He played college football with Army and was selected as a first-team All-American in 1911.

Devore grew up in Wheeling, West Virginia and was the son of J. H. Devore, a prominent West Virginia broker. He graduated from Wheeling High School and enrolled at the United States Military Academy at West Point, New York. Devore cast an imposing figure at 6 feet, 4 inches tall, 225 pounds. He was well equipped to handle the tackle position for Army's football team while attending West Point.

In 1911, Devore was selected as a first-team All-American. D Devore was also selected as the captain of the 1912 Army Black Knights football team. Devore was also the heavyweight boxing champion at the academy, the silver medalist in heavyweight wrestling, and lettered in both baseball and basketball.

He was commissioned as a lieutenant in the infantry and accompanied Gen. John J. Pershing on the Pancho Villa Expedition into Mexico in 1916. The expedition marked the first use of motorized transport trucks and cars by the U.S. Army, and Devore was selected as the Army's first motor transport officer.

Devore served as an infantry officer in France during World War I where he was wounded.

Devore spent his career in the Army and was promoted to the rank of lieutenant colonel. He died in 1939 at Washington, D. C. Devore was married to Genevieve (Welty) Devore, and the couple had a son, Leland S. Devore, Jr.

1912 Army West Point Cadets Football Coach Ernest Graves

The Army Cadets football team represented the United States Military Academy in the 1912 college football season. It was their twenty-third season of intercollegiate football. They were coached by Ernest Graves in his first and only season in his second stint as head coach of the Cadets. As an independent football entity, the team had a record of 5-3-0.

The Cadets compiled a 5-3-0 record. They shut out two of their eight opponents The Cadets offense scored 108 points, while the defense allowed 59 points. On November 9, Army battled the Carlisle Indian Academy, which featured legendary athlete Jim Thorpe.

Other than the Army-Navy Game, which was played at Franklin Field in Philadelphia, all games were played at The Plain on the Campus of the US Military Academy in West Point, NY.

Dwight D. Eisenhower (3rd from left) and Omar Bradley (far right) were members of the 1912 West Point football team.

In 1912, the value of a touchdown was increased from five to six points. The value of the points after TD remained an extra end zone was also added. Before the addition of the end zone, forward passes caught beyond the goal line resulted in a loss of possession and a touchback. The increase from five points to six did not come until much later in Canadian Football, and the touchdown remained only five points there until 1956.

The season opener for 1911 was on Oct 5. The Cadets shutout Stevens Tech W (27-0) In the second game of the season, on Oct 12, the Cadets shut out Rutgers by a score of W (18-0). The next game on Oct 21, was a close game in which Yale shutout the Cadets L (0-6). The next game shutout was on Oct 26, against Colgate W (18-7) Then, on Nov 9, the Cadets took on the Carlisle Indians with the gifted all-everything Jim Thorpe. Carlisle dominated the Cadets L (6-27).

From here, on Nov 16, the Cadets defeated Tufts W (15-6) and on Nov 23, Army followed this with a nice victory over Syracuse W (23-7). Going into the annual Army-Navy Game with two losses, the game was up for grabs. Navy hung in and shut out the Cadets L (0-6) in another nail biter at Franklin Field. They lost to Navy's midshipmen L (0-6.)

Chapter 9 Coaches Daly, Keyes, Mitchell & Daly 1913-22

Daly   Coach #15
Keyes   Coach #16
Mitchell   Coach #17

Year	Coach	Record	Conf	Record
1913	Charles Daly	8-1-0	Indep	8-1-0
1914	Charles Daly	9-0-0	Indep	9-0-0
1915	Charles Daly	5-3-1	Indep	5-3-1
1916	Charles Daly	9-0-0	Indep	9-0-0
1917	Geoffrey Keyes	7-1-0	Indep	7-1-0
1918	Hugh Mitchell	1-0-0	Indep	1-0-0
1919	Charles Daly	6-3-0	Indep	6-3-0
1920	Charles Daly	7-2-0	Indep	7-2-0
1921	Charles Daly	6-4-0	Indep	6-4-0
1922	Charles Daly	8-0-2	Indep	8-0-2

1913 Army West Point Cadets Football Coach Charles Daly

The 1913 Army Team is shown below:

The Army Cadets football team represented the United States Military Academy in the 1913 college football season. It was their twenty-fourth season of intercollegiate football. They were coached by Charles Dudley Daly, one of the best coaches in Army history. Daly was in his first season of stint one of two stints of four seasons each as head coach of the Cadets. As an independent football entity, the team had a record of 8-1-0. It was a fantastic season.

<< Coach Charles Daly

The Cadets compiled an 8-1-0 record. They shut out five of their nine opponents, and outscored all opponents by a combined total of 253 to 57 – an average of 28.1 points scored and 6.3 points allowed. The Cadets' only loss was against Notre Dame by a 35 to 13 score. All-American Knute Rockne played on that Notre Dame team. In the annual Army–Navy Game, the Cadets defeated the Midshipmen by a 22 to 9 score.

End Louis A. Merrilat was a consensus first-team player on the Team. Tackle Alex Weyand was selected as a second-team All-American by Walter Camp and was later inducted into the College Football Hall of Fame. Quarterback Vernon Prichard was selected as a second-team All-American by Harper's Weekly.

Other than the Army-Navy Game, which was played at the Polo Grounds in New York, all Army games were played at The Plain on the Campus of the US Military Academy in West Point, NY.

More About Coach Daly

After earning football letters at West Point in 1901 and 1902, Charles Daly returned to the Academy for two separate coaching stints, guiding the Black Knight gridders from 1913 to 1916 and again from 1919 through 1922. During his eight campaigns along the Army sideline, the Black Knights amassed a sparkling .804 winning percentage, forging a record of 58-13-3.

Daly directed the Black Knights to undefeated seasons in 1914, 1916 and 1922. Army's perfect 9-0 mark in 1914 was the first in the program's history. Daly's Army teams defeated Navy five times in eight meetings. And, it was Daly roaming the sideline for the Black Knights in 1913 when the Academy initiated its series with Notre Dame, beginning what would evolve into one of college football's most storied rivalries.

In 1951, Daly became the first player or coach from West Point to be enshrined in the College Football Hall of Fame, accepting his honor as part of the Hall's inaugural induction class. Daly was a founding member of the American Football Coaches Association and served as that organization's first president in 1922.

During his undergraduate playing days, which included stints as a quarterback at both Harvard and Army, Daly was named a first-team All-American four times (1898-1900 with the Crimson and 1901 at Army) before earning third-team plaudits at West Point in 1902.

Daly notably coached Army Football teams. He began his coaching career in American football with teams at Harvard before West Point. At West Point, as previously noted, he is known as one of the immortals. More specifically, he is known as the "Godfather of West Point Football.

He was coach to Dwight Eisenhower, Omar Bradley, Joseph Stilwell, Matthew Ridgway, James Van Fleet, George S. Patton and other American military luminaries of the 20th century. In 1921 he founded the American Football Coaches Association.

At West Point he was also an Assistant Professor of Military Science and Tactics from 1928 to 1934. An athletic field on the campus is named in honor of him.

In addition to the legacy Daly created on the gridiron, he also initiated a long-time family association with West Point that saw three of his sons, two grandsons and one great-grandson earn degrees from the Academy.

Here is a famous quote from Coach Daly:

A remarkable similarity exists between war and football. This is particularly manifest in their organization. In both war and football, we have the staff and the troops. In both we have the supply department, medical branch, and the instruction branch. In both, the importance of leadership is paramount. The principles of war laid down by Clausevitz are the principles of the application of force. Just so in football, we have exactly analogous principles of the application of force and a similar organization.

— *Charles Dudley Daly, American Football*

Games of the 1913 Season

The Cadets opened the season against Stevens Tech at home as usual, and came away with a fine shutout W (24-0) In the second game of the season, on Oct 11, the Cadets shut out Rutgers (State University of NJ) by a score of W (29-0). The next game on Oct 18, against Colgate was a close match in which the Cadets barely prevailed W)7-6). Other than ND< this was the closest game to a loss all season for the Cadets. On Oct 25, the Cadets played the second closest game of the season other than ND as they squeaked by Tufts in a shutout win W (2-0).

Notre Dame found the money to get to Army from South Bend and they came home with a big payoff. Coach Jesse Harper had the best passer in the country with Gus Dorais, and he had the best end in the country with Knute Rockne. Notre Dame had a passing attack when other teams were just learning about the forward pass. If this were a ground game, the Cadets would have put in an undefeated season in 1913. Notre Dame passed big and won big L (13-35).

On Nov 8, Albright had no idea how good Army really was when they came to the Plain on Nov 8 and were beaten W (77-0) Next up for a smashing was Villanova, on Nov 15—a fine team but not up to the new-found power of Army Football W (55-0).

Then on Nov 22, Springfield (MA) played tough football but lost anyway to the Cadets W (14-7) After losing the prior two years to Navy in the traditional Army-Navy Game, the Cadets would not be stopped on Nov 29 in the last game of the season and Army beat Navy W (22-9). Army had a phenomenal 8-1 season, which set them up for one of the finest West Point Seasons of all time in 1914.

1913 Player Highlights, Louis Merrillat, End

Louis Alfred "Merry" Merrilat, Jr. was born June 9, 1892. He was a great American football End and an accomplished military officer. He played college football with Army and was selected as a first-team All-American in both 1913 and 1914. He was wounded in battle while serving in France during World War I and later played in the National Football League for the Canton Bulldogs in the 1925 NFL season. He became a soldier of fortune, training Iran's Persian Guard, working with the Chinese Army in the 1930s, and serving in the French Foreign Legion.

A native of Chicago, Illinois, Merrilat gained an appointment to the USMA at West Point and matriculated as a cadet at West Point from June 1911 to June 1915. While serving as a cadet, Merrilat was an all-around athlete, competing for Army in football, baseball, basketball and track.

He gained much fame as a standout end for the undefeated 1913 Army Cadets football team and as noted, he was selected as a first-team All-American in both 1913 and The passing combo team of "Prichard to Merrilat" was one of the first great passing combinations in college football, and Merrilat was noted for playing "the western game, something, which had not been seen before in the east."

His teammates on the Army football teams included two of the leading generals of World War II – Omar Bradley, who played at the opposite end position from Merrilat, and Dwight Eisenhower, who played halfback until a leg injury sidelined him.

In 1913, he helped the Army defeat a Navy team that allowed only seven points in its other games. Army defeated Navy 22 to 9, as Merrilat scored 18 points on two touchdown passes and a 60-yard run.

Some of the game went as follows: Army capped its first undefeated season (9-0) with a "textbook perfect" 20-0 triumph over Navy. The Cadets took advantage of a blocked punt and two Navy fumbles to score their first-14 points. After forcing Navy to punt on its opening possession, Louis Merillat blocked the punt in the end zone for a safety.

The Mids' H.C. Blodgett fumbled a second-quarter punt that "Robert Neyland" picked up at the Navy 20-yard line. One play later, Louis Merillat was in the end zone after catching a 20-yard touchdown pass from Vernon Prichard. Finally, Blodgett fumbled a second punt that quarter which resulted in a Paul Hodgson one-yard touchdown run.

After graduating, Merrilat served in the U.S. Army as a second lieutenant from 1915 to 1916 and a first lieutenant from 1916 to 1917. In May 1917, one month after the entry of the United States into World War I, Merrilat was promoted to the rank of captain of the infantry. He sailed for France with the American Expeditionary Forces in March 1918 and was promoted to the rank of temporary major of the infantry in June 1918. He participated in the Battle of Château-Thierry, Second Battle of the Marne, and Meuse-Argonne Offensive. He was severely wounded by airplane machine gun fire at Avocourt and sailed for the United States on December 24, 1918.

Merrilat spent many years as a "soldier of fortune." In Iran, he trained the Persian Guard. From Iran, Merrilat traveled to China where he was a general and trained more than 40,000 Chinese troops, "the pick of their army." Merrilat developed a reputation as a soldier with "no equal as a troop trainer or an army builder."

When World War II began, Merrilat reported to the French and served on the Maginot Line. After a few months, he left and became a captain in the French Foreign Legion where he reportedly "served with bravery and distinction."

When WW II was getting underway, Merrilat resigned from the French Foreign Legion and enlisted in the U.S. Army, where he was given a position to train the troops at the rank of colonel, at Miami Beach, Florida. Ninety hotels in Miami Beach were taken over by the Army during the war, and Merrilat turned over the keys to the final building to Mayor Herbert Frink in June 1946.

1914 Army West Point Cadets Football Coach Charles Daly

The 1914 Army Team is shown on the next page:

The Army Cadets football team represented the United States Military Academy in the 1914 college football season. It was their twenty-fifth season of intercollegiate football. They were coached by Charles Dudley Daly. Daly was in his second season of stint one of two stints of four seasons each as head coach of the Cadets. As an independent football entity, the team had a record of 9-0-0. It was a phenomenal season. It was Army's best season to date.

The Cadets compiled an 9-0-0 record. They were undefeated and untied. They shut out six of their nine opponents, and outscored all opponents by a combined total of 219 to 20 – an average of 24.3 points scored and 2.2 points allowed. In the annual Army–Navy Game, the Cadets shut-out the Midshipmen 20 to 0.

The Cadets also defeated Notre Dame by a 20 to 7 score. The 1914 Army team was recognized as the 1914 national champion by the Helms Athletic Foundation, the Houlgate System, and the National Championship Foundation, and a co-national champion by Parke H. Davis.

Three Army players were recognized as first-team players on the 1914 College Football All-America Team: end Louis A. Merrilat; center John McEwan; and quarterback Vernon Prichard. Tackle Alex Weyand was selected as a third-team All-American by Walter Camp. Four players from the 1914 team were later inducted into the College Football Hall of Fame: McEwan; Weyand; Robert Neyland (later coach at Tennessee); and Elmer Oliphant.

Other than the Army-Navy Game, which was played at Franklin Field in Philadelphia, all Army games were played at The Plain on the Campus of the US Military Academy in West Point, NY.

The Cadets opened the season against Stevens Tech at home as usual, and came away with a blowout shutout W (49-0) In the second game of the season, on Oct 11, the Cadets shut out Rutgers (State University of NJ) by a score of W (13-0). The next game on Oct 18, against Colgate was a close match in which the Cadets pulled away and won handily W (21-7) On Oct 24, the Cadets played Holy Cross and did not permit a point in a fine shutout W (14-0).

Next up for a smashing was Villanova, on Oct 31—a fine team but not up to the new-found power of Army Football W (41-0). On Nov 7, the Cadets played the Fighting Irish of Notre Dame and this time, Army Was ready for Jesse Harper's Irish. Army dominated a close game and won the final score W (20-7) against what was then one of the finest football programs in the nation. f

Then on Nov 14, Maine came to play in the plain and were pushed back up country by the score of W (28-0). On Nov 21, Springfield (MA) played tough football but lost anyway to the Cadets W (13-6). The Army-Navy Game was back at Franklin Field in 1914 and Army shut-out Navy W (20-0). Army had a phenomenal 9-0-0 season, which brought many honors to the Daly coached Army Cadets. They simply had a great year.

1914 Player Highlights John McEwan L

John James "Cap" McEwan was born February 18, 1893. He was a great American football player and later a fine coach. He played from 1913 to 1916 as a center at the United States Military Academy, where he was a three-time All-American and captain of the Army football squad for three seasons.

McEwan served as the head football coach at West Point (1923–1925), the University of Oregon (1926–1929), and the College of the Holy Cross (1930–1932), compiling a career college football record of

59–23–6. He also coached at the professional level for the Brooklyn Dodgers of the National Football League (NFL) from 1933 to 1934, tallying a mark of 9–11–1. McEwan was inducted into the College Football Hall of Fame as a player in 1962.

McEwan was an innovator among players of the early 1900's, pioneering the spiral center-snap and introducing a primitive version of the defensive rover-back to Eastern football. Upon graduation from West Point in 1917, McEwan was hailed as the greatest football center the U.S. Military Academy ever had. Walter Camp labeled him first-team All-American in 1914.

John McEwan

When he was about to play football as a senior in 1916, McEwan was elected team captain by his Cadet peers. Tim Cohane, who was a longtime sports editor of LOOK MAGAZINE and author of "Gridiron Grenadiers", described McEwan in these words: "Big Mac, in his prime, weighed from 195 to 205 and stood 6 feet, 4 inches tall. He was built like a heavyweight fighter. His broad shoulders tapered down to slim hips and comparatively thin legs, which brought him frequent but not inactivating knee injuries."

McEwan was unusually fast for a man of his size and became known for his ability to cover large areas of the field while exhibiting a tremendous tackling and blocking prowess. Seven years after his graduation, the Alexandria, Minnesota native returned to West Point as head football coach. During his three coaching seasons, his Army teams rolled to an 18-5- 3 record. He went on to coach Oregon, Holy Cross and the professional Brooklyn Dodgers. He died in 1970.

1915 Army West Point Cadets Football Coach Charles Daly

Dwight D. Eisenhower practice punting for Army in the 1915 season

The Army Cadets football team represented the United States Military Academy in the 1915 college football season. It was their

twenty-sixth season of intercollegiate football. They were coached by Charles Dudley Daly. Daly was in his third season of stint one of two stints of four seasons each as head coach of the Cadets. As an independent football entity, the team had a record of 5-3-1.

The Cadets compiled an 5-3-1. They shut out four of their nine opponents, and outscored all opponents by a combined total of 114 to 57. In the annual Army–Navy Game, the Cadets lost to the Midshipmen by a 14 to 0 score.

Three Army players were recognized on the 1915 College Football All-America Team. Fullback Elmer Oliphant was selected as a first-team player by Walter Camp, Monty, and Damon Runyon. Center John McEwan was selected as a first-team All-American by Damon Runyon and a second-team player by Monty. Tackle Alex Weyand was selected as a second-team player by Monty and a third-team player by Walter Camp.

Other than the Army-Navy Game, which was played at the Polo Grounds in New York, all Army games were played at The Plain on the Campus of the US Military Academy in West Point, NY.

The Cadets opened the season on Oct 2, with a tie T (14-14) against Holy Cross at home. In the second game of the season, on Oct 9, the Cadets shut out Gettysburg by a score of W (22-0). The next game on Oct 18, against Colgate was a close match in which Colgate shut out the Cadets L (0-13). Oct 23, the Cadets played Holy Cross and did not permit a point W (10-0).

Next up for a smashing was Villanova, on Oct 30—a fine team that rose to the occasion to defeat the Cadets L (13-16). On Nov 6, the Cadets played the Fighting Irish of Notre Dame and Notre Dame got the best of the Cadets in a close shutout L (0-7).

Then on Nov 13, Maine came to play in the plain and were shut out W (24-0). Springfield (MA) was next on Nov 20 as the Cadets won the game W (17-7). The Army-Navy Game was at The Polo Grounds again and Navy shut out Army W (14-0).

1916 Army West Point Cadets Football Coach Charles Daly

The Army Cadets football team represented the United States Military Academy in the 1916 college football season. It was their twenty-seventh season of intercollegiate football. They were coached by Charles Dudley Daly. Daly was in his fourth season of stint one of two stints of four seasons each as head coach of the Cadets. As an independent football entity, the team had a record of 9-0-0. Army had a great season.

The Cadets compiled an 9-0-0. They shut out three of their nine opponents, and outscored all opponents by a combined total of 235 to 36. In the annual Army–Navy Game, the Cadets defeated the Midshipmen 15 to 7. The Cadets also defeated Notre Dame by a score of 30 to 10 and Villanova by a 69 to 7 score. The 1916 Army team was selected retroactively as the 1916 national champion by Parke H. Davis. Army itself has chosen not to claim this as a National Championship but it sure in fact was

The Army Navy Game 1916 Championship

Fullback Elmer Oliphant from the 1916 Army team was a consensus first-team All-American and was later inducted into the College Football Hall of Fame in 1955. Center John McEwan received second-team honors from Walter Camp, the United Press, the International News Service, and Walter Eckersall.

Other than the Army-Navy Game, which was played at the Polo Grounds in New York, all Army games were played at The Plain on the Campus of the US Military Academy in West Point, NY.

The Cadets opened the season on Sept 30, with a low scoring shutout W (3-0) against Lebanon Valley at home on the Campus of West Point in NY. In the second game of the season, on Oct 7, the Cadets shut defeated Washington & Lee W (14-7). The next game on Oct 14, against Holy Cross was shutout W (17-0).

United States Military Academy
West Point, N. Y.

The Army football team experienced an entirely successful season, every game being an Army victory. Possessing personnel of exceptionally high grade players, the outcome of the various games was expected. At only one period during the entire season was the team pressed. The most important games were the Army-Washington and Lee game, the Army-Notre Dame game, and the Army-Navy game. The Washington and Lee game was won by straight, hard football, the Notre Dame game by forward passing, the Navy game by a combination of the above.

Few teams have ever possessed the power of this year's Army team. With a line of powerful, rangy, experienced men and a backfield capable of performing at all times, its strength can be understood. Oliphant and Vidal in the backfield and McEwan, Meacham and Knight were the bright stars. In the modern game Oliphant, Vidal and McEwan are the equal of any players.

Football Scores

Sept. 29, Lebanon Valley, 3—0.
Oct. 7, Washington and Lee, 14—7.
Oct. 14, Holy Cross, 17—0.
Oct. 21, Trinity, 53—0.
Oct. 28, Villa Nova, 69—7.
Nov. 4, Notre Dame, 30—10.
Nov. 11, Maine, 17—3.
Nov. 18, Springfield, 17—2.
Nov. 25, Navy, 15—7.

Army Navy National Championship Game 1916

Army got its moxie back and began to wallop teams on the way to its undefeated and untied 1916 season. On Oct 21, the Cadets thumped Trinity in a shutout W (53-0). The following week on Oct 28, the Cadets routed Villanova W (69-7). The following week on Nov 4, the Cadets overpowered Notre Dame W 30-10). On Nov 11, the Cadets defeated Maine W (17-3).

From the archives: ARMY CONQUERS NAVY, 15-7, AMID CHEERS OF 45,000;

Oliphant the Chief Figure in West Point's Victory at the Polo Grounds, makes a run of 83 yards. Then, Goodstein scores for the losers by turning a blocked kick into a touchdown. There were quite a few notables in the gay throng. But, President Wilson was Absent. Yet, the crowd included men Prominent in All Walks of Life.

– New York Times – Nov 26, 1916

More than 45,000 cheering spectators saw the Army football team defeat the Navy by a score of 15 to 7 at the Polo Grounds yesterday.

Famous for its gala crowds, the annual contest never attracted a more brilliant assemblage, while spectacular playing, especially by Oliphant and Vidal, the Army stars, transformed the banks of the huge eclipse of the Brush stadium into a mass of shouting, flag-waving humanity. **Here is a great link to the original NY Times article: http://query.nytimes.com/mem/archive-free/pdf?res=9D04E1DA1F3FE233A25755C2A9679D946796D6CF**

1916 Player Highlights Elmer Oliphant, B

Elmer Quillen "Catchy" or "Ollie" Oliphant was born on July 9, 1892. He was a multi-talented athlete, starring in football, basketball, track player. He also served as a coach. He is one of the great scorers in college football history, credited with a total of 435 points in his college career – 135 at Purdue and 300 at Army. Oliphant also went on to play in the National Football League (NFL). The Elmer Oliphant story – the whole story – is fascinating to read. The was one heck of an athlete. I'd love to have the room to print it all.

Born in Bloomfield, Indiana to Marion Elsworth Oliphant and Alice V. Quillen Oliphant in 1892, he finished High School after three years at Washington, Indiana at the Linton High School after a transfer in his junior year.

He was nicknamed Catchy because he excelled as a catcher, outfielder and power hitter in baseball. It could also be because the dictionary has one meaning of catchy as "having the power to catch the attention." Supposedly one time he was playing center field for the Linton team, called a time-out, hurried to the nearby cinder track and won the 100-yard dash. Then, he returned to his position in center field and the game continued. The Indiana Football Hall of Fame states that he was All-State End while at Linton High School. He scored a school record of 60 points as Linton defeated rival Sullivan by a whopping 128–0 score.

He worked at Purdue University-- waiting tables, carrying laundry, stoking furnaces, and selling shoes to earn his way as a student. He earned 7 official varsity letters in football, basketball, baseball and track. He also swam and wrestled.

An end on the football team as a freshman, he was a starting halfback for his final three seasons at the school and distinguished himself as a runner and kicker. In one game, he single-handedly beat Wisconsin by kicking a game winning field goal with a broken ankle to give the Boilermakers a 3–0 victory and then fainted in pain.

Only 5'7" and 174 pounds, he belied his build with outstanding speed and power. In football, he helped turn Purdue's football into a winning program. He graduated with a degree in Mechanical Engineering. Perhaps to extend his time in football, he later accepted an appointment to the U.S. Military Academy at West Point upon his Purdue graduation.

At West Point, he was the first cadet athlete to letter in four major sports and it required a special act of the Athletic Council to design a suitable varsity letter containing a gold star and three stripes for him. Back at the turn of the 20th century, the criteria to receive a letter was very strict. He also monogrammed in hockey, boxing, and swimming which meant that he wasn't able to participate fully in those sports but was recognized. At that, he is listed as a Champion Boxer in the Corps of Cadets.

He still holds records that have never been broken. During his college career, he scored 135 points at Purdue and 289 points at West Point and is identified as one of the greatest scorers in collegiate history. He established the World Record in 220-yard low hurdles on grass.

Oliphant in Army letterman's jacket.

While at West Point he won the Army Athletic Association Trophy. (He won in 1918. 2004 was the 100th year the trophy was given.)

He has been inducted into several Halls of Fame. The most recent induction occurred on October 6, 2004. He was in the inaugural group of sixteen inducted into the Army Sports Hall of Fame at West Point.

On graduation day, June 12, 1918, he married Barbara "Bobbie" Benedict. World War I changed priorities at West Point, and they reverted to purely military instruction during wartime. Among his duties, he served in the U.S. Cavalry for one year at Fort Sill in Oklahoma. While in military service at West Point in 1919, he invented the intramural sports system as we know it today. The idea was copied by the Naval Academy and was soon used in colleges and universities across the country. He was appointed track instructor at

West Point by Douglas MacArthur, who was the superintendent after returning from World War I.

Although he is virtually forgotten today, he was known to every sports fan in the first quarter of the 20th century. There is a 1955 Topps All-American collectible sports card with his picture, and a Street and Smith comic book featured him in 1943 with a section "The Thrilling Story of West Point's Most Famous Athlete Four Letter Man, Ollie Oliphant."

Oliphant played for the Rochester Jeffersons in 1920 and the Buffalo All-Americans in 1921. They were some of the first members of what is now the NFL (National Football League). In 1921, Oliphant led the league in points (47), FGs (5) and PATs (26) and threw 7 touchdowns for the Buffalo All-Americans. After the 1921 season, Oliphant retired from active participation in sports.

1917 Army West Point Cadets Football Coach Geoffrey Keyes

1917 Army Football Team above and on next page

Chapter 9 Daly, Keyes, & Mitchell 1906 - 1907   143

1, Jenkins; 2, Chapline; 3, Zimmerman; 4, Rasen; 5, Grey; 6, Barton; 7, Groves; 8, Holbrook; 9, Searby; 10, Ward; 11, Moore; 12, Rockafellow; 13, Gould; 14, Gilmartin; 15, Seibert, Mgr.; 16, Robinson, Asst. Mgr.; 17, Crouch; 18, Epes; 19, Richardson; 20, Lipman; 21, Manning; 22, Dominney; 23, Bartlett; 24, Christiansen; 25, Yeager; 26, Watkins; 27, Marsden; 28, Ferenbaugh; 29, Springer; 30, Rundell; 31, Luce; 32, McQuarrie; 33, Shrader; 34, Stokes; 35, Oliphant, Capt.; 36, Knight; 37, Murrill; 38, Adams; 39, March; 40, York; 41, Major Keyes, Coach; 42, Badger; 43, Casey; 44, Kreber; 45, Monroe; 46, Johnson; 47, Estill; 48, Van de Graaff; 49, Stenzel; 50, Post; 51, Pulsifer; 52, Smith; 53, Hendricks.
Copyright, 1917, by White Studio, New York.
UNITED STATES MILITARY ACADEMY, WEST POINT, N. Y.

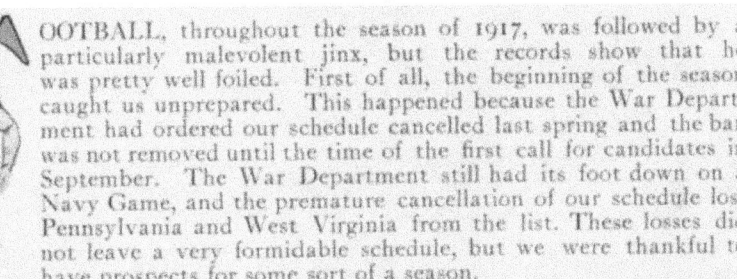FOOTBALL, throughout the season of 1917, was followed by a particularly malevolent jinx, but the records show that he was pretty well foiled. First of all, the beginning of the season caught us unprepared. This happened because the War Department had ordered our schedule cancelled last spring and the ban was not removed until the time of the first call for candidates in September. The War Department still had its foot down on a Navy Game, and the premature cancellation of our schedule lost Pennsylvania and West Virginia from the list. These losses did not leave a very formidable schedule, but we were thankful to have prospects for some sort of a season.

The early graduation of '18 deprived us of Jones, Place, Hirsch, House and Timberlake, all "A" men; also Chapman, Jack Knight, Huff, Fleming and other lesser lights. In addition there was the gap left by Big Mac, Meacham, Gerhardt, Butler, Redfield and others of 1917. Thus the team had little resemblance to our last Navy wrecker. Despite these gaps we had enough good material, but, unfortunately, various causes prevented the use of all of it.

The greatest handicap, apparent from the first, was the lack of experienced coaches. The nation being at war, no officers could be specially detailed for this purpose. Moreover, with such poor Navy Game prospects, the Athletic Council

About the 1917 Team

The Army Cadets football team represented the United States Military Academy in the 1917 college football season. It was their

twenty-eighth season of intercollegiate football. They were coached by Geoffrey Keyes in his first and only season as head coach of the Cadets. As an independent football entity, the team had a record of 7-1-0. Army had a great season.

Army Football Coach Geoffrey Keyes 1917

The Cadets compiled an 7-1-0 record. shut out four of their eight opponents, and outscored all opponents by a combined total of 203 to 24. The Cadets' sole loss came to Notre Dame by a 7 to 2 score. The Army–Navy Game was not played during the 1917 season.

Halfback Elmer Oliphant was a consensus first-team player on the 1917 College Football All-America Team and was later inducted into the College Football Hall of Fame.

All Army games were played at The Plain on the Campus of the US Military Academy in West Point, NY.

The Cadets opened the season on Oct 6 with a shutout W (28-0) against Carnegie tech at home on the Campus of West Point in NY. In the second game of the season, on Oct 13, the Cadets shut out VMI W (34-0). In the next game on Oct 20, against Tufts the Cadets dominated W (26-3).

On Oct 27, the Cadets defeated Villanova W (21-7). The following week on Oct 28, the Cadets lost a close match to the Fighting Irish of Notre Dame coached by Jesse Harper, L (2-7). On Nov 10, the Cadets shut out Carlisle W (28-0).

Then on Nov 17, the Cadets walloped Lebanon Valley W (50-0). In the season finale without an Army Navy Game, the Cadets outlasted Boston College in a fine game W (14-7).

1918 Army West Point Cadets Football Coach Hugh Mitchell

<< Coach Hugh Mitchell

The Army Cadets football team represented the United States Military Academy in the 1917 college football season. It was their twenty-ninth season of intercollegiate football. They were coached by Hugh Mitchell in his first and only season as head coach of the Cadets. As an independent football entity, the team had a record of 1-0-0.

The Cadets compiled an 1-0-0. In the only game played by the Cadets in 1918, they defeated a team from Mitchel Army Air Service in New York.

World War I had created a major demand for soldiers and football was no longer the priority of the football athletes at the academy.

1919 Army West Point Cadets Football Coach Charles Daly

The Army Cadets football team represented the United States Military Academy in the 1919 college football season. It was their thirtieth season of intercollegiate football. They were coached by Charles Dudley Daly. Daly was in his first season of stint two of two stints of four seasons each as head coach of the Cadets. (Daly had been Army's coach from 1913 to 1916 but Army regulations said he had to resign after four years.) As an independent football entity, the team had a record of 6-3-0.

The Cadets compiled an 6-3-0 record. They shut out five of their nine opponents, and outscored all opponents by a combined total of 140 to 38. In the annual Army–Navy Game, the Cadets lost to the Midshipmen by a 6 to 0 score. The Cadets also defeated Villanova by a 62 to 0 score, but lost to Notre Dame by a 12 to 9 score.

End Earl "Red" Blaik, who later went on to be a great Army Coach, was selected by Walter Camp as a third-team player on the 1919 College Football All-America Team.

Other than the Army-Navy Game, which was played at the Polo Grounds in New York, all Army games were played at The Plain on the Campus of the US Military Academy in West Point, NY.

The Cadets opened the season on Sept 27 with a shutout W (28-0) against Middlebury at home on the Campus of the USMA at West Point, In the second game of the season, on Oct 4, the Cadets shut out Holy Cross in a close game W (9-0). In the next game on Oct 11, against Syracuse, the Cadets could not keep up in the close game and lost to the Orangemen L (3-7).

On Oct 27, the Cadets shut out Maine W (6-0) The following week on Oct 28, the Cadets defeated Boston College W (13-0). On Nov 1, the Cadets beat Tufts W (24-13).

Then on Nov 8, the Cadets barely lost to big rival Notre Dame L (9-12). Notre Dame was coached by Knute Rockne in his second year. The Irish won the National Championship in 1919 with the famous George Gipp (The Gipper) doing a lot of the heavy lifting.

On Nov 15, the Cadets pounded Villanova W (62-0). On Nov 29, at the Polo Grounds in NY, Army was shut out by Navy L (0-6)

Best Army Navy Game # 7

After a two-year hiatus for World War I, the Army-Navy game returned to the football field in 1919.

President Wilson attended the 1919 Army-Navy Game

Each team entered the contest without a loss, as the Midshipmen were 5-0-3 and the Cadets were 6-0-1.

Navy finished the day with seven times more yards than Army but could not get into the end zone. However, Clyde King booted a pair of field goals to give the Midshipmen a 6-0 victory on a rainy day in a turnover-free game. It would mark the fourth time in 10 years that Navy had won the game by just kicking field goals.

The Midshipmen finished the season 6-1, while the Cadets ended up 6-3.

1920 Army West Point Cadets Football Coach Charles Daly

The Army Cadets football team represented the United States Military Academy in the 1920 college football season. It was their thirty-first season of intercollegiate football. They were coached by Charles Dudley Daly. Daly was in his second season of stint two of two stints of four seasons each as head coach of the Cadets. (Daly was Army's coach from 1913 to 1916) As an independent football entity, the team had a record of 7-2-0.

The Cadets compiled a 7-2-0 record. They shut out five of their nine opponents, and outscored all opponents by a combined total of 314 to 47. Army excelled on Offense and Defense. In the annual Army–Navy Game, the Cadets lost to the Midshipmen by a 7 to 0 score. The Cadets also defeated Lebanon Valley College by a 53 to 0 score and Bowdoin College by an embarrassing 90 to 0 score.

Two Army players were recognized on the 1920 College Football All-America Team. Fullback Walter French was selected as a first-team All-American by Football World magazine and as a second-team All-American by Walter Camp and the United Press. Guard Fritz Breidster was selected as a second-team All-American by Walter Eckersall and a third-team player by Walter Camp.

Other than the Army-Navy Game, which was played at the Polo Grounds in New York, all Army games were played at The Plain on the Campus of the US Military Academy in West Point, NY.

The Cadets opened the season on Oct 2 with a shutout W (35=0) against Union at home on the Campus of the USMA at West Point, In the second game of the season, which ironically in all of my references says it was also played on Oct 2 v Marshall, the Cadets brought home a W (38-0) shutout. If I figure this one out by book printing time, I will make the change otherwise, I admit, I just do not know.

On Oct 9, the Cadets shut out Middlebury W (27-0). In the next game on Oct 16, against Springfield (MA) the Cadets prevailed W (26-7). On Oct 23, the Cadets beat Tufts quite handily W (28-6). On Oct 30, the visiting Fighting Irish from Notre Dame, coached by Knute Rockne defeated the Cadets L (17-27) The Irish always saw Army as its most formidable opponent.

On Nov 6, the Cadets shellacked Lebanon Valley in a big W (53-0) shutout. On Nov 13, in an unusual game against a first-time opponent, the Cadets played every minute of the game against Bowdoin and literally knocked the smithereens out of the visitors W (90-0).

On Nov 27, at the Polo Grounds in NY, Army was shut out by Navy in a close match L (0-7)

1921 Army West Point Cadets Football Coach Charles Daly

The Army Cadets football team represented the United States Military Academy in the 1921 college football season. It was their thirty-second season of intercollegiate football. They were coached by Charles Dudley Daly. Daly was in his third season of stint two of two stints of four seasons each as head coach of the Cadets. (Daly was Army's coach from 1913 to 1916) As an independent football entity, the team had a record of 6-4-0.

The Cadets compiled a 6-4-0 record. They shut out five of their ten opponents, and outscored all opponents by a combined total of 217 to 65. In the annual Army–Navy Game, the Cadets lost to the Midshipmen by a 7 to 0 score. The Cadets also lost to Yale and Notre Dame, two rivals / nemeses/.

Three Army players were recognized on the 1921 College Football All-America Team. Halfback Walter French was selected as a third-team All-American by Walter Camp. Guard Fritz Breidster was selected as a third-team All-American by Jack Veiock, sports editor of the International News Service. A center named Larsen was selected as a second-team All-American by Walter Camp and Football World.

Other than the Army-Navy Game, which was played at the Polo Grounds again in 1921, in New York, all Army games were played at The Plain on the Campus of the US Military Academy in West Point, NY.

The Cadets opened the season on Oct 1 with a win against Springfield (MA) W (28-6) at home on the Campus of the USMA at West Point, In the second game of the season, which ironically in all of my references says it was also played on Oct 1 vs. New Hampshire, the Cadets lost a close game L (7-10). Like the prior year, if I figure this one out by book printing time, I will make the change otherwise, I admit, I just do not know. Too many references are the same. Army needs to clear this up.

On Oct 8, the Cadets shut out Lebanon Valley W (33-0). In the next game on Oct 8, against Middlebury, the Cadets won in a shutout W (19-0). Then, on Oct 15, the Cadets shut out Wabash quite handily W (21-0). On Oct 22, Army got out of the Plain in a real game at the Yale Bowl and were beaten in a close game v Yale L (7-14).

On Oct 29, Susquehanna got thumped by the Cadets W (53-0). After this great warm-up game, the next game was Knute Rockne's Fighting Irish on Nov 5. The Irish shut out the Cadets L (0-28). The Irish never took an Army team for granted. On Nov 12, the Cadets whooped Villanova W (49-0). Despite the great big wins, when the Midshipmen came to play at the Polo Grounds, like this year, the Cadets burped a bit, played a fine game but lost the game in another nail-biter L (0-7).

1922 Army West Point Cadets Football Coach Charles Daly

The Army Cadets football team represented the United States Military Academy in the 1922 college football season. It was their thirty-third season of intercollegiate football. They were coached by Charles Dudley Daly. Daly was in his fourth and last season of stint two of two stints of four seasons each as head coach of the Cadets. (Daly was also Army's coach from 1913 to 1916) As an independent football entity, the team had a record of 8-0-2. It was one of a rare number of times that and always well-playing Army had attained eight wins in a season.

The Cadets compiled an undefeated, twice tied 8-0-2 record. They shut out seven of their ten opponents, and outscored all opponents by a combined total of 228 to 27 – an average of 22.8 points scored and 2.7 points allowed. In the annual Army–Navy Game, the Cadets defeated the Midshipmen 17 to 14.

Two Army players were recognized as first-team players on the 1922 College Football All-America Team: guard Fritz Breidster and center Edgar Garbisch. Garbisch was later inducted into the College Football Hall of Fame.

Other than the Yale Game played at the Yale Bowl, and the Army-Navy Game, which was played at the Polo Grounds again in 1922, in New York, all Army games were played at The Plain on the Campus of the US Military Academy in West Point, NY.

The Cadets opened the season on Sept 23, with a shutout against Lebanon Valley W (12-0) at home on the Campus of the USMA at West Point, On Sept 30, the Cadets shut out Springfield (MA) W (35-0). In the next game on Oct 7, against Kansas, the Cadets won in a shutout W (13-0) On Oct 14, the Cadets beat Auburn W (19-6) On Oct 228 Army got out of the Plain in a real football game at the Yale Bowl and tied Yale T (7-7).

On Nov 4, New Hampshire was shut out by the Cadets W (33-0). After this warm-up game, the Cadets were really ready to put up a big score and they did against St. Bonaventure on Nov 4. The Cadets walloped the Bonnies in a shut out win W (53-0). Notre Dame was next on Nov 11 and they played the Cadets to a scoreless tie T (0-0) in a major defensive battle.

On Nov 18, the Cadets whooped Bates W (39-0). Despite the great big wins, when the Midshipmen came to play at any of the venues such as Franklin Field in Philadelphia PA , as in 1922, it was an exciting game. This year, the Cadets got the victory in another close match W (17-14).

1922 Player Highlights Ed Garbisch L

Edgar William "Ed" Garbisch was born April 7, 1899 n Washington, Pennsylvania; He was a fine American college football player, accomplished military officer, businessman and art collector. When servicemen came to the Army they were permitted another four years of eligibility. That would be a good way today to help boost the Army program.

Garbisch therefore played eight years of college football at Washington & Jefferson College (1917-1920) and then, the United States Military Academy (1921-1924) and was an All-American Guard each year from 1922 to 1924. He was inducted to the College Football Hall of Fame in 1954.

He stood 6 feet tall, weighed 185, and was a place kicker and drop kicker. In 1922, he place-kicked a 47-yard field goal to give Army a victory over Navy 17-14. We all know how important that kick was in this annual rivalry game.

In 1924, he drop-kicked 4 field goals as Army beat Navy 12-0. He played against Notre Dame five times; once at W&J, four times at Army - and played 60 minutes in all five games. Garbisch graduated 17th in a class of 245 at West Point, was cadet captain and captain of the tennis and football teams.

He served 20 years in the Army Engineers, worked on procurement of engineering materials for the North Africa and Normandy invasions in World War II, and retired with the rank of colonel.

He joined Grocery Products Co. as president. He collected art, specializing in Native American, and made important donations of art to the Metropolitan Museum and the National Gallery. Washington and Jefferson awarded him an honorary doctorate in fine arts in 1972. Garbisch was a trustee of Boys Club of America, a trustee of Pop Warner Little Scholars, and vice-president of the National Football Foundation.

His father wanted him to be a pianist but gave up after watching teammates carry Edgar off the field following the 1924 Navy game. "They don't do that for pianists," he said. In 1926, two years after his last college game, he was chosen to play in the first East-West Shrine Game and was East captain. Still remembered at West Point is the prayer Garbisch said before his last game: "Please, dear God, help us to acquit ourselves like men and to play the game within the rules to the best of our abilities." Garbisch was married for more than 50 years to Bernice Chrysler, the daughter of Chrysler founder Walter P. Chrysler

Chapter 10 Coaches McEwan, Jones, & Sasse 1923-1932

McEwan   Coach #18
Jones   Coach #19
Sasse   Coach #20

Year	Coach	Record	Conf	Record
1923	John McEwan	6-2-1	Indep	6-2-1
1924	John McEwan	5-1-2	Indep	5-1-2
1925	John McEwan	7-2-0	Indep	7-2-0
1926	Biff Jones	7-1-1	Indep	7-1-1
1927	Biff Jones	9-1-0	Indep	9-1-0
1928	Biff Jones	8-2-0	Indep	8-2-0
1929	Biff Jones	6-4-1	Indep	6-4-1
1930	Ralph Sasse	9-1-1	Indep	9-1-1
1931	Ralph Sasse	8-2-1	Indep	8-2-1
1932	Ralph Sasse	8-2-0	Indep	8-2-0

1923 Army West Point Cadets Football Coach John McEwan

<< Coach John McEwan

The Army Cadets football team represented the United States Military Academy in the 1923 college football season. It was their thirty-fourth season of intercollegiate football. They were coached by John McEwan in his first of three seasons as head coach of the Cadets. As an independent football entity, the team had a record of 6-2-1.

The Cadets compiled a 6-2-1 record. They shut out five of their nine opponents, and outscored all opponents by a combined total of 237 to 56. In the annual Army–Navy Game, the Cadets and the Midshipmen played to a scoreless tie.

Two Army players were recognized on the 1923 College Football All-America Team. Center Edgar Garbisch was selected as a first-team player by Tom Thorp and Percy Haughton and a second-team player by Athletic World magazine, Norman E. Brown and Davis Walsh. Garbisch was later inducted into the College Football Hall of Fame. Guard August Farwick received second-team honors from Norman E. Brown and Tom Thorp.

Other than the Notre Dame game, played at Ebbetts Field; Yale Game played at the Yale Bowl, and the Army-Navy Game, which was played at the Polo Grounds again in 1922, in New York, all Army games were played at The Plain on the Campus of the US Military Academy in West Point, NY.

The Cadets opened the season on Sept 29, with a shellacking shutout against Tennessee W (41-0) at home on the Campus of the USMA at West Point, On Oct 6, the Cadets shut out Florida W (20-0). In the next game on Oct 13, against Knute Rockne's Notre Dame at Ebbetts Field in Brooklyn, the Cadets were shut out in a close match L (0-13). On Oct 20, v Auburn, the Cadets defeated the Tigers W (28-6). On Oct 27, the Cadets walloped Lebanon Valley in a blowout shutout W (74-0).

For the third year in a row, Army got out of the Plain in another real football game at the Yale Bowl in New Haven Connecticut and lost to the Bulldogs, L (10-31). On Nov 10, the Cadets shut out Arkansas Tech W (44-0). Then, on Nov 17, it was Bethany at home defeated by the Cadets in a nice game W (20-6). On Nov 24 v. Navy at the Polo Grounds the Cadets played the Midshipmen to a scoreless tie T (0-0).

1924 Army West Point Cadets Football Coach John McEwan

The Army Cadets football team represented the United States Military Academy in the 1924 college football season. It was their thirty-fifth season of intercollegiate football. They were coached by John McEwan in his second of three seasons as head coach of the Cadets. As an independent football entity, the team had a record of 5-1-2.

The Cadets compiled a 5-1-2 record. They shut out four of their eight opponents, and outscored all opponents by a combined total of 111 to 41. In the annual Army–Navy Game, the Cadets defeated the Midshipmen by a 12 to 0 score. The team's only loss came to undefeated national champion Notre Dame by a 13 to 7 score.

Five Army players were recognized on the 1924 College Football All-America Team. Center Edgar Garbisch was selected as a first-team player by Walter Camp, Football World magazine, and All-Sports Magazine. Garbisch was later inducted into the College Football Hall of Fame. Guard August Farwick received first-team honors from the All-America Board, the Newspaper Enterprise Association, Billy Evans, and Walter Eckersall. End Frank Frazer was selected as a third-team player by Walter Camp. Harry Ellinger received third-team honors from Davis J. Walsh. Halfback Harry Wilson was selected as a third-team player by All-Sports Magazine.

This year, 1924, other than the Notre Dame game, played at the Polo Grounds; the Yale Game, played at the Yale Bowl; and the Army-Navy Game, which was played at Municipal Stadium • Baltimore, MD, all Army games were played at the brand new Michie Stadium on the Campus of the US Military Academy in West Point, NY.

The Cadets opened the season on Oct 4, with a shutout victory over Saint Louis in the inaugural game for the brand new Michie Stadium on the Campus of the USMA at West Point, On Oct 11, the Cadets shut out Detroit W (20-0). In the next game on Oct 13, against Knute Rockne's National Champion Notre Dame squad, complete with the "immortal" Four Horsemen, at the Polo Grounds, the Cadets gave the Irish a run for their money but lost in a close match, L (7-13) before a huge crowd of 55,000.

On Oct 25, v Boston University, the Cadets defeated the Terriers, W (20-0). Then, on Nov1, Army played Yale at the Yale Bowl in New Haven CT to a tie T (7-7). Nov 8, the Cadets defeated Florida's Gators at home, W (14-7). In the setup game for the Army-Navy annual battle, on Nov 15, the Cadets tied Columbia in a hard-fought contest T (14-14). Then, in the season finale, on Nov 29 v. Navy at Municipal Stadium • Baltimore, MD (Army–Navy Game), the Cadets shut out the Midshipmen W (12-0).

1925 Army West Point Cadets Football Coach John McEwan

The Army Cadets football team represented the United States Military Academy in the 1925 college football season. It was their thirty-sixth season of intercollegiate football. They were coached by John McEwan in his third and last of three seasons as head coach of the Cadets. As an independent football entity, the team had a record of 7-2-0.

The Cadets compiled a 7-2-0 record. They shut out three of their nine opponents, the Cadets offense scored 185 points, while the defense allowed 71 points, On November 28, Army beat Navy by a score of 10–3.

Babe Ruth had taken ill in 1925 and thus could not lead the Yankees to the World Series. Therefore, college football took center stage at Yankee Stadium that fall. The fiercely competitive Notre Dame–Army game moved to Yankee Stadium in 1925, where it remained until 1947.

This year, 1925, other than the Notre Dame game, played at Yankee Stadium; the Yale Game, played at the Yale Bowl; the Columbia game played at Baker Field; and the Army-Navy Game, which was played at Municipal Stadium • Baltimore, MD, all Army games were played at the brand new Michie Stadium on the Campus of the US Military Academy in West Point, NY. There seemed to be coming a day when the Cadets would be traveling to stadiums all over the country. But, not quite this year.

The Cadets opened the season on Oct 3, with a nice victory over Detroit W (31-6) at Michie Stadium on the Campus of the USMA at West Point. On Oct 10, the Cadets defeated Knox W (26-7). In the traditional third game on Oct 17, it was pay-back time against Knute Rockne's prior National Champion Notre Dame squad at Yankee Stadium. The Cadets shut out the Irish by a good margin W (27-0).

On Oct 24, v St. Louis, the Cadets shut out the Billikens W (19-0). Then, on Oct 31, Army played Yale at the Yale Bowl in New Haven CT and were defeated by a score of L (7-28). On Nov 17, the Cadets defeated Davis & Elkins W (14-6).

On Nov 14, at Columbia's Baker Field, the Cadets were defeated by the Lions L (7-21). Then, in the season finale, on Nov 28 v. Navy at the Polo Grounds in New York, NY, the Cadets defeated the Midshipmen W (10-3)

Biff Jones takes over as Cadets head coach

A PROSPECTUS of the '26 season filled us with high hopes despite the fact that our coaching staff had migrated to the West. We had lost but one regular from 25's none too successful team, and felt that from a nucleus of ten experienced men, almost any coach could mold a winning combination. Also, this was the last season during which Plebes were to be eligible; so we anxiously awaited news of their prospects. As some famous general once said, everything went as planned. Our new material proved of exceptional ability, our regulars, with one or two exceptions, were free from serious injuries, and as a result, our team was good—one of the best. A hard schedule was successfully met, and for once the Army-Navy game was a football game besides being a national exhibit.

To sketch individual performance would be too great a task, but Biff Jones must be mentioned as a first year head coach who was unusually successful. Great credit is due the men who performed; as a collection of football players we hold them unequalled.

Capt. Jones, Coach Hewitt, Captain

Biff Jones, a great coach, a Cadet favorite

Lawrence "Biff" Jones graduated from the U.S. Military Academy in 1917. He served in France as a Lieutenant of field artillery and returned to West Point in 1926 as head football coach, succeeding John McEwan.

His four-year record there was an impressive 30-8-2. His 1926 and 1927 teams lost but one game each, his 1928 Cadets but two.

In 1927, Jones did Army a great service when he brought Earl "Red" Blaik back to the Point as an assistant coach. Blaik worked for three years under Jones and would return years later to lift the Cadets to their highest success.

However, Jones moved on and enjoyed further success at Louisiana State, Oklahoma and Nebraska. He established himself as a serious, sound, hard-working mentor with a gift for organization.

In 1937, Jones retired from the Army as a Major.

Also in 1937, he left the Oklahoma Sooners to coach their rival, the Nebraska Cornhuskers, replacing coach Dana X. Bible.

Jones remained at Nebraska for five years and tallied a 28–14–4 mark. He led Nebraska to its first bowl game, the 1941 Rose Bowl, and also coached the second-ever televised college football game.

Jones left Nebraska in 1942 when he was called back to service as a colonel during World War II.

Later, he served as graduate manager at the Academy until June, 1948.

Playing career
1915–1916 Army Position: Tackle

Coaching career as Head Coach
1926–1929 Army 30-8-2
1932–1934 LSU 20-5-6
1935–1936 Oklahoma 9-6-3
1937–1941 Nebraska 28-14-4

Head coaching record Overall
87–33–15

Administrative career as Athletic Director
1935–1936 Oklahoma
1937–1942 Nebraska
1942–1948 Army

On or off the gridiron, Jones was always in command of the situation and never suffered from a lack of respect paid to him.

He was inducted into the College Football Hall of Fame in 1954, and the Nebraska Football Hall of Fame in 1971.

Jones married Elizabeth Trueman King, daughter of Mr. & Mrs. George Anderson King, in 1920, when he was a Captain in the Field Artillery at West Point. She was a graduate of Smith College.

1926 Army West Point Cadets Football Coach Biff Jones

<< Coach Biff Jones

The Army Cadets football team represented the United States Military Academy in the 1926 college football season. It was their thirty-seventh season of intercollegiate football. They were coached by Biff Jones in his first of four seasons as head coach of the Cadets. As an independent football entity, the team had a record of 7-1-1.

The Cadets compiled a 7-1-1 record. They shut out four of their nine opponents, and outscored all opponents by a combined total of 240 to 71. In the annual Army–Navy Game, the Cadets tied with the Midshipmen at a 21 to 21 score. The team's only loss came to Notre Dame by a 7 to 0 score.

Army Cadets 1926 A-Team

Four Army players were recognized on the 1926 College Football All-America Team. Tackle Bud Sprague was a consensus first-team honoree with first-team designations from the Associated Press (AP) and the Central Press Association (CP). Sprague was later inducted into the College Football Hall of Fame. Halfback Harry Wilson was selected as a first-team honoree by Walter Camp, the All-America Board, Collier's Weekly, the International News Service, and the Newspaper Enterprise Association. Guard Ernest Schmidt was selected as a first-team player by the New York Sun. Center Maurice Daly was selected as a second-team honoree by the New York Sun.

This year, 1926, other than the Notre Dame game, played at Yankee Stadium; the Yale Game, played at the Yale Bowl; and the Army-Navy Game, which was played at Soldier Field in Chicago Illinois, all Army games were played at Michie Stadium on the Campus of the US Military Academy in West Point, NY.

The Army Cadets began the 1926 season at home on Oct 2, with a nice shutout victory over Detroit W (21-0) at Michie Stadium on the Campus of the USMA at West Point. On Oct 9, the Cadets defeated Davis & Elkins W (21-7). In the third game on Oct 16, Army defeated Syracuse W (27-21) in a very close match. On Oct 23, the Cadets shut out the Eagles of Boston College W (41-0). Then, on Oct 30, at the Yale Bowl, Army shut out Yale W (33-0).

On Nov 6 v Franklin & Marshall, the Cadets shut out the Diplomats W (55-0) in a major shellacking. Then, on Nov 13, Knute Rockne's Fighting Irish shut out army by a close score L (0-7). Then, on Nov 20, the Army pounded Ursinas in a shutout W (44-0). Then, in the season finale, on Nov 27 v. Navy at Soldier Field in Chicago, IL, the Cadets tied the Midshipmen T (21-21).

About the 1926 Army Navy Game

THE GREATEST ARMY–NAVY GAME
Thanks to Ray Schmidt
PAGE 9
https://forwhattheygave.com/2007/12/11/1926-football-team/

There was a time — more difficult to remember with each passing season — when the results of the annual gridiron showdown between the teams of West Point and Annapolis (that's Army and Navy) were followed by football fans across the country, and often carried significance in the race for mythical national honors. Yet even more so, the game and its surrounding pageantry represented the best moments of college football. No other rivalry in college football consistently created such anticipation at the host cities, and then actually came through with the color, the excitement, and the spectacle that was unmatched — with even a good football game on occasion.

From this long-running series there is one game that stands above the others as the greatest Army-Navy clash ever, and one of the best in the annals of all college football history. In the early 1940s, Esquire magazine conducted a poll and named the game "the greatest in history" to that time, while the long-time prominent coach, Clark Shaughnessy, selected it as one of the 12 greatest games of all-time. Shaughnessy described it as one game "seldom matched for brilliant and courageous individual play, and for daring and spectacular team strategy." It was of course the legendary 1926 Army-Navy showdown.

In those times, the service academies alternated years in selecting the site for their annual game, and during the 1920s bids were frequently received from several cities — usually always along the Eastern Seaboard. In late 1924, a group from Chicago — supported by U.S. Representatives Fred Britten and Martin Madden of Illinois — entered the bidding to host the 1925 Army-Navy game. The other cities seeking the game included Washington D.C., Philadelphia, Baltimore, and two different groups from New York (one representing the Polo Grounds and the other the relatively new Yankee Stadium). Chicago was under a handicap because of its distance from the two schools, and West Point officials (who would be selecting the 1925 site) were on record as opposing any site that would keep the Corps of Cadets away from the school overnight — a position endorsed by War Secretary John W. Weeks.

The 1925 game was ultimately awarded to the Polo Grounds — despite Yankee Stadium's larger seating capacity — but Chicago businessmen were soon preparing another bid for the 1926 game which would be selected by Naval Academy officials. Again, the Midwest city was challenged by New York, Baltimore, and Philadelphia, but this time it was better prepared The Chicago group announced its willingness to raise $100,000 for each academies' athletic fund, in addition to the approximately $600,000 which would be required to cover the expenses of bringing the teams and students to the game. Yet the Eastern cities continued in the role of the favorites.

Political pressure upon the academies intensified, as Midwest congressmen and service men's organizations turned up the heat. No stone was left unturned — in December 1925 the Chicago Herald-Examiner ran an editorial stating that an Army-Navy game in Chicago would "arouse in youthful civilian minds a new understanding of love of country and eager appreciation of what education at West Point and Annapolis means" — this at a time when many leaders of America were urging the need for much better preparedness and training for the nation's youth, given the recent experiences of World War I. In case patriotism didn't strike the right chord, the editorial declared that, "Those great schools are not the exclusive property of the East."

In the end, political pressure and big money carried the day — along with a stadium that could seat in excess of 100,000 ticket-buying fans — and so Annapolis officials awarded the 1926 game to Chicago.

The Midwest city had built mammoth Grant Park Stadium on the banks of Lake Michigan just south of the downtown area in 1925. Some football games had been played there that first season — including Northwestern's famous 3-2 win over Michigan in the mud — yet for 1926 the stadium was being renamed as "Soldier Field" in memory of World War I military personnel, and the Army-Navy game was selected as the formal dedication event.

Soldier Field was a U-shaped arena with a seating capacity of nearly 100,000, with many of the seats at the north end well beyond the gridiron itself. In anticipation of a large ticket demand for the Army-Navy clash, the Chicago Park Board was having temporary bleachers installed to close the open north end of the stadium — with no concern that these seats would be 30-40 yards beyond the goal posts.

After holding out the seats for the two visiting student bodies and numerous dignitaries, there remained 40,000 decent seats which were priced at either $15 or $10 each, with the binocular-type seats priced lower. A full house scaled at these prices would produce gate receipts of approximately $800,000.

To say the least, the demand for tickets was overwhelming, as over 600,000 ticket requests were received for the 100,000 seats available on sale. Placed in charge of the ticket sales was Colonel H.C. Carbaugh — a 65-year old Army veteran who normally served as supervisor of the Civil Service Department for Chicago's South Park Board Members of the public seeking tickets at times became so aggressive that it was necessary for Carbaugh to have body guards while at work, and police were assigned to protect the entrances to the Park's Administration Building.

Of course, it wouldn't be Chicago without some hint of corruption, and it came to light when U.S. Representative John J. Gorman from Chicago charged that the South Park Board was violating an earlier agreement with the Chicago-area congressmen by only providing them with a hundred tickets each. Gorman added that rumors abounded that each of the park commissioners was receiving 1200 tickets. E. J. Kelly, president of the South Park commissioners, replied that everything possible was being done to distribute the tickets fairly and no attention was being given to the complaints of the congressmen.

Two days before the game Navy's traveling party arrived aboard a special train via the Pennsylvania Railroad Coach Bill Ingram spurned a practice session at Soldier Field, and instead took his Middies to a workout on a secluded grassy island in the Sherman Park lagoon while guards protected all the bridgeways leading over the water. The Army team arrived soon afterward on the Michigan Central line, and Coach Biff Jones then drilled his charges at Soldier Field before the team headed for its accommodations at the South Shore Country Club.

The day before the game the visiting student bodies from the two academies were treated to a luncheon at Marshall Field's giant department store in downtown Chicago, after which the Cadets and midshipmen staged a big parade south on Michigan Avenue as they marched to Soldier Field for the formal dedication ceremony. Meanwhile, there was also a full slate of luncheons and parties planned to entertain the service personnel throughout the weekend.

Helping to fuel the already overheated college football fans of Chicago was the fact that the two teams were among the nation's elite for 1926 — Navy coming in with a record of 9-0-0 and Army at 7-1-0, with only a narrow 7-0 defeat to Notre Dame marring the Cadets record. The Army team was slightly favored, and its powerhouse included such great players as Chris Cagle, "Lighthorse" Harry Wilson, Chuck Born, Gar Davidson, and Red Murrell; while Navy countered with standouts such as Tom Hamilton, Frank Wickhorst, Tom Eddy, and Whitey Lloyd.

When time for the kickoff finally arrived on November 27, 1926 — amidst concerns over the many counterfeit tickets which had been found in circulation — Soldier Field was jammed with approximately 110,000 fans, with thousands more standing atop every nearby building, water tower, and bridge that afforded any hopes of a glimpse of the action. A New York Times writer surveyed the scene from the rim of Soldier Field and reported that, "Looking off over the top of the stadium, there was nothing to see but people."

It was later stated that over 18,000 automobiles had been parked around the stadium, while Chicago taxi companies reported that they had made approximately 20,000 separate trips out to the arena. The massive crush of people and cars required the city to assign 1,350 police officers to direct traffic and maintain order. James Bennett of the Chicago Tribune described it as "a multitude that was worthy of the game."

It was a cold day along the Chicago lakefront, and, except for the sun breaking through on one occasion, the game was played under a gray and heavily clouded sky. Snow banks surrounded the field from an earlier storm that had required 300 men to work the entire night before the game shoveling off the seats of the stadium. Around the rim of the stadium were large American flags which rippled in the wintry breezes off Lake Michigan.

Army kicked off to open the game, and surprisingly, Coach Jones of the Cadets had a half dozen of his first-string players on the sideline.

After the teams exchanged punts, the offensive fireworks began. Starting from its 45-yard line, Navy began to mix an array of short passes with its running attack. After several plays moved the ball to Army's 34, Jim Schuber of Navy faked an end sweep but instead rifled a long pass that Hank Hardwick plucked out of the air at the eight-yard line before being dragged down at the one. Two plays later Howard Caldwell blasted in for the touchdown, and Tom Hamilton's drop-kick made it 7-0, Navy.

Again, the teams returned to an exchange of possessions although Navy clearly held the upper hand, and writer Walter Eckersall later declared that "the Middies appeared unbeatable in the first quarter." Late in the period Navy began a drive from its 43-yard line and, after a penalty set them back to the 32, Hamilton connected on a pass to Schuber that was good for 23 yards. After a couple more plays, Coach Jones rushed the rest of his Army first string into the game just before the quarter ended with the Middies at the Army 22. Several plays later Schuber blasted in from one yard out for the TD, and Hamilton's PAT made it 14-0.

Later in the second quarter Army finally got its offense on track behind the hard running of Chris Cagle and Harry Wilson. Starting from their 37-yard line after a punt, the Cadets got rolling as Wilson broke off a dazzling change of pace run of 23 yards to the Navy 40.

Two plays later, Cagle swept around right end on a 21-yard gallop, and on the next snap Wilson slashed through the left side of the line and sailed 17 yards to Army's first touchdown. Wilson's placekick made it 14-7.

The next time Army had the ball it was unable to move, and so Red Murrell dropped back to his 20, from where he boomed a towering punt that came down to the Middies' Howard Ransford on the Navy 25. Attempting a running catch, Ransford fumbled the ball and the bouncing pigskin caromed off the foot of Army's Skip Harbold and toward the Navy goal line. Catching up with the ball near the 15, Harbold picked it up and rumbled toward paydirt, and despite falling down at the one, the weary cadet managed to squirm into the end zone for the touchdown. Wilson's PAT made it 14-14, and the wild first half soon came to a close.

After the gigantic throng had been entertained by a mock battle between students of the two schools, the second half got underway as Army started from its 26 after Cagle's 20-yard runback of the kickoff. Several plays later Wilson swept around left end for a gain of 15 yards to the Navy 44, and on the next snap Cagle broke up the middle and dashed all the way for the touchdown that put Army ahead 21-14 after Wilson's PAT.

Despite the stunning comeback by the Cadets, the Middies returned to the attack. Both of the high-powered offenses fought back and forth until late in the third quarter when Navy started from its 43-yard line after a punt. Slowly the Middies headed up the field as the action moved into the fourth quarter. Hamilton completed two key passes to Alan Shapley on the drive, and Ransford chipped in a critical gain of eight yards for a first down at Army's 15. The 12-play drive was capped off in sensational fashion when Shapley swept around right end on a fourth down and three play for an eight-yard touchdown run. With the entire stadium holding its breath, Hamilton calmly drop-kicked the extra point to tie it at 21-21.

With just over seven minutes left to play, the surrounding gloom and darkness had gathered to the point where it was increasingly difficult for fans and writers in the press box to distinguish the players on the field. Still, Army mounted one last attempt at the win, starting from its 27-yard line after the following kickoff. On the second play of the series Wilson broke through left tackle for a 28-yard dash into Navy territory, and then he and Murrell alternated in pounding the Middies' line. Finally, checked just inside the 20, Wilson dropped back to attempt a place-kick from the 26. The ball was spotted directly in front of the goal posts, but incredibly Wilson's kick sailed just wide.

The final couple minutes were played in "almost total darkness," as the electric lights over the stadium's entrance tunnels and on the Scoreboard twinkled in the gloom. On the last play of the game Hamilton attempted a desperate pass for Navy, but the aerial was intercepted by (and here's where the darkness contributed to the confusion) either Wilson, Cagle, or Chuck Harding — depending on which game account you choose to accept. The runback was finally halted deep in Navy territory, and so the monumental battle ended in a 21-21 tie.

Combined with Notre Dame's shocking 19-0 loss to Carnegie Tech that same day, undefeated Navy's hard-earned tie gave its supporters plenty of ammunition to debate Stanford for the mythical national championship. Yet more significant was the 1926 game's place in football history. Walter Eckersall described it as "one of the greatest football games ever played," and it remains so to his day. No single game in college football history has ever so completely combined the color, spectacle, national media coverage, public popularity, and top-flight level of play as the Army-Navy battle of 1926 at Soldier Field. Robert Kelley of the New York Times defined the game's significance when he wrote that day: "Football had the greatest pageant, its high spot of color, and so did sport in the United States." http://www.la84.org/SportsLibrary/CFHSN/CFHSNv17/CFHSNv17n2e.pdf

Best Army Navy Game # 2

The Nov. 27, 1926 meeting between Army and Navy took place in Chicago and marked the day the stadium there was christened "Soldier Field."

The fans in attendance also saw a heckuva game.

The contest opened with a bit of gamesmanship from Cadets' coach Biff Jones.

A graduate of West Point, Jones theorized that if he started his second-teamers, the Midshipmen would get a false sense of security and not know what hit them the starters were inserted.

The plan nearly backfired, as Navy jumped out to a 14-0 lead on touchdown runs by Henry Caldwell and James Schuber.

However, Army clawed back in it, and ultimately took a 21-14 lead following a 44-yard touchdown run by Chris Cagle that concluded the third quarter.

Midshipmen Alan Shapley responded with an 8-yard touchdown run to give the game its final score.

Navy went on to win the national championship.

1926 Player Highlights Bud Sprague

Bud Sprague came to West Point from the University of Texas where he had been a star football player and track star. He was a big man at six-three and he played at 240 pounds. Yet, for all that size, Sprague was agile and quick. He once ran the 100-yard dash in 9.7. He and his large family were from Dallas.

While at West Point, Sprague won his letter for all four years. He was named All-American tackle, selected as a first-team honoree by the Associated Press (AP), the International News Service (INS), and the Central Press Association (CP). He was also honored by being elected captain of the football team in 1928.

He played in all the great games of that time and was a mainstay creating positive action on those marvelous Saturdays in the late 20's when the world was a different place. In December of 1970, he was elected to the National Football Hall of Fame.

Unlike many, Sprague chose not to make the Army a career; upon graduation. Instead he opted to resign and went straightaway to work for the Home Insurance Company of New York City, where he was employed until he retired in 968, attaining (at various times) the position of director, vice-president, and secretary of many of the subsidiary insurance companies, working in many different departments over the years, and traveling a great deal. He was president of the New York Board of Trade in 1949, and later became a director of the United States Chamber of Commerce. He remained active with his West Point associations.

When the second World War broke out, Sprague volunteered for the Army, serving in the Transportation Corps and, as part of the Planning Division, being privileged to attend the meetings at Teheran, Potsdam and Yalta. At war's end, he returned to civilian life. Many Army football heroes are also heroes in life.

1927 Army West Point Cadets Football Coach Biff Jones

The Army Cadets football team represented the United States Military Academy in the 1927 college football season. It was their thirty-eighth season of intercollegiate football. They were coached by Biff Jones in his second of four seasons as head coach of the Cadets. As an independent football entity, the team had a record of 9-1-0.

The Cadets compiled a 9-1-0 record. They shut out six of their ten opponents, and outscored all opponents by a combined total of 197 to 37. In the annual Army–Navy Game, the Cadets defeated the Midshipmen by a 14 to 9 score. The team's only loss came to national champion Yale by a 10 to 6 score.

Four Army players were recognized on the 1927 College Football All-America Team. Halfback Red Cagle was a consensus first-team honoree and was later inducted into the College Football Hall of Fame. Tackle Bud Sprague was selected as a first-team honoree by the Associated Press (AP), the International News Service (INS), and the Central Press Association (CP). End Charles Born was selected as a second-team honoree by the United Press (UP), Hearst newspapers, New York Sun, and Billy Evans. Tackle George Perry was selected as a first-team honoree by the New York Sun.

This year, 1927, other than the Notre Dame game that was played at Yankee Stadium; the Yale Game that was played at the Yale Bowl; and the Army-Navy Game, that was played at the Polo Grounds in New York, NY, all Army games were played at Michie Stadium on the Campus of the US Military Academy in West Point, NY.

The season opener was played on Sept 24. Army began the 1926 season at home with a nice shutout victory over Boston University -- W (21-0) at Michie Stadium on the Campus of the USMA at West Point. On Oct 1, the Cadets shut-out Detroit W (6-0). In the third game on Oct 8, Army defeated Marquette W (21-12). On Oct 15, Army defeated Davis & Elkins W (27-6). Then, on Oct 22, at the Yale Bowl, Army was shut out by National Champion Yale L (6-10).

On Oct 29, v Bucknell the Cadets shut out the Bisons W (34-0). Then, on Nov 5, Army shut out Franklin & Marshall W (45-0). On Nov 12, Army shut out the vaunted Knute Rockne coached Fighting

Irish W (18-0) at Yankee Stadium L (0-7). Then, on Nov 20, the Army shut out Ursinas W (13-0) In the season finale, on Nov 27 v. Navy at the Polo Grounds in NY, NY, the Cadets beat the Midshipmen W (14-9)

1927 Player Highlights Red Cagle Davis, B

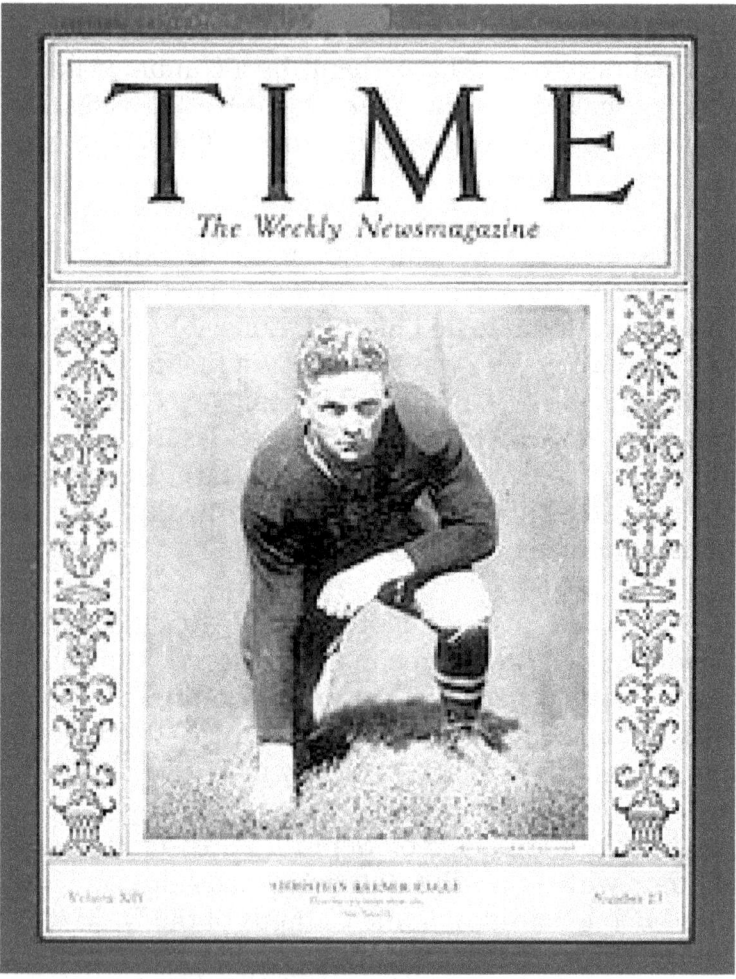

Army's Red Cagle on the Cover of TIME

Christian Keener "Red" Cagle was born on May 1, 1905. He was a talented American athlete. Born in De Ridder, Louisiana, he was one of eight children, including five brothers and two sisters. Cagle was named after an uncle, who in turn was named after the late Bishop Christian Keener of the Methodist church. He attended high school in Merryville, a small community about 20 miles (30 km) southwest of De Ridder. According to local legend, he was known for getting off the school bus and racing it to school, a race that he quite often won. The football field at Merryville High School is named Keener Cagle Field in his honor.

Cagle was a three-time All-American in football while playing for the United States Military Academy (Army). A star halfback, Cagle's powerful abilities landed him on the cover of Time magazine in 1929.

For five seasons, running from 1930 to 1934, Cagle played professional football in the National Football League. His 1932 salary with the New York Football Giants was second highest in the entire league. The following year Cagle became a co-owner of the new Brooklyn Dodgers NFL franchise, for which he also played, selling his stake upon his retirement in 1934. Cagle was inducted into the College Football Hall of Fame in 1954.

Christian "Red" Cagle had two college football careers. He first starred at the University of Louisiana at Lafayette (then named Southwestern Louisiana Institute or SLI) from 1922–1925, where he earned a degree in arts and sciences. In his career at Louisiana-Lafayette, he scored 235 points from touchdowns, extra points and field goals, a school record that lasted until 1989. His time at Louisiana Lafayette has him placed among the all-time greats of early Southern football. Besides being the football captain (1925), he also was a star in basketball and track and field sports at Louisiana-Lafayette, where he received a degree in arts and sciences.

Cagle then played college football for four years at the United States Military Academy (Army) 1926–1929 but did not graduate because he had secretly married in August 1928 in violation of Academy rules. He was forced to resign in May 1930.

Known as the "Red Thunderbolt of West Point," he was an All-American halfback for the last three years. His longest runs were 75 yards against Yale, 1928; 70 yards against Ohio Wesleyan, and 65 yards against Yale, 1929. In four years at Army he scored 169 points, averaged 6.4 yards per attempt in rushing and 26.4 yards on kickoff returns.

He was the team captain at Army in 1929, and in this role, he was featured on the September 23 cover of Time magazine of that same year. Cagle was noted for playing with the chin strap loose from his helmet, and sometimes without helmet. Sportswriters liked to refer to him as "Onward Christian" because of his ability to advance the ball.

Cagle played professional football for five seasons, including the New York Giants from 1930 to 1932. During his final year with the Giants, Cagle was the highest paid member of the team, earning a handsome $500 per game — second in the entire league to the $550 per game earned by superstar halfback Red Grange of the Chicago Bears.

Cagle died in 1942, at 37 years of age, from a peculiar mishap the day after Christmas. He was discovered unconscious at the bottom of a Manhattan subway stairwell. According to The Advertiser report, "Cagle tripped and fell the full length of a flight of subway steps." He died three days later of a fractured skull. At the time of his death he had lived in a Queens apartment house with his wife and was employed by an insurance company. What a great talent!

1928 Army West Point Cadets Football Coach Biff Jones

The Army Cadets football team represented the United States Military Academy in the 1928 college football season. It was their thirty-ninth season of intercollegiate football. They were coached by Biff Jones in his third of four seasons as head coach of the Cadets. As an independent football entity, the Army team had a record of 8-2-0.

The Cadets compiled an 8-2-0 record. The Cadets offense scored 215 points, while the defense allowed 79 points. The 1928 season was one of the few years in which Army did not play the Navy Midshipmen in the Army–Navy Game.

In the 1928 game versus Notre Dame, held at Yankee Stadium, with the score 0–0 at halftime, legendary Notre Dame coach Knute Rockne gave his "win one for the Gipper" speech (with reference to All-American halfback George Gipp, who died in 1920); Notre Dame went on to defeat Army, 12–6.

Army participated in the best-attended college football game at Yankee Stadium. The game was held on December 1, 1928, when Army lost to Stanford 26–0 before 86,000 fans.

They shut out six of their ten opponents, and outscored all opponents by a combined total of 197 to 37. In the annual Army–Navy Game, the Cadets defeated the Midshipmen by a 14 to 9 score. The team's only loss came to national champion Yale by a 10 to 6 score.

This year, 1928, other than the Notre Dame game that was always played at Yankee Stadium; the Harvard game was played at Harvard Stadium in Boston MA; The Yale Game was played at the Yale Bowl; and the Stanford Game that was played at Yankee Stadium in New York, NY, all other Army games were played at Michie Stadium on the Campus of the US Military Academy in West Point, NY.

The season opener was played on Sept 29. Army began the 1926 season at home with a nice shutout victory over Boston University -- W (35-0) at Michie Stadium on the Campus of the USMA at West Point. On Oct 6, the Cadets battled for a close win against SMU W (14-13). In the third game on Oct 13, Army shut out Providence W (44-0). On Oct 20 at Harvard's Harvard Stadium in Boston MA, the Cadets defeated the Crimson W (15-0).

On Oct 27, at Yale in the Yale Bowl New Haven CT, the Army beat Yale W (18-6). On Nov 3, at home, Army defeated DePauw W (38-12). On Nov 10, Army played a great game but were defeated by Knute Rockne's Fighting Irish L (6-12) in a very close tough played match. On Nov 17, the Army defeated Carleton W (32-7). In a first-time appearance for Nebraska at Michie Stadium, the Cadets defeated the Cornhuskers W (13-3). In the Season finale on December 1, without an Army-Navy Game, the Cadets were shut-out by the West-Coast Stanford Cardinal L (0-26) before 86,000 screaming fans at Yankee Stadium in the Bronx, NY.

1929 Army West Point Cadets Football Coach Biff Jones

The Army Cadets football team represented the United States Military Academy in the 1929 college football season. It was their

fortieth season of intercollegiate football. They were coached by Biff Jones in his fourth and last of four seasons as head coach of the Cadets. As an independent football entity, the Army team had a record of 6-4-1.

The Cadets compiled a 6-4-1 record. The 1929 game between Army and Notre Dame had the highest attendance in the series at 79,408.

The days of Army having it forever its way at home had come to an end. Army began to play as all other collegiate teams with both home games and away games. The preponderance of exceptions to Army playing at home hit five teams last year. Army chose to compete like all other teams with both home and away games.

The season opener was played on Sept 28. Army began the 1929 season at home with a nice shutout victory over Boston University -- W (26-0) at Michie Stadium on the Campus of the USMA at West Point. On Oct 5, the Cadets battled for a big score win against Gettysburg, W (33-7). In the third game on Oct 12, Army beat Davidson, W (23-7). On Oct 19 at Harvard's Harvard Stadium in Boston MA, the Cadets tied the Crimson T (20-20).

On Nov 2, at home, Army defeated South Dakota, W (33-6). On Nov 9, Army lost to Illinois, L (7-17). Then in a thunderous overpowering victory, the Cadets beat Dickinson at home, W (89-7) in a huge victory. On Nov 23, Ohio Wesleyan fought hard but list to Army by a score of W)19-6).

On Nov 30, the Cadets could not keep up with Notre Dame and lost in a shutout by a small score of L (0-7. Army played a great game but were defeated by Knute Rockne's Fighting Irish in a very close tough played match. On Dec 28, at Stanford in Stanford Stadium, Stanford, CA, Army lost its last game of 1929 L (13–34).

Because of Army regulations curtailing the tenure of head coaches to four years, the much beloved Biff Jones stepped down as head man at the end of the 1929 season, sporting an impressive 30-8-2 (.775) record. He was replaced by Ralph Sasse, another favorite.

In the last two years of Biff Jones at Army, the Cadets enjoyed another successful season in 1928 with eight wins but two losses - to

Stanford and Notre Dame. However, Army regressed to 6-4-1 in 1929, partly because its star RB, Chris Cagle, injured his shoulder. After the season, Jones was removed from his post since the Army high command considered coaching football at the Academy just another four-year assignment for an officer.

Several years later, Jones would be assigned to the ROTC program at LSU at the request of Huey Long so that Biff could coach the Tigers.

Major Ralph Sasse replaced Jones and kept future coach Red Blaik on his staff along with another assistant, Gar Davidson, whom Blaik could not stand and who would prove to be his nemesis in his quest for the top job on the Plains. Under Sasse, Red became the disciplinarian of the staff, earning the unaffectionate nickname of "The Whip" from the players.

Ralph Irvin Sasse (July 19, 1889 – October 16, 1954) was an American football player, coach, college athletics administrator, and United States Army officer. He served as the head football coach at the United States Military Academy from 1930 to 1932 and at Mississippi State College, now Mississippi State University, from 1935 to 1937, compiling a career college football record of 45–15–4.

1930 Army West Point Cadets Football Coach Ralph Sasse

The Army Cadets football team represented the United States Military Academy in the 1930 college football season. It was their forty-first season of intercollegiate football. They were coached by Ralph Sasse in his first of three seasons as head coach of the Cadets. As an independent football entity, the Army team had a great record of 9-1-1.

The Cadets compiled an 9-1-1 record. They shut out seven of their eleven opponents, and outscored all opponents by a combined total of 268 to 22, an average of 24.4 points scored and 2.0 points allowed per game. In the annual Army–Navy Game, the Cadets defeated the Midshipmen by a 6 to 0 score. The team's only loss was by a 7 to 6 score against an undefeated national champion Notre Dame team in Rockne's final year as head coach.

<< Coach Ralph Sasse

Two Army players were recognized on the 1930 College Football All-America Team. Tackle Jack Price received first-team honors from the North American Newspaper Association (NANA) and the Los Angeles Times. Guard Charles Humber received second-team honors from the International News Service (INS) and third-team honors from the Associated Press (AP).

All Army home games that were not designated to be played on a neutral field such as Soldier Field in Chicago, Yankee Stadium in the Bronx, or Franklin Field in Philadelphia were played at Michie Stadium on the campus of the US Military Academy in West Point, New York.

The season opener was played on Sept 27. Ralph Sasse's Army squad began the 1930 season at home with a nice shutout victory over Boston University -- W (39-0) at Michie Stadium on the Campus of the USMA at West Point. On Oct 4, the Cadets battled for a big score shutout against Furman, W (54-0). In the third game on Oct 11, Army shut-out Swarthmore, W (39-0). On Oct 18 at Harvard's Harvard Stadium in Boston MA, the Cadets defeated the Crimson W (6-0).

On Oct 25, at the Yale Bowl in New Haven CT, Army tied Yale T (7-7). On Nov 1, Army defeated North Dakota at home W (33-6). Then on Nov 8, the Cadets defeated Illinois, W (13-0) In in a major scoring victory, the Cadets beat Kentucky Wesleyan at home W (47-2).

On Nov 22, Army shut out Ursinas at home W (18-0). At Soldier Field, Army and Notre Dame battled like there was no tomorrow. The game was almost a tie but ND pulled it off L (6-7) Army played a great game but were defeated by Knute Rockne's National Champion Fighting Irish in what was a very close tough played match. On Dec 13, at Yankee Stadium, in the Bronx, NY, the Cadets shut out the Midshipmen in a nail-biter game W (6-0).

1931 Army West Point Cadets Football Coach Ralph Sasse

The Army Cadets football team represented the United States Military Academy in the 1931 college football season. It was their forty-second season of intercollegiate football. They were coached by Ralph Sasse in his second of three great seasons as head coach of the Cadets. As an independent football entity, the Army team had a great record of 8-2-1.

The Cadets compiled an 8-2-1 record. They shut out four of their eleven opponents, and outscored all opponents by a combined total of 296 to 72. In the annual Army–Navy Game, the Cadets defeated the Midshipmen by a 17 to 7 score. End Robert Sheridan broke his neck making a tackle in a 6 to 6 tie with Yale. The Cadets also defeated Notre Dame, 12 to 0. The team's only losses were to Harvard by a 13 to 14 score and to Pittsburgh by a 0 to 26 score.

Two Army players were recognized on the 1931 College Football All-America Team. Tackle Jack Price received first-team honors from the International News Service (INS) and Central Press Association (CP), and halfback Ray Stecker received third-team honors from the INS.

All Army home games that were not designated to be played on a neutral field such as Soldier Field in Chicago, Yankee Stadium in the Bronx, or Franklin Field in Philadelphia were played at Michie Stadium on the campus of the US Military Academy in West Point, New York.

The season home opener was played on Sept 27. Army began the 1931 season at home with a shooting shutout victory over Ohio Northern, W (60-0). As all home games, this match was played at

Michie Stadium on the Campus of the USMA at West Point. On Oct 3, the Cadets battled for a big score win against Knox, W (67-6). In the third game on Oct 10, Army beat Michigan State at home, W (20-7). Then on Oct 17 Army lost in a close home battle with Harvard L (13-14).

On Oct 24, at the Yale Bowl in New Haven CT, Army tied Yale T (6-6). On Oct 31, Army shut-out Colorado College at home W (27-0). Then on Nov 7, the Cadets shut-out LSU at home W (20-0) In one of just two losses in 1931, the Cadets were shut out by Pittsburgh L (0-26). Army then defeated Ursinas at home W (54-6). After being beaten for several years in a row by Notre Dame, in this, the first year without Knute Rockne, the Army defeated Notre Dame W (12-0). On Dec 12, at Yankee Stadium, in the Bronx, NY, the Cadets shut out the Midshipmen W (17-7).

1932 Army West Point Cadets Football Coach Ralph Sasse

The Army Cadets football team represented the United States Military Academy in the 1932 college football season. It was their forty-third season of intercollegiate football. They were coached by Ralph Sasse in his third and final season of three great seasons as head coach of the Cadets. As an independent football entity, the Army team had a great record of 8-2-0.

The Cadets compiled an 8-2-0 record. They shut out eight of their ten opponents, and outscored all opponents by a combined total of 261 to 39. In the annual Army–Navy Game, the Cadets defeated the Midshipmen by a 20 to 0 score. The Cadets also defeated Harvard, 40 to 0. The team's only losses were to Pittsburgh by an 18 to 13 score and to Notre Dame by a 21 to 0 score.

Three Army players were recognized on the 1932 College Football All-America Team. Guard Milton Summerfelt was a consensus first-team player. End Dick King received first-team honors from the New York Sun, and second-team honors from the Associated Press (AP), Newspaper Enterprise Association (NEA), and International News Service (INS). Quarterback Felix Vidal received third-team honors from the AP.

All Army home games that were not designated to be played on a neutral field such as Soldier Field in Chicago, Yankee Stadium in the Bronx, or Franklin Field in Philadelphia were played at Michie Stadium on the campus of the US Military Academy in West Point, New York.

The season home opener was played on Oct 1. Army began the 1932 season at home with a shutout victory over Furman W (13-0). As all home games, this match was played at Michie Stadium on the Campus of the USMA at West Point. On Oct 8, the Cadets battled for a big shutout win against Carlton, W (57-0). In the third game on Oct 15, Army lost to Pittsburgh at home, L (13-18). Then, On Oct 22, Army shut out Yale at the Yale Bowl in New Haven CT. W (20-0).

On Oct 29, Army shut out William & Mary W (33-0). On Nov 5, Army won a big shut-out from powerhouse Harvard at Harvard Stadium in Allston MA W (46-0) Then on Nov 12, the Cadets shut-out North Dakota big-time at home W (52-0). On Nov 19, the Cadets shut out West Virginia Wesleyan W (7-0)

Notre Dame beat Army on Nov 26 at Yankee Stadium in the Bronx L (0-21) before 78,115 fans. Then, on Dec 32, at Franklin Field in Philadelphia PA, the Army Shut out the Navy W (20-0).

Sasse asks to be relieved of duty

Ralph Sasse's 1930 Cadet squad finished 9-1-1, the only loss coming to - who else? - Notre Dame. The 1931 season brought an 8-2-1 record, including a win over the Fighting Irish. However, the season was marred by the death of E Dick Sheridan in the fifth game. The tragedy deeply affected Sasse, who asked to be relieved after the 1932 season, which ended 8 up 2 down.

Player Highlights 1932 Milt Summerfelt

It is an understatement to suggest that Milton Fredrick Summerfelt was a great athlete. He was actually one of the greatest football players of all times at West Point. He also possessed admirable qualities of character and leadership. He was open-minded, straightforward and personable in nature, with a keen interest in people and their welfare, he gained and retained the friendships of all who knew him.

Born in Benton Harbor, Michigan, he graduated from Benton Harbor High School in 1926. He waited several years for his appointment to go to West Point. During this interim, he spent two years at Western State Teachers College and one year at Northwestern University. He was a star football player in high school and in college. Named football captain for Northwestern University for 1929, he could not accept because of his entry to West Point in July 1929.

His strong leadership qualities were early recognized at West Point. In athletics, he was All American in football and lacrosse, winning three major "A"'s in both sports. He was captain of the football team in 1932 when Army blanked Navy by a score of 20-0. He made all of the All-American team selections, including, to Milt's embarrassment, the Coed's non-playing team as one of the handsomest players. He was awarded the Edgerton Saber as the outgoing football captain. After graduation, he was selected to play in the All-Star East-West football game in Chicago, but did not play because of military duties.

His first duty was with Army Air Corps flying schools in Texas. "A great, exciting and difficult year, gaining those wings," according to Milt. He received his wings on 13 October 1934 and three days later was married to Val Louise Landry, sister of Bob Landry, Class of 1932 and later a major general in the US Air Force. Milt and Val began their happy married life at Luke Field in Hawaii. Their next station was Mitchell Field in New York. Milt received high praise from the Army Ordnance Department for his support as a bomber pilot of their bomb testing, and from the Coast Artillery for his assistance in their training in the use of searchlights for anti-aircraft defense. His professional competence was recognized early in his career.

In August 1944, Milt was given command of a B-29 Very Heavy Bomb Group, the 333rd. The group was then in training but later was shipped to Okinawa for combat duty over Japan. Milt was cited for his exceptional qualities of leadership and a high degree of professional knowledge in the manning, organization, administration, flying, and technical training of his group for combat. The citation stated that his keen foresight, effective planning, sound judgement, and tireless effort were examples to his subordinates and inspired them to a greater unit achievement and esprit de corps. He was awarded the Legion of Merit and the Commendation Ribbon.

After the war, he continued to hold important positions—first, in the War Department general staff policy branch, later with the Atomic Energy Office. After finishing the National War College, he stayed on in Washington, planning for the Joint Chiefs of Staff. He then commanded the Rome Air Force Base depot for two years.

Milt was promoted to brigadier general in 1954. In 1955, he was appointed deputy chief of the US Military Advisory Group in Bonn, Germany. In 1958, he was made deputy commander of the Sacramento Air Material Area, a post he held until 1961. In 1961, he became the senior member of the Personnel Council for the Secretary of the Air Force, a position he held until his retirement in 1963.

Milt's record is replete with letters of praise for his outstanding performance of duty from numerous military and civilian authorities, including the Secretary of State, Dean Rusk; Curtis E. LeMay, Chief of Staff of the Air Force; and David Bruce, Ambassador to Germany.

Milt has left his mark on history. One that all who knew him and those who read about him all admire.

Chapter 11 Coaches Garrison Davidson & William Wood, 1933-1940

Davidson   Coach # 21
Wood   Coach # 22

Year	Coach	Record	Conference	Record
1933	Gar Davidson	9-1-0	Indep	9-1-0
1934	Gar Davidson	7-3-0	Indep	7-3-0
1935	Gar Davidson	6-2-1	Indep	6-2-1
1936	Gar Davidson	6-3-0	Indep	6-3-0
1937	Gar Davidson	7-2-0	Indep	7-2-0
1938	William Wood	8-2-0	Indep	8-2-0
1939	William Wood	3-4-2	Indep	3-4-2
1940	William Wood	1-7-1	Indep	1-7-1

1930-s Army Cadets Football

Garrison Hold Davidson replaces Ralph Sasse as Head Coach

Garrison Holt Davidson
Class of 1927

Hall of Fame Induction Class of 2014
Administrators / Football
l
Gar Davidson is a 1927 West Point graduate and is honored for a career that includes football accolades as a player, time spent as the head football coach and later, as Superintendent.

Davidson earned two varsity letters as a member of the football team and scored the first touchdown in Michie Stadium. He was also a part of a win and tie opposite Navy.

He was an assistant coach for the "plebe" team for two seasons, was the head coach of the "B" squad for one season and then moved on to head coach for the "plebe" team.

Davidson was the head football coach from 1933-37 and compiled a 35-11-1 mark, including a 3-2 record against Navy.

He later served as Senior Battalion Commander, was an instructor in the West Point Physics Department and worked for Leslie Groves building the Pentagon.

Davidson was selected by George Patton to be Deputy Engineer for Western Task Force Invasion of North Africa. He served as Seventh Army Engineer for the Sicilian Campaign, was an Assistant Division Command of the 24th Infantry and Commandant of the Command and General Staff College.

Davidson returned to West Point as the Superintendent from 1956-60 and retired in 1964 as a lieutenant general.

1933 Army West Point Cadets Football Coach Gar Davidson

The Army Cadets football team represented the United States Military Academy in the 1933 college football season. It was their forty-fourth season of intercollegiate football. They were coached by Gar Davidson in his first of five fine seasons as head coach of the Cadets. As an independent football entity, the Army team had a great record of 9-1-0.

<< Coach GAR Davidson

The Cadets compiled a 9-1-0 record. They shut out seven of their ten opponents, and outscored all opponents by a combined total of 227 to 26. In the annual Army–Navy Game, the Cadets defeated the Midshipmen by a 12 to 7 score. In the final game of the season, the Cadets lost to Notre Dame by a 13 to 12. But for the one-point difference in this one game, Army would have been undefeated and untied in 1933

Four Army players were recognized on the 1933 College Football All-America Team. Halfback Jack Buckler received first-team honors from the Associated Press (AP), United Press (UP), Newspaper Enterprise Association (NEA), Central Press Association (CP), and New York Sun. Quarterback Paul Johnson received second-team honors from the AP and NEA. Guard Harvey Jablonsky received second-team honors from the NEA, CP, and International News Service (INS). End Peter James Kopcsak received third-team honors from the CP.

All Army home games that were not designated to be played on a neutral field such as Soldier Field in Chicago, Yankee Stadium in the

Bronx, or Franklin Field in Philadelphia were played at Michie Stadium on the campus of the US Military Academy in West Point, New York.

The season home opener was played on Sept 30. Army began the 1933 season at home with a victory over Mercer W (19-6). As all home games, this opening match was played at Michie Stadium on the Campus of the USMA at West Point. On Oct 7, the Cadets battled for a shutout win against VNI W (33-0). In the third game on Oct 14, Army shellacked Delaware in a shutout victory at home, W 52-0). Then, On Oct 21, Army shut out Illinois in a close game at Cleveland Ohio W (6-0).

On Oct 28, at the Yale Bowl in New Haven CT, the Cadets shut out the Bulldogs W (21-0). On Nov 4, Army won a big shut-out from Coe at home W (34-0). Then on Nov 11, the Cadets shut-out Harvard at Harvard Stadium in Allston MA, W (27-0). On Nov 18, Army shut out the Pennsylvania Military College W (12-0)

In the big games of the year, operating with an undefeated and untied record, next up was Navy in the Army-Navy Game. Then, on Nov 25, at Franklin Field in Philadelphia PA, the Army defeated the Navy in a close match W (12-13). The next opponent on Dec 2 was a major rival and a spoiler--Notre Dame coached by Hartley Hunk Anderson. Army was undefeated and untied and it was the last game of the season. A win would mean a perfect record. The Irish beat the Cadets on Dec 2 at Yankee Stadium in the Bronx by one point, L (12-13) before 73,594 fans. It was a year that almost was. Nonetheless it was a great year for Army.

1934 Army West Point Cadets Football Coach Gar Davidson

The Army Cadets football team represented the United States Military Academy in the 1934 college football season. It was their forty-fifth season of intercollegiate football. They were coached by Gar Davidson in his second of five seasons as head coach of the Cadets. As an independent football entity, the Army team had a nice record of 7-3-0.

The Cadets compiled a 7-3-0 record. They shut out five of their ten opponents, and outscored all opponents by a combined total of 215 to 40. In the annual Army–Navy Game, the Cadets lost to the Midshipmen by a 3 to 0 score. The Cadets also lost to Notre Dame by a 12 to 6 score and to Illinois by a 7 to 0 score.

Halfback Jack Buckler was selected by the College Sports Writers as a second-team player on the 1934 College Football All-America Team.

All Army home games that were not designated to be played on a neutral field such as Soldier Field in Chicago, Yankee Stadium in the Bronx, or Franklin Field in Philadelphia were played at Michie Stadium on the campus of the US Military Academy in West Point, New York.

The Cadets opened the home season on Sept 29. Army began the 1934 season at home with a shutout victory over Washburn W (19-0). As all home games, this opening match was played at Michie Stadium on the Campus of the USMA at West Point. On Oct 6, the Cadets commandeered a shutout win against Davidson W (41-0). In the third game on Oct 13, Army shellacked Drake in a shutout victory at home, W 48-0). On Oct 27, at the Yale Bowl in New Haven CT, the Cadets defeated the Bulldogs W (20-12).

Then, On Nov 3, Army was shut out by Illinois at Memorial Stadium in Champaign, Illinois L (0-7) On Nov 10, at Harvard Stadium in Allston, MA, the Cadets beat the Harvard Crimson W (27-6). Then on Nov 17, at home, the Cadets shut-out the Citadel W (34-0).

Then, on Nov 24, at Yankee Stadium, in the Bronx, NY, Notre Dame Squeaked out a victory over Army L (6-12) before 73,594 fans. On Dec 1 in the Army-Navy Game, played at Franklin Field, Philadelphia, PA, the Midshipmen shut out the Cadets by a field goal L (0-3)

1935 Army West Point Cadets Football Coach Gar Davidson

The Army Cadets football team represented the United States Military Academy in the 1935 college football season. It was their forty-sixth season of intercollegiate football. They were coached by

Garrison H. Davidson in his third of five seasons as head coach of the Cadets. As an independent football entity, the Army team had a nice record of 6-2-1.

The Cadets compiled a 6-2-1 record. They shut out four of their nine opponents, and outscored all opponents by a combined total of 176 to 62. In the annual Army–Navy Game, the Cadets defeated the Midshipmen by a 28 to 6 score. The Cadets' two losses came against Mississippi State and Pittsburgh. They played Notre Dame to a 6–6 tie.

Two Army players were recognized on the 1935 College Football All-America Team. End William R. Shuler received first-team honors from the Associated Press (AP). Halfback Charles R. Meyer received second-team honors from the United Press(UP) and North American Newspaper Alliance.

All Army home games that were not designated to be played on a neutral field--such as Soldier Field in Chicago, Yankee Stadium in the Bronx, or Franklin Field in Philadelphia, were played at Michie Stadium on the campus of the US Military Academy in West Point, New York.

The Army Home opener was on Oct 5. Army began the 1934 season at home with a low-scoring shutout victory over William & Mary W (14-0). As all home games, this opening match was played at Michie Stadium on the Campus of the USMA at West Point. On Oct 12, the Cadets overpowered Gettysburg for a high-scoring shutout victory W (54-0). In the third game on Oct 19, Army shut out Harvard at home W (13-0). On Oct 26, at the Yale Bowl in New Haven CT, the Cadets defeated the Bulldogs W (14-8).

Then, on Nov 2, Army was defeated at home by Mississippi State L (7-13). Then, On Nov 9 at Pitt Stadium, the Cadets were defeated by the Pittsburgh Panthers L (6-29). Then, on Nov 16, at Yankee Stadium, in the Bronx, NY, Notre Dame tied Army T (6-6) before 78114. On Nov 23 at home, Army shut-out Vermont W (34-0) Then in the season finale, on Nov 30 at Franklin Field in Philadelphia, in the annual Army-Navy Game, the Cadets defeated the Midshipmen W (28-6)

1936 Army West Point Cadets Football Coach Gar Davidson

The Army Cadets football team represented the United States Military Academy in the 1936 college football season. It was their forty-seventh season of intercollegiate football. They were coached by Garrison H. Davidson in his fourth of five seasons as head coach of the Cadets. As an independent football entity, the Army team had a record of 6-3-0.

The Cadets compiled a 6-3-0 record. They shut out their opponents in three of nine games and outscored their opponents by a combined total of 238 to 71. In the annual Army–Navy Game, the Cadets lost to the Midshipmen by a 7 to 0 score. The Cadets' other two losses came against Colgate and Notre Dame.

No Army players were recognized on the 1936 College Football All-America Team.

All Army home games that were not designated to be played on a neutral field--such as Soldier Field in Chicago, Yankee Stadium in the Bronx, or Franklin Field in Philadelphia, were played at Michie Stadium on the campus of the US Military Academy in West Point, New York.

Army opened at home on Oct 3 with a shutout victory over Washington & Lee W (28-0)). As all home games, this opening match was played at Michie Stadium on the Campus of the USMA at West Point. On Oct 10, at Baker Field in New Your, NY, Army defeated Columbia W (27-16). In the third game on Oct 17, at Harvard stadium in Allston, MA, Army shut out Harvard at W (32-0). On Oct 24, Army shut-out Springfield (MA) at home W (33-0)

On Oct 31, Army lost to Colgate at home L (7-14). Then, On Nov 7, Army dominated Muhlenberg at home W (54-7). On Nov 14, at Yankee Stadium in the Bronx, the Cadets were defeated by the Fighting Irish of Notre Dame L (6-20) before 74,423. Then, on Nov 21 Army overpowered Hobart at home W (51-7). Then came the Army-Navy-Game on Nov 28. This game was played at Municipal Stadium in Philadelphia. The Midshipmen defeated the Cadets L (0-7)

1937 Army West Point Cadets Football Coach Gar Davidson

The Army Cadets football team represented the United States Military Academy in the 1937 college football season. It was their forty-eighth season of intercollegiate football. They were coached by Garrison H. Davidson in his fifth and last of five seasons as head coach of the Cadets. As an independent football entity, the Army team had a record of 7-2-0.

The Cadets compiled a 7-2-0 record. They had five games in which the defense gave up just one touchdown and of course they pitched a shutout in the Army-Navy game. Other than that, there were no shutouts. Army was terrific on offense and outscored their opponents by a combined total of 176 to 72. In the annual Army–Navy-Game, the Cadets defeated the Midshipmen by a 6 to 0 score. The Cadets' two losses came against Yale and Notre Dame.

For such a fine year, unexpectedly, there were no Army players recognized on the 1937 College Football All-America Team.

All Army home games that were not designated to be played on a neutral field--such as Soldier Field in Chicago, Yankee Stadium in the Bronx, or Franklin Field in Philadelphia, were played at Michie Stadium on the campus of the US Military Academy in West Point, New York.

On Oct 2, Army opened at home with a W (21-6) victory over Clemson. As all home games, this season opener was played at Michie Stadium on the Campus of the USMA at West Point. On Oct 9 at home, Army defeated Columbia in a close match W (21-18). In the third game on Oct 16, at the Yale Bowl in New Haven, CT, Army was defeated by Yale L (7-17) in a close match. On Oct 23, Army bested Washington (MO) big-time by a score of W (47-7). On Oct 30, Army defeated a tough Virginia Military Academy (VMI) at home W (20-7).

On Nov 6, at Harvard Stadium in Allston, MA, the Cadets defeated the Crimson W 7–6. On Nov 18, at Yankee Stadium in the Bronx, the Cadets were shut out in a tight game by the Fighting Irish of Notre Dame L (0-7) before 76,359 fans. On Nov 27 in the Army-

Navy-Game, played at Municipal Stadium in Philadelphia. The Cadets shut out the Midshipmen W (6-0)

1938 Army West Point Cadets Football Coach Gar Davidson

The Army Cadets football team represented the United States Military Academy in the 1938 college football season. It was their forty-ninth season of intercollegiate football. They were coached by William Wood in his second of three seasons as head coach of the Cadets. As an independent football entity, the Army team had a record of 8-2-0.

The Cadets compiled an 8-2-0 record. They shut out three of ten opponents and outscored their opponents by a combined total of 243 to 95. In the annual Army–Navy Game, the Cadets defeated the Midshipmen by a 14 to 7 score. The Cadets' two losses came against Columbia and Notre Dame.

For such a fine year again, unexpectedly, there were no Army players recognized on the 1938 College Football All-America Team.

All Army home games that were not designated to be played on a neutral field--such as Soldier Field in Chicago, Yankee Stadium in the Bronx, or Franklin Field in Philadelphia, were played at Michie Stadium on the campus of the US Military Academy in West Point, New York.

On Sept 24, Army got its season rolling at home with a shutout win W (32-0) victory over Wichita. As all home games, this season opener was played at Michie Stadium on the Campus of the USMA at West Point. On Oct 1 at home, Army defeated VPI in a shutout / blowout W (39-0) In the third game on Oct 8 at home, Army was beaten in a close match by Columbia L (18-20). On Oct 15, at Harvard Stadium in Allston, MA, the Cadets defeated the Crimson W (20-17)

On Oct 22, at home v Boston University, the Cadets shut out the Terriers W (40-0). On Oct 29, at Yankee Stadium in the Bronx, the Cadets were defeated in a tough fought game by the Fighting Irish of Notre Dame L (7-19) before 76,338 fans. On Nov 5 Army defeated a tough Franklin & Marshall team at home W (20-12). The Next team to take on the Army was Chattanooga who were defeated at Michie Stadium W (34-13). The Cadets then defeated Princeton W (19-7) on Nov 19. This all lead to the season finale – The Army-Navy-Game in Municipal Stadium in Philadelphia PA in which Army defeated Navy W (14-7)

1939 Army West Point Cadets Football Coach William Wood

<< Coach William Wood

The Army Cadets football team represented the United States Military Academy in the 1939 college football season. It was their fiftieth season of intercollegiate football. They were coached by William Wood in his second of three seasons as head coach of the Cadets. As an independent football entity, the Army team had a record of 3-4-2.

The Cadets compiled a 3-4-2 record. They outscored their opponents by a combined total of 106 to 105 – just one point—very unusual for Army. In the annual Army–Navy Game, the Cadets lost to the Midshipmen by a 10 to 0 score. The Cadets' three other losses came against Yale, Notre Dame, and Harvard. It was a poor year overall for Army.

It was not a great offensive or defensive season for the Army Cadets. This was a truly unusual season but it would set the stage for a worse season the following year and it would make all Army fans clamor for two years from now when the immortal Red Blaik came to town on the coaching side.

Army tackle Harry Stella was selected by the United Press (UP), International News Service (INS), and Newsweek magazine as a first-team player on the 1939 College Football All-America Team.

All Army home games that were not designated to be played on a neutral field--such as Soldier Field in Chicago, Yankee Stadium in the Bronx, or Franklin Field in Philadelphia, were played at Michie Stadium on the campus of the US Military Academy in West Point, New York.

On Sept 30, Army got off to a winning start in its season opener against Furman, W (16-7). As all home games, this season opener was played at Michie Stadium on the Campus of the USMA at West Point. On Oct 7 at home, Army defeated Centre in a close match W (9-0) In the third game on Oct 14 at Columbia's Baker Field in New York, the Cadets and the Lions played to a tie T (6-6). Then, on Oct 21, at the Yale Bowl in New Haven CT, the Bulldogs defeated the Cadets L (15-30).

On Oct 22, at home v Ursinas, the Cadets defeated the Bears W (46-13). The really tough teams were next to be played. On Oct 29, at Yankee Stadium in the Bronx, the Cadets were shut out in a tough game by the Fighting Irish of Notre Dame L (0-14) before 75,632 fans. On Nov 11 Army was shut out by a tough Harvard squad at Harvard's Stadium in Allston, MA. L (0-15). On Nov 18, just before the Army Navy game, the Cadets and the Penn State Nittany Lions played at Michie Stadium to a tie T (14-14). This all lead to the season finale – The Army-Navy-Game in Municipal Stadium in Philadelphia PA in which Navy's Midshipmen shut out Army's Cadets L (0-10).

1940 Army West Point Cadets Football Coach William Wood

The Army Cadets football team represented the United States Military Academy in the 1940 college football season. It was their fifty-first season of intercollegiate football. They were coached by William Wood in his third and final year of three seasons as head coach of the Cadets. As an independent football entity, the Army team had a record of 1-7-1, which is one of the team's all-time worst records. This would-be Wood's last year as coach before Red Blaik saved the day.

Was it Wood's fault?

Nobody from what I have researched faults William Wood for this poor year or the last poor year. Neither do they overly credit him for the fine first year he had with an 8-2-0 record. After all, in a day when colleges were hiring full-time professionals, Army had been making do with part-timers whose full-time role was being a commissioned officer. Such was the case with Coach William Wood.

The game was quickly changing from football to war at the US Military Academy when the big war was brewing in Europe. After having secured the neutrality of the Soviet Union (through the August 1939 German-Soviet Pact of nonaggression), we may all remember from our history books that Germany started World War II by invading Poland on September 1, Britain and France responded by declaring on Germany on September 3. This was the beginning of World War II

The US spent a lot of time from 1920 to 1941 analyzing its involvement in World War I. In the years after World War I many Americans quickly reached the conclusion that their country's participation in that war had been a disastrous mistake, one which should never be repeated again. During the 1920s and 1930s, therefore, the US pursued a number of strategies aimed at preventing war. In this end over time, a number of Neutrality acts had been passed to help prevent the US from engaging in such a horrific entanglement ever again.

When Hitler's Germany began the war in 1939 war with Germany on the one hand, and Britain and France on the other, President Franklin D. Roosevelt dutifully went back to American law and he invoked the Neutrality Acts. However, in his heart, Roosevelt believed that this was a fundamentally different war from World War I.

Germany, he believed (and most Americans agreed with him) was in this case a clear aggressor. Without sending troops into battle, Roosevelt therefore sought to provide assistance for the Allies. He was not prepared to have the US enter the war. He began by asking Congress to change the neutrality laws so that the US could make arms sales to the Allies. Later on, after German forces overran France, the president asked Congress for a massive program of direct military aid to Great Britain—an initiative that Roosevelt dubbed "Lend-Lease." In both cases the legislature agreed to FDR's proposals, but only after intense debate.

How involved should the US become? After all, we had an ocean separating us from the war. This issue of involvement in the "European war" deeply divided America for over two years.

On the one hand, Roosevelt and the so-called "internationalists" claimed that a program of aid to Great Britain and other countries fighting against Germany would make actual U.S. participation in the war unnecessary. On the other hand, there were those, who were called "isolationists," who wanted nothing to with foreign entanglements of war. They believed that the president's policies were making it increasingly likely that the country would wind up in another disastrous foreign war—just like World War I. The fear of such a war was real for sure as only twenty-years had passed.

As 1939 turned into 1940 and then 1940 turned into 1941, and as 1942 was approaching, the US debate on the war continued until some other country, namely Japan "woke up a sleeping giant." This debate was still raging when Japanese aircraft attacked Pearl Harbor on December 7, 1941. At this point it was clear that, like it or not, the United States would be a full participant in the Second World War.

From the first inkling of war, especially from 1939 onwards, as important as football was for the service academies, protecting the US from aggression was a much more important mission. It affected everything and football was not an exception.

However, the US Army football team being successful had some bearing on the pride of the US Army servicemen. And, so after not paying much attention to coaching for so many years, the Army Brass knew that for the sake of the Army and the Country and for Army Football, they had to change their coaching philosophy.

After William Wood showed the Brass how bad a football team can get when it is not a priority, the Brass knew things had to change big-time. Luckily, Red Blaik was in the Army coaching pipeline as a former Cadet gridiron star.

Until Blaik was appointed coach in 1941, as noted, the teams of the Army's United States Military Academy at West Point usually had been coached for a tour of duty by a career officer for four years or less at a time. The officer, was assigned to the team in much the same manner as he might be posted to Fort Leonard Wood as supply officer. But when Blaik was lured from Dartmouth, he came with his own set of rules, and Army Brass were mostly happy to play by them. For the first time, a coach was permitted to hire a professional staff and was automatically bestowed the rank of full colonel. He was also appointed athletic director, and systemized recruiting began at Army. The USMA had entered the era of big-time college football.

There are those of us Army fans who think that the same hard look at Army's football prowess needs to be reexamined today. It seems that Army is well on its way with a great 2016 and more to come in 2017. Can Jeff Monken be the new Red Blaik. Many of us on the fan line sure hope so.

Did hiring Red Blaik work? You bet it did. Hold on to your hats as after we purge this last bad chapter of early Army football from our innards, we get to be entertained through one of the finest periods of football in any American College. The United States Military Academy in the Red Blaik years made itself well known. Hold on... we'll be there soon. Let's look a little more at the scenario into which Red Blaik found himself before we finish this season.

War and Remembrances from Army-Navy Series

December 08, 1991 | By Robert Markus, Chicago Tribune.

The following includes excerpts from this great article from 1991 about what it was like to play football and be at war.

According to retired Col. Morris Herbert, head of the academy's association of graduates, of the 19 players on the Army team in a particular 1941 game (Army-Navy) that we will cover in the next chapter, six would become general officers; five would be killed in action.

Murphy, who retired a two-star general and now lives in Colorado Springs, remembers the main topic of conversation at West Point that winter-how quickly their training would be accelerated.

In previous wars, they knew, the four-year curriculum had been truncated by as much as two years. Murphy, it turned out, graduated on schedule that May. Succeeding classes were put on a three-year cycle for their diplomas.

As for the Army-Navy game itself, that 1941 game was the last in Philadelphia until after the war. It marked the debut of Army graduate Earl Blaik as coach, but that wouldn't be enough to keep Navy from scoring a 14-6 victory.

In time, Blaik would lead Army to incredible heights of glory. He had come to Army after a 45-0 loss to Cornell followed by a 48-0 defeat to Columbia convinced academy officials they needed a professional coach.

Until then, recounts Col. Morris, "They always had part-time coaches. The guy who coached from 1938-1940, Bill Wood, was a cavalry captain who would come back to the Point each fall to coach the team."

When Blaik arrived for his first spring practice, the story goes, he was in the midst of telling his squad that most football games are lost because of poor line play.

Seeing one player who appeared to be half asleep, Blaik barked out:

``Mister, where are most football games lost?``

``Right here at West Point, sir,`` came the answer.

Morris, who at 14 had seen his first Army-Navy game that year, explains why the game was moved from Philadelphia.

``They were afraid that having both cadet corps in one stadium at one time would be too inviting a target,`` he said.

``So in 1942, the game was at Annapolis. The cadet corps did not go to the game, so half of the midshipmen were ordered to root for Army. They sang the Army songs and cheered the Army cheers, though I doubt their hearts were in it.

``The next year the game was at the Point, and half the corps had to cheer for Navy.``

The 1940 Season with Coach Wood

The Cadets compiled a 1-7-1 record. They were outscored by their opponents by a combined total of 197 to 54. It was the first season since 1899 in which an Army football team had been outscored by its opponents. In the annual Army–Navy Game, the Cadets lost to the Midshipmen by a 14 to 0 score. The Cadets also suffered blowout defeats to Cornell (45-0) and Penn (48-0). It was a very poor year overall for Army.

No Army players were honored on the 1940 College Football All-America Team. Three weeks after the end of the 1940 season, the War Department ordered coach Wood back to active troop duty and named Earl Blaik as head coach for the 1941 season. The War Department had been paying attention to the football success of the Cadets. Though the Draft was in play, it was not a good recruiting tool to have an inept football team and so Army took the proper corrective action. Nobody really knew how great the team would become.

All Army home games that were not designated to be played on a neutral field--such as Soldier Field in Chicago, Yankee Stadium in the Bronx, or Municipal Field in Philadelphia, were played at Michie Stadium on the campus of the US Military Academy in West Point, New York.

On Oct 5, Army got a look at just how poor this season would be as they played Williams and barely beat this 3rd level team (Division III of today). W (20-19). Williams should have won the game.

As all home games, this season opener was played at Michie Stadium on the Campus of the USMA at West Point. This October 5 game was the first and it would be the last win of the season for the Cadets. Without laboring over all the losses and ties, we'll simply list the games from this year which we soon hope to forget completely. Though there were some bright spots, such as the close game v #2 Notre Dame L (0-7) there were not many

October 5   Williams, Michie, W (20-19
October 12   Cornell, Michie L (0–45)
October 19   Harvard, Harvard Stadium in Allston, MA T (6–6)
October 26   Lafayette, Michie, L (0–19)
November 2   Notre Dame Yankee Stadium, Bronx, NY L 0–7
November 9   Brown, Michie, L 9–13
November 16 Penn, Franklin Field, Philadelphia, PA L (0–48)
November 23 Princeton, Palmer Stadium • Princeton, NJ L (19–26)
November 30 Navy, Municipal Stadium • Philadelphia, PA L (0–14)

And that folks, is that! Let's move on to better weather.

Chapter 12 Coach Red Blaik 1941 - 1958

Blaik   Coach # 23

Year	Coach	Record	Conference	Record
1941	Red Blaik	5-3-1	Indep	5-3-1
1942	Red Blaik	6-3-1	Indep	6-3-1
1943	Red Blaik	7-2-1	Indep	7-2-1
1944	Red Blaik	9-0-0	Indep	9-0-0
1945	Red Blaik	9-0-0	Indep	9-0-0
1946	Red Blaik	9-0-1	Indep	9-0-1
1947	Red Blaik	5-2-2	Indep	5-2-2
1948	Red Blaik	8-0-1	Indep	8-0-1
1949	Red Blaik	9-0-0	Indep	9-0-0
1950	Red Blaik	8-1-0	Indep	8-1-0
1951	Red Blaik	2-7-0	Indep	2-7-0
1952	Red Blaik	4-4-1	Indep	4-4-1
1953	Red Blaik	7-1-1	Indep	7-1-1
1954	Red Blaik	7-2-0	Indep	7-2-0
1955	Red Blaik	6-3-0	Indep	6-3-0
1956	Red Blaik	5-3-1	Indep	5-3-1
1957	Red Blaik	7-2-0	Indep	7-2-0
1958	Red Blaik	8-0-1	Indep	8-0-1

Coach Red Blaik with offensive stars Doc Blanchard and Glenn Davis

Earl "Red" Blaik was everything Americans would expect a graduate of the United States Military Academy to be: an officer, a gentleman, and a winner: as West Point's head football coach from 1941 through 1958, he was one of the best coaches ever.

In his 18 years at West Point, he coached two national champions (most credit Army with three national championships—a tie with ND in 1946) and six unbeaten teams. Even more important than his 166 wins, though, was the example of leadership he provided at a place where leadership is prized.

In the mid-1940s, coincidental with the arrival of Red Blaik, Army football became one of college football's greatest dynasties. It was a tumultuous time for America, amid World War II, and college football had been shaken up like every other part of life. Some schools stopped playing. The great basketball powerhouse, Gonzaga, for example, had a nice football program going into World War II.

Like many colleges, their football program went on hiatus during World War II (in April 1942). After the war, the administration decided not to resume it. The program had been in some financial difficulty prior to the war and it seemed like a good idea at the time to forego the sport at Gonzaga.

There were more and more young men heading to combat and other roles to support the war effort. Many top players flocked to military training centers before heading overseas. And, of course, many great players chose to come to West Point. Army football had been strong before and after World War I under great coaches such as Charles Daly and Biff Jones. Army football had a storied rivalry with Notre Dame dating back to 1913 when Rockne and Dorais played for the Irish.

But in the post Rockne era, something happened to Army. From 1932-43, Army failed to beat Notre Dame, managing only two ties. That soon changed under the tutelage of Blaik. Football was maturing as an American sport and strategies were ever so much more important to have successful seasons.

Blaik was already an accomplished football master when he came to Army. It was not an easy decision for him. As a West Point grad, he made a difficult decision to leave Dartmouth, where he had gone 45-15-4 in seven seasons, finishing seventh in the AP poll in 1937. After three solid seasons back at West Point, Blaik's Black Knights went 27-0-1 from 1944-46. It was unexpected and wonderful. Army was beating everybody during the war including the Germans and the Japanese.

Army became undisputed national champions the first two years. In 1944, they didn't allow more than a TD in a game and beat Notre Dame 59-0 and Navy 23-7. In 1945, Army beat then-No. 2 Notre Dame 48-0 and then the Cadets whooped #2 Navy 32-13. In '46, Notre Dame had one of the most talented teams ever, with the war over, and the two battled to a 0-0 tie. The Fighting Irish were voted to be the # 1 college team in the final AP poll when Army barely hung on for a 21-18 win over 1-8 Navy.

Army had a 9-0-1 Army and were recognized by the CFB Research Group as champions and by the Helms group for a tie with Notre Dame. Notre dame's record was 8-0-1 and their support by AP gave the Irish the consensus championship but many consider Notre Army as having a share of the gold that year. ND backers included the National Championship Foundation, AP Poll, Helms (tie).

The below photo shows some action in what is now referred to as the 1946 championship of ND V Army. Let's examine it briefly

This opportune photo above is considered by the football scholars and pundits as the defining play of 1946's "Game of the Century." In this play as you can see clearly in the photo, Notre Dame's Bill Gompers turned the corner on 4th down and headed for Army's goal line. But alas, he did not make it. In fact, he did not even reach the 2-yard line for a first down. In this game, there were no other serious scoring threats, and so this "Game of the Century," ended in a 0-0 stalemate.

Yes it was 1946 and it had been a little more than a year since the war had ended. Army had two in a row and ND had their best team, perhaps ever... Nonetheless, without cell phones or TV and a 24-hour news cycle, somehow everybody in the country knew this game was coming. Many have said that never before had a game been hyped as much as this meeting of #1 Army and #2 Notre Dame.

Other games had been called "Game of the Century" in the past, but this was the first to be widely described as such by the press nationwide before the game.

Army had been kicked around by ND for years and now with two in a row under their belts, Army was confident that it could beat ND a third time. Hey, the Army Cadets were the 2-time defending national champion. They came into the game with a 25-game winning streak. They had whooped Notre Dame 59-0 and 48-0 the previous 2 years. But it was a different ND team this particular year. Frank Leahy, ND's coach, other coaches, and a number of players were now back from the war, and when last this group of were on campus, Notre Dame had beaten Army and had won the 1943 mythical national championship (MNC).

This game had the top greats from the period playing together on the same field. The game featured 3 Heisman Trophy winners, 3 Outland Trophy winners, and 10 Hall of Famers, not counting the Hall of Fame coaches on each side. Notre Dame claims MNCs for 1943, 1946, 1947, and 1949, and Army claims MNCs for 1944, 1945, and 1946. This was a true clash of the titans, an intersection of 2 of the greatest runs in college football history: Army going 27-0-1 1944-1946 and Notre Dame going 36-0-2 1946-1949.

Army kept its spot at #1 after the scoreless tie, but when they struggled to beat 1-8 Navy 21-18 in their final game, Notre Dame passed them up for the #1 ranking in the final AP poll. Above the picture, we showed how all of the organizations listed in the NCAA Records Book see the 1946 mythical national championship (omitting math/computer ratings, which are not generally accepted as MNCs). Both ND and Army have a right to their claims for a national championship. Since there were no official agencies like we have today, most consider that ND and Army shared the 1946 Mythical National Championship.

Army's three-year peak was nearly unmatchable, with Heisman winners Doc Blanchard and Glenn Davis sharing the backfield, but it wasn't the end of Blaik's success. While Notre Dame was getting tougher and tougher with Frank Leahy back in football action, Army was doing well with Red Blaik but ND's 36-0-2 record to 1949 was also unmatched.

With Blaik as the master, and a strict disciplinarian, nobody expected what happened to Army. An academic cheating scandal in 1951 ripped apart Blaik's team. Blaik's son was part of the scandal and he was forced to leave the Academy. Blaik persevered and after just a couple down years, including Blaiks's only losing season of 18, Army football bounced back.

Red Blaik ended his career on a high note in 1958, coaching an 8-0-1 team that finished third in the AP poll and featured Heisman winner Pete Dawkins, making it the last national powerhouse West Point football team.

In his career, Earl "Red" Blaik coached three Heisman winners and eight top-10 teams at Army, with two undisputed national championships and claims to share the '46 title as well. To enhance his legacy, Blaik produced an astounding coaching tree, headlined by five-year assistant Vince Lombardi. Now, we get to look at the action in those eighteen years, so hold on folks, we're just a few text lines away. Enjoy!

1941 Army West Point Cadets Football Coach Red Blaik

The Army Cadets football team represented the United States Military Academy in the 1941 college football season. It was their fifty-second season of intercollegiate football. They were coached by Earl "Red" Blaik in his first of eighteen seasons as head coach of the Cadets. As an independent football entity, the Army team had a record of 5-3-1.

<< Coach Blaik

Gen. Douglas MacArthur in background pic.

The Cadets compiled a 5-3-1 record. They outscored their opponents by a combined total of 105 to 87. The season represented a four-game improvement on the prior year's record of 1–7–1. In the annual Army–Navy Game, the Cadets lost to the Midshipmen by a 14 to 6 score. The Cadets also lost to Harvard and Penn and played Notre Dame to a scoreless tie.

Army halfback Hank Mazur was selected by Life magazine as a third-team player on the 1941 College Football All-America Team.

All Army home games that were not designated to be played on a neutral field--such as Soldier Field in Chicago, Yankee Stadium in the Bronx, and also Municipal Field or Franklin Field in Philadelphia; were played at Michie Stadium on the campus of the US Military Academy in West Point, New York.

On Oct 4, Army got off to a winning start in its season opener against The Citadel, W (19-6) It had been a whole season since Army had won its last game. All home games, just like this season opener were played at Michie Stadium on the Campus of the USMA at West Point. On Oct11 at home, Army defeated VMI in a close match at home, W (27-20). In the third game on Oct 18 at the Yale Bowl in

New Haven, CT, Cadets beat the Bulldogs W (20-7). Then, on Oct 25, at the Yale Bowl in New Haven CT, the Bulldogs defeated the Cadets L (15-30). On Oct 25, at home, the Cadets shut out Columbia W (13-0).

Army was 4-0 with a great start when the meat of their schedule came up beginning on Nov 1 at Yankee Stadium in the Bronx, NY v the #6 ranked Fighting Irish of Notre Dame before 75,226 fans, the Cadets played ND to a scoreless tie T (0-0) showing that this Blaik-coached team had a lot of mettle.

The first loss did not come until Nov 8 when the Cadets went to Massachusetts to Harvard Stadium to play the Crimson and they were set back by a score of L (6-20). On Nov 15 Army got its second loss against a tough Penn at Franklin Field in Philadelphia PA L (7-14)

On Nov 26, Army got its moxie back when it beat a tough West Virginia team at home W (7-6) in a nail-biter. All of this lead to the most important game of the year for Army—its season finale – The Army-Navy-Game played in Municipal Stadium in Philadelphia PA. Navy's Midshipmen outgunned Army in this close match L (6-14).

Army had recovered and Army fans could expect about seventeen more great years before it had to worry about consistently winning again.

1942 Army West Point Cadets Football Coach Red Blaik

The Army Cadets football team represented the United States Military Academy in the 1942 college football season. It was their fifty-third season of intercollegiate football. They were coached by Earl "Red" Blaik in his second of eighteen seasons as head coach of the Cadets. As an independent football entity, the Army team had a record of 6-3-1.

The Cadets compiled a 6-3-1 record.

After a long drought, Army again began pitching shutouts. This year there were two with more to come in future years. Army was back in control on offense and defense. They outscored their opponents by a combined total of 149 to 74. In the annual Army–Navy Game, the Cadets were shut out by the Midshipmen by a 14 to 0 score. The Cadets also lost to Penn and Notre Dame. Soon Army will be winning against all schools—big and small.

Army had a great team as reflected by the honors received. Four Army players were honored on the 1942 College Football All-America Team. Tackle Robin Olds was selected as a first-team player by Grantland Rice for Collier's Weekly. Tackle Francis E. Merritt was selected as a second-team player by both the Central Press Association (CP) and the Newspaper Enterprise Association (NEA) and was later inducted into the College Football Hall of Fame. Halfback Henry Mazur was selected as a second-team player by the International News Service (INS). End James Kelleher was selected as a third-team player by the Sporting News and NEA.

All Army home games that were not designated to be played on a neutral field--such as Soldier Field in Chicago, Yankee Stadium in the Bronx, Thompson Field in Annapolis; Municipal Field or Franklin Field in Philadelphia; were played at Michie Stadium on the campus of the US Military Academy in West Point, New York.

On Oct 4, Army got off to a winning start in its season opener against Lafayette with a shutout W (14-0). All home games, were played at Michie Stadium on the Campus of the USMA at West Point. On Oct 10 at home, Army defeated Cornell W (28-8) and then traveled the short distance the following week to Baker Field in New York, NY to defeat Columbia W (34-6). On Oct 24, at Harvard Stadium in Allston MA, Army Shut out the Crimson W (14-0). Next, on Oct 31 at Franklin Field in Philadelphia, the Cadets were shut out by the Penn Quakers L (0-19). Then, on Nov 7, the big rival Notre Dame Fighting Irish came to Yankee Stadium in the Bronx, NY and shut out the Cadets L (0-13).

On Nov 14, at home the Cadets defeated VPI W (19-7). Then feeling pretty good about themselves, Army crushed Princeton W (40-7 at Yankee Stadium. In the game that always counts, the Cadets came up short again against Navy at Thompson Stadium in Annapolis. Because the Army Brass did not want both service academies in the same stadium, Navy attended the game but Army did not. Half of the Navy guys learned the Army fight songs and took the places of their comrades in the other branch. The Cadets lost the game by a shutout despite all those fine Navy cheers, L (0-14)   i

The Cadets played VMI in a close match at home, W (27-20). In the third game on Oct 18 at the Yale Bowl in New Haven, CT, Cadets beat the Bulldogs W (20-7). Then, on Oct 25, at the Yale Bowl in New Haven CT, the Bulldogs defeated the Cadets L (15-30). On Oct 25, at home, the Cadets shut out Columbia W (13-0).

Army had more than recovered and Army fans had an air of confidence about each season and each game in each season forward.

1942 Player Highlights Casimir Myslinski, Center

Casimir John Myslinski was one of the great centers in Army football. He was born on 6 Mar 1920 in Steubenville, OH. He was the third of nine children of Felix and Stella Dziegelewski Myslinski. He played football at Steubenville High School, where he graduated and in HS, he was also the sports editor for the school newspaper and yearbook.

After graduation, he attended Stanton Preparatory School in Cornwall, New York. In 1941, he gained an appointment to the United States Military Academy from Ohio Congressman George H. Bender.

A classmate wrote, "From a midwestern steel town an unexcitable, self-made man came to West Point. A warm smile and a bruising brand of football gave Cas much recognition Plebe year. "Yearling year, Sid's outstanding defensive ability and 60 stellar minutes against Notre Dame and Navy won him the football captaincy. This practical-minded man will go high in this man's army."

A football teammate is quoted, "He makes 3 times as many tackles on my side of the line as I do." It is no wonder that Cas was named All-American football center in 1943 and won the Knute Rockne

Award. In addition to his spectacular football career, he was appointed Cadet Lieutenant during first class year, wrestled, and played chess.

Despite his classmate's predictions, Cas became an Air Cadet and received his silver wings on 5 Jun and his gold bars on 6 Jun 1944. His first assignments were at Smyrna for B-24 training, after which he went through a rapid succession of assignments ending at Roswell, NM, for B-29 transition. As he wrote in the 10-year Reunion Book, "Managed to escape from B-29s by going to McGill Field, FL. Escaped from SAC by going to Europe in 1947," where he participated in the Berlin Airlift.

On 28 Jun 1947, at Andrews Field, Maryland, Casimir married Eleanor (Sandy) Thuge. Cas and Sandy had 4 children: Lynda Sue was born in Mar 1950, Patricia Marie in Mar 1951, Michael Casimir in Jul 1954, and Dorothy Valentine in Aug 1956.

When Cas returned from Europe in 1951, he spent a year at Columbia University, receiving a master's degree in physical education. Casimir later reported to West Point for a year as a tactical officer before joining the Physical Education Department.

Close friend, classmate, and teammate Frank Merritt remembers, "Upon getting his degree in physical education he was to be assigned to the Naval Academy And [when] he reported to the Naval Academy, football coach Eddy Erdelac, finding out that he was there, made it necessary for Cas to be transferred because he, Erdelac, thought he would be a spy for West Point. So, Cas ended up at West Point."

(Note—Later, the Navy goat was found in the Myslinski basement!) In 1956, Cas was transferred to the Air Force Academy, first as assistant football coach and, later, as director from 1957-60.

After his tour at the Air Force Academy, Cas was back flying as commander of a jet training squadron until 1964, when he spent a year as Chief of the USAF Training Mission to Saudi Arabia. Upon his return to the States, Cas attended the Air War College and then moved to California, where he commanded a F-104 squadron at George Air Force Base.

LTC Myslinski retired from the Air Force in 1967 and sold real estate briefly before accepting the position of Athletic Director at the University of Pittsburgh, a position he occupied until his final retirement in 1982. During his tenure at Pitt, he was credited with reviving a sports program that had been plagued by losing records, poor facilities, and inadequate funding.

1943 Army West Point Cadets Football Coach Red Blaik

The Army Cadets football team represented the United States Military Academy in the 1943 college football season. It was their fifty-fourth season of intercollegiate football. They were coached by Earl "Red" Blaik in his third of eighteen seasons as head coach of the Cadets. As an independent football entity, the Army team had a record of 7-2-1. Army had begun to win the big ones. This year, the Cadets were the #11 ranked team in the country. Not bad so close to being rock bottom. Wait until 1944 for some real National Level fireworks!

The Cadets compiled a 7-2-1 record. Firing shutouts right and left, the Cadets shut out five of their ten opponents, and outscored all opponents by a combined total of 299 to 66. Wow! In the annual Army–Navy Game, the Cadets lost to the Midshipmen by a 13 to 0 score. The Cadets also lost to Notre Dame by a 26 to 0 score, but won convincing victories over Colgate(42-0), Temple (51-0), Columbia (52-0), and Brown (59-0). The fans and alums were most upset by the Navy losses but had confidence that it would end soon. It did.

Two Army players were honored on the 1943 College Football All-America Team. Center Cas Myslinski was a consensus first-team honoree, and tackle Francis E. Merritt was selected as a first-team player by Football News and a second-team player by the Associated Press.

As noted but worth repeating, after a long drought with two shutouts last year, Army had again begun to pitch shutouts. This year there were five with many more to come in future years. Army was back in the saddle on both offense and defense. Soon it would show even more so.

All Army home games that were not designated to be played on a neutral field--such as Soldier Field in Chicago, Yankee Stadium in the Bronx, Thompson Field in Annapolis, Municipal Field or Franklin Field in Philadelphia; were played at Michie Stadium on the campus of the US Military Academy in West Point, New York.

Army kicked off its 1943 season On Sept 25 with a nice shutout win at home against Villanova W (27-0) All Army home games, were played at Michie Stadium on the Campus of the USMA at West Point. On Oct 2 at home, Army shut out Colgate, W (42-0) and then invited Temple who traveled the short distance from Philadelphia to Michie the following week on Oct 9 to be shellacked W (51-0) by the Cadets. The following week at Baker Field in New York, the Cadets walloped Columbia W (52-0).

On Oct 23, at the Yale Bowl in New Haven CT, the #2 ranked Cadets whooped the Yale Bulldogs W (39-7). Moving to the big Franklin Field, #2 Army tied #6 Penn T (13-13) Harvard Stadium in Allston MA, Army Shut out the Crimson W (14-0). Next, on Oct 31 at Franklin Field in Philadelphia, the Cadets were shut out by the Penn Quakers L (0-19). Then, on Nov 7, the big rival Notre Dame Fighting Irish came to Yankee Stadium in the Bronx, NY and shut out the Cadets L (0-13).

Frank Leahy's #1 ranked Notre Dame team of 1943 had been buzzing around the country picking off all opponents like they had not brought a defense. On Nov 16, Notre Dame showed up at Michie Field in full regalia, ready for a big win against their nemesis Army. Red Blaik was still fine tuning the Cadets and though they played very well against the Irish. It was not good enough as ND went home with the W but for Army it was L (0-26). Yankee Stadium was alive with excitement as 75,121 fans cheered Army and Notre Dame for a great game.

The United States Air Force was not an entity in 1943 but it was on its way. It was created on September 18, 1947, and its academy became the best training ground for pilots and navigators and other

Air-personnel in the world, representing of course, the United States of America

So, when I saw that on Nov 13 this fine football season, that Army had played USNTS Sampson, I figured it was an Air Force operation to-be. They were tough enough to field a football team of their own good enough to take on Red Blaik's soon to-be National Champions. Army had a tough time with these upstarts but pulled out the win for Blaik at Michie on Nov 13, W (16-7). On Nov 20, Brown came to Michie to get in a good game but got a lot more. They got thumped / shut out by an enlivened Army corps who enjoyed the W (59-0) shootout.

Despite all the good Army play this year, Navy was still a formidable opponent in its baddest of years. This was not one of those. Playing for the first time at Michie Stadium with the Army contingent doing the Navy cheers and the Navy service absent from the game completely, Navy must have loved the sweet Army voices and were invigorated to win the game by shutout v Army L (0-14) Good day for Navy! Bad day for Army! But wait 'til next year!!!!!

1944 Army West Point Cadets Football Coach Red Blaik

The Army Cadets football team represented the United States Military Academy in the 1944 college football season. It was their fifty-fifth season of intercollegiate football. They were coached by Earl "Red" Blaik in his fourth of eighteen seasons as head coach of the Cadets. As an independent football entity, the Army team had a perfect record of 9-0-0. Army had learned to win the big ones.

This year, they won everything big to small to all things in-between. This year, the Cadets were the #1 ranked team in the nation Not bad for a team that four years prior was at the bottom. This year, thanks to the Brass's faith in Red Blaik, the Army celebrated with some live National Level fireworks with a consensus National Championship.

The Cadets compiled a 9-0-0 perfect record. Firing shutouts right and left, the Cadets shut out four of their ten opponents, and outscored their opponents 504 points to 35 points. At the season's end, the team won a national championship. The team captain was Tom Lombardo. Showing the guts of the Army team in all kinds of action, in 1950, Lombardo was killed in action during the Korean War.

Dewitt Tex Coulter was All American as tackle via UP2, Glenn Davis, Halfback, and Doc Blanchard fullback were All American by just about everybody's standards such as AAB, AP, FN, INS, NEA, SN, UP , LK, etc. Army had a great team and great players and a great coach.

Army began its 1944 season on Sept 30 with a whomping shutout of North Carolina W (46-0) All Army home games, were played at Michie Stadium on the Campus of the USMA at West Point. On Oct 7 at home, Army shellacked Brown W (59-7) and then invited Pittsburgh to travel to Michie the following week on Oct 14 to be whacked W (69-7) by the Cadets. The following week at Michie, the @2 ranked Cadets thumped the Coast Guard W (76-0) Army was not trained to hear the cry of "Uncle" from its opponents. Duke looked like a championship team at the Polo Grounds in NY compared to all others who so far had met the onslaught of the Cadet Offense and the quick closes of the West Point Defense. Army did need to work to dispose of Duke W (27-7)

Army scores were never so high because Army had never been quite this good and this was reflected on Nov 4 at Michie v Villanova in a shutout rout W (83-0). No team at Army had ever shellacked Notre Dame until Red Blaik came to town. Red's Cadets beat the Tar out of ND at Yankee Stadium in the Bronx, NY as big as a win v ND could ever be W (59-0).

As good as Penn was, their great team looked like mush meat at Franklin Field when on the same field with Army in 1944. The vaunted Penn got thumped just like everybody else W (62-7). Ya got to give it to the Navy. Despite all the thumping, shellacking, whomping and outright devastating opponents by large scores, Navy kept its pride. They lost big-time to Army but by a respectable W (23-7). For Army, the navy win was the sweetest of the season.

Army was as good as it gets in 1944.

Great day for Army! Bad day for Navy and it was not about to change the next year.

Army Navy Game #1 Best Game

Army came into this contest 8-0, having outscored opponents by a combined score of 481-28. But, the Cadets also came in with something to prove, having lost to Navy, 13-0, a year earlier.

Making that 1943 result even worse for Army was that the game took place in West Point.

The top-ranked Cadets got their revenge, dominating the No. 2 Midshipmen, 23-7, despite throwing five interceptions and fumbling three times.

Competing two weeks before the Battle of the Bulge and featuring a backfield that included future Heisman Trophy winners Glenn Davis and Doc Blanchard, Army outrushed its rivals, 181-71.

And after the contest, the team received a telegram from Gen. Douglas MacArthur, halfway around the world and full of pride.

"The greatest of all Army teams—STOP—We have stopped the war to celebrate your magnificent success. MacArthur."

1944 Player Highlights Hank Foldberg, End

Henry Christian "Hank" Foldberg, Sr. was born March 12, 1923. He was a great American college and professional football player who later became a college football coach. Foldberg played his first stint of college football for Texas A&M University for one year and then the United States Military Academy. Afterwards, he played professionally for Brooklyn Dodgers and the Chicago Hornets of the All-America Football Conference (AAFC). He later served as the head football coach of Wichita State University and Texas A&M University.

Foldberg played end for coach Earl Blaik's Army Cadets football team from 1944 to 1946. Army produced back-to-back undefeated 9–0 records in 1944 and 1945, and the Cadets were recognized as the Associated Press national champions following both seasons. As a senior in 1946, Army was again undefeated at 9–0–1, with one tie v Notre Dame. Foldberg was recognized as a consensus first-team All-American at End. As a cadet athlete, he also earned varsity letters in lacrosse and baseball.

Foldberg resigned from the U.S. Military Academy in 1948, a year short of graduation, citing family financial hardship.

Hank signed with the Washington Redskins of the National Football League (NFL) after being drafted in the fifth round (twenty-eighth pick overall) in the 1947 NFL Draft. Instead, he decided to remain in school at West Point for another year. He did play professional football in 1948 and 1949, first with Branch Rickey's Brooklyn Dodgers of the AAFC in 1948, and then with the AAFC's Chicago Hornets in 1949. In his two seasons as a pro, he played in twenty-five games, and started fifteen, while catching thirty-one passes for 331 yards. Three teams from the AAFC merged into the NFL in 1950, and the AAFC ceased to exist thereafter.

Foldberg was married to the former Margaret Smith, and they had a son and a daughter. After he left the coaching profession, he entered the real estate business in Arkansas. Foldberg's son, Hank Foldberg, Jr., later played tight end for the Florida Gators football team from 1971 to 1973. Foldberg passed away at his home in Bella Vista, Arkansas. He was 77 years old.

1944 Player Highlights Glenn Davis, B

Glenn Davis 1947 Yearbook Photo

Glenn Woodward Davis was born on the day after Christmas, on December 26, 1924. The Canadians celebrate Boxer day on December 26. Davis was a college and professional American football player for Army and then for the Los Angeles Rams. He is best known for his college football career for the United States Military Academy at West Point from 1943 to 1946. Davis was known as "Mr. Outside." He was named a consensus All-American three times, and in 1946, he won the Heisman Trophy and was named Sporting News Player of the Year and Associated Press Athlete of the Year. He was one of the best football players of all time on one of the best teams of all time.

The son of a Bank Manager, Glenn Davis was born and raised in Southern California. He and his twin brother Ralph played high school football at Bonita High School in La Verne, California. They both loved the game and both were exceptional players. In 1942, Davis led the Bearcats to an 11–0 record and the school's first-ever football championship, earning the Southern Section Player of the Year award. In 1989, Bonita High's stadium was dedicated in his name. The brothers were close and had originally planned to attend USC in Los Angeles, but when their U.S. Representative agreed to sponsor them with appointments to West Point, they decided to go there. Twin brother Ralph became an outstanding shot-putter at West Point

At West Point, under coach Earl Blaik, Davis played fullback in his freshman season. Blaik moved him to halfback for his three varsity seasons, while Doc Blanchard took over at fullback. With Davis and Blanchard, Army went 27–0–1 in 1944, 1945, and 1946. Davis was nicknamed "Mr. Outside", while Blanchard was "Mr. Inside".

Davis averaged 8.3 yards per carry over his career and 11.5 yards per carry in 1945; both results are records which still stand today. Davis led the nation in 1944 with 120 points. He scored 59 touchdowns, including eight on his freshman squad, in his career. His single-season mark of 20 touchdowns stood as a record for 10 years.

Blanchard and he set then-record 97 career touchdowns by two teammates. The record was broken by USC backs Reggie Bush and LenDale White, who garnered 99 career touchdowns in their time. In 2007, Davis was ranked #13 on ESPN's list of Top 25 Players in College Football History.

Davis depicted with the Rams in 1950

Davis' service obligation ended in 1950, and he finally joined the Rams for their 1950 season. Despite his knee injury, Davis was an effective player, and was even named to the 1950 Pro Bowl, but in 1951, he injured his knee again. He was out for the 1952 season. In September 1953, the Rams released him, ending his professional career.

Davis moved to Texas to work in the oil industry, but returned to California a few years later. He became special events director for the Los Angeles Times, organizing and directing the newspaper's charity fundraising events. He held this job until his retirement in 1987.

Davis was married three times. In 1948, he dated actress Elizabeth Taylor. From 1951 to 1952 he was briefly married to film actress Terry Moore. In 1953, Davis married Ellen Slack; they were married for 42 years, until her death in 1995. They had one son, Ralph.

In 1974, his exploits, and those of the 1944 Army team, are mentioned by Lou Grant while discussing football with another man in a public bar in season five, episode 16 of The Mary Tyler Moore Show (1970–77), which aired on Saturday, January 4, 1975. In 1996, Davis married Yvonne Ameche, widow of NFL star Alan Ameche. Davis passed away in 2015

1945 Army West Point Cadets Football Coach Red Blaik

The Army Cadets football team represented the United States Military Academy in the 1945 college football season. It was their fifty-sixth season of intercollegiate football. They were coached by Earl "Red" Blaik in his fifth of eighteen seasons as head coach of the Cadets. As an independent football entity, the Army team had a perfect record of 9-0-0 for the second year in a row. Hard as it is for most humans to believe, this is the same record that Army posted last year and it is not a duplicate. That's how good the Army team had gotten because of Red Blaik and the Army Brass loosening up on items in the agenda that were not football oriented.

Army had already learned to win the big ones. This year, they won everything again. The Cadets were the #1 ranked team in the nation

The Cadets compiled a 9-0-0 perfect record. The Cadets shut out five of their nine opponents, and they outscored their opponents 412 points to 46 points. At the season's end, the team won a national championship.

Doc Blanchard won the Heisman Trophy in 1945. Army All Americans are listed below with their positions, and sponsoring group to the right

Glenn Davis--Halfback—AAB, AFCA, AP, COL, FWAA, INS, LK, NEA, SN, UP, CNS, CP, NL, NYS, OF, WC, YA
Doc Blanchard—Fullback—AAB, AFCA, AP, COL, FWAA, INS, LK, NEA, SN, UP CNS, CP, NL NYS, OF, WC, YA
Tex Coulter--Tackle—AAB, AFCA, AP, COL FWAA, INS, NEA, SN, UPCNS, CP, NL, NYS, OF, WC
John Green—Guard—AAB, AFCA, COL, FWAA, LK, SN, UP, CNS, CP, WC

Army began its 1945 season on Sept 30 with a shutout of Louisville AAF, W (32-0). This home opener and all Army home games, were played at Michie Stadium on the Campus of the USMA at West Point. On Oct 6 at home, Army shellacked and shut out Wake Forest W (54-0) and then invited Michigan to Yankee Stadium for a neutral game. The Cadets beat the Wolverines W (28-7) On Oct 20, #1

Army played against the Melville PT Boats in a big win W (55-13). On Oct 27, the Cadets beat Duke at the Polo Grounds in NY W (48-13)

On Nov 3, the Cadets defeated Villanova at home at Michie in a blowout W (54-0). The Cadets had blowout fever as they kept it up another week this time blowing Notre Dame out of Yankee Stadium W (48-0). On Nov 17, the Cadets pounced on the Penn Quakers in at Franklin Field a big rout W (61-0). In the Army Navy-Game on Dec 1, Army defeated Navy in a tough game but the score was very convincing as to who the best was in the battle of the service academies. W (32-13). Army, for the second year in a row, 1945, was as good as it gets.

Dec 1 was a great day for Army! It was a bad day for Navy and it was not about to change the next year.

Best Army Navy Game #3

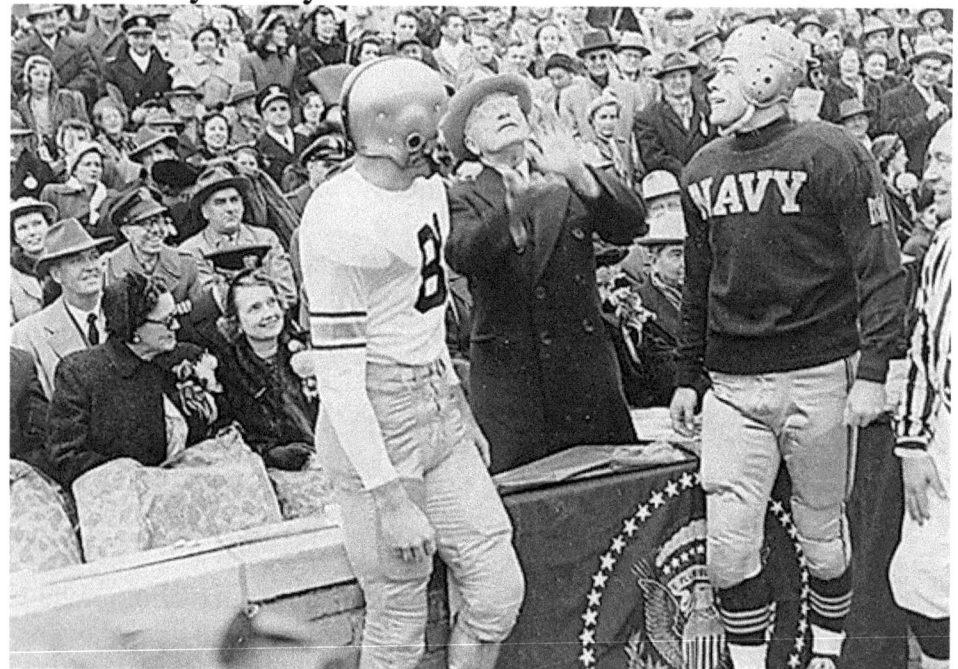

President Truman Tossing the Coin

This is well before 2011's LSU-Alabama game was designated the first "Game of the Century."

And this one was all Army.

Behind the play of eventual Heisman Trophy winner Felix "Doc" Blanchard, the top-ranked Cadets topped No. 2 Navy, 32-13.

Blanchard finished the day with three touchdowns, one of which came on an interception.
His backfield mate, Glenn Davis, who also left West Point with a Heisman, made up for throwing an early interception by running for a 28-yard touchdown late in the game.

Army would go on to win the national championship.

1945 Player Highlights John Green L

John "Jack" Green was born on September 15, 1924. He was a great American football player and coach. A native of Shelbyville, Kentucky, he started his college playing career as a letterman for Tulane in 1942. He was then appointed to the United States Military Academy where he played from 1943 to 1945. At Army, Green was a two-time All-American and played on consecutive national championship-winning undefeated teams in 1944 and 1945. Green stood 5-11, weighed 190-pounds and was one of the finest guards ever to play for Army.

He was named to Collier's All-America team in 1944 and was a consensus All-America selection in 1945 and Green was captain of the 1945 team. He was also on the wrestling team. Green served as assistant Army coach under Earl Blaik in 1946, then completed a five-year tour of duty and retired from the Army with the rank of captain. He went into coaching for a 14-year period.

This included four years as head coach at Vanderbilt 1963-1966 and service as assistant coach at Tulane, Florida, Kansas and Baylor. He went into business in Nashville, Tennessee. He was elected to the College Football Hall of Fame as a player in 1989.

1945 Player Highlights Tex Coulter, L

Tex Coulter was born on Oct 2, 1924 in Red Springs Community, Smith County, Texas. He grew up in an orphanage in Fort Worth. It is said that whatever security he found at first stemmed from his huge six-foot-five, 270-pound frame. After service in World War II he earned an appointment to West Point, played two seasons at tackle on the great Blanchard-Davis football teams of 1944-1945. Later he turned to the pro game with the New York Giants and the Montreal Alouettes.

Coulter, known as Tex, was an all-American on Army's 1945 national championship team. He paid Blanchard and Davis a great compliment in this quote: "He and Doc were both easy to block for," says DeWitt (Tex) Coulter, an All-America tackle on the Blanchard-Davis teams. "You didn't really need to get in a solid lick, because they had this sense of where to go, that great running instinct."

"I never regarded Glenn as exactly shy, but Doc was looser, less straitlaced," says former teammate Coulter. "He was just a lot of fun. I remember Colonel Blaik asking each of us before our first practice if we drank. Well, most of us dodged that one, but Doc just said, 'Oh, sure.'"

He then played left tackle for the Giants from 1946 to 1952 and made the All-Pro team in 1948 and 1949.

A high school star at Masonic Home in Fort Worth during the 1940s, Coulter was inducted into the Texas Sports Hall of Fame in 1997.

1944 Player Highlights Doc Blanchard, B

Doc Blanchard Yearbook Picture

Felix Anthony "Doc" Blanchard was born in 1924. He was a great athlete and especially a great college football player. He led Army to three consecutive National Championships in 1944-1946 and as a junior, became the first college football player to win the James E. Sullivan Award, as the nation's "outstanding amateur athlete" while also grabbing both the Heisman Trophy and Maxwell Award that same year (1945).

He had led his St. Stanislaus College high school team to an undefeated season as a senior, and thus, he was highly recruited and he chose to play for the University of North Carolina Tar Heels. However, in 1943, during World War II, "Doc" (named for his father's profession as a boy), enlisted in the United States Army and his father secured him an appointment to West Point where he played three more seasons.

In 1944, as Army faced Notre Dame, Doc Blanchard compiled 56 of the teams 59 points in their 59-0 rout of the Fighting Irish. Following the game, Notre Dame coach Ed McKeever quipped, "I've just seen Superman in the flesh. He wears number 35 and goes by the name of Blanchard." He served as fullback for the Cadets, but also played linebacker, placekicker and punter with Army and in 1944, he earned All-American honors (his first of three selections) as he led them to the first of three straight College Football National Championships – the only three in school history to date, though there are some mythical championships and a lot of undefeated seasons that may count over time.

Blanchard, also known as "Mr. Inside" to Davis' "Mr. Outside", won the Heisman Trophy, Maxwell Award and the first ever James E. Sullivan Award in 1945, becoming the first junior to garner all three awards. Displaying the duo's absolute dominance of their era, Davis won the Maxwell Award in 1944 and then took home the Heisman in 1946. Playing under Earl "Red" Blaik, Blanchard and his backfield partner in crime Glenn Davis led the Cadets to an undefeated 27-0-1 record, with the only blemish coming in a 0-0 tie with Notre Dame in 1946.

In the 1946 NFL Draft, the Pittsburgh Steelers selected Doc third overall, but he chose a career in the United States Air Force as a fighter pilot. After a 25-year career in the Air Force, receiving multiple commendations for bravery and service, Doc Blanchard retired in 1971 as a full colonel. He then spent a number of years as the commandant of Cadets at the New Mexico Military Institute. In 1959, Doc Blanchard was inducted into the College Football Hall of Fame.

Since 2004, Rotary International has presented the Doc Blanchard Award and the Glenn Davis Award to the top two high school football players participating the U.S. Army All-American Bowl as the players "who best exemplify the U.S. Army's high standard of excellence in community service, education and athletic distinction."

1946 Army West Point Cadets Football Coach Red Blaik

The Army Cadets football team represented the United States Military Academy in the 1946 college football season. It was their fifty-seventh season of intercollegiate football. They were coached by Earl "Red" Blaik in his sixth of eighteen seasons as head coach of the Cadets. As an independent football entity, the Army team had an undefeated record of 9-0-1 with a tie to spoil it from being perfect.

The Cadets spent most of the season as the #1 ranked team in the nation. The Cadets compiled a 9-0-1 undefeated record. The Cadets shut out five of their nine opponents, and they outscored their opponents 263 points to 80 points. At the season's end, the team came in #2 according to AP. The squad was also recognized as national champions for the 1946 season by several selectors. The 1946 Army vs. Notre Dame football game at Yankee Stadium is regarded as one of college football's Games of the Century. 1946 college football season.

The 1946 NCAA football season finished with the Notre Dame Fighting Irish crowned as the national champion in the AP Poll, with the United States Military Academy named as national champion in various other polls and rankings. In history, most observers give both teams credit as National Champions. Their 0-0 head to head battle proved both teams were great.

Glenn Davis won the Heisman Trophy in 1946. Army All Americans are listed below with their positions, and sponsoring group to the right

Glenn Davis—Halfback—AAB , AFCA, AP, CO, FWAA, INS, NEA, SN, UP, CP, WC

Doc Blanchard—Fullback—AAB, AFCA, AP, CO, FWAA, INS, NEA, SN, UP   CP, WC
Hank Foldberg—End—CO, INS, NEA, UP

The 1946 Army football season began later in September earlier later than usual on Sept 21 with a shutout of Villanova, W (35-0) This home opener and all Army home games, were played at Michie Stadium on the Campus of the USMA at West Point. On Sept 28, at home, Army defeated Oklahoma W (21-7). On Oct 5. On Oct 12 at Michigan Stadium in Ann Arbor, MI, the #2 Cadets defeated the #4 Wolverines W (20-13). On Oct 19, at home, the Cadets defeated the Columbia Terriers W (48-14)

On Oct 26, at the Polo Grounds in NY City, NY, the Cadets shut out the Duke Blue Devils, W (19-0). home, Army then shut out West Virginia by the same score W (19-0) a week later on Nov 2.

On Nov 9 at Yankee Stadium in the Bronx, NY. the Cadets and the Fighting Irish played what many call the best college football game in history. If you like high scoring games, you would not like this game but if you like tough, smash-mouth football, this was the best game ever. It was a battle of #1 Army coached by the immortal Red Blaik, v #2 Notre Dame coached by the immortal Frank Leahy. Neither team would give an inch—literally and the game wound up in a scoreless tie T (0-0).

On Nov 16, the Cadets still ranked #1 after the tie, defeated the #5 ranked Penn Quakers W (34-7). At the end of the season, Navy was all that mattered to Army and the Cadets had a real tough game against the Midshipmen but prevailed by the close score of W (21-18). At Philadelphia's Municipal Stadium in PA.

1947 Army West Point Cadets Football Coach Red Blaik

The Army Cadets football team represented the United States Military Academy in the 1947 college football season. It was their fifty-eighth season of intercollegiate football. They were coached by Earl "Red" Blaik in his seventh of eighteen seasons as head coach of the Cadets. As an independent football entity, the Army team had a record of 5-2-2.

The Cadets compiled a 5-2-2 record. They shut out four of their nine opponents, and they outscored their opponents 220 points to 165 points. At the season's end, the team came in #11 in the National standings.

The Black Knights offense scored 220 points, while the defense allowed 165 points. At season's end, the team ranked eleventh in the National standings.

Army had six players in the running for All-American honors as follows: **First Team:** Center: Jimmy Hartinger (Army) First Defense: John McEnery (Army); **Second Team**: First Defense: Hank Foldberg (Army) Goal: John Rust (Army) **Third Team:** Attack: Ted Marley (Army); **Honorable Mention:** Bob Montague (Army):

On Sept 27, the 1947 Army football season began with a light shutout over Villanova W (13-0). This home opener and all Army home games, were played at Michie Stadium on the Campus of the USMA at West Point. After a week off, the Illini of Illinois met the Cadets in Yankee Stadium and played to a scoreless tie T (0-0). On Oct 4, my wedding anniversary, the Cadets blew out the Colorado Buffalos at home in a shootout W (47-0). On Oct 18, at home, Army shutout VPI in a fine win W (40-0). Then, playing a tough Columbia team, at Baker Field in New York, on Oct 25, the Cadets could not bring home the win in a very tough loss L 20-21)

On Oct 26, at the Polo Grounds in NY City, NY, the Cadets shut out the Duke Blue Devils, W (19-0). home, Army then shut out West Virginia by the same score W (19-0) a week later on Nov 2.

On Nov 1 at home v Washington & Lee, the Cadets put their offense in gear and whooped the generals in a shootout W (65-13). After a heartbreaking 0-0 tie the prior year at Yankee Stadium, Frank Leahy's Notre Dame squad was back at Yankee Stadium and they were ranked #1 in the nation. They were preparing to play the #1 ranked team, Army on Nov 8. This year, Leahy got the best of Blaik as ND defeated the Cadets L (7-27) before 59,171. Penn, a recent add-on team to the Army schedule was as tough as it gets for many years and 1947 was no exception. The Penn Quakers and the Army Cadets played to a low scoring tie T (7-7).

On Nov 29, Army had hit the end of its scheduled season and it was time for the raison d'etre (reason for being). This of course was the traditional season finale v the Midshipmen of Navy. Navy was all that mattered to Army and the Cadets had a real tough game against the Midshipmen but managed to shut them out W (21-0) in Philadelphia's Municipal Stadium in PA.

1947 Player Highlights Joe Steffy G

Joe Steffy was one of Army's greatest guards. He spent a good part of his football playing time opening the way for the Heisman Trophy winners Doc Blanchard and Glenn Davis to burst through opposing lines for Army's undefeated national football championships of the mid-1940s.

Joe Steffy All American Guard

In one season at the University of Tennessee and three at West Point, Steffy played on teams that lost only three games. He was a first-team all-American in 1947, when he became the second recipient of the Outland Trophy as the nation's best interior lineman. He was elected to the College Football Hall of Fame in 1987.

Steffy's No. 61 jersey was retired by Army in 2009. He joined Blanchard, the hard-driving fullback known as Mr. Inside, along with Davis, the speedy halfback called Mr. Outside, and the Heisman-winning halfback Pete Dawkins as the only West Point football players to receive that honor.

Red Blaik, the West Point coach who recruited many of America's leading college football players during World War II, called Steffy "one of the best guards in Academy history."

He did not possess great physical size but his heart and his attitude made up for it. At feet 10 inches and 190 pounds, he was a tough cookie, playing guard on offense and at the center of the line on defense. Coach Red Blaik remembered him in his memoir "The Red Blaik Story." He related how Steffy could deliver a crushing blow while opening up holes. In the 1947 game against Navy, Blaik said, "Joe took out an end with one of the two most devastating blocks in my memory." Blaik used that block as a training video. Here he is below, in a photo op with his coach Red Blaik.

<<< Joe Steffy, right, with Coach Red Blaik in 1947.
Credit Sam Falk/New York Times

Born on April 3, 1926, in Chattanooga, Tenn, Joseph Benton Steffy Jr. played for the 1944 Tennessee team that went undefeated in the regular season but lost to Southern California in the Rose Bowl. After Tennessee, Steffy transferred to West Point where he played for the unbeaten Army teams of 1945 and 1946 and then was named captain of the 1947 team, which had just two losses.

Steffy graduated from West Point in 1949 and married the former Ann Brown in April 1950. His best man was John Trent, the captain of Army's 1949 football team (he played end and he was a fellow Tennessean)

Two months later, the Korean War began. Lt. John Trent was killed in action near the port of Wonsan in November 1950. A month after that, Lieutenant Steffy was struck in the foot by a grenade while in combat. Suffering from frostbite as well, he was evacuated to Japan from the port of Hungnam and received a Bronze Star.

Steffy loved football. He coached the Army freshman football team in the early 1950s, then owned an auto dealership in Newburgh. He was a regular at Army football games for many years and spoke to Army's players about the times when West Point ruled college football.

Steffy told stories about when sportswriters in New York would often ask him about the most intense game he played in. For all his memories of West Point, his thoughts went back to a 0-0 tie in his first year of college football.

With no disrespect to the tough games he had at Army, he related the answer to The Chattanooga Times Free Press in 1999: "I told 'em, Tennessee and Alabama. You determined who won that game by the number of teeth you had left when the game was over." Steffy was quite a whip.

1948 Army West Point Cadets Football Coach Red Blaik

The Army Cadets football team represented the United States Military Academy in the 1948 college football season. It was their fifty-ninth season of intercollegiate football. They were coached by Earl "Red" Blaik in his eighth of eighteen seasons as head coach of the Cadets. As an independent football entity, the Army team had an undefeated record of 8-0-1.

The Cadets compiled an 8-0-1 record. They shut out two of their nine opponents, and they outscored their opponents 294 points to 89 points. At the season's end, the team came in #6 in the National standings.

During the season, head coach Earl Blaik implemented a two-platoon system, using specialists strictly for offense and defense. Offensive coach Gillman left Army after the season to become the head coach at the University of Cincinnati.

The 1948 Army football season began with a shutout over Villanova W (28-0). This home opener and all Army home games, were played at Michie Stadium on the Campus of the USMA at West Point. On Oct 2, at home, Army won by a blowout over Lafayette W (54-7). Then, on Oct 9, at Illinois Memorial Stadium in Champaign IL, the Cadets barely defeated the Illini W (26-21) but brought home the win nonetheless. On Oct 16, Harvard was back on the schedule at #5 Army. The Cadets got the best of the Crimson W (20-7)

On Oct 23, #5 ranked Army defeated # 12 Cornell at Schoellkopf Field at Cornell W (27-6)) On Oct 30, the Cadets ripped apart VPI at home W (49-7). On Nov 6, unranked Stanford played Army and were shut out at Yankee Stadium in the Bronx, NY, W (43-0). Next up on Nov 13, in a very good Army year was a tough team, Penn, playing at Franklin Field, Philadelphia PA. The Cadets beat the Quakers in a tough battle W (26-20).

As happens just about every year, after a good or bad season, Army gets to play in the Army-Navy-Game. This year, the game was played on Nov 27 in Philadelphia Municipal Stadium in Phila., PA. Army was undefeated but that did not matter to Navy and they pulled out all the stops and the Midshipmen were able to tie the Cadets in a tough encounter T (21-21).

Going into the game undefeated, one must ask what impact the tie to Navy had on the Red Blaik team's opportunities for another National Championship. Well, we know it did not help one bit, no matter how tough a game it was.

1949 Army West Point Cadets Football Coach Red Blaik

The Army Cadets football team represented the United States Military Academy in the 1949 college football season. It was Army's sixtieth season of intercollegiate football. They were coached by Earl "Red" Blaik in his ninth of eighteen seasons as head coach of the Cadets. As an independent football entity, the Army team had an undefeated and untied record (perfect) of 9-0-0.

The Cadets compiled a 9-0-0 record. Is that not impressive in its frequency? They shut out two of their nine opponents, and they outscored their opponents 354 points to 68 points. Army was phenomenal and had a perfect record but it was not good enough for those calling the shots. At the season's end, the team came in #4 in the National standings. You cannot do much better than a perfect record.

Arnold Galiffa was the starting quarterback. Blaik had picked him ahead of his own son, Bob. Johnny Trent was the team captain. The Cadets won the Lambert-Meadowlands Trophy as the best college team in the East. At season's end, Red Blaik confessed that he thoughts of retiring. Why no National Championship with a perfect record? They are not too easy to come by. Red Blaik was simply a great coach. Even he wondered what was wrong with "perfect." Looking at the schedule, one must conclude that the teams Army played were not slackers.

The 1949 Army football season began with a blowout on Sept 24, over Davidson, W (47-7) This home opener and all Army home games, were played at Michie Stadium on the Campus of the USMA at West Point. On Oct 1, at home, Army won by a blowout over Penn State by the same exact score W (47-7). Feeling good about winning, the Army Cadets took on the #1 ranked Michigan team in Michigan Stadium on Oct 8, and put a hurt on the Wolverines creating a W 21-7) victory for Army. On Oct 15, at Harvard's Harvard Stadium in Boston MA, the Cadets beat the Crimson in a shootout W (54-14).

On Oct 22, #2 ranked Army defeated Columbia at home W (63-6). Then, on Oct 29, at home, #2 Army beat VMI w (40-14). On Nov 5, at home, the Cadets shut out Fordham W (35-)

Next up on Nov 12, in another very good Army year a tough Penn Team showed up and demanded to be played. This game was at Franklin Field, Philadelphia PA. The Cadets beat the Quakers in another tough battle W (14-13).

Regardless of how Army or Navy played through any season, either can have a fan/alumni resurrection with a victory over the other in the Army-Navy-Game. This year, the game was played on Nov 26 in

Philadelphia Municipal Stadium in Philadelphia, PA. Army was undefeated but that did not matter to Navy and the Midshipmen tried to do what it could to shape the game's eventuality. Since Army dominated by a shutout win of W (38-0). I am really not sure what Navy could have done to look better other than to have been able to play better against a phenomenally tough Army team/

Going into this game undefeated, one must ask what impact a great win over Navy had on the Red Blaik team's opportunities for another National Championship. Well, we know it did not happen and many wonder to this day, Why Not? To Army, Red Blaik was like Knute Rockne was to Notre Dame. And, form a guy who studied both; he should have been. Blaik, who retired in 1958, is recognized as is Rockne, as one of college football's true immortals.

1949 Player Highlights Arnold Galiffa B

ARNOLD ANTHONY GALIFFA was a gifted athlete in all sports. He was a leader of men and according to reliable sources, he was a truly nice guy. He hailed from the smoky valley of Donora, Pennsylvania, near the plants of the United States Steel Corporation. His athletic ability in high school brought Arnold 12 varsity letters and was responsible for his being named to two all-Pennsylvania teams. This attracted the attention of Red Blaik, and Arnold joined the USMA Class of 1950 on 2 July 1946 as a football prospect. He did not ever disappoint Coach Blaik.

At West Point, he continued playing multiple sports and he earned 11 major varsity letters in football, baseball and basketball. This achievement had been bettered by only by one graduate and equaled by only one other. He was the quarterback of the football team and captain of the basketball team. In his first class-year, he led a football team with a 9-0 record, ranking 4th in the nation.

While some believe the game against Michigan in 1949 (Army won in an upset, 21-7) was his finest hour as a quarterback, he showed his leadership best in the Pennsylvania game in 1948. No one will ever forget the final quarter. Army was behind 20-19 on their own 26-yard line with three minutes to play when Galiffa engineered a masterful drive. Army advanced to the Pennsylvania 15-yard line in six plays, with Galiffa completing several passes in succession. With time running out, he threw a pass to John Trent in the end zone for a touchdown and an Army victory of 26-20.

Arnold was named to five All-American teams for 1949, including the Chicago Tribune, United Press International, Look magazine and others. At graduation, he was presented with three Army Athletic Association trophies: one as the cadet who rendered the most valuable service to athletics while at West Point; one as the most outgoing basketball captain; and one as the most valuable football player of 1949. He also played in the East-West game in San Francisco in 1950. In 1983, Arnold was inducted into the National Football Hall of Fame, and in March 1990 he was inducted into the National Italian Sports Hall of Fame, Pittsburgh Chapter.

Arnold graduated in June 1950 and married his long-time girlfriend, Peggy Perdock. As Arnold's roommates knew very well, he had a habit of humming "Peg of My Heart." But the honeymoon was cut short, as Arnold and many of the Class of 1950 went to the war in Korea. Arnold was assigned as a platoon leader in the 3rd Infantry Division. He received a Bronze Star and was mentioned in the press for throwing a hand grenade a record distance of 75 yards in combat. After completing his tour on the line, Arnold was reassigned to Tokyo as aide de camp to Generals Ridgway and Mark Clark while they were supreme commanders.

In 1953 Arnold resigned from the Army to enter civilian life. He was contacted by Vince Lombardi, who was then backfield coach for the New York Giants. Arnold played four years of professional football - a year with the New York Giants, another with the San Francisco Forty-Niners, and two years in the Canadian Football League. Injuries plagued him the entire four years.

Arnold and Peggy returned to Pennsylvania in 1955. For the next 23 years, Arnold worked for United States Steel. In March 1978, Arnold was diagnosed with a major illness. After six months, he died in September 1978 and was buried in Pennsylvania.

Arnold was a happy person and a great sport. He loved his family and his life. He is missed by all.

1950 Army West Point Cadets Football Coach Red Blaik

The Army Cadets football team represented the United States Military Academy in the 1950 college football season. It was Army's sixty-first season of intercollegiate football. They were coached by Earl "Red" Blaik in his tenth of eighteen seasons as head coach of the Cadets. As an independent football entity, the Army team had a great, almost perfect record of 8-1-0. Try and do better yourself.

The Cadets compiled n 8-1-0 record. Considering how frequently Earl Blaik brought in a great team, that is another impressive record. They shut out five of their nine opponents, and they outscored their opponents 267 points to 40 points. Bob Blaik, the son of the coach, was the starting quarterback.

Army had a phenomenal one-loss (to Navy) record and the team did quite well finishing #5 in the Coaches' poll and #2 in the AP poll. Nothing including a championship level record mattered in the

Army-Navy Game. All Army's great record did was make a poor Navy team ((2-6 going into the game) want to play better and they did. They topped the Cadets L (2-14), finishing their season at 3-6.

During this season, Tom Lombardo, the captain of the 1944 Army team, was killed in action in Korea. Two weeks before the Army–Navy Game, Johnny Trent, the captain of the 1949 Army team, was killed in action. Trent, and Arnold Galiffa, the starting quarterback of the 1949 Army team, has officers in the Army, had been sent with the Eighth Army to Korea. With President Harry S. Truman in attendance, Navy beat Army by a score of 14–2.

It was the first time Navy had beaten Army since 1943. Tough teams meet tough challenges. Tough soldiers always play to win but sometimes, despite their best, they are stopped from achieving. There are many heroes in the Army and the Navy and in the graves that hold the bones of those brave men, who gave it all up for God and country.

The 1950 Army football season began with a shutout on Sept 30, over Colgate, W (28-0) This home opener and all Army home games, were played at Michie Stadium on the Campus of the USMA at West Point. On Oct 7, at home, Army won by a wide margin over Penn State W (41-7). With a 2-0 undefeated record, the Cadets took on the Wolverines of Michigan at Yankee Stadium in the Bronx, NY on Oct 14, and prevailed W (27-6). Harvard was no longer a world-class football team but they were tough enough when the Crimson suffered a major blowout at the hands of the Cadets W (49-0) on Oct 21.

On Oct 28, a top-ten ranked Army team shut out Columbia at Baker Field, NY, W (34-0). Then, on Nov 4, a very tough Penn Quakers team was challenged and beaten at Franklin Field in Philadelphia, PA by the Cadets W (28-13). On Veterans Day, Nov 11, a National Holiday for all, especially Army Veterans, the Cadets whooped New Mexico in a blowout, W (51-0). Stanford, always a tough opponent, hosted the Cadets at Stanford and played a close match but lost nonetheless W (7-0).

Army had sailed through its second undefeated season in a row, except for one thing. The Cadets had to meet the poorly playing Midshipmen at Municipal Stadium for a season finale on Dec. 2.

With a really lousy 2-6 record few pundits gave Navy a chance to avoid an embarrassment at the hands of Army. The Cadets were big favorites but then again, this was the Army-Navy Game when all bets are off. Navy kept Army in a hole the entire game and the Cadets blew an opportunity for being undefeated two years in a row simply because a stubborn Navy team would not let them win. Navy prevailed L (2-14))

1950 Player Highlights Dan Foldberg, End

John Daniel Foldberg graduated from Sunset High School in Dallas, Texas. He was a great athlete as a football player and he was also an American military officer. He played as an end for the Army Cadets at the United States Military Academy. Army head coach Earl Blaik rated him the best end he had ever coached. He was selected in the 1951 NFL Draft, but pursued a 27-year military career. Foldberg served as an infantry officer in the Korean and Vietnam Wars.

Dan Foldberg & Red Blaik

Foldberg was born in Texas on April 22, 1928. He played basketball as part of the 1944 state championship team. His older brother, Hank, had played football at Texas A&M before transferring to West Point where he was named a consensus All-American in 1946, and graduated from West Point in 1947.

Like his brother, Dan Foldberg chose to attend the United States Military Academy in West Point, New York. He played football there as an end. During the 1948 season, Foldberg was described as a consistently impressive player on what was a dominating Army team. The Cadets' only close game that year was a 14–13 victory over Penn. One source described the Army team as "the nearest thing to a paragon of perfection in the East."

That same year, Foldberg was named a United Press second-team All-American. For his senior year in 1950, Foldberg returned as the Cadet's only starting offensive lineman and was named the team captain. In 1950, Dan was also named a first-team All-American by unanimous consensus.

During the 1950 season, legendary Army head coach Earl Blaik called Foldberg the best end he had ever coached. Foldberg finished eighth in the vote for the Heisman Trophy, which is awarded annually to college football's most outstanding player. He was invited to participate in the 1950 Blue-Gray Classic all-star game, where he served as the captain of the Rebel squad.

A gifted athlete, Foldberg also played on the Army lacrosse team as a defenseman. The United States Intercollegiate Lacrosse Association(USILA), the college sport's governing body, named him a second-team All-American as senior in 1951. He graduated from West Point as a member of the Class of 1951. and
He was selected in the 22nd round of the 1951 NFL Draft by the Detroit Lions as the 261st overall pick. Instead, he remained in the Army as a career officer.

Besides his athletic honors in his long military career, he was awarded the Silver Star, Bronze Star, and the Purple Heart. In 1978, having attained the rank of colonel, Foldberg retired from the military to Tulsa, Oklahoma.

1951 Army West Point Cadets Football Coach Red Blaik

The Army Cadets football team represented the United States Military Academy in the 1951 college football season. It was Army's sixty-second season of intercollegiate football. They were coached by

Earl "Red" Blaik in his eleventh of eighteen seasons as head coach of the Cadets. As an independent football entity, the Army team had its worst season under coach Red Blaik 2-7-0, their legacy immortal coach. It proved just one thing. Even Red Blaik was human.

The Cadets compiled a 2-7-0 record. Considering how frequently Earl Blaik brought in a great team, this was a major anomaly. at is another impressive record. The Cadets offense scored 116 points, while the defense allowed 183 points. There were no shutouts either way in 1951.

From the moment Army lost to Navy in 1950 after going undefeated, Coach Blaik was agitated by the loss. He held on to the agitation long after Army suffered the loss to Navy in 1950—well into the off-season. Blaik had another peeve that really frosted him. Around Army guys all his career, he was upset over the dismissal of General Douglas MacArthur.

Sam Galiffa, who was part of the 1949 team, and who, at the time was a decorated aide to General Matthew Ridgway, arranged for members of the Army coaching staff to come to Japan in the off-season to visit the troops.

Vince Lombardi and Doug Kenna first visited Tokyo and conducted several football clinics for the troops stationed there. Although defensive coordinator Murray Warmath helped the discharged players relocate to other schools, it was his last year at Army. He left at the end of the season to become the head coach for Mississippi State.

Red Blaik ultimately had more to worry about than the Navy loss. The Cadets, working hard to become soldiers in the shortest route possible, engaged in a massive honor code academic violation. It was revealed in the spring of 1951. There were accusations that football players were distributing unauthorized academic information to help assure that their "brothers" made it through the rigors and got their commissions.

This travesty was reported to Colonel Paul Harkins on April 2. It was later revealed that Red Blaik's son, Bob, was part of the honor code violation. On August 3, the violations were announced and several athletes were implicated in the scandal. Army Cadets do their best at all times to avoid black marks on themselves and the Academy. They did not get away with this one.

Joseph P. Kennedy spoke to assistant coach Doug Kenna, and he helped pay the way for several discharged players to attend Notre Dame. Bob Blaik, son of the Coach, left Army for Colorado College. Of the players that were discharged, three went on to careers in the National Football League: Al Pollard, Gene Filipski and Ray Malavasi. Malavasi also become head coach of the Los Angeles Rams. The message is that without the gradebook, the season would have been lost healthier than 2-6.

With such top Army talent playing for other colleges after the scandal, the makeshift team that was assembled was clean of honor violations, but their lack of strong talent was still a reminder of the reason why Army was in the doldrums in 1951. After losing several games to Ivy League schools, Army's scrappy team defeated Columbia for its first win. The team received a congratulatory note for this effort from General Douglas MacArthur. There would be few accolades this season.

In week 6 of the season, the Cadets played the great NY Giant Halfback Frank Gifford, who was a mainstay of the USC Trojans squad. The game, which Army lost by a respectable score, 28-6, was played at Yankee Stadium.

Going into the Army–Navy game, the Cadets had a very poor record of 2 wins and 6 losses. This was Blaik's only losing season at Army. In the Army–Navy game, Navy scored two touchdowns before Army even ran an offensive series. Army could not keep up with Navy and the Cadets were thumped by the aggressive Midshipmen W (42-7). Red Blaik coached a 2-7 team and it really was about as good a season as any coach could have made it.

Army kicked off the 1951 season with its first of seven kicks in the behind. This one came from Villanova on Sept 29, L (7-21). This home opener and all Army home games, were played at Michie Stadium on the Campus of the USMA at West Point. On Oct 6, at Dyche Stadium in Evanston, IL, Army lost to Northwestern L (14-

20). On Oct 13, with a 0-2 winless record, the Cadets took were beaten by Harvard L (21-22) at Harvard Stadium in Boston, MA.

On Oct 27, Army defeated Columbia at home W (14-9) for its first win of the campaign. This was followed on Nov 3, with another defeat L (6-28) at Yankee Stadium, Bronx, NY, against USC. On, Nov 10, the Army defeated The Citadel W (27-6) giving the Army its second and last win of the season. Then, before the Army-Navy Game, On Nov 17, at Penn in a game played in Franklin Field in Philadelphia, PA, the scrappy Cadets were beaten by the tough Quakers L (6-7).

Army was at the end of its worst season in the Red Blaik Era. No matter how bad the Army-Navy loss of 1950 was for the psyche of Red Blaik and Army, this season was a killer. It was as if a big magic marker had erased a big part of the playing squad and Army was dared to compete. They competed and nobody pushed them over—well nobody other than Navy. So now in the final game of the year, there was hope that this scrappy group of courageous Cadets would find something from a season of Blaik coaching and at least look good. It did not happen as Navy loved beating Army as bad as it could and the Midshipmen would not let go until they had a big victory over Army L (7-42). Navy did everything but shut out Army in this game but it sure tried to do so. Army does not forget easily.

1952 Army West Point Cadets Football Coach Red Blaik

The Army Cadets football team represented the United States Military Academy in the 1952 college football season. It was Army's sixty-third season of intercollegiate football. They were coached by Earl "Red" Blaik in his twelfth of eighteen seasons as head coach of the Cadets. As an independent football entity, the Army team had its second worst season under coach Red Blaik 4-4-1, their legacy immortal coach. It proved just one thing. Even Red Blaik was human.

The Cadets compiled a 4-4-1 record. After having the better players on his 1950 team stripped from ever becoming upperclassmen, Blaik had himself an unwanted rebuilding year in 1952. It was not so bad as 1951, which had set the bottom of the troth for Army. Yet, it was not so good so nobody was cheering Army while the Cadets were losing four games, gaining zero shutouts, and suffering two shutouts on the way to a medsa medsa season.

After a 2-7 season, Army got back on the winning side of its games, right from its opening day on Sept 27 at South Carolina at home W (28-7). All Army home games were played at Michie Stadium at West Point NY. The good winning feelings from an opening day victory had not quite set in when on Oct4, the #7 USC Trojans defeated the unranked Cadets and shut them out clean as a whistle, L (0-22).

Recovering again, Army defeated Dartmouth W (37-7) at home on Oct 11. Then, on Oct 18, the Cadets found the need again to recover after being defeated by the Panthers of Pittsburgh L (14-22) at home. Then, On Oct 25, in a tough game, Columbia played the Army to a tie T (25-25).

On Nov 1, the Cadets pounded the VMI Keydets W (42-14) at home and then traveled to Grant Field in Atlanta GA to take on the #3 ranked Georgia Tech Bulldogs in a losing effort L (6-45). Then, it was off to Franklin Field in Philadelphia on Nov 15, to play the Penn Quakers and grab a nice win in a very close match W (14-13).

Nobody in New York State was looking for a loss against the Midshipmen in the Army Navy Game but that is exactly what Navy delivered at Municipal Field in Philadelphia PA. Army and Navy played well but Navy won the game in a nail-biter L (0-7).

1953 Army West Point Cadets Football Coach Red Blaik

The Army Cadets football team represented the United States Military Academy in the 1953 college football season. It was Army's sixty-fourth season of intercollegiate football. They were led by Coach Earl "Red" Blaik in his thirteenth of eighteen seasons as head coach of the Cadets. As an independent football entity, the Army team had another fine season under coach Red Blaik 7-1-1,

The Cadets compiled a 7-1-1 record. After his 1952 building year, the building was done, and the Red Blaik Army team was ready to kick butt. Not sure if "Kick Butt" was an appropriate Army slogan but the fans did not care. Army was back. The Cadet fans were cheering for Army while the Cadets were winning most of their games. The Army Cadets finished the season by winning the Lambert-Meadowlands Trophy, awarded to the top college team in the East.

The Cadets had lost six players, including Freddie Myers, to academic ineligibility. The Cadets defeated Furman 41–0, the team's first shutout since the 1951 scandal, and the goings became bright.

After a tough loss to Northwestern, the Cadets were undefeated for the rest of the season. In a scoreless tie against the Tulane Green Wave, future Green Bay Packer Max McGee played exceptionally for Tulane. After too many years in a row of losses to Navy, in the Army-Navy game, Army's 20–7 victory over Navy was embraced and celebrated as it was the first since 1949.

The turning point of the season was an October victory over #7 ranked Duke University. Duke had the great named players such as Red Smith and Worth (A Million) Lutz. Tommy Bell ran up the middle and got his due. Quarterback Pete Vann switched the ball to his left hand, and made a southpaw pass. Red Smith was tackled by Bob Mischak in the final minutes of the game. Mischak ran 73 yards to make the tackle catching up eight yards of separation to save a touchdown.

Inspired by Mischak, Army held Duke inside the one-yard line, took over on downs, and eventually won the game. " Army had gotten the sludge behind them and had begun enjoying football again...And, the results wowed in the scores for Red Blaik's team produced throughout this great season.

"When Bob Mischak made that unlikely play, what Blaik called "a marvelous display of heart and pursuit," the Army football team regained its soul." Direct quote from Maraness.

Army restarted its football season program for 1953 on September 26 against Furman at home with a great shutout win W (41-0). All Army home games were played at Michie Stadium in West Point NY as was this season's opener. In the second game, the Cadets rolled out to play at Dyche Stadium in Evanston IL against a very tough

Northwestern team and it they got beaten for the only time in 1953 L (20-23) On Oct 10, v Dartmouth at home, the Cadets shut out the Big Green W (27-0). In a nail-biter on Oct 17 vs. Duke at the Polo Grounds in New York, NY, the Cadets skimmed by the Blue Devils W (14–13). Next was Oct 24 at home vs. Columbia, the Cadets beat the Lions W (40–7).

The following week on Oct 31 at Tulane in a game played at Tulane Stadium in New Orleans, LA, the Cadets managed a tie against the Green Wave. On Nov 7 at home, Army defeated NC State W (27–7). Then, on Nov 14, the Cadets traveled to Franklin Field, Philadelphia, PA to beat the Penn Quakers W (21–14).

The season-making or breaking encounter with the Midshipmen in the Army-Navy Game on Nov 28 at Municipal Stadium, Philadelphia, PA, Army put Navy away W (20–7)

1954 Army West Point Cadets Football Coach Red Blaik

The Army Cadets football team represented the United States Military Academy in the 1954 college football season. It was Army's sixty-fifth season of intercollegiate football. They were led by Coach Earl "Red" Blaik in his fourteenth of eighteen seasons as head coach of the Cadets. As an independent football entity, the Army team had another fine season under coach Red Blaik 7-2-0.

The Cadets compiled a 7-2-0 record. Army outscored all opponents by a combined total of 325 to 127. In the annual Army–Navy Game, the Cadets lost to the Midshipmen by a close 27 to 20 score. The Cadets also lost to South Carolina by a 34 to 20 score in the first game of the season.

Four Army players were honored on the 1954 College Football All-America Team: halfback Tommy Bell (FWAA, INS-1, NEA-2); end Don Holleder (AFCA, INS-2, NEA-1, UP-1, CP-1); guard Ralph Chesnauskas (AP-1, UP-3); and quarterback Pete Vann (INS-2, UP-3, CP-2).

Army began the 1954 football season on September 25 against South Carolina at home with a loss to the Gamecocks L (20-34). All Army home games by default were played at Michie Stadium in West Point NY as was this season's opener. On Oct 2, at Michigan Stadium • Ann Arbor, MI, the Cadets defeated the Wolverines W (26–7). On Oct 9, the Cadets got the show in gear as they pitched a blow-out against the Dartmouth Big Green at home W (60-6). After an extra week's rest, on Oct 23 at Columbia in Baker Field, New York, NY, Army won handily in a blow0ut W (67–12).

On Oct 30, in as close a battle as you can have, Army beat Virginia at home, W (21-20). Then, on Nov 6 at the Yale Bowl in New Haven CT, for the first game in twelve years (1943), the Cadets whooped the Bulldogs W (48-7). On Nov 13, at Franklin Field in Philadelphia, the Cadets shut out the Penn Quakers W (35-0).

On Nov 27, with a 7-1 record, Army played the #6 ranked Navy Midshipmen at Municipal Stadium Philadelphia, PA in the annual (Army–Navy Game). The game was close but it resulted in an Army loss L (20–27).

1955 Army West Point Cadets Football Coach Red Blaik

The Army Cadets football team represented the United States Military Academy in the 1955 college football season. It was Army's sixty-sixth season of intercollegiate football. They were led by Coach Earl "Red" Blaik in his fifteenth of eighteen seasons as head coach of the Cadets. As an independent football entity, the Army team had another fine season under coach Red Blaik 6-3-0.

The Cadets compiled a 6-3-0 record. Army shut out two opponents and outscored all opponents by a combined total of 256 to 72. In the annual Army–Navy Game, the Cadets defeated the Midshipmen by a score of 14 to 6. The Cadets also lost to Michigan, Syracuse, and Yale. No Army players were honored on the 1955 College Football All-America Team.

Army got its 1955 football season started on September 24 against Furman at home with a nice blowout win W (81-0). All Army home games by default were played at Michie Stadium in West Point NY as was this season's opener. On Oct 1, Army beat #18 Penn State at home W (35–6). The next week on Oct 8, the Cadets lost the first of two in a row to Michigan at Michigan Stadium, Ann Arbor, MI L (2-

26) On Oct 15, the Cadets were shut out by the Syracuse Orangemen at home L (0-13). Army got back on track on Oct 22 at home vs. Columbia winning in a big shutout W (45-0).

Then, on Oct 29, at home, Army defeated Colgate W (27–7). After this, on Nov 5 at the Yale Bowl in New Haven CT, Yale's #19 Bulldogs defeated the Cadets in a close match L (12-14). This was followed on Nov 12, at Franklin Field, Philadelphia PA, with a shutout win against the Penn Quakers W (40-0)

On Nov 26, with a 5-3 record, unranked Army played the #11 ranked Navy Midshipmen at Municipal Stadium Philadelphia, PA in the annual (Army–Navy Game). The game was close but it resulted in an Army win W (14–6).

1956 Army West Point Cadets Football Coach Red Blaik

The Army Cadets football team represented the United States Military Academy in the 1956 college football season. It was Army's sixty-seventh season of intercollegiate football. They were led by Coach Earl "Red" Blaik in his sixteenth of eighteen seasons as head coach of the Cadets. As an independent football entity, the Army team had another fine season under coach Red Blaik 5-3-1.

The Cadets compiled a 5-3-1 record. Army shut out two opponents and outscored all opponents by a combined total of 223 to 153. In the annual Army–Navy Game, the Cadets tied the Midshipmen by a score of 7 to 7. The Cadets also lost to Michigan, Syracuse, and Pittsburgh. No Army players were honored on the 1955 College Football All-America Team.

Army guard Stan Slater was honored by the United Press as a third-team player on the 1956 College Football All-America Team.

The Cadets got the 1956 football season going on September 24 against VMI at home with a nice tough win W (32-12). All Army home games by default were played at Michie Stadium in West Point NY as was this season's opener. On Oct 6, at home against Penn State, the Cadets beat the Nittany Lions by one touchdown W (14-7). On Oct 13, at Michigan Stadium in Ann Arbor MI, the Cadets were beaten by the Wolverines L (14–48). On Oct 20, at Syracuse's Archbold Stadium in Syracuse, NY, Army took it on the chin from the Orangemen in a close shutout L (0–7). Oct 27 at Columbia in a game played at Baker Field in New York, NY, Army recovered well and whomped Columbia in a shut-out W (60-0).

On Nov 3, at home, the Cadets beat the Colgate Raiders W (55-46) in a shootout. On Nov 10, at home, Army defeated William & Mary W (34–6). Then on Nov 17 Pittsburgh got the best of Army at Pitt Stadium, Pittsburgh, PA L (7–20).

On Nov 26, with a 5-3 record, the unranked Army Cadets played the unranked Navy Midshipmen at Municipal Stadium Philadelphia, PA in the annual (Army–Navy Game). The game was as close as it could get and it ended in a tie T (7-7).

1957 Army West Point Cadets Football Coach Red Blaik

The Army Cadets football team represented the United States Military Academy in the 1957 college football season. It was Army's sixty-eighth season of intercollegiate football. They were led by Coach Earl "Red" Blaik in his seventeenth of eighteen seasons as head coach of the Cadets. As an independent football entity, the Army team had another fine season under coach Red Blaik 7-2-1.

The Cadets compiled a 7-2-0 record; shut out one opponents and outscored all opponents by a combined total of 251 to 129. In the annual Army–Navy Game, the Cadets lost to the Midshipmen by a score of 14 to 0. The Cadets also lost to Notre Dame by a score of 23 to 21.

Two Army players were honored on the 1957 College Football All-America Team. Back Bob Anderson was a consensus first-team selection. Center Jim Kernan was a second-team selection of the International News Service (INS). The Cadets finished at #13 in the Coaches poll and #18 in the AP poll.

Army began the 1957 football season going on September 28 at home against Nebraska at home with a blowout shutout W (42-0). All Army home games by default were played at Michie Stadium in

West Point NY as was this season's opener. On Oct 5 at #8 Penn State's New Beaver Field in University Park, PA, the Cadets beat the Nittany Lions in a close match W 27–13. On Oct 12, the # 12 Notre Dame Fighting Irish came to Municipal Stadium in Philadelphia, PA to play the #10 ranked Cadets. The Irish went home with the win L (L 21–23). The game was played before 95,000. On Oct 19 at home, the Cadets beat the Panthers of Pittsburgh W (29–13).

On Oct 26 October 26 at Scott Stadium in Charlottesville, VA, Army beat Virginia W (20–12). The following week, the Cadets beat the Raiders of Colgate at home in a shootout W (53-7). Next, on Nov 9, Utah came to Michie Stadium and in a close match were beaten by Army W (39-33) Then, on Nov 16, the Tulane Green Wave lost to the Cadets W (20-14).

On Nov 306, with a 7-1 record, the #10 ranked Army Cadets played the unranked Navy Midshipmen at Municipal Stadium Philadelphia, PA in the annual (Army–Navy Game). The game was close but Navy got the win in a shutout W (0-14).

1958 Army West Point Cadets Football Coach Red Blaik

The Army Cadets football team represented the United States Military Academy in the 1958 college football season. It was Army's sixty-ninth season of intercollegiate football. They were led by Coach Earl "Red" Blaik in his eighteenth and last of eighteen seasons as head coach of the Cadets. As an independent football entity, the Army team had an undefeated season under coach Red Blaik 8-0-1.

Legendary Army coach Earl "Red" Blaik with talented halfback, Bob Anderson, in 1958.

The Cadets compiled an 8-0-1 record; shut out two opponents and outscored all opponents by a combined total of 264 to 49. In the annual Army–Navy Game, the Cadets beat the Midshipmen by a score of 22 to 6. The Cadets also tied Pittsburgh 14 to 14. At season's end, the team was third in the national rankings by both major polling organizations. Red Blaik had a phenomenal record at Army and is the premiere Army immortal coach with an overall record of 121-33-10. Just phenomenal!

On Sept 27, #8 ranked Army got its 1958 football season underway at home against South Carolina Nebraska at home with a major victory W (45-8). All Army home games by default were played at Michie Stadium in West Point NY as was this season's opener. Penn State was the next victim of this superior Army team on Oct 4 as #5 ranked Army pitched a shutout W (26-0). On Oct 11 at #4 Notre Dame, Army controlled the game and beat the big guns of ND at

Notre Dame Stadium South Bend, IN for a very nice win W (14-2). Next game was at home vs. Virginia as the #1 ranked Army squad laid it on for a fine W (35-6) victory.

Pete Dawkins was honored after this season with the Heisman Trophy.

On Oct 25, At Pittsburgh's Pitt Stadium in Pittsburgh, PA, Army suffered its only blemish of the year as the Panthers tied the Cadets T (14-14). It was enough to drop Army to #3 and the Cadets never got the top spot back. On Nov. 1, the #3 ranked Cadets defeated the Raiders of Colgate in a major shootout W (68-6). On Nov 8, still at #3, the Cadets defeated the Rice Owls at Rice Stadium Houston, TX, W (14–7). Next was a shutout against Villanova at home W (26-0)

For whatever reason, perhaps because of the low score against Rice, Army slipped to #5 right before the Army-Navy Game at Municipal Stadium on Philadelphia. The Cadets beat the Midshipmen for a nice win (22-6).

This was a unique Army Navy game with two legends playing – one on each team. The game featured a matchup of two Heisman Trophy winners — Army's Pete Dawkins, the 1958 winner, and Navy's Joe Bellino, the 1960 winner. These two exceptional players were also exceptional men; Dawkins was ultimately a Rhodes Scholar, Brigadier General and candidate for Senate, while Bellino played for the AFL's Boston Patriots and served in the Navy and Naval Reserve for 28 years. Dawkins' Cadets finished the 1958 season unbeaten with a 22–6 win over the Midshipmen. Army had other fine years but this year would be Army's last unbeaten season and of course it was legendary coach Red Blaik's last at the helm.

Chapter 13 Coaches Hall & Dietzel 1959-1965

Hall   Coach # 24
Dietzel   Coach # 25

Year	Coach	Record	Conference	Record
1959	Dale Hall	4-4-1	Indep	4-4-1
1960	Dale Hall	6-3-1	Indep	6-3-1
1961	Dale Hall	6-4-0	Indep	6-4-0
1962	Paul Dietzel	6-4-0	Indep	6-4-0
1963	Paul Dietzel	7-3-0	Indep	7-3-0
1964	Paul Dietzel	4-6-0	Indep	4-6-0
1965	Paul Dietzel	4-5-1	Indep	4-5-1

Dale Hall replaces Red Blaik

Army Picks Dale Hall as Coach

DALE HALL
... unanimous choice.

West Point, N. Y., Jan. 31 [UPI]—Dale Hall, an unsung halfback on the outstanding Army football teams that included Doc Blanchard and Glenn Davis, Saturday was named head football coach at the United States military academy to succeed Earl [Red] Blaik.

The 34 year old Hall, who has been Blaik's No. 1 assistant for the past three seasons, thus becomes one of the youngest head coaches ever put in charge of the Cadets.

Hall, the unanimous choice of the five man athletic board at West Point, signed a three year contract at an undisclosed salary. The appointment was announced by Lt. Gen. Garrison H. [Gar] David-

Tulsa, and Johnny Green, who played guard on the same teams with Hall and who now is an assistant coach at Tulane.

Blaik, one of the nation's most successful coaches, announced on Jan. 13 that he

letics during his cadet career."

Hall served four years in the infantry and held the rank of 1st lieutenant at the time he was separated from the service in 1949. Then he launched his coaching career, serving as an assistant coach at Purdue, New Hampshire, and Florida before returning to the Point in 1956.

Hall was a member of Army's 1944 national championship team that went thru the season undefeated and untied. Altho Blanchard and Davis were on the same team, they did not play in the same backfield with Hall. The Cadets had such a wealth of talent that season, Blaik platooned two offensive backfields.

Dale Hall is like the guy who replaced Knute Rockne at Notre Dame – Hunk Anderson. Earl "Red" Blake who retired at 62-years of age was an immortal legacy at Army while he was still living. It is always a better deal to replace a bum coach or a poor manager and not typically a good deal to replace a legend who is loved by everybody.

Though nobody could have brought the big winning seasons of Red Blaik back to Army, Dale Hall did reasonably well following one of the best coaches of all time, Earl Blaik.

Ironically, Red Blaik had a fine assistant besides Dale Hall who might have done a bit better with the team. I am not second guessing here. The war years were over and high school graduates were not lining up for football at West point like they once did. Some might think that Army lost a big opportunity in hindsight when the Brass chose not to offer their own Vince Lombardi the job. Wanting the head coaching job at Army and yet also wanting a job, Lombardi is said to have asked for permission to call Green Bay. We all know the rest of that story.

Coach Dale Stanly Hall (June 21, 1924 – August 23, 1996) was an American football and basketball player and coach. He was good at sports, period and he was smart as a whip. He played football and basketball at the United States Military Academy, where he was a two-time All-American in basketball and was named the Sporting News Men's College Basketball Player of the Year in 1945. Hall served as the head football coach at West Point from 1959 to 1961, compiling a record of 16-11-2. He was also the head basketball coach at the University of New Hampshire during the 1951-52 season, tallying a mark of 11-9.

Dale Hall was an all-around athlete. At the U.S. Military Academy at West Point, N.Y., Hall was a Helms Foundation All-American basketball first-team selection in 1944 and 1945 and led Army to a 29-1 record, averaging 23 points a game.

He scored 23 touchdowns for the 1944 national champion football team and shared the backfield with a pair of Heisman Trophy winners, Doc Blanchard and Glenn Davis, who won the trophy the following two seasons. Hall graduated first in a West Point class of over 800. He had major athletic skills and had a vertical leap of 39 inches. He earned seven letters in three sports at Army and was a 4.0 student. Hall succeeded the legendary Earl "Red" Blaik as Army's football coach in 1959 and as noted, he led his team to a 17-11-2 record in three seasons.

He was always good. In high school, he is the only Parsons H.S. football player to have his number retired.

Hall retained Coach Blaik's staff when he took over in 1959. Hall was only the second civilian in the modern era to coach Army. After eighteen years with the same coach, one could expect a burp when a new guy took the rains. The burp was Hall's first season at 4-4-1 followed by two 6-win winning seasons.

1958 Player Highlights Pete Dawkins, B

In the fall of 1959 Bill Carpenter, West Point's Lonesome End, was named captain of the Army football team. As the story goes, Carpenter, upon hearing the news, climbed to the top of Lusk Reservoir on the West Point campus and began removing his shoes. When asked what he was doing, Carpenter said, "They want me to follow in Pete Dawkins's footsteps. I have to learn how to walk on water."

The picture on the next page is taken from a great biography article from Aug 25, 1997 Issue of Original Layout. Pete Dawkins was born March 8, 1938.

Technically speaking, Dawkins was not alive from the beginning of time nor did he ever walk on water, but he did everything else as a senior at West Point. Not only was he a Heisman Trophy-winning halfback for Army's undefeated team of 1958 who landed on many covers, but he was also class president, first captain of Cadets and graduated in the top 5% of his class.

After three years at Oxford on a Rhodes Scholarship, Dawkins spent 24 years in the Army, serving in Korea and Vietnam. In 1981, at 43, he became the Army's then youngest brigadier general. Along the way he earned a Ph.D. in public policy from Princeton and became a White House fellow while playing a mean jazz trumpet, piano, guitar, clarinet, trombone and French horn. Walk on water? Who has time? "I was, uh, sort of intense," the 59-year-old Dawkins says sheepishly.

Indeed, when Dawkins arrived at West Point in 1955, football players were told not to train with weights because the extra muscle was thought to be too cumbersome. So, he hid barbells under his mattress and a bar under his bunk and lifted in the dark following taps.

Pete Dawkins, Army Great

After retiring from the Army in '83, he worked as an investment banker on Wall Street and was soon a millionaire. In 1988, he was handpicked by New Jersey governor Tom Kean to run as the state's Republican nominee for the U.S. Senate. Though he lost to incumbent Frank Lautenberg in a bitterly contested race, Dawkins treasured his time on the campaign trail. "I would have hated to have gone to my grave without having taken a shot at it," he says, "but it's a full-contact sport. My daughter (Noel) said, 'You did great, Dad. You got the silver medal.'"

Today Dawkins lives in Rumson, N.J., with Judi, his wife of 36 years, and is the chairman and CEO of the direct-marketing subsidiary of the Travelers Group, a financial services conglomerate. He doesn't plan to run again for public office, but he still seems, uh, sort of intense. "You're a fool if you don't realize there comes a time when you slow down, but I haven't seen that coming yet," he says. "I still get up every morning at 4:50, lace up my shoes and feel like there's important work to be done."

1959 Player Highlights Bill Carpenter, End

William Stanley "Bill" Carpenter, Jr. was born on September 30, 1937. He is a retired American military officer who also played some great football at West Point. He gained national prominence as the "Lonesome End" of the Army football team. During his military service in the Vietnam War, he again achieved fame when he saved his company by directing airstrikes on his own position. For the action, he was awarded the Distinguished Service Cross.

His dad, Private First Class Carpenter, Sr. served in the U.S. Army as an ammunition bearer in the 393rd Infantry Regiment, 99th Infantry Division and was killed in action in the Ruhr Pocket. He is interred in Margraten, Netherlands at the Netherlands American Cemetery.

The Lonesome End was a 1955 graduate of Springfield High School, Springfield, Pennsylvania and later attended the Manlius School (now Manlius Pebble Hill School) in Manlius, New York. Carpenter married Toni M. Vigliotti in 1961 and had three children: William S.

Carpenter III (1962), Kenneth Carpenter (1964), and Stephen Carpenter (1965).

While attending the United States Military Academy at West Point, Carpenter played as a split end on the football team, alongside Heisman Trophy-winning halfback and fellow combat infantryman Pete Dawkins. Carpenter earned the nickname the "Lonesome End" as a result of the team's tactic of aligning him near the far sideline and leaving him outside of huddles. He played on the undefeated 1958 West Point team, and in 1959, while team captain, was named an All-American. Legendary Army head coach Earl Blaik, who spent twenty years on the Army coaching staff, called Carpenter "the greatest end I ever coached at West Point." In 1982, Carpenter was inducted into the College Football Hall of Fame.

Upon graduation, Carpenter was commissioned as an infantry officer and went on to serve at least two tours in Vietnam. In 1964, he was an adviser assigned to an airborne brigade of the Army of the Republic of Vietnam. That unit came under heavy enemy fire immediately after being inserted by helicopter into a sugar cane field. Bill Carpenter was wounded by a gunshot through the arm while changing rifle magazines. His radio set was hit with another bullet and he was spun around and knocked to the ground. He proceeded to eliminate the source of the enemy fire, by knocking out a bunker with a hand grenade.

For his actions, he was awarded the Silver Star, the U.S. Army's third highest award for valor in combat.

In 1984, Carpenter went on to take command of the newly activated 10th Mountain Division and, finally, the Combined Field Army in Korea. He eventually retired as a lieutenant general and settled in Montana.

1959 Army West Point Cadets Football Coach Dale Hall

The Army Cadets football team represented the United States Military Academy in the 1959 college football season. It was Army's seventieth season of intercollegiate football. They were led by Coach Dale Hall in his first of three seasons as head coach of the Cadets. As an independent football entity, the Army team had a .500 season under coach Dale Hall 4-4-1.

The Cadets compiled a 4-4-1 record; shut out one opponent, and outscored all opponents by a combined total of 174 to 141. In the annual Army–Navy Game, the Cadets lost to the Midshipmen by a score of 43 to 12. The Cadets also lost to Illinois, Penn State, and Oklahoma.

<< Coach Dale Hall

Army end Bill Carpenter was a consensus first-team player on the 1959 College Football All-America Team.

On Sept 26, Army began its 1959 football season at home against Boston College at home with a major victory W (44-8). All Army home games by default were played at Michie Stadium in West Point NY as was this season's opener. On Oct 3, at Illinois Memorial Stadium Champaign, IL, Army lost to Illinois, L (14–20). Then, on Oct 10, Army lost at home to # 16 Penn State L (11-17). Next, the Cadets traveled to Duke Stadium in Durham, NC and beat the Blue Devils W (21–6). Then it was Colorado State on Oct 24 at home for the win, W (25-6.

Air Force came to Yankee Stadium for another battle of the Service Academies on Oct 31. They played the Army to a tie T (13-13). Then it was a shutout win against Villanova at home on Nov 7, W (14-0). Next in the schedule was a tough Oklahoma squad in a losing effort in a game played at Oklahoma Memorial Stadium Norman, OK L (20–28).

On November 28, like clockwork came the Army–Navy Game at Municipal Stadium in Philadelphia, PA, the Cadets lost to the Midshipmen L (12–43) The Army team was clearly missing Red Blaik after just one year.

1960 Army West Point Cadets Football Coach Dale Hall

The Army Cadets football team represented the United States Military Academy in the 1960 college football season. It was Army's seventy-first season of intercollegiate football. They were led by Coach Dale Hall in his second of three seasons as head coach of the Cadets. As an independent football entity, the Army team had a fine season under coach Dale Hall 6-3-1.

The Cadets compiled a 6-3-1 record; shut out two opponents, and outscored all opponents by a combined total of 222 to 95. In the annual Army–Navy Game, the Cadets lost to the Midshipmen by a score of 17 to 12. The Cadets also lost to Penn State, and Nebraska.

Army guard Al Vanderbush was selected by the Central Press Association as a first-team player on the 1960 College Football All-America Team. He was also selected by the UPI as a second-team player.

Army began its 1960 football season at home very early on Sept 17, against Buffalo with a major shutout victory W (37-0). All Army home games by default were played at Michie Stadium in West Point NY as was this season's opener. On Sept 24, Boston College played Army at home and the Eagles were defeated by the Cadets W (20–7). On Oct 1, the Cadets got a big plane ride out to play California at California Memorial Stadium Berkeley, CA. For the Cadets, it was a nice trip and a fruitful trip as they beat California W (28–10). On October 8, at home, Penn State's Nittany Lions again beat the Army Cadets L (16–27).

On Oct 15 at Nebraska's Memorial Stadium in Lincoln, NE, the Cornhuskers had the Army's number in their close victory L (9–14). On Oct 22 Villanova played Army at home and were whooped in a big shutout W (54–0). Then, on Oct 29, the Cadets defeated Miami of Ohio at home W (30-7). A tough Syracuse team was next on the schedule Nov 5 at Yankee Stadium Bronx, NY. The Cadets gained the big Win, in a close match W (9–6). The next game was right before Army-Navy. It was Nov 12, at Pitt Stadium in Pittsburgh, PA. The Cadets played the Panthers to a tie   T (7–7).

On November 26, undeniably, the Army-Navy game would be at Municipal Stadium in Philadelphia, PA. The Cadets lost again to the

Midshipmen L (12–17) The Army team had yet to win one against Navy in the post Blaik years.

Best Army Navy Game # 6

The 1960 game saw Navy senior Joe Bellino clinch the Heisman Trophy by accounting for 192 all-purpose yards (including defense and special teams) in a 17-12 victory by the Midshipmen.

Nicknamed "The Slasher" by legendary sports writer Red Smith, Bellino carried 20 times for 85 yards, catch a pair of passes for 16 yards and return two kickoffs for 46 yards. He also intercepted a pass and took at 45 yards.

That said, Navy nearly lost a heartbreaker, as the Cadets came back from a 17-0 deficit to cut the Midshipmen's lead to five points after a pair of touchdowns by Al Rushatz.

Army had the ball on the Navy 32 with 1:50 remaining in the contest when Bellino intercepted Tom Blanda's pass in the end zone to seal the win—and the Heisman.

1961 Army West Point Cadets Football Coach Dale Hall

The Army Cadets football team represented the United States Military Academy in the 1961 college football season. It was Army's seventy-second season of intercollegiate football. They were led by Coach Dale Hall in his third and last of three seasons as head coach of the Cadets. As an independent football entity, the Army team had a respectable season under coach Dale Hall 6-4-0.

The Cadets compiled a 6-4-0 record; shut out no opponents, and outscored all opponents by a combined total of 224 to 118. In the annual Army–Navy Game, the Cadets lost to the Midshipmen by a score of 13 to 7. The Cadets also lost to Michigan, West Virginia, and Oklahoma. No Army players were selected on the 1961 College Football All-America Team.

Army initiated its 1961 football season at home on Sept 23, against Richmond, with a major nice victory W (24-6). All Army home games by default were played at Michie Stadium in West Point NY as was this season's opener. On Sept 30th, the University in Boston, not the College came to West Point to play Army and were beaten W (31-7). Big Ten Teams are always tough as was Michigan on Oct 7 at Michigan Stadium in Ann Arbor, MI as the Wolverines dominated the Cadets L (8–38). Always tough to beat, Rip Engle's Penn State Nittany Lions invited Army to Beaver Stadium at University Park, PA, and Army paid for the invitation with a nice but close victory W (10–6).

Idaho showed up at Michie Stadium on Oct 21 and were beaten back big time W (51–7). West Virginia played tougher than Idaho and got the W on Oct 28 L (3-7). Detroit took its shot at Army at Michie Stadium but failed W (34-7). Next game was William & Mary on Nov 11 at home as the Cadets put on their steam-roller personality and crushed the opponent's W (48–13). A big game was next against Oklahoma on Nov 18 at Yankee Stadium Bronx, NY, and the Cadets got their third loss of the year to the Sooners

On December 2, the Army-Navy game went on as scheduled at Municipal Stadium in Philadelphia, PA the Cadets lost again to the Midshipmen L (7-13) The Army team had yet to win one against Navy in the post Blaik years. Yes, we are counting!

Paul Dietzel replaces Dale Hall at season-end

Coach Dietzel coached for seven seasons at LSU and produced a 46-24-3 record. His tenure included coaching Heisman Trophy winner Billy Cannon in 1959 and an SEC title in 1961.

He left after that season to be head coach at Army. Dietzel had served as a bomber pilot in the U.S. Army Air Corps in World War II and had two stints as an assistant coach there before becoming LSU's head coach.

Dietzel spent four seasons at West Point before moving on to coach at South Carolina. His nine seasons there included the 1969 Atlantic Coast Conference title.

His overall record as a college head coach was 109-95-5. He was inducted into the Louisiana Sports Hall of Fame in 1988.

Dietzel also spent several years as an athletics administrator, serving as AD at South Carolina from 1966-75, at Indiana from 1976-78 and at LSU from 1978-82. He also served a year as commissioner of the Ohio Valley Conference in 1975.

1962 Army West Point Cadets Football Coach Paul Dietzel

The Army Cadets football team represented the United States Military Academy in the 1962 college football season. It was Army's seventy-third season of intercollegiate football. They were led by Coach Paul Dietzel in his first of four seasons as head coach of the Cadets. As an independent football entity, the Army team had another respectable season under coach Dietzel identical to the last year of Coach Dale Hall 6-4-0.

<< **Coach Paul Dietzel**

The Cadets compiled a 6-4-0 record; shut out two opponents, and outscored all opponents by a combined total of 152 to 104. In the annual Army–Navy Game, the Cadets lost to the Midshipmen by a score of 34 to 14. The Cadets also lost to Michigan, Oklahoma State, and Pittsburgh. No Army players were selected on the 1962 College Football All-America Team.

Army started its 1962 football season at home on Sept 22, against Wake Forest, with a major victory W (40-14). All Army home games by default were played at Michie Stadium in West Point NY as was this season's opener. On Sept 29 vs. Syracuse at the Polo Grounds in New York, NY, Army prevailed W (9–2). Then, on Oct 6 at Michigan Stadium in Ann Arbor, MI the Wolverines prevailed on the Cadets L (7–17). Moving through the schedule, on Oct 13 at home, Army barely got by Penn State W (9-6). This was followed by a win at home vs. VPI on Oct 27

W (20-12). Then, on Oct 27, the Cadets shut out George Washington in DC Stadium, Washington, DC W (14–0).

On Nov 3 at Boston University in a game played at Nickerson Field, Boston, MA, the Army won a nice one W (26–0). On Nov 10 Oklahoma State played Army at home and beat the Cadets in a close match L (7–12). On Nov 17, vs. Pittsburgh, the Cadets played and lost by one point in Yankee Stadium in The Bronx, NY, L (6–7).

In the annual Army-Navy game on December 1 at Municipal Stadium in Philadelphia, the Cadets lost again to the Midshipmen L (14-34) The Army team had yet to win one against Navy in the post Blaik years. Yes, we are counting!

1963 Army West Point Cadets Football Coach Paul Dietzel

The Army Cadets football team represented the United States Military Academy in the 1963 college football season. It was Army's seventy-fourth season of intercollegiate football. They were led by Coach Paul Dietzel in his second of four seasons as head coach of the Cadets. As an independent football entity, the Army team had a fine season under coach Dietzel--7-3-0. This would be the last winning season for Army under Coach Dietzel.

The Cadets compiled a 7-3-0 record; shut out four opponents, and outscored all opponents by a combined total of 177 to 97. In the annual Army–Navy Game, the Cadets lost to the Midshipmen by a score of 21 to 15. The Cadets also lost to Minnesota and Pittsburgh.

Army guard Dick Nowak was selected by the UPI and the American Football Coaches Association as a second-team player on the 1963 College Football All-America Team.

Army started its 1963 football season at home on Sept 22, with a shutout against Boston University W (30-0). All Army home games by default were played at Michie Stadium in West Point NY as was this season's opener. On Sept 28, at home, the Cadets shut out the Cincinnati Bearcats W (22-0) Entering October with two wins and no losses, the Cadets met Minnesota at Memorial Stadium in Minneapolis, MN and were defeated by the Gophers L (8–24). The Cadets got back on the track on Oct 12 at Beaver Stadium in

University Park, PA when they beat the Nittany Lions in a close match W (10-7). Next, at home, the Cadets blew-out the Wake Forest Demon Deacons W (47-0).

Army's third shutout of the season came on Oct 26 at home vs. Washington State W (23-0). On Nov 2, a tough Airforce team gave Army a tough time at Soldier Field in Chicago, IL, but lost in the end W (14-10). On Nov 9, Utah played the Cadets at home and Army prevailed by one point over the Utes W (8-7. Then, at Pittsburgh's Pitt Stadium in Pittsburgh, PA on Nov 17, the Cadets were shut out by the Panthers L (0–28)

On Dec. 7 at Municipal Stadium in Philadelphia, PA, in the traditional Army–Navy Game, the Midshipmen again got the upper hand defeating the Cadets L (15–21). Losing had become the norm in this game for the Cadets and nobody was happy about it. The Army team had yet to win one against Navy in the post Blaik years.

Best Army Navy Game # 4

The 1963 Army-Navy game was postponed a week following the assassination of President John F. Kennedy in Dallas.

1963 Army Navy Game

The game itself featured a starring performance by Navy's Pat Donnelly in a 21-15 victory.

A halfback, Donnelly scored three touchdowns to give the Midshipmen a 21-7 lead with four minutes gone in the fourth quarter.

However, the Cadets made it interesting, going 52 yards (all on running plays), culminating with a 1-yard touchdown and then successful two-point conversion run by quarterback Rollie Stichweh.

Stichweh then recovered the onside kick at the Navy 40.
He led Army all the way to the Midshipmen 4 when time ran out.

1964 Army West Point Cadets Football Coach Paul Dietzel

The Army Cadets football team represented the United States Military Academy in the 1964 college football season. It was Army's seventy-fifth season of intercollegiate football. They were led by Coach Paul Dietzel in his third of four seasons as head coach of the Cadets. As an independent football entity, the Army team had a losing season under coach Dietzel—4-6-0.

The Cadets compiled a 4-6-0 record; shut out one opponent, and were outscored by all opponents by a combined total of 118 to 147. In the annual Army–Navy Game, the Cadets defeated the Midshipmen by a score of 11 to 8. The Cadets also lost to #1 Texas, Penn State, Virginia, Duke, Syracuse, and Pittsburgh.

All Army home games other than those in neutral fields are played on the West Point campus at Michie Stadium in West Point NY. This year's home opener was on Sept 19 vs The Citadel., the Cadets shut out the Bulldogs W (34–0). On Sept 26, the Cadets defeated the Eagles of Boston College at home W (19-13). On Oct 3, at Texas Memorial Stadium in Austin, TX, the Cadets were defeated by the #1 Longhorns L (6–17). Penn State then added to the pain with a sliver close victory over Army L (2-6).

The third loss in a row came from Virginia on Oct 17 at Scott Stadium in Charlottesville, VA L (14–35). The fourth loss in a row came from Duke at home in a close shutout L (0-6). Army recovered in defeating Iowa State W (9-7) on Oct 31. Another loss for the Cadets came on Nov 7 at Yankee Stadium in the Bronx, NY. The Orangemen defeated the Cadets L (15-27). Then, on Nov 14, the

Cadets suffered another loss. This time it was to the Panthers of Pittsburgh at home L (8-24).

On November 28, after losing five Army-Navy-Games in a row, the Cadets broke the streak and defeated the Midshipmen at JFK Stadium in Philadelphia, PA W (11-8).

JFK Stadium was built as part of the 1926 Sesquicentennial International Exposition. Originally known as Sesquicentennial Stadium when it opened April 15, 1926, the structure was renamed Philadelphia Municipal Stadium after the Exposition's closing ceremonies. In 1964, it was renamed John F. Kennedy (JFK) Stadium in memory of the 35th President of the United States who had been assassinated the year before.

1965 Army West Point Cadets Football Coach Paul Dietzel

The Army Cadets football team represented the United States Military Academy in the 1965 college football season. It was Army's seventy-sixth season of intercollegiate football. They were led by Coach Paul Dietzel in his fourth and last of four seasons as head coach of the Cadets. As an independent football entity, the Army team had a losing season under coach Dietzel—4-5-1.

The Cadets compiled a 4-5-1 record; shut out one opponent, and were outscored by all opponents by a combined total of 132 to 119. In the annual Army–Navy Game, the Cadets tied the Midshipmen by a score of 7 to 7. The Cadets also lost to Tennessee, Notre Dame, Stanford, Colgate, and Air Force. No Army players were recognized on the 1965 College Football All-America Team.

Other than those games played in neutral fields, all Army home games are played on the West Point campus at Michie Stadium in West Point NY. This year's home opener was on Sept 18 vs The Tennessee Volunteers. The Cadets were shut out by the Volunteers L (0-21) in a rare opening season loss. On Sept 25, the Cadets defeated VMI at home W (21-7). On Oct 3, at home, the Cadets shut-out Boston College W (10-0). On Oct 9, at Shea Stadium in Flushing, the Fighting Irish of Notre Dame shut out the Army Cadets L (0-17).

On Oct 16 at home, Army defeated Rutgers W (23-6). Then the Cadets traveled to Stanford California and played in Stanford Stadium against the Stanford Cardinal and were defeated L (14-31). On Oct 30, Colgate's Raiders came to Michie Stadium and beat the Cadets by one-point L (28-29). Next, the Cadets were bean by the Air Force Fighting Falcons on Nov 6 at Soldier Field in Chicago, IL L (3-14. As a great prep for the Army-Navy Game, the Cadets shut out Wyoming at home W (13-0)

On November 27, the Army Cadets tied the Midshipmen of Navy in the annual Army-Navy-Game at JFK Stadium in Philadelphia, PA T (7-7).

Chapter 14 Coaches Tom Cahill & Homer Smith 1966-1978

Cahill   Coach # 26
Smith   Coach # 27

Year	Coach	Record	Conference	Record
1966	Thomas Cahill	8-2-0	Indep	8-2-0
1967	Thomas Cahill	8-2-0	Indep	8-2-0
1968	Thomas Cahill	7-3-0	Indep	7-3-0
1969	Thomas Cahill	4-5-1	Indep	4-5-1
1970	Thomas Cahill	1-9-1	Indep	1-9-1
1971	Thomas Cahill	6-4-0	Indep	6-4-0
1972	Thomas Cahill	6-4-0	Indep	6-4-0
1973	Thomas Cahill	0-10-0	Indep	0-10-0
1974	Homer Smith	3-8-0	Indep	3-8-0
1975	Homer Smith	2-9-0	Indep	2-9-0
1976	Homer Smith	5-6-0	Indep	5-6-0
1977	Homer Smith	7-4-0	Indep	7-4-0
1978	Homer Smith	4-6-1	Indep	4-6-1

Coach Cahill

Army Coach Tom Cahill, right, talks with four of his team stars on whom he'll depend in today's game against Navy in Philadelphia. From left Ken Johnson, captain; quarterback Steve Lindell, tight end Gary Steele and fullback Charlie Jarvis. (AP)

Thomas Cahill was hired in 1959 by Earl (Red) Blaik to coach freshman football and baseball at Army. He was then promoted to head coach in 1966 when Paul Dietzel resigned to take over at South Carolina.

Cahill exceeded the two losing seasons at the end of Dietzel's tenure immediately by finishing with an 8-2 record in his first season. This included an 11-0 victory over Penn State in Joe Paterno's first year there. Cahill was voted 1966 Coach of the Year by the American Football Coaches and the Football Writers and Touchdown Club of Washington, D.C.

"Life can change so quickly," Cahill said that first season. "For 20 years I put my shoes on the same way, then all of a sudden people want to know--'How does it look, Tom?'--people who never asked me anything before."

Army had another fine year in at 8-2 again in 1967 and then 7-3 in 1968. But Cahill's squads ran into some trouble winning games as they closed out the 1960s with a 4-5-1 mark. Then, his 1970 squad went 1-9-1. Army was 6-4 in each of the next two seasons, then in an unexplainable happening, went winless in 1973.

Before the 1973 finale against Navy, West Point administrators assured reporters that Cahill would return as coach, no matter the outcome. However, after Navy won by 51-0, the worst defeat in the history of the rivalry, Cahill was fired.

His coaching record at Army was 40-39-2 in eight years, including a 5-3 mark against Navy.

Coach Cahill later put in five seasons at Union College in Schenectady, going 12-27-1. In 1984, Cahill returned to West Point and became a fixture in the press box at Michie Stadium as an analyst on the Army radio network. He was scheduled to broadcast a game but died at 73-years of age on the Thursday before the Oct 31 Army v Eastern Michigan game. He would have enjoyed chirping about this game as the Cadets won big 57-17.

Cahill was quite an athlete in his prime. Born in Fayetteville, N.Y., Tom was a three-sport star in football, baseball and basketball at Niagara.

1966 Army West Point Cadets Football Coach Thomas Cahill

The Army Cadets football team represented the United States Military Academy in the 1966 college football season. It was Army's seventy-seventh season of intercollegiate football. They were led by Coach Thomas Cahill in his first of eight seasons as head coach of the Cadets. As an independent football entity, the Army team had a fine record this season under coach Cahill—8-2-0.

The Cadets compiled an 8-2-0 record; shut out three opponents, and outscored all opponents by a combined total of 141 to 105. In the annual Army–Navy Game, the Cadets defeated the Midshipmen by a score of 20 to 7. The Cadets also lost to Notre Dame (35-0) and Tennessee (38-7).

Army linebacker Townsend Clarke was selected by the Central Press Association as a first-team player on the 1966 College Football All-America Team.

No Army players were recognized on the 1965 College Football All-America Team.

This year's home opener was on Sept 17 vs Kansas State. The Cadets defeated the Wildcats W (21-6). Other than those games played in neutral fields, all Army home games are played on the West Point campus at Michie Stadium in West Point NY. On Sept 24 at home, Army shut-out Holy Cross W (14-0). On Oct 1, in a close game at Michie Stadium, the Cadets defeated W (11-0) It was joe Paterno's first year as head coach for the Nittany Lions. The next week, Army traveled to South Bend, Indiana to face the Fighting Irish of Notre Dame. The Irish shut out the Cadets L (0-35).

The following week, Oct 22, at home, the Cadets roughed up Pittsburgh in a shutout W (28-0). Just one week later, Oct 29, Army was playing Tennessee at Memphis Memorial Stadium in Memphis, TN, and as tough as they played, the Cadets were roughed up a bit by the Volunteers in a losing effort L (7-38). On Nov 5 at home, the

Cadets beat George Washington W (20–7). After traveling across the country on Nov 12, the Cadets could only muster up six points but California only managed to get just three points v the tough Cadet defense. This game was played at California Memorial Stadium in Berkeley, CA, and the Cadets beat the Golden Bears W 6–3.

On November 26, the Army Cadets defeated the Midshipmen of Navy in the Annual Army–Navy-Game at JFK Stadium in Philadelphia, PA W (20-7).

1967 Army West Point Cadets Football Coach Thomas Cahill

<< Coach Thomas Cahill

The Army Cadets football team represented the United States Military Academy in the 1967 college football season. It was Army's seventy-eighth season of intercollegiate football. They were led by Coach Thomas Cahill in his second of eight seasons as head coach of the Cadets. As an independent football entity, the Army team had a fine record this season under coach Cahill—8-2-0.

The Cadets compiled an 8-2-0 record; shut out one opponent, and outscored all opponents by a combined total of 183 to 94. In the annual Army–Navy Game, the Cadets lost to the Midshipmen by a score of 14 to 19. The Cadets also lost to Duke by a 7 to 10 score. No Army players received first-team honors on the 1967 College Football All-America Team

This year's home opener was on Sept 23 vs Virginia. The Cadets defeated the Wahoo's W (26-7). Other than those games played in neutral fields, all Army home games are played on the West Point campus at Michie Stadium in West Point NY. On Sept 30, the Cadets played at Boston College's Alumni Stadium in Chestnut Hill, MA and gained the win W (21–10). Duke's Blue Devils beat the Cadets at Michie Stadium on Oct 7 in a close match L (7-10). Then, at the Cotton Bowl in Dallas Texas, on Nov 13, the Cadets defeated SMU W (24–6)

One week later on Oct 21, Rutgers played tough in a Cadet home game but lost the match to the Cadets W (14-3). A rough and tough Stanford team played the Cadets at home on Oct 28 and went back to California with a loss W (24-20). The always-ready Air Force Squad played a tough match on Nov 4 at Falcon Stadium in Colorado Springs, CO but it was not enough to avoid being beaten by the Cadets W (10-7). The Cadets shut out Utah at home on Nov 11 W (22-0). The next week, at Pitt Stadium in Pittsburgh PA, the Cadets beat Pittsburgh W (21-12).

With an 8-1 record, yet unranked, on December 2, the Army Cadets were defeated by the Midshipmen of Navy in the Annual Army-Navy-Game at JFK Stadium in Philadelphia, PA L (14-9).

During the 1967 season, despite having a fine record for the second year in a row, the Army Cadets had not received the favor in any week of being in the top 20. I would suspect that it was because Army was an Independent team and many other collegiate programs were affiliated with conferences. After the drought of fine seasons after Red Blaik, it's like Army had been forgotten by the Sports press. This would be the best Army record for thirty years as the team spun into a period of darkness and Army was awakened in a 10-2 season until 1996. In 1996, with Coach Sutton, Army was not favored again by the press as they were ranked 24th in the country despite a nice 10-2 record.

1968 Army West Point Cadets Football Coach Thomas Cahill

The Army Cadets football team represented the United States Military Academy in the 1968 college football season. It was Army's seventy-ninth season of intercollegiate football. They were led by Coach Thomas Cahill in his third of eight seasons as head coach of the Cadets. As an independent football entity, the Army team had a fine record this season under coach Cahill—7-3-0.

The Cadets compiled a 7-3-0 record; shut out two opponents, and outscored all opponents by a combined total of 270-137. In the annual Army–Navy Game, the Cadets defeated the Midshipmen by a score of 24 to 14. The Cadets lost to Vanderbilt by a 13 to 17 score, and to Missouri by a 3 to 7 score.

Army linebacker Ken Johnson was selected by the American Football Coaches Association as a first-team player on the 1968 College Football All-America Team.

This year's home opener was on Sept 21 vs The Citadel. Attendance was 23,000. The Cadets defeated the Bulldogs W (34-14). Other than those games played in neutral fields, all Army home games were played on the West Point Campus at Michie Stadium in West Point NY. On Sept 28, at home, Vanderbilt defeated the Cadets L (13-17).

On Oct 5, at Missouri's Memorial Stadium in Columbia, MO, the Tigers got the best of the Cadets L (3-7) before 58,576. Then on Oct 12, the Cadets squeaked out a win against the visiting California Golden Bears W (10-7) before a sellout of 32,000.

On Oct 19, the Cadets shut out Rutgers W (24-0). A week later the Cadets went into high gear and pitched a blow-out against Duke W (57-25). On Nov 2, at Beaver Stadium in the Nittany Valley of Pennsylvania, before 49,122, Joe Paterno's Lions defeated the Cadets L (24-28). On Nov 9, the Cadets pounded Boston College at home to the tune of W (58-25). Then, on Nov 16 at Pittsburgh's Pitt Stadium in Pittsburgh, PA, the Cadets shut-out the Panthers W (26–0)

With a 6-3 record, on November 30, the Army Cadets defeated the Midshipmen of Navy in the Annual Army-Navy-Game at JFK Stadium in Philadelphia, PA W (21-14). The game was available for viewing on ABC TV and it was seen by 102,000 at JFK. My dad and I were watching it at home that day.

1969 Army West Point Cadets Football Coach Thomas Cahill

The Army Cadets football team represented the United States Military Academy in the 1969 college football season. It was Army's eightieth season of intercollegiate football. They were led by Coach Thomas Cahill in his fourth of eight seasons as head coach of the

Cadets. As an independent football entity, the Army team had a losing record this season under coach Cahill—4-5-1.

The Cadets compiled an 4-5-1 record; shut out one opponent, and outscored all opponents by a combined total of 161 to 160. Despite the poor season, the Cadets came alive for Navy. In the annual Army–Navy Game, the Cadets shut-out the Midshipmen by a score of 27-0. The Cadets lost five games this year—one more than they had won. No Army players received first-team honors on the 1969 College Football All-America Team

This year's home opener was on Sept 20 vs New Mexico. The Cadets defeated the Lobos W (31-14). Other than those games played in neutral fields, all Army home games are played on the West Point campus at Michie Stadium in West Point NY. On Sept 27 at Vanderbilt's Dudley Field in Nashville, TN, the Cadets beat the Commodores W (16–6). Back at home on Oct 4, my wedding anniversary, Texas A&M got the best of the Cadets by a touchdown L (13–20). Ready for a rumble, Notre Dame shut out the Cadets at Yankee Stadium in the Bronx, NY by a big score L 0–45.

On Oct 18, taking on Utah State at home, the Cadets were beaten by the Aggies, L (7–23). Hosting Boston College on Oct 25, the Cadets prevailed with a nice win W (38-7). On Nov 1, the Fighting Falcons of Air Force never gave up the fight in this game and beat the Cadets by a touchdown L (6-13). After getting on a big plane on Nov 8 to Sutzen Stadium in Eugene Oregon, the Cadets had all they could do to tie the Ducks in a great football game T (17-17). Then, back from the jet lag, the Cadets were not ready for Pittsburgh at home and lost to the Panthers L (6-15).

On November 30, the Army Cadets recouped their whole season by this one victory over Navy. That's how big this service rivalry actually is. They shut out the Midshipmen of Navy in the Annual Army-Navy-Game at JFK Stadium in Philadelphia, PA W (27-0).

1970 Army West Point Cadets Football Coach Thomas Cahill

The Army Cadets football team represented the United States Military Academy in the 1970 college football season. It was Army's

eighty-first season of intercollegiate football. They were led by Coach Thomas Cahill in his fifth of eight seasons as head coach of the Cadets. As an independent football entity, the Army team had a terrible losing record this season under coach Cahill—1-9-1.

The Cadets compiled a 1-9-1 record; shut out one opponent, Holy Cross in their only win, and were outscored by all opponents by a combined total of 151 to 281. With their poor season, and Navy's equally one victory season, the Cadets did not come alive for Navy. In the annual Army–Navy Game, the Navy won by scoring four more points in a game that had no offense L (7-11)

Nobody got shut out but all players knew there was a big war (Vietnam) going on outside the confines of the stadium, and the great officers playing in this game would soon be participants. It was another year that was as bad as the honor scandal, but nobody is talking. The Cadets' only victory came in the season opener, a 26 to 0 victory over Holy Cross. No Army players were selected as first-team players on the 1970 College Football All-America Team.

This year's home opener was on Sept 12 vs Holy Cross. The Cadets shut out the Crusaders W (26-0) It was the first win of the season for the Cadets and the only win. Other than those games played in neutral fields, all Army home games were played on the West Point campus at Michie Stadium in West Point NY. The list of losses in this poor football year for Army are shown below. No amount of scribing can make this a better season:

September 19 Baylor, home L (7–10)
September 26 at Nebraska L (0–28)
October 3 at Tennessee L (3–48)
October 10 at Notre Dame L (10–51)
October 17 at Virginia L (20–21)
October 24 Penn State, home L (14–38)
October 31 at Boston College L (13–21)
November 7 Syracuse, home, L 29–31
November 14 Oregon, home, T (22–22)
November 28 Navy, site neutral @JFK L (7–11)

Before I finish this book, my plan is to find out whether my supposition that the Service Academy's preoccupation with the

Vietnam war had a major impact on their being able to attract the best college athletes and/or the war itself took officers often before they were ready. I am not sure yet and if this paragraph stays here in this book, I will be working on the answer.

1971 Army West Point Cadets Football Coach Thomas Cahill

The Army Cadets football team represented the United States Military Academy in the 1971 college football season. It was Army's eighty-second season of intercollegiate football. They were led by Coach Thomas Cahill in his sixth of eight seasons as head coach of the Cadets. As an independent football entity, the Army team had an OK record this season under coach Cahill—6-4-0.

The Cadets compiled a 6-4-0 record; shut out no opponents, and were outscored by all opponents by a combined total of 146 to 206. This was not a bad season for Army but Navy had a terrible 3-8 season. Navy's three victory season gave them little hope in the annual battle. The Cadets were ready for Navy. In the annual Army–Navy Game, the Cadets beat the Midshipmen by the skin of their teeth 24 to 23.No Army players were selected as first-team players on the 1971 College Football All-America Team.

This year's home opener was on Sept 18 vs Stanford. The Cardinal kept up the pressure the whole game and defeated the Cadets in a rare opening game loss L (3-38). Other than those games played in neutral fields, all Army home games were played on the West Point campus at Michie Stadium in West Point NY. The Cadets then traveled to Grant Field in Atlanta GA to defeat the Georgia Tech Yellow Jackets W (16-13).

The next win was at home on Oct 2vs. Missouri W (22–6). Joe Paterno's Penn State Nittany Lions shut out the Cadets on Oct 9 in a lop-sided game at Beaver Stadium in University Park PA L (0-42). Air Force's Fighting Falcons then got the best of the Cadets on Oct 16 at Falcon Stadium in Colorado Springs, CO L (7–20). On Oct 23, at home, the Cadets beat the Virginia Wahoo's in a close match W (14-9). This was followed by a one-point loss to the Miami Hurricanes that was played in the Miami Orange Bowl in Miami, FL L (13–24)

On Nov 6 at home, the Cadets solidly beat the Rutgers Scarlet Knights W (30-17) On Nov 13, the Cadets kept the win streak going by defeating Pittsburgh at home W (17-14).

In the Army-Navy-Game on November 27 at JFK Stadium in Philadelphia, the Cadets got by the Midshipmen by one point in a really exciting nail-biter W (24-23)

Best Army Navy Game # 8

Army captured the 1971 game, 22-20, after Kurt Heiss made one of the longest field goals in the rivalry's history.

In a contest that mostly was about the Cadets' ground game (they rushed for 373 yards) and Navy's passing game (quarterback Jim Kubiak threw for 361 yards), it came down to a 52-yard kick by Heiss with 6:19 remaining to win.

The game featured six lead changes and more than its share of big plays, mostly by Navy, as tailback Michael Jefferson had a 73-yard touchdown run and Kubiak threw a 56-yard scoring pass to tight end Kevin Hickman.

Still, it wasn't enough to overcome the Cadets that day.

1972 Army West Point Cadets Football Coach Thomas Cahill

The Army Cadets football team represented the United States Military Academy in the 1972 college football season. It was Army's eighty-third season of intercollegiate football. They were led by Coach Thomas Cahill in his seventh of eight seasons as head coach of the Cadets. As an independent football entity, the Army team had an OK record this season under coach Cahill—6-4-0.

The Cadets compiled a 6-4-0 record; shut out no opponents, and were outscored by all opponents by a combined total of 160 to 282. This was a bad season for Army but Navy had as terrible a season also at 4-7. Navy's six loss season before the game gave them little hope in the annual battle other than that Army was doing just as poorly. The Cadets, who had problems with their D all year, were ready for Navy. In the annual Army–Navy Game, the Cadets beat the Midshipmen by the skin of their teeth 23 to 15. No Army players were selected as first-team players on the 1972 College Football All-America Team.

This year's home opener was on Sept 23 vs Nebraska. The visitors were relentless in the Cornhuskers win against the Cadets L (7-77). Other than those games played in neutral fields, all Army home games were played on the West Point campus at Michie Stadium in West Point NY.

The Nebraska game was a travesty for Army and a major triumph for Nebraska. Army pride kept the Cadets from ending the season right then and there. It is hard to believe. I was so curious about this game that I began to read game recaps to find out what went wrong with Coach Cahill's team in an otherwise OK 6-4 season.

Simply put, Nebraska's Cornhuskers completely overwhelmed Army, 77-7, before a sellout crowd of 42,239 at Michie Stadium. Millions saw the game on ABC-TV's regional telecast. There was no escaping

The Cornhuskers scored two TDs in the first quarter, added three in the second, four in the third and two in the fourth before Army finally scored with 35 seconds left in the game. All 49 of Nebraska's players saw action, with the reserves taking over midway in the third quarter. The 77 points were the most scored in the nation in 1972.

Nebraska's Johnny Rodgers scored three touchdowns, while Dave Goeller and Steve Runty each scored twice. Dave Humm set a Nebraska and Big 8 percentage record when he hit 14 of 18 passes for 160 yards.

As might be expected, Nebraska dominated the total offense statistics, 481 yards to 124. The Husker Black Shirts held Army to minus 12 yards rushing.

After this game, the Cadets beat Texas A&M on Sept 30 at KLE Field in College Station Texas. The Cadets did not give up but came back. This win put the Cadets on track for a winning season.

On Oct 7, the Cadets beat Lehigh at home W (26-21). The Cadets played another Pennsylvania team, # 15 ranked Penn State the following week and were not so fortunate, being shut-out L (0-45). On Oct 14, the Cadets beat the Scarlet Knights of Rutgers by a TD W (35-28). After this win came another loss on Oct 28, against Miami of Florida at home L (7-28). The next week, Army slipped by Air Force for the win in a close match at home W (17-14).

Then on Nov 11, the Cadets lost to Syracuse in Archbold Stadium • Syracuse, NY L (6–27). The following week, Army won the first of two in a row, defeating Holy Cross in a close match at home W (15-13).

In the Army-Navy-Game on December 2, at JFK Stadium in Philadelphia, the Cadets defeated the Midshipmen to win the Commander-in-Chief's Trophy in the Army-Navy game) W (23–15).

1973 Army West Point Cadets Football Coach Thomas Cahill

The Army Cadets football team represented the United States Military Academy in the 1973 college football season. It was Army's eighty-fourth season of intercollegiate football. They were led by Coach Thomas Cahill in his eighth and last of eight seasons as head coach of the Cadets. As an independent football entity, the Army team had its worst record ever under any coach 0-10-0.

That means the Cadets compiled a 0-10-0 record; shut out no opponents, and were outscored by all opponents by a combined total of 382 to 67. This was a bad season for Army. Navy had a bad season but at least they had some wins at 4-7. Navy's six loss season before the big game gave them little hope in the annual battle other than that Army had not even won any games. The Cadets, who had problems with their game all year, were not ready for Navy or any other team this year.

In the annual Army–Navy Game, the Midshipmen clobbered the Cadets in a shutout W (53-0). They also lost to Notre Dame by a whopping 62 to 3. Nothing could explain such a poor season and Tom Cahill would not be around the following year to offer an explanation. No Army players were selected as first team players on the 1972 College Football All-America Team.

The season record for 1973 follows

The results of this dismal season follow:

22-Sep	Tennessee	Home	L 18–37
29-Sep	California	Home	L 6–51
6-Oct	at Georgia Tech	Atlanta, GA	L 10–14
13-Oct	at Penn State	Beaver Stadium	L 3–54
20-Oct	Notre Dame	Home	L 3–62
27-Oct	Holy Cross	Home	L 10–17
3-Nov	at Air Force	Falcon Stadium	L 10–43
10-Nov	Miami (FL)	Home	L 7–19
17-Nov	Pittsburgh	Home	L 0–34
1-Dec	vs. Navy	JFK Stadium	L 0–51

This article by Gordon S. White is from the New York Times. It was written right after the Army-Navy-Game.

PHILADELPHIA, Dec. 1—In the most-one-sided contest of the 74 Army-Navy football games, Navy trounced the Cadets, 51-0, today to make a bright ending to another Navy losing season but also to create one of the darkest days in the 84-year history of Army football.

Never has a team so dominated this service rivalry that began at West Point, N. Y., in 1390 when Navy accepted an Army challenge and traveled up the Hudson River to beat the Cadets, 24-0. And never before has an Army team had such a poor season record as these 1973 Cadets.

College Football -- ?? who lost all 10 of their games.

The first Army team in 1890, which played only that one game against Navy, was the only other Cadet squad to go through a season without at least one victory.

After scoring a touchdown on the opening drive of the game for a 6-0 lead, Navy made a complete rout of the game in the second period with four touchdowns and a field goal to hold a 37-0 lead at half-time before 91,926 persons in John F. Kennedy Stadium. Two- more touchdowns in the third quarter established Navy's triumph as the largest margin of victory in an Army-Navy game. Navy's scoring fell only 4 points short of the series record of scoring by both teams set in 1959 when Navy beat Army, 43.12, for a 55-point total.

It was a big day for George Welsh, who ended his first season as Navy's head coach. His fourth victory of the season for Navy did much to erase the memory of the seven losses the Middies suffered along the way this year.

Welsh, a former Navy quarterback who beat Army in the 1954 game, must have thought he was still at Penn State, where he was an assistant coach for the past 11 seasons and where victories came often and in lopsided fashion.

Navy's success came on the strength of a penetrating ground attack led by Cleveland Cooper, the fine junior tailback. He picked up 102 yards on 18 runs and tied an Army-Navy game record by scoring three touchdowns against the Cadets.

Cooper joined Joe Bellino (Navy, 1959), Pat Donnelly (Navy, 1963) and Charlie Jarvis (Army, 1968) in scoring three touchdowns in one of these service clashes. The Navy tailback scored on runs of 7, 6 and 1 yards before leaving the game as Welsh called off the first-stringers early in the third period. Cooper and others ran through and around Army for a total of 366 yards on the ground. Welsh tried to ease the pain for Army and its coach, Tom Cahill, as the Navy coach used all 59 Midshipmen suited for the game and used each of them for at least one full quarter of action.

Ed Gilmore, Cooper's substitute and the man who scored the final touchdown on a 1-yard play, was the leading ground-gainer with 123 yards. But he did most of his rushing long after Army Was completely whipped and a beaten and saddened team. Steve Dykes contributed a 44-yard field goal on the last play of the first half, aided by a strong tailwind, as if Navy needed any help.

The 91,926 fans established this gathering as the smallest since the Army-Navy game moved back to the big concrete dish in Philadelphia in 1946. During World War II the game was played at Annapolis, West Point and Baltimore, 1942-45, in much smaller arenas.

A bright sun kept the fans warm despite a strong northwest wind and temperatures in the 40's. Most of the crowd was seated tong before the kickoff to witness the ritual marching entrance of the Brigade and the Corps.

That happened when there still was hope for Army. The game had not begun. There was the annual gathering of military celebrities headed by John W. Warner, Secretary of the Navy, and Howard H. Callaway, Secretary of the Army.

It wasn't long before Warner and the Brigade were smiling. The rout began in the second quarter when the midshipmen scored four touchdowns and a field goal in the last 9 minutes 36 seconds of that period. That was scoring at a rate of nearly 4 points a minute.

As if things weren't going bad enough for Army all game long, Navy got 2 points on its last conversion when it wasn't even trying for more than 1. Holding for a placement extra point, Navy's Mike Yeager reached for a high snap from center and could not get the ball down for Dykes to kick. So, Yeager took off and scored 2 points on a run.

It was just a bad day for Army as Cahill suffered his third loss to Navy against five victories since becoming the head coach of the Cadets in 1966.

Homer Smith replaces Tom Cahill

Homer Smith got an extra year after his 1977 winning season at Army. It was not a sure thing. Army's head football coach converted what many believed was a "mission impossible" into a successful Army football season by doing exactly as he was ordered to do—win seven games and beat Navy in 1977. So, Smith, whose original four-year contract at West Point expired at the end of the year got the word that he had satisfied the Army enough to be rewarded with a new contract.

Army brass initially refused to comment on Smith's future, although they had already met to determine just what to do and when to announce it. Meanwhile, Homer Smith was not about to be jobless. Princeton appeared to be waiting in the wings to possibly offer Smith the Princeton head-coaching job if Army did not sign him to a new contract.

Following Army's third straight losing season under Coach Smith in 1976, the Board of Athletic Control at the United States Military Academy called in Smith last January and told him he had to win or else. They quantified it that he had to win at least seven games in 1977, including the Navy game, in order to remain as Army's head coach. That was the meets minimum requirements number. Most fans and pundits felt Army would not be able to win that many games or beat Navy. That's why it appeared to be a "mission impossible" for Smith and his staff.

But the Army players and coaches turned experts into know-nothings as the Cadets concluded a 7-4 won-lost season with a gratifying 17-14 triumph over Navy, which was Army's first victory over Navy in Smith's four years as head coach. Luck would not be so kind in 1978.

1974 Army West Point Cadets Football Coach Homer Smith

The Army Cadets football team represented the US Military Academy in the 1974 college football season. It was Army's eighty-fifth season of inter-collegiate football. They were led by Coach Homer Smith in his first of five seasons as head coach of the Cadets. As an independent football entity, the Army team had a poor record of 3-8-0.

Overall, the Cadets compiled a 3-8-0 record; shut out no opponents, and were outscored by all opponents by a combined total of 306 to 156. This was a bad season for Army. Navy also had a bad season but they out won army by one game-- 4-7. Both teams had three wins when they met. The Navy, who had a few problems with their game all year, were ready for Army this year. In the annual Army–Navy Game, the Midshipmen shut out the Cadets W (19-0). No Army players were selected as first-team players on the 1974 College Football All-America Team.

<< Coach Homer Smith

This year's home opener was on Sept 14 vs Lafayette. The Cadets prevailed in a close match W (14-7) Other than those games played in neutral fields, all Army home games were played on the West Point campus at Michie Stadium in West Point NY. On Sept 21, the Cadets defeated the Green Wave of Tulane at home W (14-31). On Sept 28, the Cadets traveled to California to play the Golden Bears and lost the match L (14-27). The next game was against Joe Paterno's Nittany Lions on Oct 5. The Cadets could not keep up with Penn State but lost by just one TD L (14-21). e

On Oct 12, at Duke's Wallace Wade Stadium in Durham, NC the Cadets lost to the Blue Devils L (14–33). On Oct 19 at Notre Dame's Notre Dame Stadium, the House that Rick Built in South Bend, IN, the Cadets were shut out by the Fighting Irish L (0–48). On Oct 26, the Cadets beat Holy Cross in a close match at home W 13–10. Then, on Nov 2, at home, the Vanderbilt Commodores beat the Cadets L (14-38.

The next week on Nov 9, at home, Army squeaked out a victory over Air Force for the Commander-in-Chief's Trophy W (17–16). In the game before the Army-Navy Game, the Cadets lost a close match in a shootout against North Carolina at Kenan Memorial Stadium in Chapel Hill, NC L (42–56).

In the Army-Navy-Game on November 30, at JFK Stadium in Philadelphia, the Cadets were defeated in a shutout by the Midshipmen to win the Commander-in-Chief's Trophy (Army-Navy-Game) L (0-19).

About the Commander-In-Chief's Trophy

Since Air Force is now involved in the Army schedule for the last several seasons and we have been noting the existence of the Commander in Chief's Trophy, we pause below to explain it.

The Commander-in-Chief's Trophy is awarded to each season's winner of the American college football triangular series among the teams of the U.S. Military Academy (Army Black Knights), the U.S. Naval Academy (Navy Midshipmen), and U.S. Air Force Academy (Air Force Falcons).

The Navy–Air Force game is traditionally played on the first Saturday in October, the Army–Air Force game on the first Saturday in November, and the Army–Navy Game on the second Saturday in December. In the event of a tie, the award is shared, but the previous winner retains possession of the trophy. Along with the Florida Cup, the Michigan MAC Trophy, and the Beehive Boot, the Commander-in-Chief's Trophy is one of the few three-way rivalries that awards a trophy to the winner.

Through 2016, the Air Force Falcons hold the most trophy victories at 20 and the Navy Midshipmen have won 15. The Army Black Knights trail with only six; their last came 21 years ago in 1996. The trophy has been shared on four occasions, last in 1993.

1975 Army West Point Cadets Football Coach Homer Smith

The Army Cadets football team represented the United States Military Academy in the 1975 college football season. It was Army's

eighty-sixth season of intercollegiate football. They were led by Coach Homer Smith in his second of five seasons as head coach of the Cadets. As an independent football entity, the Army team had a poor record of 2-9-0.

Overall, the Cadets compiled a 2-9-0 record; shut out no opponents, and were outscored by all opponents by a combined total of 337 to 165. This was another bad season for Army. Navy had a fine season including a nice win against Army but they met. The Midshipmen beat the Cadets 6 to 30.No Army players were selected as first-team players on the 1974 College Football All-America Team.

This year's home opener was on Sept 13 vs Holy Cross. The Cadets won in a blowout W (44-7) Other than those games played in neutral fields, all Army home games were played on the West Point campus at Michie Stadium in West Point NY. On Sept 20, Army defeated Lehigh in a shootout W (54-32). This would be the last Army victory if the 1975 season.

The losses for the rest of the Cadets season follow in tabular form

27-Sep	Villanova	Home	L 0–10
4-Oct	at Stanford	Stanford CA	L 14–67
11-Oct	Duke	Home	L 10–21
18-Oct	Pittsburgh	Home	L 20–52
25-Oct	at Penn State	Beaver Stadium	L 0–31
1-Nov	at Air Force	Falcon Stadium	L 3–33
8-Nov	Boston College	Home	L 0–31
15-Nov	at Vanderbilt	Dudley Field	L 14–23
29-Nov	vs. Navy	JFK Stadium	L 6–30

1976 Army West Point Cadets Football Coach Homer Smith

The Army Cadets football team represented the United States Military Academy in the 1976 college football season. It was Army's eighty-seventh season of intercollegiate football. They were led by Coach Homer Smith in his third of five seasons as head coach of the Cadets. As an independent football entity, the Army team had a poor record of 5-6-0.

Overall, the Cadets compiled a 5-6-0 record; shut out no opponents, and were outscored by all opponents by a combined total of 267 to 201. This was another poor record for Army, though they played well and lost a number of close games. Navy had a poor season also (4-7) but they were able to get a nice win against Army in the traditional rivalry game. The Midshipmen beat the Cadets 10 to 38. No Army players were selected as first-team players on the 1974 College Football All-America Team.

This year's home opener was on Sept 11 vs Lafayette The Cadets won in a close match W (16-6). Other than those games played in neutral fields, all Army home games were played on the West Point campus at Michie Stadium in West Point NY. On Sept 18, Army defeated Holy Cross in a very tight game W (26-24). On Sept 25, North Carolina defeated Army by just two points W (26-24). The Cadets won by even less (one point) vs Stanford the following week on Oct 2 W (21-20.

On Oct 9, Joe Paterno's Penn State squad beat the Cadets at beaver Stadium in University park, PA L (16-38) in the first of three losses in a row. The next loss was on Oct 16 against Tulane's Green Wave at The Louisiana Superdome in New Orleans, LA L (10–23). The third loss was on Oct 23 at home against Boston College L (10-27). The Cadets recovered against the Fighting Falcons of Air Force on Oct 30 at home with a nice win W (24-7) competing for the Commander-in-Chief's Trophy.

On Nov at No. 2 Pittsburgh, the Panthers got the best of the Cadets L (7-37). The next game was Colgate at home. The Cadets played well and defeated the Raiders W (29-13)

In the Army-Navy-Game on November 27, at JFK Stadium in Philadelphia, the Cadets had a tough time scoring while Navy put 38-points on the board to defeat Army. The Midshipmen won this leg of the Commander-in-Chief's Trophy (Army-Navy-Game) L (10-38).

1977 Army West Point Cadets Football Coach Homer Smith

The Army Cadets football team represented the United States Military Academy in the 1977 college football season. It was Army's

eighty-eighth season of intercollegiate football. They were led by Coach Homer Smith in his fourth of five seasons as head coach of the Cadets. As an independent football entity, the Army team had a respectable record of 7-4.

Overall, the Cadets compiled a 7-4-0 record. They finished with their first winning season since 1972. Army's win over UMass was the 500th in school history. Leamon Hall threw five touchdown passes, including three to freshman Mike Fahnstock. Homer Smith– Eastern Coach of the Year (New York Football Writers Association). In the Army-Navy Game, the Cadets beat the Midshipmen 17 to 14 at JFK Stadium. Army won the Commander in Chief's Trophy.

This year's home opener was on Sept 10 vs UMass The Cadets won handily W (34-10) before 22,101. Other than those games played in neutral fields, all Army home games were played on the West Point campus at Michie Stadium in West Point NY. On Sept 17 at home vs VMI, the Cadets had what it takes to win the game and won W (27-14. On the road at 2-0, Army traveled to Alumni Stadium in Chestnut Hill, MA on Sept 24, where they found a tough and stubborn Boston College Eagles team that would not give up until they had pounded the Cadets defense for 49-points. BC won this match handily L (28-49).

Next on Oct 1 was a tough Colorado Buffaloes team that shut out the Cadets at home L (0-31). With two losses in a row, Army pulled out all the stops to beat a determined Villanova Squad W (34-32) in a nail-biter. The next week it was Dan Devine's Fighting Irish playing in Giants Stadium before 72, 594 fans. The Irish shut out the Cadets in a tough battle L 90-24). Lafayette was next at Michie Stadium and the Cadets made quick work of the Leopards W (42-6).

Holy Cross came next to battle the Cadets but the Cadets were too big, too powerful and too determined and so they beat the Crusaders in a shootout W (48-7) before a packed house of 41,376. The Cadets then traveled to Falcon Stadium in Colorado Springs CO on Nov 5 to face the Air Force for the Commander in Chief's Trophy. The Cadets earned the win W (31-6). On Nov 12, Pittsburgh beat the Cadets by two to one at Giants Stadium in East Rutherford, NJ L (26-52)

In the season finale, the Cadets played in the annual Army-Navy-Game, which this year was played on November 27 at JFK Stadium in Philadelphia. It was a low scoring game but the Cadets hung in there to defeat the Midshipmen by a field goal W (17-14). Since the Cadets also beat Air Force, they won the Commander-in-Chief's Trophy for 1977

1978 Army West Point Cadets Football Coach Homer Smith

The Army Cadets football team represented the United States Military Academy in the 1978 college football season. It was Army's eighty-ninth season of intercollegiate football. They were led by Coach Homer Smith in his fifth of five seasons as head coach of the Cadets. As an independent football entity, the Army team had a respectable record of 4-6-1.

Overall, the Cadets compiled a 4-6-1 record. They finished with another losing season. Coach Smith would not get to coach the following year. Army pitched no shutouts against its opponents and they were outscored by their opponents by a combined total of 255 to 188. In the annual Army–Navy Game, the Cadets lost to the Midshipmen by a 28 to 0 score.at JFK Stadium. No Army players were selected as first-team players on the 1978 College Football All-America Team.

This year's home opener was on Sept 16 vs Lafayette. The Cadets won in a tough battle W (24-14). Other than those games played in neutral fields, all Army home games were played on the West Point campus at Michie Stadium in West Point NY. On Sept 23, Virginia busted into Michie Stadium ready to take a victory home with them. In a very close game, the determined Wahoo's got their win L (17-21) and there were no happy Cadets. On Sept 30, a tough Washington State Squad played Army to a tie at Michie T (21-21).

On Oct 7, no team volunteered to lose but the Tennessee Volunteers played the best that day and they got the big W against the Cadets L (13-31). Then, on Oct 14, a team that once was a pushover for the Cadets decided to win and win big. Holy Cross whose days of fame were just in front of it, grabbed some fame in 1978 when they shut out the once vaunted Army Cadets big time L (0-31). As nice as it was for Holy Cross, nobody at Army was smiling.

On Oct 21, the up and coming Florida Gators whose dark days were way behind them turned their tricks on the Cadets at Florida Field • in Gainesville, FL, and they walked away with a nice win over Army L (7–31). Colgate was struggling sometimes in Division II and Army simply overpowered the Raiders on Oct 28, W (28-3). On Nov 4, the Air Force Fighting Falcons came to beat the Cadets but did not. It was just the opposite W (28-14). On Nov 11, BC almost upset the Cadets at home but the Cadets scored a few more points than the Boston College Eagles, winning the game at home W (29-26) by three points. That's all it takes sometimes to win. On Nov 18, the Cadets lost by a 2 to 1 margin to Pittsburgh at Pitt Stadium in Pittsburgh, PA L (17–35).

In the season finale for Army, despite loving each other in real battles, on the gridiron, the Midshipmen were always looking to make the Army look bad. The Cadets again dutifully played in the annual Army-Navy-Game, planning to rip out a slice of the Navy squad. So, on December 2, at JFK Stadium in Philadelphia. It was a low (0) scoring game for Army but nobody told Navy to keep their guns silent. The Midshipmen walked out of JFK with a win W – a (28-0) shutout over the Cadets and they, not Army, won the Commander-in-Chief's Trophy for 1978

Chapter 15 Coaches Saban, Cavanaugh & Young 1979 - 1989

Saban   Coach # 28
Cavanaough   Coach # 29
Young   Coach # 30

Year	Coach	Record	Conference	Record
1979	Lou Saban	2-8-1	Indep	2-8-1
1980	Ed Cavanaugh	3-7-1	Indep	3-7-1
1980	Ed Cavanaugh	3-7-1	Indep	3-7-1
1982	Ed Cavanaugh	4-7-0	Indep	4-7-0
1983	Jim Young	2-9-0	Indep	2-9-0
1984	Jim Young	8-3-1	Indep	8-3-1
1985	Jim Young	9-3-0	Indep	9-3-0
1986	Jim Young	6-5-0	Indep	6-5-0
1987	Jim Young	5-6-0	Indep	5-6-0
1988	Jim Young	9-3-0	Indep	9-3-0
1989	Jim Young	6-5-0	Indep	6-5-0
1990	Jim Young	6-5-0	Indep	6-5-0

1979 Army West Point Cadets Football Coach Lou Saban

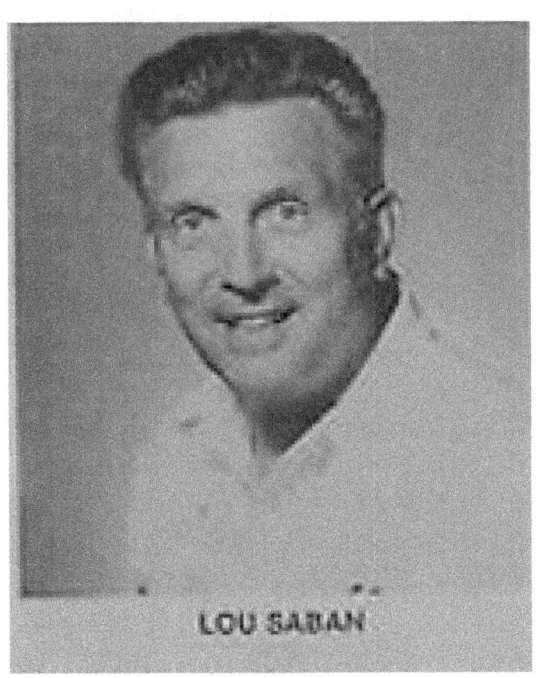
LOU SABAN

The Army Cadets football team represented the United States Military Academy in the 1979 college football season. It was Army's ninetieth season of intercollegiate football. They were led by Coach Lou Saban in his first and last of one season as head coach of the Cadets. As an independent football entity, the Army team had a terrible record of 2-8-1

Overall, the Cadets compiled a 2-8-1 record. They finished with another losing season. Coach Saban would choose not to coach the following year. Army pitched no shutouts against its opponents and they were not only outscored by their opponents but they had three shutouts thrown against them.

In the annual Army–Navy Game, the Cadets lost to the Midshipmen by a 31 to 7 score.at JFK Stadium. No Army players were selected as first-team players on the 1978 College Football All-America Team.

Coach Lou Saban could have brought victories to Army's flailing program at the time but his temperament did not blend in well with the Army Brass.

By the time Lou Saban joined the Army coaching "team," he had developed a reputation as an itinerant coach, a "notorious job-hopper" who was nevertheless respected for rebuilding teams in poor condition. Lou Saban needed to hold the steering wheel in his hand to steer the ship and he found others with a tight grip on the wheel that only a Superman and a super management negotiator could release. Saban was a coach and did not want that kind of job.

Saban said he wanted to stay at Army "until they put me out to pasture". I think he meant it but he needed to have the tools in his hand. Saban stayed at Army for only one season. He said he was unhappy with the academy's unwillingness to invest more in its football program. "This is a desperate situation", he said near the end of the 1979 season. "To fight alone as a football staff is impossible." He resigned in July 1980 after leading Army to a 2–8–1 record the previous season. Nobody missed him but they would have if he had control of the program. He was quite a coach with a 50-year career.

This year's home opener was on Sept 15 vs Connecticut. The Cadets won in a tough battle W (26-10). Other than those games played in neutral fields, all Army home games were played on the West Point campus at Michie Stadium in West Point NY. On Sept 22 at Stanford, in Stanford Stadium, Stanford, CA, the Cadets got the best of the Cardinal W (17–13). Then on Sept 29, at home, North Carolina came in tough and beat the Cadets L (3–41). Next up on Oct 6, was the Duke Blue Devils, who played the Cadets to a tie T (17-17).

Joe Paterno's Penn State squad played the Cadets at on Oct 13 at Beaver Stadium in University Park, PA and hung in for a games worth and got the win L (3–24). In the Army's first game against Baylor on Oct 20, that I can recall, things did not go well as the Bears decided to claw and pound the Cadets to the tune of a big loss L (0-55)

Once in a losing mode, the Cadets tried to recover but were defeated by Boston College at home on Oct 27 L (16-29). No games after the first two were wins so the losses came and came and came and did not go way for the whole season. At Air Force, the score was L (7-28). At Rutgers, the shutout score was L (0-20) and Pittsburgh at home was even worse L (0-40). The usual end of season Army-Navy-Game was also a stinker for Army with Navy whooping Army at the usual place and time (Dec 1) by the score of L (7-31)

1980 Army West Point Cadets Football Coach Ed Cavanaugh

The Army Cadets football team represented the United States Military Academy in the 1980 college football season. It was Army's ninety-first season of intercollegiate football. They were led by Coach Ed Cavanaugh in his first of three seasons as head coach of the Cadets. As an independent football entity, the Army team had a terrible record of 3-7-1

Overall, the Cadets compiled a 3-7-1 record. They finished with another losing season. Army pitched no shutouts against its opponents and they were outscored by their opponents 295 to 204. Army had worst numbers with other coaches. They had no shutouts thrown against them. In the annual Army–Navy Game, the Cadets lost to Navy by a definitive 33 to 6 score. It was no fluke.

This year's home opener was on Sept 13 vs Holy Cross. The Cadets won W (28-7). Other than those games played in neutral fields, all Army home games were played on the West Point campus at Michie Stadium in West Point NY. On Sept 20, an always formidable foe, California's Golden Bars came to play at Michie and were held back by a determined Cadet Team W (26-19). There would be no transcontinental win for California this day. Heading out to the West Coast for the game the following week, the Cadets were defeated by Washington State L (18-31). Back on the schedule after many years,

Harvard showed they were the team they always had been by defeating the Cadets at home L (10-15).

On Oct 11, Lehigh played Army to a tough earned tie T (24-24). On Oct 18, the Cadets traveled to play Notre Dame at Notre Dame Stadium in South Bend, IN, and were outscored by the Irish L (3–30). The following week, and always tough Boston College Squad met the Army at Alumni Stadium in Chestnut Hill, MA L (14–30). The Cadets lost this one. Then on Nov 1 Rutgers Scarlet Knights defeated the Cadets at home L 21–37. The next outing was Nov 8 at home against Air Force for the Commander-in-Chief's Trophy. The Cadets won the game W (47–24). On Nov 15, the Cadets lost big time to Pittsburgh at home L (7–45)

In the usual end of season Army-Navy-Game, the Cadets misfired for Army with Navy whooping Army at the usual place and time (Nov 29) by the score of L (6-33)

1981 Army West Point Cadets Football Coach Ed Cavanaugh

The Army Cadets football team represented the United States Military Academy in the 1981 college football season. It was Army's ninety-second season of intercollegiate football. They were led by Coach Ed Cavanaugh in his second of three seasons as head coach of the Cadets. As an independent football entity, the Army team had a terrible record of 3-7-1

Overall, the Cadets compiled a 3-7-1 record. They finished with another losing season. Army pitched one shutout against Princeton and no others and they were outscored by their opponents 212 to 126. The team had two shutouts thrown against them – Rutgers & Pittsburgh. In the annual Army–Navy Game, the Cadets played the Midshipmen to a 3-3 tie.

This year's home opener was on Sept 12 vs Missouri. The Cadets lost L (10-24) to the Tigers. Other than those games played in neutral fields, all Army home games were played on the West Point campus at Michie Stadium in West Point NY. On Sept 19 at home, the Cadets were defeated by VMI by one TD L (7–14). Then, on Sept 26, the Cadets beat Brown W (23-17) at home. On Oct 3, Army beat Harvard W (27-13) in a game played at Harvard Stadium in Allston,

MA. Then on Oct 10, the Cadets were shut out by Rutgers at home L (0-17).

On October 17, the Cadets got their only shutout of the year vs. Princeton and they won this home game W (34-0). On Oct 24 at home, Boston College pounded the Cadets L (6-41). In the Commander in Chief game v Air Force on Oct 31, the Fighting Falcons defeated the Cadets in a low-scoring close match L (3-7). Holy Cross then got the best of Army on Nov 7 L (13-28). The next week on Nov 14 at Pittsburgh's Pitt Stadium in Pittsburgh, PA, the Panthers whomped the Cadets in a big shutout L (0-48).

On December 1, in the end of season Army-Navy-Game, the Midshipmen tied the Cadets at Veterans Stadium in Philadelphia Cadets T (3-3)

1982 Army West Point Cadets Football Coach Ed Cavanaugh

The Army Cadets football team represented the United States Military Academy in the 1982 college football season. It was Army's ninety-third season of intercollegiate football. They were led by Coach Ed Cavanaugh in his third and last of three seasons as head coach of the Cadets. As an independent football entity, the Army team had a terrible record of 3-7-1

Overall, the Cadets compiled a 3-7-1 record. They finished with another losing season. Army pitched no shutouts and had no shutouts thrown against them. They were outscored by their opponents 271 to 164. In the annual Army–Navy Game, the Cadets lost to the Midshipmen by a 24-7 score.

This year's season opener was on Sept 11 vs Missouri at Faurot Field, Columbia, MO. The Cadets lost L (10-23) to the Tigers. Other than those games played in neutral fields, all Army home games were 7played on the West Point campus at Michie Stadium in West Point NY. On Sept 18 at home, the Cadets defeated Lafayette W (26–20). Then, on Sept 25, the Cadets traveled to North Carolina's Kenan Memorial Stadium in Chapel Hill, NC, and they were pounded by the Tar Heels L (8–62). On Oct 2 at home, the Cadets defeated Harvard's Crimson W (17–13)

On Oct 9 at Giants Stadium in East Rutherford, NJ, the Cadets lost to Rutgers 3–24. Then on Oct 16 at Princeton's Palmer Stadium in Princeton, NJ, the Cadets came through with the win W (20–14). The following week at home, on Oct 23, Boston College defeated Army L (17–32). At the end of October, on the 30th, the Cadets beat the Columbia Raiders at home W (41–8). Next game on Nov 6, at home v Air Force, the Fighting Falcons defeated the Cadets L (9–27). Then it was Pitt at home on Nov 13. The Panthers defeated the Cadets L (6-24).

In the season finale on December 1, the Army-Navy-Game, the Midshipmen defeated the Cadets at Veterans Stadium in Philadelphia L (7-24)

Jim Young to replace Ed Cavanaugh as Army Head Coach

Football, even football at the college level service academies, is a tough business. Ed Cavanaugh was fired Monday, Dec. 6, 1982 after his third losing season. Ironically, it was Cavanaugh's best winning season of the three. As head football coach at Army, Cavanaugh sensed the inevitable after a loss to Navy on Saturday Dec. 4.

'I like to eat, but I'm realistic also,' Cavanaugh said after Saturday's defeat in the 83rd renewal of the classic rivalry.

'I'm very understanding about the situation and I know that coaching is judged by wins and losses.'

Cavanaugh succeeded Lou Saban after the 1979 season and registered a 10-21-2 record. The Cadets posted identical 3-7-1 records during the 1980 and '81 seasons. This year, they finished with a 4-7 mark.

'Cavanaugh worked very hard to improve the program according to the West Point Athletic Director, Carl Ulrich: "… we are grateful for his efforts. Though some progress has been made, we feel that it's time to make a change."

Ulrich planned to replace Cavanaugh by year end.

At a National Football Foundation and Hall of Fame lunch in New York City, Brig. General Bill Carpenter, Army's famed 'lonely end' of the late 1950's, said the Point's failure to recruit all-star high school and prep school talent contributes to the Academy's football failures. Some say overall leadership. One thing for sure, Army after Coach Blaik was a different program. Jim Young after his 2-9 start in 1983 was a breath of fresh air for the Army program.

On Nov. 10, 1984, the Pittsburgh Post-Gazette wrote an inspiring article that they make available today on their web site. Thank you for that. Jim Young in many ways brought back an Earl "Red" Blaik spirit to the Army Cadets.

WEST POINT, N Y. –

The kaleidoscope of colors swirling around Army's Michie Stadium fades with each passing frost; the scarlets and auburns and golds give way to shades of sepia along the palisades that plunge into the Hudson River. Yet the scene remains breathtaking and just a bit arrogant, like the brittle brown photographs of West Point graduates Robert E. Lee and Stonewall Jackson.

For the better part of the last decade, the autumn view was the only reason to climb Michie's bleachers on a Saturday afternoon. "I know Sports Illustrated came out and said this is the best place to watch a college football game," Army Athletic Director Carl Ullrich said. "I'm sick and tired of all that. I want to get to the point where they say it's a great place to watch a great college football team."

Army, now 5-2-1, isn't great. But by beating Air Force, 24-12, Saturday night at West Point, the Black Knights moved closer to a bowl trip -- their first ever. Scouts from the Hall of Fame, Liberty, Bluebonnet and Independence bowls watched Saturday's game.

"All four said before the game that they were as interested in us as they were in Air Force now 5-4," Ullrich said. "You're always looking for teams that have a good following, and the service academies will always bring people out," said Bill Oakley of the Hall of Fame Bowl committee. Said the Bluebonnet's Ted Nance: "Army and Virginia are two teams that have never been to a bowl; certainly, Army is a logical draw."

If Army loses at Boston College today and beats Montana (2-6-1) in Tokyo Nov. 17, it will be 6-3-1 going into its open weekend of Nov. 24, when the bowl committees announce their selections. Bowl scouts would be willing to take a chance on Army, banking that the Black Knights could beat Navy, Dec. 1 at Philadelphia.

Beat Navy. The plea is painted in letters, 20 feet tall, on the roof of Cullum Hall. You see it from anywhere at West Point, contrasting sharply with the staid gray granite walls of the nearby Cadet barracks and its adjacent parade ground, where the grass is clipped as close as a military buzz cut. Army last beat Navy in 1977; its record against the Midshipmen since 1973 stands at 1-9-1...

In 1973 the Black Knights went 0-10, losing to Navy 51-0. Homer Smith followed Cahill and introduced a passing offense that produced the only winning season in the last decade: 7-4 in 1977. The next year, however, Army went 4-6-1, losing to Navy 28-0. Smith was gone. He retreated to the Harvard School of Divinity and later resurfaced as offensive coordinator at UCLA. His dismissal was a bitter one "He didn't fit the image of Army football" - one Army official said, and Smith later took a list of alleged violations to the NCAA. The NCAA investigated and issued a warning, telling Army to clean up its record-keeping.

Meanwhile, Army hired Lou Saban. "That was one of our worst mistakes," said Col. Al Vanderbush, a deputy athletic director who played guard and linebacker on Army's last undefeated team: the 1958 squad that finished No. 3 in the nation with Heisman Trophy winner Pete Dawkins in the backfield.

"With Saban's track record and his age (57), why in the world did we hire him if we were trying to rebuild?" Vanderbush asked. "Then when he quit after one year he has a habit of doing that, we hired his assistant, Ed Cavanaugh. He (Ed) just didn't have the charisma; as far as I know, nobody here liked him."

From 1980 through 1982, Cavanaugh's teams went 10-21-2, continuing the trend that was set in motion after Blaik (121-33-10) retired. "In the 50's, we were comparable to the best teams in the country, but our program stagnated as other programs started getting better and better," Vanderbush said.

For a while, there was a Vietnam excuse, which sufficed. But then George Welsh arrived at Navy in 1973 and took the Midshipmen to three bowl games. Air Force took it from there, winning the 1982 Hall of Fame Bowl and the 1983 Independence Bowl. Ullrich spent 11 years at Navy, five as an assistant athletic director, before becoming the Army athletic director in 1980. "When I got here, we were 10 years behind the Naval Academy," said Ullrich, 56.

Army players were still required to go to class Saturday mornings before home games, getting out of Chemical Engineering 301 at 11 a.m. and running up the hillside to Michie in time for pregame warm-ups. They had no weight program; they waited in line with the rest of the Cadets at the academy's only weight room. They had no training table. Ullrich pushed for the new weight room and locker room complex. He adjusted players' schedules so they take fewer credit hours in the fall, ' more in the spring. He eliminated the Saturday morning classes.

Finally, he hired Jim Young. The road winds up the hill to Michie Stadium, passing the Cadet Chapel and taking a sharp right at Lusk Reservoir. There, at the bend, stands a statue as striking as Washington's Iwo Jima Memorial. Called "The American Soldier," it captures three GIs straining forward into battle. "Presented to the Corps of Cadets," the inscription reads. "The lives and destinies of valiant Americans are entrusted to your care and leadership."

All Cadets take classes in leadership, through the psychology department, the military science department, the philosophy department. Upon graduation, they are appointed second lieutenants in the regular U.S. Army.

"Military folks like to look to a confident leader," Vanderbush said. "People here at the academy, from the Cadets to the instructors to the career military men, became kind of cynical when they saw the lack of leadership in some of our recent football coaches." Jim Gentile is a senior linebacker who leads Army in tackles this season.

"You meet a lot of leaders here; you know what it takes. As soon as Coach Young got here, we knew it would be different." Karl Heineman, a senior offensive tackle, started all 11 games as a sophomore in Cavanaugh's first season. "In the last game, he called me No. 62," Heineman said.

"Coach Young knew all our name-; by the second day of practice." Some at the academy doubted Ullrich's judgment when he hired Young. They wanted someone with experience at a service academy preferably a West Point graduate. Ullrich, however, refused and looked to Young's credentials. He worked nine years as an assistant to Bo Schembechler. First at Miami of Ohio and then at Michigan.

In 1972, he left Michigan to become head coach at Arizona. He compiled a 31-13 record before becoming head coach at Purdue. Purdue had a great run with Young. Reaching three bowl games. Young, at 49, left coaching and took a year off as an associate athletic director at Purdue. Young hedged when asked why he gave up coaching and then one year later returned to the profession, at Army of all places.

"I thought I had quit coaching for good; I got rid of all my books." lie said. "But I missed the association with the players and coaches, and 1 missed the ups and downs of (-very Saturday ... I like it here. You never have to worry about the kids going to class, yet you play to win."

Last season, Young's first, his team went 2-9, so he scrapped the pro-style offense he installed at Purdue and reverted to the wishbone. "The Air Force Academy was having great success with it, and we had similar personnel," he said. Strapped by Army's entrance requirements, Young knew he'd have to make do with a slower offensive line more suited to run-blocking," Young generously commented.

The new Army coach started the grand experiment last spring. At the time. Nate Sassaman was a back-up defensive back, and Doug Black was trying to make the varsity after being cut as a freshman and spending his sophomore season in the Army intramural league. Both played the wishbone in high school, so Young made Sassaman his starting quarterback and Black his starting fullback.

When trying to explain Army's sudden success this year, Young flinches at the mention of the Army-Navy game, preferring to put it on hold until Thanksgiving weekend. But to understand football at West Point is to realize why this year's prospects for a bowl trip haven't sent the Army brass into frenzied celebration. "I don't want to sound too ho-hum; we are thrilled with how the season is going," Ullrich said after the victory over Air Force. "There was lots of hugging and cheering, but it wasn't boisterous because here, our season is not going to be complete unless we beat Navy."

No wonder Army's mascot is a mule. The stubborn streak inherent among the straight-backed officers at West Point greatly aided the decline and fall of Army football. They were Cadets in the halycon days when Doc Blanchard and Glenn Davis led coach Earl Blaik's troops to national championships in 1944 and 1945 - and they greeted Army's fall from grace with much wringing of hands. But they wouldn't change.

Tradition is everything at West Point, where the "Long Gray Line" of graduates includes Lee, Jackson, Douglass C. MacArthur, George S. Patton and Dwight D. Eisenhower. The place has a certain timeless grace, a sense of history as tangible as the musty smell of the Cadet Chapel's stone foundation. "It's a thrill for me to live here; 20 yards from my house are the ruins of a Revolutionary War fort," Young said. "It's like Camelot. A place that doesn't exist anymore." That's the romantic view. Those involved with Army football after Blaik retired in 1958 saw the program get trapped in a time warp it took decades to escape.

The latest bowl talk draws a cynical smile from Tom Cahill, who coached Army to a 40-39-2 record from 1966 to 1973. In his first season, the Black Knights went 8-2 and Cahill was proclaimed coach of the year. In 1967 Army beat Pitt to go 8-1 and earn an invitation to the Sugar Bowl. But the Secretary of the Army, the honorable Stanley R. Resor, declined the bid. "Because American troops were fighting in Vietnam, he decided it was inappropriate for Army to play in the carnival like atmosphere of New Orleans," said Cahill, who now does radio color commentary of all Army games for WNBR in Beacon, N.Y.

After the 2-9 season, Jim Young brought Army a lot of smiles going 8-3, then 9-3, then 8-5 before a losing season in 1987 5-6. He finished up as you will soon see with a great 9-3 season in 1988 followed by two 6-5 seasons before he turned the reins over to Bob Sutton in 1991. I can still smell the fresh air.

1983 Army West Point Cadets Football Coach Jim Young

The Army Cadets football team represented the United States Military Academy in the 1983 college football season. It was Army's ninety-fourth season of intercollegiate football. They were led by Coach Jim Young in his first of eight seasons as head coach of the Cadets. As an independent football entity, the Army team had a terrible record of 2-9-0

Overall, the Cadets compiled a 2-9-0 record. They finished with another poor season. Army pitched no shutouts and had no shutouts thrown against them. They were outscored by their opponents 304 to 140. In the annual Army–Navy Game, the Cadets lost to the Midshipmen by a 42-13 score.

This year's opener was on Sept 10 vs Colgate at home. The Cadets lost to the Red Raiders in a close match L (13-15). Other than those games played in neutral fields, all Army home games were played on the West Point campus at Michie Stadium in West Point NY. On Sept 17 at Louisville's Cardinal Stadium in Louisville, KY, the Cardinals defeated the Cadets L (7–31).

With no victories yet in the season, Army determination helped the Cadets on Sept 24 to defeat the Dartmouth Big Green in a close, hard fought match W (13-12). On Oct 1, the Cadets lost to Harvard at Harvard Stadium in Allston, MA L (21–24). The Cadets second and last win of the season came on Oct 8 v Rutgers at home W (20-12).

On Oct 15, the Cadets took on Gerry Faust's Notre Dame Fighting Irish at Giants Stadium in East Rutherford, NJ and were defeated by the Irish L (0–42). Then, on Oct 22, at home, Lehigh's Mountain Hawks defeated the Cadets in a one-point game L (12-13). On Oct 29 at Air Force's Falcon Stadium in Colorado Springs, CO in the Commander-in-Chief's Trophy) game, the Fighting Falcons beat the Cadets L (20–41). On Nov 5 at home, Boston College defeated Army handily L (14–34). Then in a precursor to the Army-Navy game, the Pitt game was always a tough one. This year was not different played at Pitt Stadium in Pittsburgh, PA, the Panthers defeated the Cadets L (7–38)

On November 25, in the season finale Army-Navy-Game, the Midshipmen beat the Cadets in Rose Bowl Stadium in Pasadena, CA in the Commander-in-Chief's Trophy game L (13–42).

1984 Army West Point Cadets Football Coach Jim Young

The Army Cadets football team represented the United States Military Academy in the 1984 college football season. It was Army's ninety-fifth season of intercollegiate football. They were led by Coach Jim Young in his second of eight seasons as head coach of the Cadets. As an independent football entity, the Army team had a fine record of 8-3-1

Overall, the Cadets compiled an 8-3-1 record. They finished with a fine season record. Army pitched no shutouts and had no shutouts thrown against them. They outscored their opponents 320 to 218. In the annual Army–Navy Game, the Cadets defeated the Midshipmen by a 28-11 score. The Cadets also defeated Michigan State, 10–6, in the 1984 Cherry Bowl.

This year's home opener was on Sept 15 vs Colgate. The Cadets got the season off the right way with a convincing win against the Red Raiders W (41-15). Other than those games played in neutral fields, all Army home games were played on the West Point campus at Michie Stadium in West Point NY. On Sept 22, at Tennessee's Neyland Stadium in Knoxville, TN, the Volunteers played the Cadets to a tie T (24–24). On Sept 29 at home, the Cadets defeated the Duke Blue Devils W 13–9. With their best start in years at 3-0, on Oct 6, Army kept the streak going with their 4th win in a row v Harvard W (33-11).

Finally, the Cadets lost their first game of the season on Oct 13 to Rutgers L (7-14). On Oct 20, they got back on track by defeating Penn at home W (48–13). On Oct 27, after a trip to the Carrier Dome, Syracuse's new Stadium, the Cadets lost to the Orangemen L (16-27). Then, on Nov 3, Army defeated Air Force at home W (24-12). The following week in a tough game v Boston College on Nov

10, the Cadets lost to the Eagles L (31-45). On Nov 17 vs Montana in a game played in Tokyo Japan's Mirage Bowl, the Cadets won W (45-31)

On Dec 1 in the season finale, the Army-Navy-Game, the Cadets beat the Midshipmen at Veterans Stadium in Philadelphia, PA (Commander-in-Chief's Trophy) W (28–11)

In their first post-season Bowl game, the Cherry Bowl vs. Michigan State at the Pontiac Silverdome in Pontiac, MI, the Cadets prevailed W (10–6). Despite a fine year, Army was unranked by the major polling units.

1985 Army West Point Cadets Football Coach Jim Young

The Army Cadets football team represented the United States Military Academy in the 1985 college football season – from 1890. It was Army's ninety-sixth season of intercollegiate football. They were led by Coach Jim Young in his third of eight seasons as head coach of the Cadets. As an independent football entity, the Army team had a fine record of 9-3-0

Overall, the Cadets compiled a 9-3-0 record. They finished with a fine season record. Army pitched no shutouts and had no shutouts thrown against them. They outscored their opponents 396 to 232. In the annual Army–Navy Game, the Cadets were defeated by the Midshipmen by a 7-17 score. The Cadets also defeated Illinois in the Peach Bowl, 31-29.

This year's opener was on Sept 14 vs Western Michigan at home. The Cadets got the season off the right way with a convincing win against the Broncos W (48-6). Other than those games played in neutral fields, all Army home games were played on the West Point campus at Michie Stadium in West Point NY. On September 21 at home, the Cadets defeated the Rutgers Scarlet Knights W (20–16). Then on Sept 28 at Penn in a game played at Franklin Field in Philadelphia, PA, the Cadets defeated the Quakers W (41-3). The following week on Oct 5, at home the Cadets defeated the Yale Bulldogs W (59-16)

Then, on Oct 12 Boston College came to Michie Stadium and were defeated by Army W 45–14. On Oct 19, Army had a close loss against Gerry Faust's Fighting Irish in a game played at Notre Dame Stadium in Notre Dame, IN L (10–24). On Oct 26, Colgate played a tough game against Army but the Red Raiders lost in a shootout by just two points to the Cadets W (45–43). Next on Nov 2, at home, the Cadets defeated the Holy Cross Crusaders W (34–12).

On Nov 9, the Cadets were beaten handily by the Air Force Fighting Falcons at Falcon Stadium in Colorado Springs, CO (Commander-in-Chief's Trophy). L (7–45). On Nov 16, Army defeated Memphis State at home in a blowout, W (49-7).

On Dec 7 in the season finale, the Army-Navy-Game, the Midshipmen beat the Cadets at Veterans Stadium in Philadelphia, PA (Commander-in-Chief's Trophy) L (7-17).

In their second post-season Bowl game in a row—The Peach Bowl vs. Illinois at Atlanta–Fulton County Stadium in Atlanta, GA, Army prevailed by a slim margin W (31–29)

1986 Army West Point Cadets Football Coach Jim Young

The Army Cadets football team represented the United States Military Academy in the 1986 college football season. It was Army's ninety-seventh season of intercollegiate football. They were led by Coach Jim Young in his fourth of eight seasons as head coach of the Cadets. As an independent football entity, the Army team had a winning record of 6-5-0

Overall, the Cadets compiled a 6-5-0 record. They finished with a respectable season record. Army pitched no shutouts and had no shutouts thrown against them. They were outscored by their opponents 292 to 276. In the annual Army–Navy Game, the Cadets defeated the Midshipmen 27-7 score. There was no Bowl Game this year.

This year's opener was on Sept 13 vs Syracuse at home. The Cadets got the season off the right way with a win against the Orangemen W (33-28). Other than those games played in neutral fields, all Army home games were played on the West Point campus at Michie Stadium in West Point NY. On Sept 20 at Northwestern's Dyche Stadium in Evanston, IL, the Wildcats defeated the Cadets L (18–25). On Sept 27, at home, Wake Forest delivered another losing blow to the Cadets in a lopsided loss L (14–49). Next on Oct 4, my Wedding Anniversary, at Yale's Yale Bowl in New Haven, CT, the Cadets defeated the Bulldogs, W (41–24).

Then on Oct 11 at Tennessee's Neyland Stadium in Knoxville, TN, the Cadets pulled out a close one W (25–21). Then a week later, the Cadets could not keep up with the crusaders of Holy Cross in a close loss L (14–17). Army suffered another loss on Oct 25 vs. Rutgers in Giants Stadium in East Rutherford, NJ L (7–35). The losses kept coming as Boston College defeated Army on Nov 1 at home L (20-27). Army recovered from the three-fall on Nov 8, defeating Air Force at home (Commander-in-Chief's Trophy) W (21–11). On Nov 15, in a scoring shootout, the Cadets defeated the Lafayette Leopards at home W (56–48).

On Dec 4 in the annual season finale, the Army-Navy-Game, the Cadets defeated the Midshipmen at Veterans Stadium in Philadelphia, PA (Commander-in-Chief's Trophy) W (27-7).

1987 Army West Point Cadets Football Coach Jim Young

The Army Cadets football team represented the United States Military Academy in the 1987 college football season. It was Army's ninety-eighth season of intercollegiate football. They were led by Coach Jim Young in his fifth of eight seasons as head coach of the Cadets. As an independent football entity, the Army team had a losing record of 5-6-0

Overall, the Cadets compiled a 5-6-0 record. They finished with a poor season record. Army pitched no shutouts and had no shutouts thrown against them. The Cadets were outscored by their opponents 277 to 223. In the annual Army–Navy Game, the Cadets defeated the Midshipmen by a 17-7 score. There was no Bowl Game this year.

This year's opener was on Sept 12 vs Holy Cross at home. The Cadets did not get the season off the right way and suffered a loss against the Crusaders L 24-34). Other than those games played in neutral fields, all Army home games were played on the West Point campus at Michie Stadium in West Point NY. On Sept 19 at Kansas State's KSU Stadium in Manhattan, KS, the Cadets beat the Wildcats W (41–14). Then on Sept 26 at home, Army defeated The Citadel W (48–6).

The next loss was Wake Forest in a close home match on Oct 3, L (13–17). The Eagles made it two losses in a row on Oct 10 at Boston College's Alumni Stadium in Chestnut Hill, MA, L (24–29) Three losses in a row came too quickly on Oct 17 as Colgate won in a nail-biter over the Army L (20–22)

Nobody wanted to be able to spell four losses in a row but had to do so on Oct 24 as a determined Rutgers squad beat the Cadets at home L (14–27). Temple helped the Cadets break the string of losses as Army beat the Owls at home W (17–7). Air Force put it together to beat the Army on Nov 7 at Falcon Stadium in Colorado Springs, CO (Commander-in-Chief's Trophy) L (10–27). That was it for 1987 losses. There would be two more wins. On Nov 14, in a shootout, the Cadets defeated the Leopards of Lafayette W (49–37).

On Dec 5 in The Army-Navy-Game, the Cadets defeated the Midshipmen at Veterans Stadium in Philadelphia, PA (Commander-in-Chief's Trophy) W (17–3).

1988 Army West Point Cadets Football Coach Jim Young

The Army Cadets football team represented the United States Military Academy in the 1988 college football season. It was Army's ninety-ninth season of intercollegiate football. They were led by Coach Jim Young in his sixth of eight seasons as head coach of the Cadets. As an independent football entity, the Army team had a nice winning record of 9-3-0.

Overall, the Cadets compiled a 9-3-0 record. They finished with a great season record. Army pitched no shutouts and had no shutouts thrown against them. They Cadets outscored their opponents 336 to 226. In the annual Army–Navy Game, the Cadets defeated the

Midshipmen by a 20-15 score. They also lost a very close game (one point) to Alabama by a score of 28 to 29 in the 1988 Sun Bowl.

This year's opener was on Sept 19 vs Holy Cross at home. The Cadets got the season off the right way with a nice win against the Crusaders W (23-3). Other than those games played in neutral fields, all Army home games were played on the West Point campus at Michie Stadium in West Point NY. Traveling to the West Coast on Sept 17, to Husky Stadium in Seattle, WA the Cadets were defeated by the Washington Huskies L (17-31) On Sept 24 at home. The Cadets defeated the Northwestern Wildcats W (23–7). Bucknell was next on Oct 1 as the Cadets smothered the Bisons in a blowout W (58-10).

On Oct 8 at Yale's Yale Bowl in New Haven, CT, the Cadets beat the Bulldogs W (33–18). Next up was Lafayette at home on Oct 15. The Cadets played tough in a close match and got the W by a score of W (24-17) On Oct 22 vs. Rutgers in Giants Stadium, East Rutherford, NJ, the Cadets hit their marks and came home with the victory W (34–24). On Nov 5, at home for (Commander-in-Chief's Trophy) vs Air Force, Army did better than the Fighting Falcons and the Cadets won the match W (28–15).

On Nov 12, The Vanderbilt Commodores tried to beat the Army Cadets at home but failed by a score of 24–19. Then, on Nov 19 at Boston College, playing in Lansdowne Road • Dublin, Ireland in the (Emerald Isle Classic), it was too much Irish all at once for the Cadets in a loss L (24–38).

On Dec 12, the Army-Navy-Game ended the football season for both Army and Navy. In this game, the Cadets defeated the Midshipmen at Veterans Stadium in Philadelphia, PA (Commander-in-Chief's Trophy) W (20-5).

Back in action again on December 24 in El Paso TX, the site of the 1988 Sun Bowl, in the post Bear Bryant years at Alabama, this Bill Curry coached Crimson Tide squad barely defeated our Army Cadets in the 1988 Sun Bowl L (28-29).

1989 Army West Point Cadets Football Coach Jim Young

The Army Cadets football team represented the United States Military Academy in the 1989 college football season. It was Army's one hundredth season of intercollegiate football. They were led by Coach Jim Young in his seventh of eight seasons as head coach of the Cadets. As an independent football entity, the Army team had a winning record of 6-5-0.

Overall, the Cadets compiled a 6-5-0 record this season. They finished with a respectable season record but every Army fan of course was looking for more. Army pitched no shutouts and had no shutouts thrown against them. They Cadets outscored their opponents 316 to 212. In the annual Army–Navy Game, the Cadets were defeated by the Midshipmen by a 19-17 score.

This year's opener was on Sept 16 vs Syracuse at the fantastic Carrier Dome in Syracuse NY. As a football fan for many years, while at IBM for about twenty years, I ran a trip on behalf of the IBM Club and then after IBM I still ran the bus trip. There was nothing the kids on the bus liked better than parking our bus next to the Army bus and watching the Cadets in full regalia in the parking lot across from the stadium. No matter how cold the weather was later in the season, it was always 69 degrees in the Carrier Dome.

The Cadets began the season with a tough loss against the Orangemen L (7-10). Other than those games played in neutral fields, all Army home games were played on the West Point campus at Michie Stadium in West Point NY. Traveling On Sept 23, at home, the Cadets defeated Wake Forest in a close match W (14–10). Then, on Sept 30 at home, Harvard and Army kept pounding at each other but the Cadets pounded twice as hard to defeat the Harvard Crimson W (56-28).

On Sept 16 at Duke's Wallace Wade Stadium in Durham, NC, the Cadets lost a close match to the Blue Devils L (29–35). Gaining back their strength after the Duke loss, the Cadets found enough at home to pound the Holy Cross Crusaders W (45–9). Next up was the Lafayette Leopards on Oct 21 at home and the Cadets prevailed again W (34–20). Rutgers came in to Michie Stadium looking for a win but left with a kudo for a nice game played as the Cadets prevailed v the Scarlet Knights W (35-14).

On Nov 4, the flying academy got in the act for the (Commander-in-Chief's Trophy), at Air Force's Falcon Stadium in Colorado Springs, CO. The Air Force did not give an inch in this tough loss for the Cadets L (3–29). On Nov 11, Boston College took on the Cadets at home and the Eagles got the best of the game L (17–24). On Nov 18 at home, Colgate got a whooping from the Army W (59–14)

On Dec 9, always late in the season, the Army-Navy-Game ended the football season for both Army and Navy. In this game, the Cadets were defeated by the Midshipmen at Giants Stadium in East Rutherford, NJ (Commander-in-Chief's Trophy) L (17-19).

Best Army Navy Game # 10

Occurring in the same year (1989) that many of the players in this year's contest were born, Navy junior Frank Schenk kicked a 32-yard field goal with 11 seconds to play to give the Midshipmen a 19-17 victory.

The result snapped a run of three straight losses by Navy, allowing the team's seniors to graduate from Annapolis with a win against their most heated rivals.

The joy was short-lived, however, as coach Elliot Uzelac was fired the next day with a year remaining on his contract. He found out about his dismissal the morning of a planned celebration—one that included fellow students cheerfully throwing snowballs at players—but did not tell the team until after the party had concluded.

Uzelach compiled a record of 8-25 in three seasons with the Middies, but no doubt left on a memorable note.

1990 Army West Point Cadets Football Coach Jim Young

The Army Cadets football team represented the United States Military Academy in the 1988 college football season. It was Army's

one-hundred-first season of intercollegiate football. They were led by Coach Jim Young in his eighth and last of seven seasons as head coach of the Cadets. As an independent football entity, the Army team had a winning record of 6-5.

Overall, the Cadets compiled a 9-3-0 record. They finished with an OK season record. Army pitched one shutout (Lafayette 56-0) and had no shutouts thrown against them. The Cadets outscored their opponents 295 to 264. In the annual Army–Navy Game, the Cadets defeated the Midshipmen by a 30-20 score. Knowing the importance of this game to Army, it was one of Young's great achievements in his final year as coach.

As an independent football entity, the Army team had a winning record of 6-5-0 in Jim Young's final season. Young had a masterful tenure while at Army and he is credited with having resurrected the program from where it had been.

Please enjoy this AP article which does a crisp summary of Jim Young's years at Army. After this we will pick up with the games of the season.

Army Coach Jim Young Will Retire

August 28, 1990 | From Associated Press

WEST POINT, N.Y. — Jim Young, Army football coach for the last seven years, said today that he will retire after this season because of personal reasons.

Young, 55, will be replaced next year by Bob Sutton, 39, the associate head coach and defensive coordinator. Sutton, who came to Army in 1983, the same year as Young, has never been a head coach.

Young, who has resurrected the Army football program, has compiled a record of 45-34-1. Overall, including stints at Purdue and Arizona, his record is 114-66-2.

After this season, Young will remain at West Point as a member of the Performance Enhancement Program staff.

Since 1984, when Young installed the wishbone offense, the Cadets have ranked no lower than fifth in rushing offense in the nation. In the first year of the wishbone, they were No. 1 in rushing.

Big Bravo to a great coach – Jim Young!

Games of the 1990 Season

This year's opener was on Sept 15 vs Holy Cross at home. The Cadets got the season off the right way with a nice win against the Crusaders W (24-7). Other than those games played in neutral fields, all Army home games were played on the West Point campus at Michie Stadium in West Point NY. On Sept 22 at home vs. VMI, the Cadets prevailed W (41–17). At 2-0 In the third game at Wake Forest played in Groves Stadium Winston-Salem, NC, the Cadets were beaten by the Demon Deacons L (14–52). Duke's Blue Devils beat the Cadets at home a week later on Oct 6 L (16-17). This was quickly followed by the third loss on Oct 13 at Boston College's Alumni Stadium Chestnut Hill, MA L (20–41).

On Oct 20, the Cadets got their oomph back by shutting out Lafayette in a blowout game W (56-0). It was the first shutout in years for the Cadets. On Oct 27, at home, the Cadets lost to the Orangemen of Syracuse L (14-26). Then, the Cadets found a W at Rutgers in a close match W (35-21). On Nov 10, at home, the Cadets lost to the Fighting Falcons of the Air Force. (Commander-in-Chief's Trophy) L (3-15). On Nov 17 at Vanderbilt's Vanderbilt Stadium • in Nashville, TN, the Cadets picked up their fifth win of the season W (42–38).

On December 8 in the annual (Army–Navy Game/Commander-in-Chief's Trophy), the Cadets defeated the Midshipmen, which put a smile on the faces a lot of Army supporters. The game was played at Veterans Stadium in Philadelphia, and the final score was W (30–20)

1990 Player Highlights Michael Mayweather B

With Doc Blanchard, Glenn Davis, and Pete Dawkins, Mayweather's very accomplished predecessors rushing to Heisman seasons, pundits are asking why Michael Mayweather didn't hoist the award himself. He finished 10th in Heisman voting in 1990. However, in his four seasons at West Point, Mayweather completely rewrote the running back record books as if the three Heisman winners did not compete. Mayweather was that good.

Michael Mayweather Army

He is the only Army running back to rush for three 1,000-yard seasons. A gifted runner, he'd already surpassed Glenn Davis' record career rushing mark of 2,959 by the end of his junior season and set the single-season rushing standard to 1,338 yards in his season year. Among his other accolades, Mayweather holds the Army mark in all-purpose yards (5,594) and 100-yard games (21).

Chapter 16 Coaches Bob Sutton & Todd Berry 1991-2002

Sutton   Coach # 31
Berry   Coach # 32

Year	Coach	Record	Conference	Record
1991	Bob Sutton	4-7-0	Indep	4-7-0)
1992	Bob Sutton	5-6-0	Indep	5-6-0
1993	Bob Sutton	6-5-0	Indep	6-5-0
1994	Bob Sutton	4-7-0	Indep	4-7-0
1995	Bob Sutton	5-5-1	Indep	5-5-1
1996	Bob Sutton	10-2-0	Indep	10-2-0
1997	Bob Sutton	4-7-0	Indep	4-7-0
1998	Bob Sutton	3-8-0	C-USA	2-4-0
1999	Bob Sutton	3-8-0	C-USA	1-5-0
2000	Todd Berry	1-10-0	C-USA	1-6-0
2001	Todd Berry	3-8-0	C-USA	2-5-0
2002	Todd Berry	1-11-0	C-USA	1-7-0
2003	Todd Berry	0-7	C-USA	0-4-0

Coach Bob Sutton happy with the team

Bob Sutton is a great coach. Sutton served as the head football coach at the United States Military Academy from 1991 to 1999, compiling a record of 44–55–1. He had one phenomenally great year and the rest were medsa medsa. Before becoming head coach at Army in 1991, Sutton spent eight years as an assistant coach at Army.

His nine-year tenure as the head football coach at Army (1991 to 1999) is second in length only to Earl "Red" Blaik. His 44–55–1 record was not the best but he is well known for leading the 1996 Army squad to a 10–2 record, an appearance in the Independence Bowl, and a top 25 finish in both major polls. For his efforts that season, Sutton was awarded the Bobby Dodd Coach of the Year Award.

1991 Army West Point Cadets Football Coach Bob Sutton

The Army Cadets football team represented the United States Military Academy in the 1991 college football season. It was Army's one hundred-second season of intercollegiate football. They were led by Coach Bob Sutton in his first of nine seasons as head coach of the Cadets. As an independent football entity, the Army team had a losing record of 4-7-0.

Coach Bob Sutton at Work

Overall, the Cadets compiled a 4-7-0 record. They finished with a poor season record. Army pitched one shutout (against Akron 19-0), and had one shutouts thrown against them (Air Force—0-25). The Cadets were outscored by their opponents 226 to 196. In the annual Army–Navy Game, the Cadets lost to the Midshipmen by a 3-24 score.

This year's opener was on Sept 14 vs Colgate at home. The Cadets got the season off the right way with a shootout win against the Red Raiders W (51-22). Other than those games played in neutral fields, all Army home games were played on the West Point campus at Michie Stadium in West Point NY. On Sept 21, at home. The Cadets were defeated by the Tar Heels of North Carolina L (12-20) Then on Sept 28 at home, the Cadets beat Harvard's Crimson W (21-20). On Oct 5, the Army lost to The State University of New Jersey (Rutgers Scarlet Knights) in a close battle L (12-14). This was followed one week later on Oct 12 by a tough loss against The Citadel L (14-20).

On Oct 19, at Louisville's Cardinal Stadium • in Louisville, KY, the Cadets picked up the win W (37–12). Next up was Boston College on Oct 26 at home and the Eagles defeated the Cadets L 17-28) On Nov 2 at home, the Cadets lost to Vanderbilt L (10–41). On Nov 9, the Army was shut out by Air Force at Falcon Stadium Colorado Springs, CO (Commander-in-Chief's Trophy) L (0–25). On Nov 16, Army, 4-6, shut out a Div. I-A opponent for the first time since a 27-0 victory over Navy in 1969. Akron, 4-6, had not won on the road this season. The final score was W (0-19).

November 16 Akron Michie Stadium • West Point, NY W 19–0
December 7   vs. Navy   Veterans Stadium • Philadelphia, PA (Army-Navy game/Commander-in-Chief's Trophy)   L 3–24

On December 7 in the annual (Army–Navy Game/Commander-in-Chief's Trophy), the Midshipmen got the best of the Cadets L (3-24) The game was played at Veterans Stadium in Philadelphia.

1992 Army West Point Cadets Football Coach Bob Sutton

The Army Cadets football team represented the United States Military Academy in the 1992 college football season. It was Army's one hundred-second season of intercollegiate football. They were led by Coach Bob Sutton in his second of nine seasons as head coach of the Cadets. As an independent football entity, the Army team had a losing record of 5-6-0.

Overall, the Cadets compiled a 5-6-0 record. They finished with a poor season record. Army pitched no shutouts, and had no shutouts thrown against them. The Cadets were outscored by their opponents 251 to 225. In the annual Army–Navy Game, the Cadets defeated the Midshipmen by a 25-24 score.

This year's opener was on Sept 12 vs Holy Cross at home. The Cadets got the season off the right way with a win against the Crusaders W (17-7). Other than those games played in neutral fields, all Army home games were played on the West Point campus at Michie Stadium in West Point NY. The next week on Sept 19, the Cadets lost to the Tar Heels at North Carolina's Kenan Memorial Stadium Chapel Hill, NC L (9–22). Then On Sept 26 at home, Army lost by one point to The Citadel L (14–15). In another nail biter, the two weeks later on Oct 10, Army beat Lafayette at home W (38-36).

On Oct 17, a tough Rutgers team pounded Army at Giants Stadium in East Rutherford, NJ, L (10–45). Another loss came on Oct 24 at Wake Forest's Groves Stadium in Winston-Salem, NC L (7–23). Then on Halloween, 1992, at home, Army trounced Eastern Michigan W (57–17). Next loss came against Air Force on Nov 7 at home (Commander-in-Chief's Trophy) L (3–7). The Cadets would win two of their last three games. First up was Northern Illinois on Nov 14 at home W (21–14). Next was Boston College at home on Nov 21 for a loss L (24–41).

And, so on December 5 in the Army Navy Game, the Cadets defeated the Midshipmen at Veterans Stadium Philadelphia, PA (Commander-in-Chief's Trophy Game) W (25–24).

1993 Army West Point Cadets Football Coach Bob Sutton

The Army Cadets football team represented the United States Military Academy in the 1993 college football season. It was Army's one hundred-third season of intercollegiate football. They were led by Coach Bob Sutton in his third of nine seasons as head coach of the

Cadets. As an independent football entity, the Army team had a winning record of 6-5-0.

Overall, the Cadets compiled a 6-5-0 record. They finished with a respectable season record. Army pitched one shutout (Colgate 30-0), and had no shutouts thrown against them. The Cadets outscored their opponents 289 to 243. In the annual Army–Navy Game, the Cadets defeated the Midshipmen by a 16-14 score.

This year's opener was on Sept 11 vs Colgate at home. The Cadets got the season off the right way with a shutout win against the Red Raiders W (30-0). Other than those games played in neutral fields, all Army home games were played on the West Point campus at Michie Stadium in West Point NY. The next week (Sept 11) Army lost to Duke L (21-42). On Sept 25 at home, Army beat VMI W (31-9) The next week at home against Akron, the Cadets won again W (35-14). Three in a row came on Oct 9 at Temple in Veterans Stadium in Philadelphia, PA W (56—21)

Rutgers broke the Army win streak at three on Oct 16 at Michie Stadium L (38-45). Boston College piled on another loss the following week on Oct 23 at Alumni Stadium Chestnut Hill, MA L (14–41). Then on Oct 30, Western Michigan made it three losses in a row for the Cadets at home L (7-20). On Nov 6, Air Force made it four season losses in a row at Falcon Stadium Colorado Springs, CO (Commander-in-Chief's Trophy) L (6–25). Before the Army Navy game, the Cadets began a mini-two-game win streak to close out the season. The first up was Lafayette on Nov 13. The Cadets defeated the Leopards at home W (35-12).

On December 5 in the Army Navy Game, a nail biter again, the Cadets defeated the Midshipmen at Giants Stadium East Rutherford, NJ (Commander-in-Chief's Trophy Game) W (16-14).

1994 Army West Point Cadets Football Coach Bob Sutton

The Army Cadets football team represented the United States Military Academy in the 1993 college football season. It was Army's one hundred-fifth season of intercollegiate football. They were led by Coach Bob Sutton in his fourth of nine seasons as head coach of the

Cadets. As an independent football entity, the Army team had a losing record of 4-7-0.

Overall, the Cadets compiled a 4-7-0 record. They finished with a poor season record. Army pitched no shutouts, and had no shutouts thrown against them. The Cadets were outscored by their opponents 252 to 215. In the annual Army–Navy Game, the Cadets defeated the Midshipmen by a 22-20 score.

This year's opener was on Sept 10 vs Holy Cross at home. The Cadets got the season off the right way with a blowout win against the Crusaders W (49-3). Other than those games played in neutral fields, all Army home games were played on the West Point campus at Michie Stadium in West Point NY. On Sept 15 at Duke's Wallace Wade Stadium in Durham, NC, the Blue Devils defeated the Cadets L (7–43). Then on at home on Sept 24, Temple beat Army by a field goal L (20-23). On Oct 1, at Wake Forest's Groves Stadium Winston-Salem, NC, the Demon Deacons got the best pf the Cadets. In its fourth loss in a row on Oct 8, the Cadets fell to Rutgers L 14-16).

Then it was Louisville at Michie for a nail biter Cadet win W (30-29). On Oct 22, the Citadel came in tough and lost by just one point giving the Cadets the W (25-24). Struggling over the years with BC, 1994 was no different as the Eagles of Boston College made short work of the Cadets again L (3-30). Air Force kept on enjoying its victory streak at home in Michie and the Cadets endured another loss to the Fighting Falcons L (6-10). Boston University, the less talented cousin to Boston College came in and would not give the Cadets a home win before the Army-Navy Game L (12-21)

On December 3 in the Army-Navy-Game, a nail biter again, the Cadets defeated the Midshipmen at Veterans Stadium Philadelphia PA (Army-Navy-Game/Commander-in-Chief's Trophy) W 22–20

1995 Army West Point Cadets Football Coach Bob Sutton

The Army Cadets football team represented the United States Military Academy in the 1995 college football season. It was Army's one hundred-sixth season of intercollegiate football. They were led by Coach Bob Sutton in his fifth of nine seasons as head coach of the

Cadets. As an independent football entity, the Army team had a break-even record of 5-5-1.

Overall, the Cadets compiled a 5-5-1 record. They finished with an OK season record. Army pitched no shutouts, and had no shutouts thrown against them. The Cadets were outscored by their opponents 325 to 211. In the annual Army–Navy Game, the Cadets defeated the Midshipmen by a 14-13 score.

This year's opener was on Sept 9 vs Lehigh at home. The Cadets got the season off the right way with a blowout win against the Mountain Hawks W (42-9). Other than those games played in neutral fields, all Army home games were played on the West Point campus at Michie Stadium in West Point NY. On Sept 16, the Duke Blue Devils defeated the Cadets L (21-23). On Sept 23, the Cadets lost again at Washington L (13-21).

Next was the Rice Owls, who played the Cadets to a tie, on Sept 30 T (21-21). Next up was Lou Holtz's Notre Dame Fighting Irish who played the Cadets to an almost tie but the Irish got the win L (27-28)

This year, the Cadets were able to put away the other Irish guys from Boston, Boston College without all the work it took to lost to Notre Dame. On Oct 21, the Cadets beat BC's Eagles in a blowout W (49-7). Go Cadets! The Cadets had begun a powerful win streak that began with BC and continued through this Colgate encounter.

In another unprecedented blowout, the Cadets destroyed the Red Raiders of Colgate. It was short lived as East Carolina mounted an attack that was enough to defeat the Army team on Nov 4, L (25-31). Next up was the new nemesis of the Service Academies, Air Force, and the Fighting Falcons kept their win streak against the Cadets going in this latest L (20-38) win. Army got their moxie back on Nov 18 when they would not stop against Bucknell in a nice victory W (37-6).

The Bucknell win got the Army ready to keep winning and with the next game being long-time nemesis Navy, the practice game helped the Cadets focus.

On December 2 in the Army-Navy-Game, an even closer nail biter, the Cadets defeated the Midshipmen at Veterans Stadium Philadelphia PA (Army-Navy-Game/Commander-in-Chief's Trophy) W 14-13).

1996 Army West Point Cadets Football Coach Bob Sutton

The Army Cadets football team represented the United States Military Academy in the 1996 college football season. It was Army's one hundred-seventh season of intercollegiate football. They were led by Coach Bob Sutton in his sixth of nine seasons as head coach of the Cadets. As an independent football entity, the Army team had a fine regular season record of 10-1-0. With the Bowl Game, it was a 10-2-0 record

Overall, the Cadets compiled a 10-2-0 record. They finished with an excellent season record – the best in thirty years. Yet, with such a great record, Army pitched no shutouts, and had no shutouts thrown against them. The Cadets outscored their opponents 379 to 224. In the annual Army–Navy Game, the Cadets defeated the Midshipmen again, by a larger margin yet it was just four points. Navy and Army always played best against each other. In such a season with a few losses, somebody plays better than your team. In this case, after losing to Syracuse near the end of the season, 17-42, Army lost to Auburn, 32–29, in the 1996 Independence Bowl.

This year's opener was on Sept 14 vs Ohio at home. The Cadets got the season off the right way with a win W (27-20) (30,500 fans). Other than those games played in neutral fields, all Army home games were played on the West Point campus at Michie Stadium in West Point NY. On Sept 21, the Cadets knocked off the Duke Blue Devils W (35-17). On Sept 28, at North Texas's Texas Stadium • in Irving, TX, the Cadets prevailed W (27–10). Then, on Oct 5, Yale came back to Michie Stadium to be defeated by the Cadets W (39–13). On Oct 12, at home, the Cadets finished off another opponent that had been a nemesis in the prior years, W (42-21) Rutgers lost big at Giants Stadium in East Rutherford, NJ before a small crowd of 19,101.

On Oct 19, the Cadets whipped Tulane at home W (34-10). On Oct 26, at Miami (OH)'s Yager Stadium Oxford, OH, Army was the victor W 27–7 before 16,543. On Nov 2, Lafayette came with guns a blazing but in this 10-1 regular season year Army was enjoying, the Cadets snuffed out their guns and turned in a double your bet win W (42-21) at home before 39,269. On Nov 9, Air Force finally could not withstand the constant pressure from Army and the Fighting Falcons had to give up a loss to the Cadets at home in the (Commander-in-Chief's Trophy) W (23–7) before a max crowd of 41,251 at Michie.

On Nov 16, at 6:00 p.m., Syracuse was in the top twenty and they were gunning for Army to get to the championship consideration area. Army was # 22 and undefeated and ready to block #19 Syracuse no matter how many men it took. The game was played at the Carrier Dome in Winter weather but in 69-degree comfort in Syracuse, NY. Army could not keep up and lost the game L (17–42) before 49,257. It was an exciting game because of the stakes.

On December 7 in the Army-Navy-Game, in a close game as usual, the #23 ranked Cadets defeated the Midshipmen at Veterans Stadium Philadelphia PA (Army-Navy-Game/Commander-in-Chief's Trophy) W 28-24) before 69,238.

Best Army Navy Game # 9

In a matchup featuring two teams headed for bowls, Army defeated Navy, 28-24, following a late defensive stand.

Headed for the Poulan Weedeater Independence Bowl, the Cadets stopped the Jeep Eagle Aloha Bowl-bound Midshipmen eight times inside the 10, highlighting the final four minutes of the tight contest. After falling behind 21-3 in the second quarter (21-13 at the half), the game turned for Army early in the third quarter on an 81-yard touchdown run by Bobby Williams. However, the two-point conversion attempt failed, and kept Navy ahead, 21-19.

After the Midshipmen missed a 42-yard field goal try on its next series, the Cadets took a 25-21 lead on a 3-yard touchdown run by Demetrius Perry.

Navy's Tom Vanderhorst atoned for his previous miss by nailing a 31-yard field goal late in the third quarter to cut the deficit to a point. Army responded with a 21-yard field goal by J. Parker to give the game its final margin.

The Midshipmen drove inside the Cadets' 10 twice in the latter stages of the fourth quarter but were stopped each time.

Because Army qualified for a Bowl Game, the season was not over.

On December 31, New Years' Eve at 3:30 p.m. vs unranked Auburn, the #24 ranked Cadets lost this game— (The Independence Bowl)— played at Independence Stadium in Shreveport, LA. The final score was L (29–32). Army had played a fine game yet had lost. It would be a long time for another coach to take Army so far.

1997 Army West Point Cadets Football Coach Bob Sutton

The Army Cadets football team represented the United States Military Academy in the 1997 college football season. It was Army's one hundred-eighth season of intercollegiate football. They were led by Coach Bob Sutton in his seventh of nine seasons as head coach of the Cadets. As an independent football entity, the Army team had a losing season record of 4-7-0.

Overall, the Cadets compiled a 4-7-0 record. They finished with a poor season record after one of the best in the prior year. In 1997, Army pitched no shutouts, and had two shutouts thrown against them (Tulane 0-41) and (Air Force 0-24). The Cadets were outscored by their opponents 311 to 221. In the annual Army–Navy Game, after many years on top, the Midshipmen defeated the Cadets big time. Army might well have not showed up for the game. Navy and Army always played best against each other but not this year.

This year's opener was on Sept 6 vs Marshall at home. The Cadets got the season off the wrong way with a loss L (25-35) Other than those games played in neutral fields, all Army home games were played on the West Point campus at Michie Stadium in West Point NY. On Sept13, the Cadets beat Lafayette's Leopards W (41-14).

Then, on Sept 20, the Cadets took it on the chin from Duke's Blue Devils at Durham NC L (17-20) Then Miami of Ohio tried to put on the hurt to the Cadets and they succeeded L (14-38> On Oct 4, my wedding anniversary, the Cadets were shut out by Tulane in a big loss L (0-41)

On Oct 18, the Cadets beat Rutgers at home W (37-35). In another close win, the victim was Colgate a team that went down by a small margin to Army W (35-27). On Nov 8, Air Force pounded the Cadets in a shutout L (0-24) North Texas was ready to win on Nov 15 but lost nonetheless as the Cadets would not permit it W (25-14). Boston College felt the same way in the game, played in Chestnut Hill, Mass. The Eagles picked up a big win against the Cadets L (0-24)

On December 6 in the Army-Navy-Game, in an unusual runaway game, the Midshipmen whooped the Cadets L (7-39) in a big loss at Giants Stadium in East Rutherford NJ . (Army-Navy-Game/Commander-in-Chief's Trophy)

1998 Army West Point Cadets Football Coach Bob Sutton

The Army Cadets football team represented the United States Military Academy in the 1998 college football season. It was Army's one hundred-ninth season of intercollegiate football. They were led by Coach Bob Sutton in his eighth of nine seasons as head coach of the Cadets. As a new member of Conference USA, the Army team had a losing season record of 3-8-0.

Overall, the Cadets compiled a 3-8-0 record. The Cadets were 2-4 in the C-USA Conference. They finished with a very poor season record after one of the best just two years prior. In 1998, Army pitched no shutouts, and had no shutouts thrown against them. The Cadets were outscored by their opponents 325 to 257. In the annual Army–Navy Game, the Cadets defeated the Midshipmen in a close match W (34-30).

This year's opener was on Sept 12 vs Miami of Ohio at home. The Cadets got the season off the wrong way with a loss L (13-14) Other than those games played in neutral fields, all Army home games were played on the West Point campus at Michie Stadium in West Point NY. On Sept 19, at home, the Cadets defeated the Cincinnati Bearcats W (37-20). The second loss of the season came on Sept 26 when Rutgers from the Big East defeated Army in New Jersey L (15-27). Next up was a game at East Carolina on Oct 3 which resulted in another Army loss L (25-30). On Oct 10, at Houston the Army squad snapped back and gained the victory W (38-28).

On Oct 17, at home, Army lost to Southern Mississippi L (13-37). Defeated. The next week at Notre Dame, in a close match, the Fighting Irish defeated the Cadets L (17-20). On Nov 7 Air Force continued its dominance over Army at home L (7-35). This was followed at home on Nov 14 in the Army's fourth loss in a row. This time Tulane's green wave triumphed in a shootout L (35-49). At Louisville on Nov 21, the Army lost its fifth in a row L (25-35).

On December 5 in the Army-Navy-Game, the Cadets defeated the Midshipmen W (34-30) in a big win at Veterans Stadium in Philadelphia--(Army-Navy-Game/Commander-in-Chief's Trophy)

1999 Army West Point Cadets Football Coach Bob Sutton

The Army Cadets / Black Knights football team represented the United States Military Academy in the 1998 college football season. It was Army's one hundred-tenth season of intercollegiate football. They were led by Coach Bob Sutton in his ninth and last of nine seasons as head coach of the Cadets / Black Knights. As a new member of Conference USA, the Army team had a losing season record of 3-8-0.

Overall, the Black Knights compiled a 3-8-0 record. The Cadets were 1–5 in the C-USA Conference. They finished with a very poor season record after one of the best two years prior. In 1998, Army pitched no shutouts, and had two shutouts (Southern Miss – 0-24 and Air Force – 0-28) thrown against them. The Black Knights were outscored by their opponents 317 to 225. In the annual Army–Navy Game, the Cadets lost to the Midshipmen in a close match L (9-19)

Throughout the years from 1890 onward, Army teams were known as the "Cadets." In the 1940s, several papers called the football team "the Black Knights of the Hudson." From then on, "Cadets" and "Black Knights" were used interchangeably until this season (1999), when the team was officially nicknamed the Black Knights. Some pundits continue to call the team either Army or the Cadets and though not official, those names are most acceptable

Another change happened during this time. Between the 1998 and 2004 seasons, Army's football program was a member of Conference USA, but starting with the 2005 season Army reverted to its former independent status. Army competes with Navy and Air Force for the Commander-in-Chief's Trophy. When there is a tie, all are winners but the trophy stays in the last clean winner's locale.

This year's opener was on Sept 11 vs Wake Forest at home. The Cadets got the season off the wrong way again with a loss against the Demon Deacons L (15-34) Other than those games played in neutral fields, all Army home games were played on the West Point campus at Michie Stadium in West Point NY. On Sept 18, at Tulane, the Green Wave prevailed in a shootout L (28-48). On Sept 25, Army defeated Ball State W (41-21). Then on Oct 2, Army lost to East Carolina at home L (14-33). On Oct 7, at home in a rare Thursday game, Army defeated Louisville in a wild shootout W (59-52).

Then, on Oct 16 @ Southern Mississippi, the Golden Eagles shut out the Cadets L 0-24). On Oct 23, Army defeated New Mexico State at home W (35-18). On Nov 6, Army was shut out by the Air Force L (0-28) On Nov 13, at Memphis, the Cadets lost to the Tigers L (10-14). On Nov 20, at home, Houston defeated Army L (14-26).

On December 4 in the Army-Navy-Game, the Midshipmen defeated the Cadets L (9-19) at Veterans Stadium in Philadelphia--(Army-Navy-Game/Commander-in-Chief's Trophy)

Despite being the winningest coach against Navy in the modern era and despite Navy victories being so important, the Army Brass forgot how hard it was always to defeat the Midshipmen and they fired Bob Sutton because he did not bring in his last Navy opportunity.

As I look at all the coaches at Army, I find it tough to fault them. In 2000, as Bob Sutton passed the keys to Todd Berry, nobody expected Todd Berry, another qualified coach to fail. Todd Berry had rebuilt Illinois State football and had led the school to the Division I-AA playoffs the past two seasons. Army brought him into the bigger leagues but he was already a fine coach.

Berry of course replaced Bob Sutton, who had a rough go of it for three years after his 10-2 season. Many think Sutton should have been retained but who knows what was going on behind the scenes. Bob Sutton was fired two days after Army lost to Navy on Dec. 4 in the 100th meeting between the teams. The accolades coming in for the new coach Todd Berry were deafening. Nobody anticipates failure with any new coach or they don't hire them.

"Coach Todd Berry is an inspiring coach," Army superintendent Lt. Gen. Daniel Christman said in announcing Berry's hiring today. "Anyone who comes into contact with him cannot help but be impressed with his commitment to this institution."

Berry has a history with players and coaches across College Football. He reunited in this hiring with athletic director Rick Greenspan, Illinois State's athletic director for six years and the man who hired Berry in 1995. Greenspan took the Army AD job in April and chose to fire Sutton after the 19-9 loss to Navy.

"I have never been as inspired by a place until I got here," Berry said. "I expect that in the near future we'll be 11-0. Anything else would be an injustice to this institution." Considering Berry's actual record at Army, he might have easily predicted that Army would be winning the football Championships on both the Moon and Mars in the near future.

Greenspan said the 39-year-old coach had all the attributes West Point was looking for. He said Berry has "passion, recruiting skills, he's a teacher of the game, a tireless worker, and someone who appreciates the values of Army." Berry however, never had to deal with the Army Leadership to be successful in life before taking the job.

It is true that he had rebuilt Illinois State football, leading the Redbirds to the Gateway Conference title this season and an 11-3 record. Illinois State lost to Georgia Southern 28-17 in last week's I-AA semifinals.

Berry was voted the league's coach of the year. His overall record at the school is 24-24 in four seasons.

"He's been just incredible for our program," Illinois State assistant athletic director Kenny Mossman said. I wonder if Army would be happy with 24-24?

He was an assistant coach for 13 years before taking the job at Illinois State, including four years as offensive coordinator at East Carolina. He also was an assistant at Southeast Missouri State, Mississippi State and Tennessee-Martin.

Sutton, Army's coach for nine years, was fired just three seasons after guiding Army to a school-record 10 wins. His record against Navy was 6-3, and he left with a 44-55-1 record. Some would say that 24-24 is a better percentage than Sutton achieved. The verdict came in quick when Coach Todd Berry put the Black Knights on the field against opponents.

2000 Army West Point Cadets Football Coach Todd Berry

The Army West Point Black Knights football team represented the United States Military Academy in the 2000 college football season. It was Army's one hundred-eleventh season of intercollegiate football. They were led by Coach Todd Berry in his first of four seasons as head coach of the Black Knights. As a new member of Conference USA, the Army team had a losing season record of 1-10-0.

Overall, the Black Knights compiled a 1-10-0 record. They were 1–6 in the C-USA Conference. They finished with a very poor season record. In 1998, Army pitched no shutouts, and had no shutouts

thrown against them. The Cadets were outscored by their opponents 372 to 224. In the annual Army–Navy Game, the Cadets lost to the Midshipmen in a close match L (28-30)

<< Coach Todd Berry

This year's opener was on Sept 4 at Cincinnati. The Black Knights got the season off the wrong way again with a loss against the Bearcats L (17-23) Other than those games played in neutral fields, all Army home games were played on the West Point campus at Michie Stadium in West Point NY. The only game the Black Knights won this year was against Tulane W (21-17) on Oct 21. All other games as listed below were losses:

Sept 9	Boston College	L 17-55
Sept 16	at Houstom	L 30-31
Sept 23	at memphis	L 16-26
Oct 7	at New Mexico State	L 23-42
Oct 14	at East Carolina	L 21-42
Oct 21	Tulane	W 21-17
Nov 4	Air Force	L 27-41
Nov 11	Louisville	L 17 – 38
Nov 18	UAB	L 7 – 27

On December 2 in the classic Army-Navy-Game, the Midshipmen defeated the Cadets L (28-30) at Baltimore (Army-Navy-Game/Commander-in-Chief's Trophy)

2001 Army West Point Cadets Football Coach Todd Berry

The Army West Point Black Knights football team represented the United States Military Academy in the 2001 college football season. It was Army's one hundred-eleventh season of intercollegiate football. They were led by Coach Todd Berry in his second of three seasons as head coach of the Black Knights. The Army team had a losing season record of 3-8-0.

Overall, the Black Knights compiled a 3-8-0 record. They were 2-5 in the C-USA Conference. They finished with another very poor season record. In 1998, Army pitched no shutouts, and had no shutouts thrown against them. The Black Knights were outscored by their opponents 365 to 229. In the annual Army–Navy Game, the Midshipmen defeated the Black Knights W (12-58). Army changed its nickname from the Cadets to the Black Knights.

This year's opener was on Sept 8 at home vs Cincinnati. The Cadets got the season off the wrong way again with a loss against the Bearcats L (21-24) Other than those games played in neutral fields, all Army home games were played on the West Point campus at Michie Stadium in West Point, NY. On Sept 22, at the University of Alabama Birmingham (UAB), the Blazers bombed the Army West Point Black Knights in a blowout L (3-55).

Boston College at Alumni Stadium in Massachusetts added to the pain, sticking the Army with their third straight loss without a win this season L (10-31) Finally in game four the Black Knights got a win against Houston at home W (28-14). Then, along came two more losses with the first against East Carolina at home on Oct 13, L (26-49) and on Oct 20, it was L (20-38) at Texas Christian (TCU).

Army came up for air on Oct 20 to defeat Tulane at home W (42-35). This was followed by another loss at Air Force on Nov 3 L (24-34). Then at home on Nov 10, Army lost to Buffalo L (19-26). On Nov 17, at Memphis, the Tigers defeated Army L (10-42).

On December 1 in the classic Army-Navy-Game, the Black Knights defeated the Midshipmen W (17-3) at Veterans Stadium in Philadelphia, PA (Army-Navy-Game/Commander-in-Chief's

Trophy). This gave the Black Knights their third victory of the season and to many Army fans a win over Navy is a successful season.

2002 Army West Point Cadets Football Coach Todd Berry

The Army West Point Black Knights football team represented the United States Military Academy in the 2002 college football season. It was Army's one hundred-thirteenth season of intercollegiate football. They were led by Coach Todd Berry in his third and last of three seasons as head coach of the Black Knights.

Overall, the Black Knights compiled a 1-11-0 record. They were 1-7 in the C-USA Conference. They finished with another very poor season record. In 1998, Army pitched no shutouts, and had one shutout thrown against them (Rutgers 0-44). The Cadets were outscored by their opponents 365 to 229. In the annual Army–Navy Game, the Cadets were pounded by the Midshipmen W (12-58). Army changed its nickname in 1999 from the Cadets to the Black Knights.

This year's opener was on Sept 7 at home vs Holy Cross. In another poor record year, the Black Knights got the season off the wrong way again with a loss against the Crusaders L (21-30) Other than those games played in neutral fields, all Army home games were played on the West Point campus at Michie Stadium in West Point NY. On Sept 14, at Rutgers, the Scarlet Knights shut out the Black Knights of Army L (0-44). The Black Knights won just one game the whole season and lost 11. The win came on Nov 16 at Tulane W (14-10). Since the rest of the year were all losses, rather than prolong the misery, I provided the rest of the season for your edification in tabular form below:

Sept 21	Louisville	L (14-45)
Sept 28	Southern Mississippi	L (6-27
Oct 5	at East Carolina	L (24-59)
Oct 12	TCU	L (27-46
Oct 19	Houston	L (42-56)
Oct 26	UAB	L (26-29)
Nov 9	Air Force	L (30-49)
Nov 23	Memphis	L (10-38)
Dec 7	Navy	L (12-58)

On December 7 in the classic Army-Navy-Game, the Black Knights were blown-out by the Midshipmen L (12-58) at Giants Stadium in East Rutherford, NJ (Army-Navy-Game/Commander-in-Chief's Trophy). This gave the Black Knights their eleventh loss of the season and to many Army fans this loss was the worst of the year.

2003 Army West Point Cadets Football Coach Todd Berry

Todd Berry Lasted six games in 2003 before he was fired. The season record was 0-6 before he was replaced mid-season The losses in 2003 for Todd Berry are as follows:

Sept 6	Connecticut	L (21-48)
Sept 13	Rutgers	L (21-36
Sept 20	Tulane	L 33-50)
Sept 27	South Florida	L (0-28)
Oct 4	at TCU	L (0-27)
Oct 11	at Louisville	L 10-34
Oct 18	East Carolina	L (32-38)
Oct 25	at Cincinnati	L (29-33)
Nov 1	UAB	L (9-24)
Nov 8	at Air Force	L (3-31)
Nov 15	Houston	L (14-34)
Nov 22	at Hawaii	L (28-59)
Dec 6	Navy	L (6-34)

The other games were by Coach Mumford – Chapter 17—

Army became the first team to finish 0-13 in major college history. The Arizona Sun published this short story of what happened to Coach Berry

WEST POINT, N.Y. (AP) — Army coach Todd Berry was fired Monday with the team 5-35 in his four seasons and mired in an eight-game losing streak.

"The Corps of Cadets and the fans of Army football deserve a competitive program that is representative of this great institution," said Lt. Gen. William Lennox Jr., superintendent of the U.S. Military Academy.

Army (0-6) has just one win in its last 17 games. The Black Knights are averaging 63.8 yards rushing to rank last in the nation and are the only team averaging under 2 yards per carry.

South Florida, playing its inaugural Conference USA game last month, shut out Army 28-0 at Michie Stadium, marking the first time the Black Knights had been blanked at home since 1981.

Here is one of my favorite quotes from me:

"Nothing in life worth having, is easy"

Here is another quote of mine that I just came up with from having read about Coach Berry's Black Knights.

"11-0 has the same numbers as does 0-11 but the meaning is a lot different!"

Chapter 17 Coaches Mumford, Ross, Brock, & Ellerson 2003 – 2013

Mumford   Coach # 33
Ross   Coach # 34
Brock   Coach # 35
Ellerson   Coach # 36

Year	Coach	Record	Conference	Record
**2003	John Mumford	0-13	C-USA	0-8
2004	Bobby Ross	2-9	C-USA	2-6
2005	Bobby Ross	4-7	Indep	4-7
2006	Bobby Ross	3-9	Indep	3-9
2007	Stan Brock	3-9	Indep	3-9
2008	Stan Brock	3-9	Indep	3-9
2009	Rich Ellerson	5-7	Indep	5-7
2010	Rich Ellerson	7-6	Indep	7-6
2011	Rich Ellerson	3-9	Indep	3-9
2012	Rich Ellerson	2-10	Indep	2-10
2013	Rich Ellerson	3-9	Indep	3-9

** Todd Berry coached six losses listed under Mumford in 2003

Coach John Mumford checking things out

2003 Army West Point Cadets Football Coaches Todd Berry / John Mumford

The Army West Point Black Knights football team represented the United States Military Academy in the 2003 college football season.

It was Army's one hundred-fourteenth season of intercollegiate football. They were led by Coach Todd Berry, in his fourth and last season. Berry was fired after six games in. John Mumford coached the last seven games. Things were not going well for Army and Coach Mumford did not provide a fix.

Overall, the Black Knights compiled a 1-11-0 record. They were 0-8 in the C-USA Conference. They finished with another very poor season record. In 1998, Army pitched no shutouts, and had two shutouts thrown against them (TCU & Louisville – Berry's last two games). The Cadets were outscored by their opponents 476 to 206. In the annual Army–Navy Game, the Cadets defeated the Midshipmen W (6-34).

This year's opener was on Sept 6 at home vs Connecticut. In another poor record year, the Black Knights got the season off the wrong way again with a loss against the Huskies L (21-48). Other than those games played in neutral fields, all Army home games were played on the West Point campus at Michie Stadium in West Point NY. On Sept 13, the Black Knights lost its second of thirteen games this season.

The full 2003 season's games are listed as follows. All Games on the list are losses. It was Army's worst record ever.

Sept 6	Connecticut	L (21-48)
Sept 13	Rutgers	L (21-36
Sept 20	Tulane	L 33-50)
Sept 27	South Florida	L (0-28)
Oct 4	at TCU	L (0-27)
Oct 11	at Louisville	L 10-34
Oct 18	East Carolina	L (32-38)
Oct 25	at Cincinnati	L (29-330
Nov 1	UAB	L (9-24)
Nov 8	at Air Force	L (3-31)
Nov 15	Houston	L (14-34)
Nov 22	at Hawaii	L (28-59)
Dec 6	Navy	L(6-34)

On December 7 in the classic Army-Navy-Game, the Black Knights were blown-out by the Midshipmen L (12-58) at Lincoln Financial

Field in Philadelphia PA (Army-Navy-Game/Commander-in-Chief's Trophy). This gave the Black Knights their thirteenth loss of the season.

Bobby Ross

Bobby Ross was the next Army coach in the pipeline. When you look at Ross's record, 9-25, with three losing seasons, you can see a similarity with Bob Sutton, except for one thing. Sutton showed that if he got the players, he could bring out their talents as in his 10-2 season.

2004 Army West Point Cadets Football Coach Bobby Ross

The Army West Point Black Knights football team represented the United States Military Academy in the 2004 college football season. It was Army's one hundred-fifteenth season of intercollegiate football. They were led by Coach Bobby Ross in his first of three seasons. As an independent football entity, the Army team had a very poor season record of 2-9.

Coach Bobby Ross at work

Overall, the Black Knights compiled a 2-9 record. They were 2-6 in the C-USA Conference (their last year). They finished with another very poor season record. In 1998, Army pitched no shutouts, and had no shutouts thrown against them. In the annual Army–Navy Game, the Midshipmen defeated the Black Knights W (13-42).

This year's opener was on Sept 11at home vs Louisville. In another poor record year, the Black Knights got the season off the wrong way again with a loss against the Cardinals L (21-52). Other than those games played in neutral fields, all Army home games were played on the West Point campus at Michie Stadium in West Point NY. On Sept 18, the Black Knights lost its second of nine games this season and # 2 of four in a row at Houston L (21-35) It would be two more losses to get to the first win of 2004. Loss #3 on Sept 25, was at Connecticut L (3-40). The next loss of the four was against Texas Christian L (17-21).

The Black Knights then defeated the Bearcats of Cincinnati on Oct 9 W (48-29 at Cincinnati The second win in a row and last win of the year came a week later on Oct 16 at South Florida W (42-35. The rest of the season was one loss after another for five in a row. The first was at East Carolina on Oct 30, L (28-38). The next loss of five was against Air Force on Nov 6, L (22-31). Next was at Tulane on Nov 13, L (31-45) Then it was UAB on Nov 20 L (14-20). All those came before # 5, the big one against Navy.

On December 4 in the classic Army-Navy-Game, the Black Knights were well-handled by the Midshipmen L (13-42) at Lincoln Financial Field in Philadelphia PA (Army-Navy-Game/Commander-in-Chief's Trophy). This gave the Black Knights their ninth loss of the season.

2005 Army West Point Cadets Football Coach Bobby Ross

The Army West Point Black Knights football team represented the United States Military Academy in the 2005 college football season. It was Army's one hundred-sixteenth season of intercollegiate football. They were led by Coach Bobby Ross in his second of three seasons. Out of conference play for good, as an independent football entity, the Army team had another very poor season record of 4-7.

Overall, the Black Knights compiled a 4-7 record. They had exited the C-USA Conference in 2004. They finished with another very poor season record. Army pitched one shutout 20-0 v Akron) and had no shutouts thrown against them. In the annual Army–Navy Game, the Midshipmen defeated the Black Knights W (23-42).

This year's opener was on Sept 10at home at Boston College In another 4-win, poor record year, the Black Knights got the season off the wrong way again with a loss against the Eagles L (7-44). The game was played at Alumni Stadium Chestnut Hill MA. Other than those games played in neutral fields, all Army home games were played on the West Point campus at Michie Stadium in West Point NY. On Sept 17, at home, the Black Knights were defeated by the Baylor Bears L 10-20). There would be four more losses before the first win.

On Sept 23 at home, #22 Iowa State defeated the Black Knights L (21-28) before 25,007 fans. On Oct 1, Connecticut got its licks in the defeat of Army in a high scoring win L (13-47), Before a max Michie Stadium crowd of 38, 482. On Oct 8, at home, Central Michigan beat Army L 10-14). The final loss before the first win was at # 25 TCU's Amon G. Carter Stadium Fort Worth, TX L 17-38). The Black Knights got sick of losing and won the next four games. The first was at Akron W (20-0) before 12,203 fans. The next win was against Air Force at Falcon Stadium Colorado Springs, CO (Commander-in-Chief's Trophy) W (27–24)

On Nov 12, it was #5 UMass at home. The Black Knights won in a close match W (34–27). The final win of a four-win season came on Nov 19 at home when the Black Knights took Arkansas State for a losing ride W (38-10). The last game was the Army Navy Game.

On December 3 in the classic Army-Navy-Game, the Black Knights were again pushed back by the Midshipmen L (23-42) at Lincoln Financial Field in Philadelphia PA (Army-Navy-Game/Commander-in-Chief's Trophy). This gave the Black Knights their seventh loss of the season

2005 Player Highlights Carlton Jones B

Carlton Jones played in Coach Bobby Ross's two-back option. He emerged as a premier running back for the Black Knights, leading the team in rushing from 2002 to 2005. By the end of his collegiate career, he ranked near the top of every rushing statistic. Jones went from third string to starter and becoming the first freshman to lead the Black Knights in rushing since Michael Mayweather (762 yards in 1989).

In his junior season, Jones broke Glenn Davis' 59-year-old single-season rushing touchdown record with 17 touchdowns. Jones rushed for a career high 225 yards and five touchdowns against South Florida in a 41-35 stunner in 2004. He left the academy second in all-time in career rushing yards (3,536) and tied for second in career 100-yard rushing games (11). But despite his many accomplishments as a running back, Jones won only seven games in his four-year career (7-40). One great player does not make a team.

2006 Army West Point Cadets Football Coach Bobby Ross

The Army West Point Black Knights football team represented the United States Military Academy in the 2006 college football season. It was Army's one hundred-seventeenth season of intercollegiate football. They were led by Coach Bobby Ross in his third and final season of three seasons. The Army team had another very poor season record of 3-9.

Overall, the Black Knights compiled a 3-9 record. They finished with another very poor season record. Army pitched no shutouts and had no shutouts thrown against them. In the annual Army–Navy Game, the Midshipmen defeated the Black Knights L (23-42).

This year's opener was on Sept 2 at Arkansas State's ASU Stadium in Jonesboro, AR. In a 3-win, poor record year, the Black Knights got the season off the wrong way again with a loss against the Red Wolves L (6-14). Other than those games played in neutral fields, all Army home games were played on the West Point campus at Michie Stadium in West Point NY. On Sept 9, at home, Army defeated Kent State W (17-14). On Sept 16, at Texas A &M, in the Alamodome, in

San Antonio, TX, the Black Knights did not have enough juice and gave up the ghost L (24-28). On Sept 23, at Baylor's Floyd Casey Stadium in Waco, TX, the Black Knights prevailed W (27–20).

Moving through the season, on Sept 30, the Rice Owls came to Michie Stadium and defeated the Army Black Knights in a shootout L (14–48). Then, on Oct 7 at home, Army defeated VMI in a rout W 62–7 before 31,069. On Oct 14, at Connecticut's Rentschler Field in East Hartford, CT, the Huskies beat the Black Knights L 7–21. On Oct 21 at home, Army lost to TCU L 17–31 before 33,614.

On Oct 28, at the Louisiana Superdome in NO LA, Tulane got the better of the Army L (28–42) before 21,053. Air Force came back after last year's loss to torment Army again at home in a big win L (7-43). On Nov 18, the Big Guns from Notre Dame invited Army to Notre Dame Stadium in South Bend, IN (Army-Notre Dame football rivalry). The Irish stole the win L (9–41) before 80,795.

On December 2 in the classic Army-Navy-Game, the Black Knights were again defeated by the Midshipmen L (14-26) at Lincoln Financial Field in Philadelphia PA (Army-Navy-Game /Commander-in-Chief's Trophy). This gave the Black Knights their ninth loss of the season.

There are a lot of great coaches who took their turns at Army. Some are great people and some are simply great coaches. Army was always looking for great coaches but sometimes stumbled on great people who could not coach as well as they might have. Bobby Ross got three years at Army and in a tough scenario, he did not perform up to expectations So, he retired. As the good man that he is, he expressed profound gratitude for the opportunity to coach the storied Black Knights of Army West Point.

Ross Retires After Three Years At Army; Brock Is New Coach
By Adam Kilgore
Washington Post Staff Writer
Tuesday, January 30, 2007; E04

Bobby Ross retired as head coach of Army yesterday, ending a three-year stint in which his teams finished 9-25 and did not beat Navy. Ross, 70, who coached Maryland for five seasons in the 1980s and took the San Diego Chargers to the Super Bowl in 1994, will be succeeded by offensive line coach Stan Brock, 48.

"I think there's a point in time when you feel like it's your time to retire, and I think I've reached that time," Ross said at a news conference at West Point. "I think there is an issue of having a certain degree of energy, which I feel is very important for anyone leading a college football program. I feel that I was lacking in that area as well."

As head coach of Maryland from 1982 to '86, Ross became known for high-scoring, quick-strike offenses and compiled a 39-19-1 record while grooming Boomer Esiason, and Frank Reich to become NFL quarterbacks. He won ACC titles from 1983 to '85, going undefeated in the league each season. He was the last Terrapins coach to win the ACC before Ralph Friedgen did so in 2001.

Friedgen spent 14 seasons as an assistant to Ross, a union that began when Friedgen was a graduate assistant at Maryland from 1969 to '72 while Ross was an assistant coach. Friedgen served as an assistant at The Citadel in 1973, when Ross accepted his first head coaching job. Friedgen also worked under Ross as offensive coordinator and offensive line coach at Maryland in 1982 and then became an assistant to Ross at Georgia Tech, where they won a national championship in 1990, and the Chargers.

Ross was a head coach for 28 seasons, 18 in college and 10 in the NFL with San Diego and the Detroit Lions.

At the news conference yesterday, Army Athletic Director Kevin Anderson gave the names of several coaches he's worked with, including Bill Walsh of the San Francisco 49ers, and said, "Coach Ross ranks on top of that list, both as a coach and a man."

Army went 3-9 last season and lost its last six games, including a 26-14 defeat against Navy.

Brock played for Ross in the NFL.

"I am not going to replace Bobby Ross. No way," Brock said. "He is the best coach I ever played for."

Upon his hiring at Army, Ross spoke about how his military background shaped his decision to accept the position. Ross graduated from the Virginia Military Institute and served in the U.S. Army from 1960 to '62 as a lieutenant. He sent one son to the Air Force Academy and another to the Naval Academy.

"My desire to always coach at West Point was a great one," Ross said in a statement. "I will be indebted to our administration forever for providing me the opportunity to do that."

2007 Army West Point Cadets Football Coach Stan Brock

The Army West Point Black Knights football team represented the United States Military Academy in the 2007 college football season. It was Army's one hundred-eighteenth season of intercollegiate football. They were led by Coach Stan Brock in his first of two seasons. The Army team had another very poor season record of 3-9. It was the second 3-9 season of three in a row.

Stan Brock before the Tulane game

Overall, the Black Knights compiled a 3-9 record. They finished with another very poor season record. Army pitched no shutouts and had no shutouts thrown against them. In the very important annual Army–Navy Game, the Midshipmen defeated the Black Knights L (3-38).

This year's opener was on Sept 1 at Akron in the Cleveland Browns Stadium Cleveland In another 3-win, poor record year, the Black Knights got the season off the wrong way again with this loss against the Zips L (14-22). Other than those games played in neutral fields, all Army home games were played on the West Point campus at Michie Stadium in West Point NY. On Sept 8, Army defeated Rhode Island at home in OT W (14-7). On Sept 15 at Wake Forest's BB&T Field Winston-Salem, NC, army lost by L (10-21). On Sept 22, at #14 Boston College's Alumni Stadium Chestnut Hill, MA, the Eagles defeated the Black Knights L (17–37) before 40,329.

On Sept 29 at home, Army defeated Temple W (37–21) before 34,176. Then on Oct 6, Army grabbed another win, two in a row, at home from Tulane W (20–17) in OT. The Black Knights then lost to Central Michigan on Oct 13 at Central Michigan's Kelly/Shorts Stadium Mount Pleasant, MI L (23–47) before 21,013. On Oct 20 at Georgia Tech's Bobby Dodd Stadium Atlanta, GA, the Yellow Jackets got the best of the Black Knights L (10–34) before 50,242 fans.

On Nov 3 at Air Force's Falcon Stadium Colorado Springs, CO, the Army was beaten by the Air Force, L (10–30) before a packed crowd of 46,144. On Nov at home, Rutgers put a lick on Army at home L (6-41). On Nov 17, at home, Tulsa defeated Army L (39-49).

On December 1 in the classic Army-Navy-Game, the Black Knights were again defeated handily by the Midshipmen L (3-38) at Lincoln Financial Field in Philadelphia PA (Army-Navy-Game /Commander-in-Chief's Trophy). The attendance was overflowing the field for this game at 71,610. This again gave the Black Knights their ninth loss of the season.

2008 Army West Point Cadets Football Coach Stan Brock

The Army West Point Black Knights football team represented the United States Military Academy in the 2008 college football season. It was Army's one hundred-nineteenth season of intercollegiate football. They were led by Coach Stan Brock in his second and last of two seasons. The Army team had another very poor season record of 3-9. It was the third 3-9 season of three in a row.

Overall, the Black Knights compiled a 3-9 record. They finished with another very poor season record. Army pitched no shutouts and had one shutout thrown against them in the Army-Navy-Game. In the very important annual Army–Navy Game, the Midshipmen defeated the Black Knights L (0-34).

This year's opener was on August 29 at home against Temple. This was the first time that an Army opener was played in August. It was part of another 3-win, poor record year. The Black Knights got the season off the wrong way again with this loss against the Owls L (7-35) before 1`,822. Other than those games played in neutral fields, all Army home games were played on the West Point campus at Michie Stadium in West Point NY. On Sept 6, in a home encounter at 1:00 PM for good TV viewing on a Saturday afternoon, New Hampshire took Army for a losing spin L (10-28).

Then, on Sept 20 at home, Akron beat Army L (3-22) before 27,040. On Sept 27, at Texas A&M's Kyle Field College Station, TX, Army went down L 21–17 before 84,090 fans, then on Oct 4, my wedding Anniversary, at Tulane's Tad Gormley Stadium New Orleans, LA, Army whooped the Green Wave W 44-13. On Oct 11, at home, Eastern Michigan could not keep up with Army at home W (17–13) before 27,096.

On Oct 18 at Buffalo's UB Stadium Buffalo, NY, the Bulls beat the Black Knights L (27–24) in OT. Then on Oct 25 at home, Army beat Louisiana Tech W (14–7) before a crowd of 27,383.

On Nov 1, at home, Air Force, fighting for the (Commander-in-Chief's Trophy) beat Army L (16–7) before a packed house of 37,409. Then, on Nov 8 at Rice in Rice Stadium Houston, TX, Army lost the match L 31-38) before 19,243. On Nov 22 at Rutgers' Rutgers

Stadium in Piscataway, NJ, Army lost another game L (3-30) before 42,212 Rutgers fans.

On December 6 in the classic Army-Navy-Game, the Black Knights were again defeated in a shutout by the Midshipmen L (0-34) at Lincoln Financial Field in Philadelphia PA (Army-Navy-Game /Commander-in-Chief's Trophy). The attendance was huge again for this meeting at 69,144.

This again gave the Black Knights their ninth loss of the season. Navy had always been the lesser player but in the recent years, the Midshipmen had begun to play better football than Army all season long and this trend affected the Army-Navy Game.

Since Navy was doing well, and since Air Force was doing well during this period, what is clear is that Army West Point, a fine service academy had not yet figured out how to win in the modern age. Out of nowhere, Navy is now ten games ahead in the win-loss coulmn.

We have been walking through some of the years in which this happened. However, this occurred, a team of generals ought to be able to figure out how to help their Cadets win football games in the same fashion as they always win wars. There should be no excuses. That's what I think.

Stan Brock took a lot of heat in 2008 from critics after changing from the pro-style offense to a triple option-like offensive scheme after the previous season. Some pundits dubbed it the "Brock Bone" or "quadruple" option, due to an added passing element. The team as noted above finished the season with a disappointing 3–9 record, with the biggest disappointment being the 34–0 rout by archrival Navy.

Brock was subsequently fired and replaced this year by former Cal Poly head coach, Rich Ellerson. The 2008 Army–Navy Game was the first shut-out of Army by Navy since 1978. One consolation was that in the game's final play, Army fullback Collin Mooney, in the last play of his college football career, broke the school record for single-season rushing by a single yard.

Brock Out; Ellerson In at Army from NY Daily News

WEST POINT, N.Y. - Army filled its football coaching vacancy by heeding a core West Point value: History matters.

Rich Ellerson grew up around Black Knights football and is leaving his coaching job at Cal Poly to come to a place he knows well. His father and two brothers graduated from the U.S. Military Academy, where brother John led the 1962 team to a 6-4 record. And he's worked before with former Army coaches known for running successful schemes on both sides of the ball.

Ellerson replaces Stan Brock, who was fired Dec. 12 after a pair of 3-9 seasons. This season ended with a 34-0 loss to Navy. Brock, a former New Orleans Saints offensive lineman, was Army's offensive line coach for three years before replacing Bobby Ross in early 2007.

Academy officials, who announced the selection Friday, said Ellerson expressed interest in the position when it was open in the past. They were impressed by his familiarity with a program in need of a quick turnaround.

"I will never receive, nor have I ever received a finer compliment professionally or personally than to be entrusted with the Army football program at this point in its history," said Ellerson, who turns 55 on Jan. 1.

Before his eight years as Cal Poly's coach, Ellerson worked with former Army coach Jim Young at Arizona, where Ellerson was an assistant. Young, who ran a successful option attack at Army, had retired from the Black Knights after the 1990 season and assumed a volunteer role on the Arizona coaching staff.

Ellerson also assisted Army coach Bob Sutton when he installed his "Desert Swarm" defense at West Point, which helped carry the Black Knights to a 10-2 record and a berth in the Independence Bowl in 1996.

Cal Poly made it to the Football Championship Subdivision playoffs four times under Ellerson and was ranked as high as No. 3 this season. He was 56-34 in his eight years at Cal Poly.

Athletic director Kevin Anderson said he's long admired Ellerson's work with the triple option at Cal Poly.

"One of our primary goals of the search was to find someone capable of turning around our program immediately, and we are confident Rich is the perfect individual to accomplish that," he said.

Despite all the confidence like many before him, Rich Ellerson was unable to deliver more than just one slightly winning season out of five. Most of the squad's seasons with Coach Ellerson were well underplayed. Four losing seasons out of five says a lot.

2009 Army West Point Cadets Football Coach Rich Ellerson

The Army West Point Black Knights football team represented the United States Military Academy in the 2009 college football season. It was Army's one hundred-twentieth season of intercollegiate football. They were led by Coach Rich Ellerson in his first of five seasons. The Army team had a losing season record of 5-7. They won two games more than the prior year.

Overall, the Black Knights compiled a 5-7 record. They finished with another relatively poor season record. Army pitched no shutouts and had no shutouts thrown against them. In the very important annual Army–Navy Game, the Midshipmen defeated the Black Knights L (3-17).

Rich Ellerson coaching for Army Black Knights

This year's opener was on Sept. 5 at Rynearson Stadium Ypsilanti, MI against Eastern Michigan. The Black Knights began the season with a win against the Eagles W (27-14) before 14,449. Other than those games played in neutral fields, all Army home games were played on the West Point campus at Michie Stadium in West Point NY. On Sept 12, at home Army picked up its first loss of the season under Coach Ellerson against Duke L (19-35) On Sept 19, Army recovered from the loss to Duke and came back to win against Ball State W (24-17).

The Black Knights were defeated on Sept 26 at Iowa State's Jack Trice Stadium, Ames, IA L 10–31 before 50,532. Then on Oct 3, the Army Homecoming, Tulane spoiled the day by sneaking in a one-point win against the Black Knights L (16-17). On Oct 10 at home, the Black Knights defeated the Commodores in OT W (16–13). Temple then beat Army L (13-27) on Oct 17 at Temple in a game played at the Lincoln Financial Field in Philadelphia, PA. Attendance was 14,275. On Oct 23, Army lost to Rutgers at home L (10-27).

On Nov 7, the Black Knights were defeated at Air Force's Falcon Stadium Colorado Springs, CO (Commander-in-Chief's Trophy), by the Fighting Falcons L (7–35) before 46,212. On Nov 14 at home the

Black Knights defeated VMI W (22-17). Army picked up its 2nd win in a row against North Texas on Nov 21 at Fouts Field Denton, TX W 17-13 before 23,647.

On December 12 in the classic Army-Navy-Game, the Black Knights were again defeated by the Midshipmen L (3-17) at Lincoln Financial Field in Philadelphia PA (Army-Navy-Game /Commander-in-Chief's Trophy). The attendance was high again for this meeting 69,541. This game was the seventh loss for the Black Knights this season.

2010 Army West Point Cadets Football Coach Rich Ellerson

The Army West Point Black Knights football team represented the United States Military Academy in the 2010 college football season. It was Army's one hundred-twenty-first season of intercollegiate football. They were led by Coach Rich Ellerson in his second of five seasons. The Army team had a winning season record of 7-5, their first season above 500 since 1996. They won two games more than the prior year.

Overall, the Black Knights compiled a 7-5 record. They finished with an OK season record. Army pitched a shutout against North Texas – 24-0, and had no shutouts thrown against them. In the very important annual Army–Navy Game, the Midshipmen defeated the Black Knights L (17-31).

By winning 6 regular season games, Army became bowl-eligible for the first time since the 1996 season. They were invited to the Armed Forces Bowl against SMU, in University Park, Texas replacing a team from the Mountain West Conference. They defeated SMU 16–14 in the bowl to finish the season 7–6, their first winning season since 1996.

This year's opener was on Sept. 4 at Rynearson Stadium Ypsilanti, MI against Eastern Michigan. The Black Knights began the season with a win against the Eagles W (31-27) before 11,318. Other than those games played in neutral fields, all Army home games were played on the West Point campus at Michie Stadium in West Point NY. On Sept 11, Army lost to Hawaii at home L (28-31). Next up was North Texas on Sept 18. The Black Knights picked up a shutout win W (24-0). On Sept 25, the Black Knights defeated the Duke Blue Devils W (35-21). Then on Oct 2, Temple won a close game (one TD) from Army L (35-42).

At Tulane on Oct9, playing in the Louisiana Superdome, the Black Knights defeated the Green Wave W (41-23). Rutgers was next at New Meadowlands Stadium in East Rutherford, NJ on Oct 16. Army got the loss L (20-23) in a close match. On Oct 30, at home vs VMI, Army won handily W (29-7). On Nov 6, first weekend in November, Air Force defeated Army L 922-42). On Nov 13, at Kent State's Dix Stadium in Kent, OH, Army won another W (45–28). In the game before THE GAME, Notre Dame defeated Army in Yankee Stadium Bronx, NY L (3-27).

On December 11 in the classic Army-Navy-Game, the Black Knights were again defeated by the Midshipmen L (17-31) at Lincoln Financial Field in Philadelphia PA (Army-Navy-Game /Commander-in-Chief's Trophy). The attendance was high again for this meeting 69,541. This game was the sixth of six losses for the Black Knights this season.

On December 30, 12:00 p.m. at SMU in the Armed Serviced Bowl played at Gerald J. Ford Stadium University Park, TX, the Black Knights defeated the Mustangs W 16–14 before a crowd of 36,742.

2011 Army West Point Cadets Football Coach Rich Ellerson

The Army West Point Black Knights football team represented the United States Military Academy in the 2011 college football season. It was Army's one hundred-twenty-second season of intercollegiate football. They were led by Coach Rich Ellerson in his third of five seasons. The Army team had a losing season record of 3-9. They lost four more games than the prior year.

Overall, the Black Knights compiled a 3-9 record. They finished with a poor season record. Army pitched a shutout against Fordham 55-0, and had no shutouts thrown against them. In the very important annual Army–Navy Game, the Midshipmen defeated the Black Knights 21-27.

This year's opener was on Sept. 4 at Northern Illinois' Huskie Stadium against Northern Illinois. The Black Knights began the season with a loss to the Huskies L (26-49) before 17,003. Other than those games played in neutral fields, all Army home games were played on the West Point campus at Michie Stadium in West Point NY. On Sept 10, Army lost to San Diego State at home L (20-23).

Next up was Northwestern on Sept 17. The black Knights picked up their first win of the season W (21-14). On Sept 24, the Black Knights were defeated L (21-48) by Ball State at Scheumann Stadium • Muncie, IN. Then on Oct 1, at home Army pounded Tulane W (45-6).

On Oct 8 at Miami (OH)'s Yager Stadium Oxford, OH, the Black Knights were defeated by the Red Hawks. L (28–35). Next was Vanderbilt at Vanderbilt Stadium Nashville, on Oct 22 L (21–44). Then on Oct 29, the Black Knights walloped Fordham's Rams W 55–0 before 39,481 fans at Michie.

On Nov 5 at Falcon Stadium • Colorado Springs, CO, the Air Force's Fighting Tigers defeated the Army Black Knights L 14–24 before an attendance of 46,709. On Nov 2, at Yankee Stadium Bronx, NY, Rutgers defeated Army L (12-27) before 30,028. On Nov 19, at Temple in a game played at Lincoln Financial Field in Philadelphia, PA, the Army lost the match L (14-42) by a wide margin.

On December 10 in the classic Army-Navy-Game, the Black Knights were again defeated by the Midshipmen L (21-27) at FedEx Field in Landover MD (112th Army-Navy-Game /Commander-in-Chief's Trophy). The attendance was high 80,789. This game was the ninth loss for the Black Knights this season.

2012 Army West Point Cadets Football Coach Rich Ellerson

The Army West Point Black Knights football team represented the United States Military Academy in the 2012 college football season. It was Army's one hundred-twenty-third season of intercollegiate football. They were led by Coach Rich Ellerson in his fourth of five seasons. The Army team had a losing season record of 2-10. They lost one more game than the prior year.

Overall, the Black Knights compiled a 2-10 record. They finished with a poor season record. Army pitched no shutouts, and had no shutouts thrown against them. In the very important annual Army–Navy Game, the Midshipmen defeated the Black Knights again 13-17. Things were not looking good for Coach Ellerson or the Army program.

This year's opener was on Sept 8 at San Diego State's Qualcomm Stadium San Diego, CA. The Black Knights began the season with a loss to the Aztecs L (7-42) before 30,799. Other than those games played in neutral fields, all Army home games were played on the West Point campus at Michie Stadium in West Point NY.

On Sept 15, Army lost a one-pointer to Northern Illinois at home L (40-41). On Sept 22, at Wake Forest's BB&T Field Winston-Salem, NC, the Black Knights were defeated by the demon Deacons L (37-49). On Sept 29, at home Army was defeated by Stony Brook L (3-23)

On Oct 6 at home vs Boston College, Army prevailed by a close margin W (34-31). Next was Kent State on Oct 13 at home in a losing effort L (17-31) Eastern Michigan was next to defeat Army on Oct 20 at Rynearson Stadium Ypsilanti, MI L (38-48).

Then on Oct 27, the Black Knights lost to the Ball State Cardinals L (22-30). Air Force was ready as always on Nov 3 for Army but not ready enough as the Black Knights defeated the Fighting Falcons W (41-21) at home before 37,707. On Nov 10 at Rutgers in High Point Solutions Stadium Piscataway, NJ, the Scarlet Knights defeated the Black Knights L (7-28) On Nov 17, at home, Temple pounded Army L (32-63) in a shootout win.

On December 8 in the classic Army-Navy-Game, the Black Knights were again defeated by the Midshipmen L (13-17) at Lincoln Financial Field in Philadelphia PA (113th Army-Navy-Game /Commander-in-Chief's Trophy). This game was the tenth loss for the Black Knights this season. Rich Ellerson's team brought in just two wins.

2013 Army West Point Cadets Football Coach Rich Ellerson

The Army West Point Black Knights football team represented the United States Military Academy in the 2013 college football season. It was Army's one hundred-twenty-fourth season of intercollegiate football. They were led by Coach Rich Ellerson in his fifth and last of five seasons. The Army team had a losing season record of 3-9. They won just one more game than the prior year.

Overall, the Black Knights compiled a 3-9 record. They finished with a poor season record. Army pitched no shutouts, and had no shutouts thrown against them. In the very important annual Army–Navy Game, the Midshipmen smothered the Black Knights 7-34. Following the loss to Navy on December 14 and finishing the season 3-9, head coach Rich Ellerson was fired.

This year's opener was on Aug 30 at Morgan State at home. The Black Knights began the season with a nice win against the Bears W (28-12) before 24245. Other than those games played in neutral fields, all Army home games were played on the West Point campus at Michie Stadium in West Point NY. On Sept 7, Army lost to Ball State at Scheumann Stadium Muncie, IN L (14-40). On Sept 14, against Stanford at home, the Black Knights lost to the Cardinal L (20-34). Before 39, 644. On Sept 21, Wake Forest defeated Army at home L (11-25). Then, on Sept 28, against Louisiana Tech, playing in Cotton Bowl Stadium Dallas, TX (Heart of Dallas Classic), Army picked up the win W (35–16).

On Oct 5 at Boston College's Alumni Stadium at Chestnut Hill, MA, the Eagles defeated the Black Knights L (27-48). Then on Oct 12 at home, Army defeated Eastern Michigan in a shootout W (50-25). On Oct 19 at Temple, played at Lincoln Financial Field Philadelphia, PA, the Owls defeated the Black Knights L (14–33). On Nov 2, at Air Force's Falcon Stadium Colorado Springs, CO (Commander-in-Chief's Trophy), the Fighting Falcons defeated the Army Black Knights L (28–42) before 36,512.

On Nov 9 at home against Western Kentucky (WKU), the Hilltoppers defeated the Black Knights L 17–212. On Nov 30, 11:00 p.m. at Hawaii's Aloha Stadium in Honolulu, Hawaii, the Black

Knights were defeated by the Rainbow Warriors L 42–49 before 32,690.

On December 14 in the classic Army-Navy-Game, the Black Knights were again defeated by the Midshipmen L (7-34) at Lincoln Financial Field in Philadelphia PA (114th Army-Navy-Game /Commander-in-Chief's Trophy). This game was the ninth loss for the Black Knights this season. 65,612 fans were in attendance.

Our acknowledgment to ESPN for this article about Rich Ellerson.

Army fires coach Rich Ellerson

Dec 16, 2013

Army has fired Rich Ellerson after five seasons, the school confirmed Sunday.

Ellerson was 20-41 at Army, including 0-5 against Navy.
The firing comes one day after Army lost 34-7 to Navy, the Black

Knights' 12th straight loss in the lopsided series.

Rich Ellerson's 34-7 loss to Navy on Saturday turned out to be his last game on Army's sideline.

"I love that football team,'" Ellerson said after the game. "I want desperately for them to have a better feeling today. That's what is killing me."

Army finished 3-9 this season.

"Obviously, in the body of work, we've made some progress," Ellerson said Saturday. "But I wasn't brought in to make progress. I was brought in to win some football games and beat Navy. I've lost to our rival five times."

The Midshipmen haven't lost to Army since 2001 and lead the series 58-49-7. Navy's 12-game run is the longest in the history of the rivalry that began in 1890.

"I thought we closed the gap the last two years, but that gap opened back up," Ellerson said.

In 2010, Ellerson led Army to its first bowl win since 1985 by beating SMU in the Armed Forces Bowl. But the last three years, Army went 8-28.

The triple-option wasn't the problem. Ellerson's offense averaged more than 300 yards rushing the past three seasons, but the rest of the team never developed. He had two years left on his contract.

"Rich Ellerson has represented West Point and the Army football program extremely well since taking over as our head coach five years ago," Army athletic director Boo Corrigan said in a statement. "Unfortunately, our team has not experienced the level of success on the football field that we expect, and we feel it is necessary to make a change in the leadership at this time."

Corrigan said deputy athletic director Col. Joe DeAntona will assume day-to-day operations of the football program until a new coach is hired.

Ellerson, 60, came to Army after eight seasons in charge of Cal Poly, where he went 56-34 with two NCAA playoff appearances. Information from The Associated Press was used in this report

Chapter 18 Coach Jeff Monken 2014-2016

Monken   Coach # 37

Year	Coach	Record	Conference	Record
2014	Jeff Monken	4-8	Indep	4-8
2015	Jeff Monken	2-10	Indep	2-10
2016	Jeff Monken	8-5	Indep	8-5
2017	Jeff Monken			

Coach Jeff Monken with the Army Team

Who is Coach Jeff Monken?

Jeff Monken is the new Sherriff in town. Others who came before him could not turn this seemingly lawless team around. Nobody has been blaming the Sherriff per se but every few years, the Army gets rid of the Sherriff and brings in a "better" lawman to bring justice to the people of Dodge City. But, the same old things happen. The bad guys come into Michie Stadium and face the ravage the townspeople.

Will this happen again? It was a good question in 2014 for sure as the new Sheriff, Jeff Monken had not even checked out his posse.

When 2014 was said and done, there was a lot of devastation (4-8 record) and the townspeople had been hurt like the olden days. But, they figured that Sherriff Monken was still getting his posse together so the Town Council kept him on.

Then came 2015, and the posse was getting formed and they looked stronger. But, the bad guys played harder than the prior year (2-10). While this was going on, Sherriff Monken was culling his posse into the best there ever was. Despite a 2-10 bad guy record, twice as bad statistically as the prior year, the townspeople also looked at the posse and they figured protection and victories over adversaries would come in 2016.

It did!

Jeff Monken, who was named Army's 37th individual head coach on Dec. 24, 2013, is now ready to begin his fourth season as head football coach. The Sherriff now has a fine posse.

Monken shows a 50-39 career record as a head coach and a 6-18 mark at Army.

Last year, 2016, was a breakout season for the Black Knights under Monken. He led them to their first win over Navy since 2001 and they won a bowl game for the first time in six seasons. The last time the Black Knights accomplished both feats in the same season was in 1984.

In 2016, Army was second in the nation in rushing offense and ran for an Army single-season record of 46 touchdowns, which eclipsed the 1945 national championship team. On the defense side, Army was consistently in the top 10 in total defense and finished the year fourth in the nation. They handled the bad guys on both sides of the ball.

In 2015, Sherriff Monken led Army to a pair of wins over Bucknell and Eastern Michigan. Under coach Monken, the Black Knights had five players reach 100 yards rushing in a game in 2015 and had three different quarterbacks throw for 100 yards. Signal callers Ahmad Bradshaw and Chris Carter ran and threw for 100 yards each in their career debuts. Army won on the road for the first time since 2010 with a 58-36 win over Eastern Michigan. The townspeople, the fans, and the Academy were beginning to believe.

Army finished the season ranked 12th in the country in rushing offense at 244.3 yards per game. Linebacker Andrew King was the top player in the national rankings. He was 21st in tackles for loss with an average of 2.1 per game and 26th in fumbles recovered with two.

In Monken's first season at Army, he guided the Black Knights to home victories over Buffalo, Ball State and Fordham, in addition to a dramatic win against Connecticut at Yankee Stadium.

Under his guidance, running back Larry Dixon, linebacker Jeremy Timpf, defensive back Josh Jenkins and offensive lineman Matt Hugenberg earned 11 citations on postseason all-star teams and two players, Joe Drummond and Dixon competed in The Medal of Honor Bowl Game and East-West Shrine Game, respectively.

Army was fifth in the country in rushing offense at 296.5 yards per game in Monken's first season and sixth in fewest penalties per game with just 4.08 infractions per contest.

Monken tutored a host of players who listed in the national rankings. Timpf was seventh in the nation in solo tackles per game and 23rd in tackles per game. Jenkins was eighth in the country in blocked kicks and 33rd in interceptions per game and both Lamar Johnson-Harris and Xavier Moss ranked 11th in punt return touchdowns. Dixon listed nationally in rushing yards per carry (30th), rushing yards (39th) and rushing yards per game (41st).

With a 47-39 win against Buffalo, Monken became the first head coach to win his first game since Bob Sutton did so in 1991 with a victory over Colgate. Prior to Monken, the last Army coach to win his first game against a Football Bowl Subdivision opponent was Ed Cavanaugh in 1980.

Monken came to the banks of the Hudson River following a successful stint as a head coach at Georgia Southern.

He spent four seasons as head coach at Georgia Southern after learning the triple-option offense under one of the nation's premier option proponents, Paul Johnson, during assistant coaching stints at Navy and Georgia Tech.

During his four seasons at Georgia Southern, Monken authored a 38-16 mark and spearheaded the programs transition to the elite Football Bowl Subdivision level from the Football Championship Subdivision (FCS) ranks.

Georgia Southern, which joined the Sun Belt Conference following Monken's tenure, was a member of the FCS and qualified for the NCAA playoffs in all three eligible seasons under Monken, advancing to the national semifinals each year while posting double-digit victory totals.

Monken guided tradition-rich Georgia Southern to some of the biggest wins in school history, with the most memorable arguably a 26-20 victory at Florida in November at the vaunted "Swamp." Despite that headline-grabbing victory, Georgia Southern was not eligible for the FCS playoffs this season due to its transitional status.

"I am thrilled to accept the head coaching position at West Point," said Monken at the time of his hiring. "Not only is the United States Military Academy one of the most prestigious academic institutions in the world, it boasts one of the nation's richest, most historic traditions in all of college football.

"There are so many people I would like to thank for this tremendous opportunity, starting with Director of Athletics Boo Corrigan and our Superintendent, Gen. Bob Caslen. I am honored and humbled by their trust in me to lead the West Point football program. I have had the privilege of serving as a coach for several outstanding institutions and am thankful to all of the student-athletes, coaches, and administrators with whom I have worked. Because of their commitment, dedication, and loyalty, this opportunity to serve at West Point has been afforded to me. More than anyone else, I want to thank the men and women who have served and continue to serve our nation in the United States Army. I am proud to be your head football coach."

Monken and Johnson are the only coaches in Georgia Southern school history to win at least 10 games in each of their first three seasons.

"Jeff Monken is an outstanding football coach. He is a tireless worker who will do the right things to build a program and he will be a great leader," said Johnson.

A finalist for the 2012 Liberty Mutual Coach of the Year award, Monken guided Georgia Southern to 10 wins his first season, 11 his second and 10 in his third. His 2013 squad posted a 7-4 mark, including the stunning, season-ending upset of Florida in Gainesville.

Under Monken's guidance, Georgia Southern was one of the top rushing teams at the FCS level, claiming the NCAA rushing title in 2012 at 399.36 yards per contest. Walter Payton Award candidate Jerick McKinnon and running back Dominique Swope established the NCAA record for rushing yards by teammates with 3,063.

Monken coached a lengthy list of all-stars, including the school's highest-ever National Football League draft choice, safety J.J. Wilcox, a third-round selection of the Dallas Cowboys in 2013.

In 2011, Georgia Southern was ranked No. 1 in both FCS polls for seven weeks and stopped Wofford, 31-10, to win its ninth Southern Conference championship. Five players were named All-America, Brent Russell was selected Southern Conference Defensive Player of the Year, Monken earned conference Coach of the Year plaudits and Swope was named Southern Conference Freshman of the Year. Home playoff wins against Old Dominion and Maine were part of the Eagles' memorable 11-3 campaign.

Monken got off to a great start in his first year as Georgia Southern's head coach, knocking off top-ranked and previously unbeaten Appalachian State as part of a 10-5 season. Georgia Southern ended the season with three straight wins to qualify for the postseason and registered three playoff victories to advance to the national semifinals.

In addition to the success on the field, Monken helped Georgia Southern reemerge academically with the team's cumulative grade point average ranking as the highest in school history in each of his first two seasons. Not only was Georgia Southern successful in the classroom and on the football field under Monken, but the players and staffs were part of several community service programs and local events.

Monken was named Georgia Southern's head coach in November of 2009, continuing a family history of football coaches. Jeff's father, Mike, and a dozen family members have coached at the high school, collegiate or professional levels.

Monken's first head coaching job came after accumulating 20 years of experience as an assistant, 13 of them with his mentor Johnson. Monken coached slotbacks at Georgia Southern from 1997 to 2001 before joining Johnson first at Navy and then Georgia Tech.

As an assistant coach at Georgia Southern, Monken was part of two NCAA FCS National Championship squads (1999 and 2000) and five straight playoff teams. Georgia Southern was among the top-five rushing teams in all five seasons and twice led the nation in rushing. Four out of five seasons, the Eagles ranked in the top-15 in scoring as well.

After serving as an assistant at Georgia Southern, Monken accepted a position on Johnson's coaching staff at Navy. Monken not only mentored slotbacks, he later added special team's coordinator duties.

In Annapolis, Monken helped the Midshipmen to five straight Commander in Chief trophies and five consecutive bowl appearances, including a 10-win season in 2004. Following his time at Navy, Monken moved to Georgia Tech where for two seasons he served as slotbacks coach and special teams coordinator. The Yellow Jackets posted double-digit wins in 2009 and captured the Atlantic Coast Conference championship, although that title was later vacated.

Monken began his coaching career in 1989 as a graduate assistant at the University Hawaii and later spent one season at Arizona State

University. Monken moved to University of Buffalo as the wide receivers and tight ends coach and also handled recruiting. He served on the staffs at Morton (Ill.) High School as head coach and at Concordia University in Illinois as the offensive line coach as well.

A native of Joliet, Ill, Monken played wide receiver for four years and earned two varsity letters in track and field while earning his bachelor's degree from Millikin University in 1989. He was inducted into the school's Athletic Hall of Fame in October and collected his master's degree from Hawaii in 1991.

Monken and his wife Beth now reside at West Point with their three daughters, Isabelle, Amelia and Evangeline. We of the Army Football Community know Jeff Monken can produce great teams. We are sure wishing and hoping and praying that his energy holds out and that he gets the support of the institution for the long haul.

When the fan base and the pundits begin to put the word "Red" in between Jeff and Monken, I think we (Army) will have more than arrived.

2014 Army West Point Cadets Football Coach Jeff Monken

The Army West Point Black Knights football team represented the United States Military Academy in the 2014 college football season. It was Army's one hundred-twenty-fifth season of intercollegiate football. They were led by Coach Jeff Monken in his first of three seasons. Monken is also the current coach and he had a good year in 2016 so we hope he is around for a while. The Army team had a losing season record of 4-8. They won one more game than the prior year.

Overall, the Black Knights compiled a 4-8 record. They finished with a poor season record, losing twice as many games as they won. Army pitched no shutouts, and were shut out by Stanford 0-35. In the very important annual Army–Navy Game, the Midshipmen smothered the Black Knights 10-17. Assistant Coach Danny Verpaele brought back the tight end position to Army

This year's opener was on Sept 6 at home against Buffalo. The Black Knights began the season with a shootout win against the Bulls (47-39) before 28643. Other than those games played in neutral fields, all Army home games were played on the West Point campus at Michie Stadium in West Point NY. On Sept 13, Army was shut out L (0-35) by #15 Stanford in Stanford Stadium—Stanford, CA, Wake Forest played army at BB&T Field Winston-Salem, NC for the win L (21-24), On Sept 27 at Yale's Yale Bowl New Haven, CT, the Bulldogs defeated the Black Knights in OT L (43–49) before 34,142

On Oct 4, my wedding anniversary to my beautiful Bride, Pat, Army defeated Ball State at home W (33–24) before a fairly packed house of 31,384. On Oct 11, at home, Rice defeated Army L (21-41) in an even more packed house of 37,011. Then, on Oct 18   3:30 p.m. at Kent State's Dix Stadium Kent, OH, the Army lost another away game L (17–39). Air Force was always ready for Army and again this year, at home, the Fighting Falcons defeated the Black Knights (Commander-in-Chief's Trophy) L 6–23 before an overflow crowd of 40,479. On Nov 8, at Yankee Stadium in the Bronx, NY, Army defeated Connecticut W 35–21 before 27,453.

Then on Nov 15 at Houchens Industries–L. T. Smith Stadium Bowling, KY, Army was defeated by WKU in a shootout L (24–52) before 16,819 On Nov 22 at home, the Black Knights defeated the Fordham Rams at home W (42–31) before 33,793.

On December 13 in the classic Army-Navy-Game, the Black Knights were once again defeated by the Midshipmen L (10-17) M & T Bank Stadium Baltimore MD (115th Army–Navy Game/Commander-in-Chief's Trophy) This game was the eighth loss for the Black Knights this season. 70, 935 fans were in attendance.

2015 Army West Point Cadets Football Coach Jeff Monken

The Army West Point Black Knights football team represented the United States Military Academy in the 2015 college football season. It was Army's one hundred-twenty-sixth season of intercollegiate football. They were led by Coach Jeff Monken in his second of three seasons. Monken is also the current coach and he had a good year in 2016 so we hope he is around for a while. The Army team had a losing season record of 2-10. They won two less games than the prior year.

Overall, the Black Knights compiled a 2-10 record. They finished with a very poor season record, losing five times as many games as they won. Army pitched no shutouts, and were not shut out by any opponent. In the very important annual Army–Navy Game, the Midshipmen smothered the Black Knights 17-21. This game was close but no cigar. Would Coach Jeff Monken get to light up a cigar in 2016? We'll see soon!

This year's opener was on Sept 4 at home against Fordham. The Black Knights began the season with a poor showing against a second-tier team with this loss against the Rams L (35-37) before 22523. Other than those games played in neutral fields, all Army home games were played on the West Point campus at Michie Stadium in West Point NY. On Sept 12, Army lost in a close match L (17-22) at Connecticut's Connecticut Rentschler Field East Hartford, CT before 28,301.

Wake Forest played Army at home on Sept 19, and the Demon Deacons defeated the Black Nights by no more than a hair L (14-17). On Sept 26 at Eastern Michigan's Rynearson Stadium Ypsilanti, MI, Army got the win in a shootout W (58–36). On Oct 3 with Coach Franklin leading PSU at Penn State's Beaver Stadium University Park, PA, Army played to a one touchdown differential but lost L (14–20) before a massive crowd of 107,387.

On Oct 10, at home, the Duke Blue Devils overpowered the Army Black Knights in a rout L 3–44 before 39,712. On Oct 17, Army beat a willing Bucknell team W (21–14) before 33,257. The Black Knights went on the road the next week to play Rice's Owls at Rice Stadium Houston, TX and Army almost came home with the bacon but missed out by a TD L (31–38) before 24,409. On Nov 7 at Air Force's Falcon Stadium Colorado Springs, CO (Commander-in-Chief's Trophy), Army could not match the Air Power and succumbed L (3–20) before 37,716.

Next against a team from New Orleans, the non-gambling Fun Capitol of America, on Nov 14, in a homecoming game played at West Point, the Black Knights almost gave the home team a big victory against Tulane but it was a field goal off L (31-34). Wrapping up the non-Navy part of the season. The Black Knights faced the Scarlet Knights of Rutgers on Nov 21. Rutgers got the best of Army that day L (21-31) before 31,217 at home. The people are counting on Jeff Monken to deliver lots less seasons like this one.

On December 12, before 69,277 fans in the classic Army-Navy-Game, the Black Knights were once again defeated by the Midshipmen L (17-21). Now the difference to overcome is just four points and we all think Jeff Monken is the modern coach to get the job done. This game was played a Lincoln Financial Field Philadelphia PA (116th Army–Navy Game/Commander-in-Chief's Trophy) This game was the tenth loss for the Black Knights this season.

2016 Army West Point Cadets Football Coach Jeff Monken

The Army West Point Black Knights football team represented the United States Military Academy in the 2016 college football season. It was Army's one hundred-twenty-seventh season of intercollegiate football. They were led by Coach Jeff Monken in his third if XXXX seasons. Monken is the current coach and he had a good year this year in 2016 so we all hope he is around for a while. The Army team had a winning record of 8-5. They won six more games than the prior year. Looks like Monken is what the doctor ordered!

Overall, the Black Knights compiled an 8-5 record. They finished with the best season since air was invented or so it seemed. Army pitched no shutouts, but the Black Knights were not shut out by any opponent. In the very important annual Army–Navy Game, the Midshipmen were finally defeated by the neve-say-die Black Knights 38-31. This game gained the Army Black Knights a big Cigar. It was close but the Cigar was achieved. Coach Jeff Monken got to light up a big cigar in 2016? We'll see about 2017 soon! Army fans are confident in making sure their cigar lighting lighters are available for the 2017 season.

This year's opener was on Sept 2 at home against Temple in a game played at Lincoln Financial Field • Philadelphia, PA. The Black Knights began the season with a fine showing against a first-tier team with this win against the Owls W (28-13) before 34005. Other than those games played in neutral fields, all Army home games were played on the West Point campus at Michie Stadium in West Point NY. On Sept 10, at home, Army defeated Rice W (31-14). It had been so long ago that the Black Knights won its two opening games that Army was filled with confidence. Army won its third game in a row against UTEP in a major shootout on Sept 17 in the Sun Bowl Stadium El Paso, TX W (66-16).

On Sept 24 at Buffalo's UB Stadium in Amherst, NY, the Bulls got enough steam going to defeat the Black Knights L (20–23) in OT. On Oct 8, at Duke's Wallace Wade Stadium Durham, NC. Duke's Blue Devils triumphed over the Black Knights L (6–13) in a close match. On Oct 15, at home, Lafayette lost in a shootout to the Army Team in a big win W (62–7) before 38,394.

Then on Oct 22 at noon, Army took on North Texas at home and were saddled with a defeat from the Mean Green L (18–35) before 31,127. Then on Oct 29, Army beat Wake Forest W (21-13) at Wake Forest in BB&T Field Winston–Salem, NC. On Nov 5 at home, Air Force chose to win and did (Commander-in-Chief's Trophy) L (12–31) before 38,443 at Michie.

Even in a good year, Army had trouble with Air Force and other great teams such as Notre Dame which they played the next week at the Alamodome in San Antonio, TX. ND defeated a very game Army Team L 6–44 before a stadium fan set of 45,762 On Nov 19, at home, Army beat Morgan State W 60–3 in front of 28,290 fans.

On December 10, before 71,600 fans in the classic Army-Navy-Game, the Black Knights, coached by Jeff Monken played to win the game. They were not only not defeated by the Midshipmen by any score, they kept with Navy through the whole game, and hung in and won. This is our father's Army team. Last year's L (17-21) four-point differential was reversed and though the score was the same Army had beaten Navy W (21-17) this time. Bravo!

This game was played at M&T Bank Stadium • Baltimore, MD (117th Army–Navy Game/Commander-in-Chief's Trophy) This game was the seventh win for the Black Knights this season. Win # 8 came in the heart of Dallas Bowl game.

Army Navy Game 2016

On December 27 at 11:00 a.m. when the NY revelers were ready to celebrate early, Army gave lots of reasons why. Army played North Texas in the Cotton Bowl Stadium in Dallas, TX celebrating the (Heart of Dallas Bowl). The Black Knights prevailed in OT W (38–31) before 39,117

The article immediately below is courtesy of USA today. It offers a look at the status of Army Football right before the Army-Navy Game of 2016. The next article is a writeup of the game by the sports press:

Army building winning culture behind coach Jeff Monken

Ted Berg, USA TODAY Sports Published 6:02 p.m. ET Dec. 8, 2016
Updated 12:02 a.m. ET Dec. 10, 2016

Previewing the annual Army-Navy game

The 117th edition of the game will kick off on Saturday.
USA TODAY Sports

(Photo: Matt Cashore, USA TODAY Sports)

WEST POINT, N.Y. — Army's first bowl game in six seasons seems likely to serve more as a coda to a successful season than a climax, given the gravity of its annual matchup against Navy on Saturday.

But the berth nonetheless stands as Army's first since 2010 and only its second since 1996, and a step forward for a program that has finished with a losing record in 18 of the past 20 seasons.

The Dec. 27 matchup with North Texas in the Heart of Dallas Bowl also represents a rematch of a regular-season contest that North Texas won at Michie Stadium in October.
"Playing in a bowl game is a measure of success for everybody that plays at this level," coach Jeff Monken told USA TODAY Sports. "So, to say we're going to play in a bowl game is certainly an accomplishment. I'm proud of our kids and I'm proud of our

coaches, and I'm proud for West Point to be able to represent our academy in that fashion."

Army dominates on both sides in 60-3 win over Morgan State

In his third season as Army's head coach, Monken endeavors the huge challenge of restoring to respectability a program that was one of college football's most successful in the early days of the sport but which last saw back-to-back winning seasons in 1989-90. An assistant coach at Navy from 2002-2007, Monken took over as Army's head coach already familiar with the particulars of recruiting top-flight high school players to a military academy, a prospect that comes with both rigorous academic standards and, for most, a five-year service commitment following graduation. It means Monken must draw on a different group of recruits than most other Division I head coaches.

"The pool's smaller — or gets smaller in a hurry — because of the military commitment," he said. "And it's a challenge. No matter how much they understand that this is a world-class degree and an opportunity to play a very high level of football, there's still the fact that we're a military school.

Navy looks beyond injuries as it readies for Army

"It is an environment — a university or college environment — that's not traditional. Our guys don't go out and drink beer until 4 in the morning on a Tuesday night. You can do that other places. (At other schools), they can sleep in and miss math class if they want — hey, they might get in trouble. But you can't do that here.
"That's the challenge in recruiting here: You've got to find the right guy. It doesn't have to be a guy that necessarily has dreamed of being in the Army his whole life; it has just got to be the right kind of guy."

College football bowl schedule, results for 2016-17

Cadets at West Point pay no tuition, so the program need not consider NCAA scholarship limitations. For some, the service commitment seemed an inevitability.

Jeremy Timpf, a senior linebacker and team captain prepping for an assignment in field artillery next year, always intended to enroll at a military academy. Another senior linebacker, Andrew King, said the opportunities associated with attending West Point made it "a perfect fit" as he was "not really a party-goer."

But for others, the commitment gave some pause.

"You hear about the service commitment, and it kind of shakes you a little bit," said Christian Poe, a sophomore receiver who followed his older brother, Edgar, to Army. "It's just something you've got to do. You're getting paid when you serve; it's not like you're serving for free. You're doing something for millions of people and you're getting paid to do it. It's a beautiful thing: You get a job coming straight out of here. It's more exciting than anything, once you get the hang of it."

Focus of coaching carousel lands on American Athletic Conference

Until the spring of 2016, committing to Army — or any of the military academies — meant postponing any NFL dreams, as prospective pro players were expected to fulfill at least two years' worth of active duty before applying to the department of defense for a special waiver allowing for a transfer to selective reserve service so they could pursue pro careers. But after the Baltimore Ravens drafted Navy quarterback Keenan Reynolds in the sixth round of the NFL draft in April, Defense Secretary Ashton Carter announced that Reynolds and teammate Chris Swain would be allowed to defer their commitments to immediately join NFL teams.

"If they're good enough to play in the NFL, they can do that from here, too," Monken said. "That's absolutely a possibility."

Though Monken and defensive coordinator Jay Bateman contended coaching Cadets differed little from coaching Division I athletes at other schools, Bateman pointed out the type of player drawn to the Army program could help the team secure a strategic advantage: A playbook hardly seems daunting to minds tasked with the school's arduous academics and officer training.

"The kids that come here, the biggest thing is how bright they are," Bateman said. "Schematically, you have a lot of different options because they understand it; they're able to process things — if/then equations, calls. They're not always compliant — they're Division I football players, so they're tough dudes. But the kid that comes here, certainly, is a bright kid that's willing to commit to something bigger than himself, so I think the brotherhood, the team, is a big part of our success here."

Follow Berg on Twitter @OGTedBerg

Army beats Navy 21-17 to end 14-year losing streak in series

Published December 10, 2016 Associated Press

Army running back Andy Davidson (40) celebrates his touchdown with teammates in the first half of the Army-Navy NCAA college football game in Baltimore, Saturday, Dec. 10, 2016. (AP Photo/Patrick Semansky) (Copyright 2016 The Associated Press. All rights reserved.)

Army ended a 14-year run of frustration against Navy, using an overpowering running game and opportunistic defense to carve out a long overdue 21-17 victory Saturday.

With future commander in chief Donald Trump looking on, the Black Knights blew a 14-point lead before quarterback Ahmad

Bradshaw scored on a 9-yard run with 6:42 left to give Army the win it had been waiting for since 2001.

The Black Knights' 14-game losing streak was the longest by either academy in a series that began in 1890. Army (7-5) now trails 60-50-7 in one of the nation's historic rivalries.

Navy (9-4) was coming off a physical 34-10 loss to Temple in the American Athletic Conference title game and had only one week to prepare for Army with a new quarterback, sophomore Zach Abey, who was making his first college start. Abey took over Will Worth, who broke his foot against Temple.

Abey ran for two touchdowns but passed for only 89 yards and was intercepted twice. Navy had four turnovers, three in the first half.

By halftime, Army led 14-0 and owned a 14-1 advantage in first downs.

After watching from the Navy side of the field before halftime, Trump visited the TV booth on the Army side in the third quarter. The interview with the president-elect coincided with a big shift in momentum.

Andy Davidson lost a fumble on the Black Knights' first possession of the second half and the Midshipmen recovered at the Army 32. A screen pass for 16 yards set up a 1-yard touchdown run by Abey to get Navy to 14-7.

Minutes later, the Midshipmen got a field goal after a replay overturned a lost fumble by Abey at the Army 11.

A 41-yard touchdown run by Abey gave Navy the lead with 12:42 remaining. But Army wasn't done.

The Black Knights put together a 12-play, 80-yard drive that lasted nearly seven minutes and ended with Bradshaw's TD with 6:42 remaining.

Bradshaw went 2 for 4 for 35 yards and an interception in Army's first win in Baltimore since 1944.

Davidson ran for 87 yards and two first-half scores, and Kell Walker carried

Chapter 19 Coach Jeff Monken 2017-

Monken   Coach # 37

Year	Coach	Record	Conference	Record
2017	Jeff Monken	To-be	Indep	To-Be

Celebration over 2016 Navy Victory

The 2017 Schedule is as follows:

Date	Opponent	Location
9/1/2017	**Fordham**	**West Point, NY**
9/9/2017	**Buffalo**	**West Point, NY**
9/16/2017	Ohio State	Columbus, OH
9/23/2017	Tulane	New Orleans, LA
9/30/2017	**Texas-El Paso**	**West Point, NY**
10/7/2017	Rice	Houston, TX
10/14/2017	**Eastern Michigan**	**West Point, NY**
10/21/2017	**Temple**	**West Point, NY**
11/4/2017	Air Force	USAF Academy, CO
11/11/2017	**Duke**	**West Point, NY**
11/18/2017	North Texas	Denton, TX
12/9/2017	*Navy*	*Philadelphia, PA*

2017 Commentary

Army's Black Knights have had a lot of devastating near misses over the years, and these classic Army-Navy Game from December 2016 nearly went down among the worst. But, it did not! Now, Army is set for 2017.

As we know, Army dominated the first half and staked themselves to a two-touchdown lead at the break. Jeff Monken's team was clearly intent on not leaving another tight finish to chance. In the end, however, as the game rolled on, the Black Knights had to sweat it out again. To Monken and the team's credit, they managed to do it, and maybe with the closeness of the game, it is all sweeter in the end.

Navy had some personnel issues but nobody was making excuses. Sophomore Zach Abey made his first career start for Navy, in relief of the injured Will Worth. It was a tough situation for an inexperienced player to get tossed into. Army was able to get Abey off balance. At the half, the substitute QB completed more passes (two) to Army players than Navy players (one), and the Midshipmen had run 13 first-half total plays to the Knights' 14 first downs. Things just were not clicking at all for Navy—at least not at first.

Of course, Navy's opportunity was coming and they were ready to take it. The Middies cut the lead to 14-10 by the start of the third quarter. Abey found the end zone for Navy's first touchdown. Then the newbie QB ripped off a 41-yard scoring run to give Navy its first lead with 12:42 left.

The Black Knights were taken back but were not laying down. Army answered the call. After Abey's score, the Knights mounted a 12-play, 80-yard drive that ended with Bradshaw's critical score. It was a game-turning response, right as Army was in trouble. The Black Knights then forced a punt after that, and they drained the clock along with Navy's spirit upon getting the ball back.

That was the game.

Like all Army-Navy Games, this game mattered a ton. It always does.

Navy lost more than just this game. The Midshipmen fell short of an American Athletic Conference title and a potential Cotton Bowl bid this year. Their chance to make it 15 in a row against arch rival Army meant everything to them and it did not happen. The Black Knights entered with their best record since 2010 and their best shot in years at ending the streak. The Black Knights ended the streak.

Navy entered as a 5-point favorite with a scoring total over/under around 47, meaning Vegas forecasted a final score in the area of Navy 26, Army 21.

With fourteen wins in a row and having a fine season, Navy began the day with the country's No. 25 offense, despite being down to their third-string QB Abey. Army hadn't been nearly as lethal on offense this year, but the Black Knights had been much better than Navy on defense. Wait 'til we all see how well Army does in 2017.

What should we expect in 2017?
Courtesy of SBNation.com

Army is finding its niche with Monken in charge. The Black Knights broke through in 2016 with a lineup far from senior-heavy, and they did so with clear, obvious areas for future improvement — passing downs offense, pass defense, special teams, etc. Recruiting has improved a bit, returning production is high, and the Cadets appear well suited to further mastery of the underdog script.

The schedule is still pretty light, but it appears to get at least a little bit more difficult this fall. Last year the Black Knights played two FCS opponents and three teams among FBS' bottom 10 in S&P+. The bottom feeders are there, but there's only one FCS foe, and four opponents are projected 71st or better.

This could be a situation a lot like last year's, where the Knights were .500 late and needed late triumphs to become bowl eligible. Or they could engineer a strong start instead. It all depends on the relative tossups — they have five games with win probability between 40 and 54 percent. With overachievement or strong close-game execution, a

6-1 start is possible. That'll take the suspense right out of the equation.

Regardless, it's great to have Army back. College football is more fun with three different service academy teams serving as a pain in the butt and proving that you can win games with two-star recruits and a disciplined system.

Monken brought the Black Knights back to the party; now we get to find out if they can stay there this time. Signs point to yes.

There is no question this past 2016 season was a great one. The Army-Navy-Game was at its best again. Of course, Army plans to get through the whole season successfully and not just make its season by winning the Navy Game. Jeff Monken is aware that Navy overcame injuries to finish 9-5 in its past season that surpassed expectations.

However, when it came to one of the game's most historic rivalries with Army (8-5), the Black Knights ended the 14-year drought with a 21-17 win. Now, with both programs coming off impressive seasons, the 2017 edition of the rivalry is expected to be another classic. I would suggest that we all circle our calendars for Dec. 9, when the two armed-forces face off again at Lincoln Financial Field at 3 p.m. ET. I sure plan to be there. Bring your copy of the book and I would be happy to sign it for you. The best.

Chapter 20 The Army, Notre Dame Football Rivalry Part I of II

Army vs. Notre Dame – Early Game

A rivalry through the ages

The Army–Notre Dame football matchup is an American college football rivalry that goes back to when teams were struggling just to get opponents. The rivalry stages the Army Black Knights football team of the United States Military Academy and Notre Dame Fighting Irish football team of the University of Notre Dame. Though both teams had been playing for over twenty-years at the time. They did not play each other until 1913. At that time, both teams were among the top college football programs in the United States.

In this book, you have found that we picked ten of the top Army-Navy-Games and we report on them within the season in which they occurred. Since Notre Dame is Army's other famous competitor, and since the meetings are not annual as in the navy encounter, we decided to create a new chapter that describes the ins and outs of the

Army v Notre Dame rivalry from its beginning to the late 20th century when Army and Notre Dame were competing regularly.

The first Army–Notre Dame game in 1913 is generally regarded as the game that established the national reputation of the Fighting Irish. Army already was viewed as one of the toughest competitors in the nation. In that game, Notre Dame revolutionized the notion of the forward pass as a major offensive weapon as the Irish pulled off a crowd stunning 35–13 victory.

For years it was "The Game" on Notre Dame's schedule, played at Yankee Stadium in New York as the small fields available in West Point could not accommodate the many spectators wanting to see the game of the year. Of course, there were many who preferred the Army Navy Game but nothing prevented fans from attending both of these smash-mouth football contests.

During the 1940s, the rivalry with the Army Black Knights reached its zenith. This was because both teams were extremely successful and met several times in key games (including one of the Games of the Century, a scoreless tie in the 1946 Army vs. Notre Dame football game). Notre Dame's Coach Frank Leahy at the time had brought in several National Championships and Army's Red Blaik did likewise. Army and Notre Dame were National powerhouses.

In 1944, the Black Knights administered the worst defeat in Notre Dame football history, crushing the Fighting Irish, 59–0. Notre Dame might suggest that in 1944 and 1945 their coach, Frank Leahy was doing his own time in the military as a Navy Officer and missed both seasons. But, it was more than that. Army had two of the best teams ever to play on a gridiron.

The following year, 1945, it was more of the same punishment for Notre Dame, with a 48–0 blitzkrieg. After meeting every year since 1919, the series went on a ten-year hiatus starting in 1947 and that lasted until 1957. The game was played in South Bend for the first time and the Fighting Irish won 27–7. Since then, there have been infrequent meetings over the past several decades, with Army's last win coming in 1958. We go through the details of that game later in this chapter.

Like Navy, due to the small capacity of Army's Michie Stadium, the Black Knights would play their home games at a neutral site, which for a number of years was Yankee Stadium and before that, the Polo Grounds. In 1957, the game was played in Philadelphia's Municipal (later John F. Kennedy Memorial) Stadium while in 1965, the teams met at Shea Stadium in New York. They last met at the old Yankee Stadium in 1969.

The 1973 contest was played at West Point with the Fighting Irish prevailing, 62–3. In more recent times, games in which Army was the host have been played at Giants Stadium in East Rutherford, New Jersey. Notre Dame leads the series 39–8–4 with most of Notre Dame's wins coming after Army's heyday in the 1940's.

Their latest matchup came in 2016, when the teams met for the 2016 Shamrock series in the Alamodome in San Antonio. Notre Dame won the game, 44-6. As of this meeting, the Irish have won the last 15 meetings, the longest in the rivalries history. But, Coach Jeff Monken has other ideas for the future success against Notre Dame, and all of Armies opponents.

Coaches Charles Dudley & Jesse Harper

In 1913, while Notre Dame was trying to convince its Administration to fund collegiate football at ND, Army was well established and had just brought in a coach who was going to bring Army some great success. Charles Dudley Daly was Army's head football coach from 1913-1916 and he had another stint from 1919-1922. He was successful both times. His Army teams were tough on opponents. Notre Dame in particular respected Army's power. Daly had a great 58-13-3 record. His 1914, 1916, 1922 teams were undefeated. All teams were winners. Daly never had a losing season in eight years.

At the same time as Dudley was preparing for more undefeated seasons, Jesse Clare Harper, a fine coach, became head coach in 1913 and remained so until he retired in 1917. Harper had a five-year head coaching career with a great record of 34-5-1 with a 7-0 undefeated record in 1913. Two of the stars on Harper's 1913 team were Knute Rockne, who played End, and Gus Dorais, QB. Dorais would pitch them and Rockne would catch them. Both made all American.

Prior to Harper, Notre Dame would take games with High Schools and athletic clubs and just about any team that would play them. During his tenure, the Irish began playing only intercollegiate games. This period also marked the beginning of the rivalry with <u>Army</u> and the continuation of rivalries with <u>Michigan State</u>. In an effort to gain respect for a regionally successful but small-time Midwestern football program, Harper scheduled games in his first season with national powerhouses <u>Texas</u>, <u>Penn State</u>, and <u>Army</u>.

By most standards, Notre Dame never should have been able to get the game with Army. As the story goes, two major factors combined to make the 1913 meeting with Army possible. Army had been stiffed by Yale. They were deemed not good enough to compete with Yale by Yale, a major Eastern superpower football team. Yale broke off its series with Army that had been played for 20 consecutive years from 1893 through 1912. Army therefore had a "hole" in its schedule. Jesse Harper knew it was his job to fill that hole with a team named Notre Dame. He did.

The Army Series against Notre Dame would itself make a great book and probably a better movie. We share some of the facts in this chapter.

Coach Jesse Harper & ND Player Knute Rockne

As noted previously, Army needed a game and Notre Dame was willing to travel. Harper was not the only ND coach that had to travel to play Army. In fact, until the 1947 game, Notre Dame's long list of great coaches after Harper agreed to travel every year from 1913 to 1946. ND had no home games. Army was home every game. Sometimes, since the Black Knights had such a small stadium, their home field was often a larger "neutral" east coast venue such as Yankee Stadium, the Polo Grounds and even Shea Stadium when it was built.

Now, let us move on with the Jesse Harper Notre Dame / Army Saga continuing from 1913. Historians and Notre Dame fans admire Harper for helping Knute Rockne make Notre Dame Stadium the House that Rockne built. The hard facts suggest that without a sharp guy like Harper coming to Notre Dame when he did, Rockne would have had few materials to build the House.

Harper was relentless and there was no email or text messaging back then. So, he did what he could to communicate with the fine teams that he hoped would play the Fighting Irish – home or away. He went on a letter-writing campaign. For 1913, he received positive responses from Army, Penn State, Texas, South Dakota, Ohio Northern, Christian Brothers of St. Louis and Alma, where he had formerly coached. From the eyes of many, Harper had already succeeded.

Let's go back again to Army as this was a real coup and it is fun to recount. The meeting arrangements against powerhouse Army had begun during the spring of 1912. Jesse Harper was the varsity baseball coach. The Notre Dame baseball team had made a successful excursion along the East Coast. From May 9-22, 1912. Harper was finishing up at Wabash until the end of the 2012-2013 Academic year but it did not stop him from writing and writing and writing.

Notre Dame played baseball games at West Virginia, Penn State, Mount St. Mary's, Catholic University, Seton Hall, Brown, Deerfield Academy, Tufts and Vermont before returning home. Harper would reach these schools after he took over as baseball coach while on the road to book some football games. He was the Notre Dame Head Coach in football, basketball and baseball from 1913-17. He was the baseball coach and he used his baseball contacts to help Notre Dame in all ways.

The Army Cadet (Black Knights) football manager at the time was Harold Loomis. He got his letter from Harper to schedule a contest as soon as possible. Loomis was ready. He offered Harper $600 to come to West Point. Unfortunately, the train ride would cost about $1000 for the Train tickets to transport all 18 members of the traveling squad the 875 miles to West Point. Harper asked for full expenses from Loomis. Loomis reluctantly agreed to pay the $1000 for the 24-hour train ride from South Bend.

"My letter to West Point," Harper recalled later, according to author Frank Maggio, "arrived at a time when the Army-Yale series ended somewhat abruptly. And the Cadets had an open date." Army agreed to a Nov. 1, 1913 game, and offered Harper the $600 revenue guarantee but as noted upped the ante to $1000.00

Though desperately wanting to close the deal for the game, Harper could not afford to lose money on the travel arrangements. The coach knew that he did have one thing that gave him an edge in getting the $1000.00. A number of Eastern college teams had already refused to play Army in light of its admissions policy.

West Point used its own set of rules for recruiting and did not pay attention to the NCAA. After all they were the US Army and the US was in a long war that was just ending. Army recruited football players who had exhausted their eligibility at another college, and to help soldier morale, West Point gave them three more years of varsity play.

Academy officials said they needed the extra time to train officers to fight in wars. Here is an outrageous example: Army halfback Elmer Oliphant played three years at Purdue before graduating in 1914. He was a two-time, first-team All-American at West Point in 1916-1917, and entered the College Football Hall of Fame in 1955.

Army's recruiting practices finally grated on the Naval Academy so badly that in the late 1920s, Navy refused to play Army. How about that for some great half-time trivia at the next ND game? Navy would not play Army! Check out the final few paragraphs in the last chapter as I suggest we go back to those recruiting days to help the service academy programs.

Coach Jesse Harper had a lot of jobs at ND as discussed. As the Athletic Director, the budget was very close to his heart. ND was so strapped for cash that the team had to cover its own "food expenses" when it traveled to Army. They ate sandwiches that were prepared in the Notre Dame campus dining hall.

Additionally, the boys had to carry their own equipment. Things were tough? How tough? It is reported that only fourteen pair of football shoes were made available to 18 Notre Dame players. Many of the substitutes in the two-way (Defense & Offense) player "rotation," had to use the shoes that were on the feet of the players coming out of the game. There was no guarantee that the shoes would fit.

The trip to West Point cost $917, and so ND had in fact made an $83 profit. Using the Alan Shepard quote as a basis to describe this phenomenon, we would characterize ND playing Army as "one small step for Notre Dame ... one giant leap toward helping brand its name, especially with the stunning W (35-13) victory."

Rockne racing with a pass from Gus Dorais vs. Army on November 1, 1913

On Nov. 1, Notre Dame met Army for the first time in West Point, N.Y. Led by head coach Jesse Harper, the Irish debuted the forward pass. Their offensive scheme surprised the Cadets and shocked the sporting world. It helped counteract Army's size advantage. Dorais was almost perfect, completing 14 of 17 attempts to Rockne for 243 yards

Notre Dame literally stunned the much bigger and more experienced Army Cadets with an offense that featured both the expected Notre Dame powerful running game but also their new and innovative long and accurate downfield forward passes from Dorais to Rockne. Dorais was a smaller player but he had a powerful, accurate arm, and Rockne had taught himself how to catch the ball with perfection. This game was the first major contest in which a team used the recently legal forward pass throughout the game so frequently that it secured their victory.

As noted above, even later in November, Notre Dame would add a great cap to its season with victories at Penn State W (14-7), at Christian Brothers in St. Louis W (20-7) and at Texas W (30-7) to finish 7-0. Because of the great work of Jesse Harper, Notre Dame's football program was literally and figuratively ahead of schedule.

Ironically, the first ND home game in South Bend against Army was in 1947. After delivering two major "home thumping's" in a row at Yankee Stadium L (0-59) and L (0-48) to Notre Dame in 1944 and 1945 right near the end of the war when Army had its best teams, the Black Nights tied the Irish in 1946 T (0-0).

Army went to Notre Dame for the first time ever, after 33 years of "home" play. The teams played every year during this period except for 1918. As we know, World War I ended November 11, 1918. When Army came to Notre Dame in 1947, they were defeated W (27-7). From 1913 to 1922, all games were played at the Plain, a small field with few stands at West Point. Then games were scheduled at the big stadiums until 1947.

After the ND home win, following the 1947 season, the teams did not play during what has been called a ten-year hiatus. The last game of the series was played in South Bend for the first time and the Fighting Irish prevailed, W (27–7).

A Notre Dame Student Jim Butz had this to say quoting another student about the 1947 game.

> *"The death knell for Army hopes was sounded in the opening 18 seconds by Terence Patrick Brannan who gathered in Mackmull's kickoff on his five-yard line with a fine over-the-shoulder catch and threaded his way 95 yards down the west sidelines to score. Brennan was aided by some fine blocks thrown by Jim Martin, George Connor, Bill Fischer, and Bill Walsh, but he used each block skillfully and picked his way through until he reached his 25 from where he simply out-ran everyone. Earley added the seventh point as the crowd went delirious with joy at the prospect of an Irish scoring orgy."*

It was not a scoring orgy but any win for either side was met with many cheers.

The Army / ND series was picked up again in 1957 and has been off and on ever since with both teams taking turns for home game games. Notre Dame played Army in the fall of 2016 on November 12, in San Antonio Texas.

Knute Rockne's 1927 ND team beat Biff Jones' Army club. Both are legendary coaches. Rockne had a 4-2 record in 1928 going into the Army Game when the teams met again. Biff Jones' army unit was 6-0. Army was favored. ND wound up the year at 5-4, one of its worst records in history

It was clearly Coach Rockne's worst record ever.

Despite it being a bad season for ND, nobody was laying down on the job. A lot of history was made when Coach Rockne delivered his famous "Gipper Speech" at halftime of the Army game. Rockne was trying to salvage something from his worst season as a coach at Notre Dame. To inspire the players, he told them the story of the tragic death of the greatest player ever at ND, George Gipp. Rockne could really motivate the troops. After this speech, Notre Dame looked like a different team.

Here's how that one went down in history: On November 10, 1928, when Rockne's Notre Dame team was tied with Army 0-0 at the end of the half, Coach Rockne entered the locker room and he recounted the words that he heard from George Gipp's lips while on his deathbed in 1920:

"I've got to go, Rock. It's all right. I'm not afraid. Some time, Rock, when the team is up against it, when things are going wrong and the breaks are beating the boys, tell them to go in there with all they've got and win just one for the Gipper. I don't know where I'll be then, Rock. But I'll know about it, and I'll be happy."

Rockne delivered this short speech as only he could. It fully inspired the team, which then went out and outscored Army in the second half and won the game 12-6. The phrase "Win one for the Gipper" was infused into the lexicon of American society and was later used as a political slogan by Ronald Reagan, who in 1940 portrayed Gipp in *Knute Rockne, All American.*

Rockne's Irish stormed onto the field in this famous game after the inspirational talk. Ironically, it was Army that scored first in the second half. But, ND came right back. Jack Chevigny, who got Rockne's halftime message loud and clear then answered with a 1-yard plunge on fourth down. He announced, "That's one for the Gipper!" – yelling it out as loud as he could as he plowed into the end zone. Or so legend has it.

Like Army, Notre Dame is a school blessed with many legends and the 1929 Gipper story is just one of them. But, that plunge did not get the game won. The Irish did not get the point after. Even with Chevigny's plunge for a TD, ND was still tied 6-6 with Army.

The second legend from this game came when a real speedster from Los Angeles named Johnny O'Brien who had become a track star and held the world record for the 60-yard hurdles, got his first chance to play football for Notre Dame. O'Brien was on the football team, but seldom played. He was on the bench for the whole game, until, in an inspired moment, Rockne turned to the fleet Johnny, and with the score 6-6 sent his speedster onto the field.

The ball was snapped, the quarterback retreated and threw it in the general vicinity of Johnny O'Brien. Johnny got under the ball, caught it, and then quite literally, he sprinted as only he could into the end zone for the final 12-6 margin of victory.

Therefore, on this one day that the Irish won one for the Gipper, Johnny O'Brien made that ONE PLAY that ever after labeled him Johnny "One Play" O'Brien.

Biff Jones' team was 6-3 when facing ND, the following year, 1929 Rockne's team was undefeated and heading for the National Championship. ND barely defeated Army 7-0 in a real tough played game.

Chris Cagle of Army offered his take: "The Army-Navy Game this year was the greatest I have ever had the pleasure to take part in during my college career. I am thankful that I had the opportunity to play against men, who could execute their assignments so well on that frozen field and I am glad that we were a real barrier before the national champions for it may be years before another tram has such a successful season."

Notre Dame rebounded in 1929 as noted when Rockne was diagnosed with life-threatening phlebitis in his leg, missed some games and at times directed the team from a wheelchair or a cot. Rockne's ND team went 9-0, and was very tough to beat. Their season was punctuated by a 13-12 victory over powerful USC, and the Irish won the national title for Notre Dame. Rockne was on a roll and followed up with a 10-0 record and another national championship in 1930 as Rockne regained his health.

Army, then coached by Major Ralph Sasse, was again Notre Dame's toughest opponent and for want of an extra point, there would have been another tie on the records of both teams. The 1930 Army-ND game at Soldier Field in Chicago before 110,000 fans was won in a nail-biter by Notre Dame W (7-6).

Let's look at the very close Army-ND game as again without the victory over Army, Notre Dame could not have won the national championship. Though there are some ND student writer biases shown in this article We have picked the game summary facts as noted in the Student written ND Scholastic magazine to portray this game because it does report most of what happened in the game:

> *NOTRE DAME 7, Army 6. And Notre Dame still holds the trail of unbeaten football teams. For the third successive year Notre Dame has taken the measure of the Cadets in this annual grid classic. Playing on the rain-soaked sod of Soldier field, Chicago, the Fighting Irish annexed their eighteenth straight victory.*
>
> *It was Notre Dame's game from start to finish but not until the last four minutes were the Rocknets able to score. On the same play that gave Notre Dame a victory over Northwestern a week before, Marchmont Schwartz galloped 55 yards behind perfect interference for a touchdown. Frank Carideo place-kicked the extra point that won the game.*
>
> *Army scored on a blocked punt just six plays later. King, left end for the Cadets, leaped in the way of Carideo's punt and fell on the ball behind the Notre Dame goal line. Army sent in Broshous, their drop-kick specialist, to try for the extra point but he was smothered by five Notre Dame linemen before he could get the ball away.*
>
> *The heavy going made anything but straight football impossible and both teams resorted to punting and watching for fumbles. Carideo gave*

the Rocknets a big advantage with his kicks, averaging 42 yards for 14 punts, and on two occasions kicking more than 65 yards.

Notre Dame's shock troops started the game and outplayed the Cadets during the first quarter. They penetrated to the Army 10-yard line but lacked the launch to score.

In the second quarter, the Notre Dame varsity entered the game, and Army substituted a new backfield. All the playing during this quarter was done on the Army half of the field and Notre Dame had the ball on the 12-yard line when the half ended.

Twice during the third quarter the Fighting Irish threatened, but they lost the ball once on a fumble and again on downs. Notre Dame recovered Stecker's fumble on the Army 11-yard line as the quarter ended. Schwartz tossed a lateral to Brill which put the ball on the six, Brill hit guard for two yards, and then Schwartz was stopped on the line of scrimmage. Carideo dropped back to try for a field goal but his kick barely left the ground.

The ball was brought out to the 20-yard line, and after two exchanges of punts the fireworks started. A clever sequence of plays drew the left side of the Army line out of position. A simple off-tackle smash executed to perfection and Schwartz was off for 55 yards and a touchdown. The sloppy grid prevented any side-stepping, Schwartz depending on speed alone, but that was enough. This run of Schwartz's was only a sample of what might have occurred quite frequently had the footing been good.

Army's touchdown was the result of relaxation on the part of the Notre Dame linemen. The Fighting Irish forwards crashed through on the next play so decisively that they atoned in full for their one mistake of the game.

The Cadets' heavy line had a distinct advantage because of the condition of the field but they were outplayed during all four quarters. The West Pointers failed to make a first down in the second half, and two of the three that they made during the first half were the results of penalties against Notre Dame. Carlmark and Messinger, the Army ends, caused many Notre Dame plays to go awry, but they were out of the picture completely when Schwartz was galloping towards their goal line. Stecker was the outstanding Army player and is undoubtedly one of the best defensive backs of the year.

This was the seventeenth game between Notre Dame and West Point and became Notre Dame's twelfth victory. Army has won... four of the contests and one game ended in a scoreless tie. Army's defeat was the first of the season for them and also the first that they have suffered under the regime of their new coach, Major Sasse.

On November 28, 1931 archrival ND, always one of the finest competitors the Army Cadets would meet, a team that had never played Army as a home game, went into Yankee Stadium ready to win. It did not happen Army beat Notre Dame L (12-0) at Yankee Stadium before a crowd of 78,559. Coach / Major Ralph Sasse's team enjoyed an 8-2-1 record in 1931.

Chapter 21 Army-Notre Dame Rivalry Part II of II

Red Blaik v Frank Leahy

In Leahy's first season in 1941, Notre Dame was at its best and it was just beginning the Leahy dynasty. Its record in Coach Leahy's first year was (8-0-1). It could have been a National Championship but for a tie against the Army Cadets. Notre Dame was proud to clock in with four home wins out of four tries. Home wins came from Arizona W (38-7), Indiana W (19-6), Illinois W (49-14), and USC W (20-18).

Leahy's Irish also did well in the "away" victories category with a big win against Georgia Tech W (20-0) to begin the away game triumphs. Then there was Carnegie Tech W (16-0), Navy W (20-13) and Northwestern W (7-6).

The only blemish on # 3 AP Notre Dame's record was Army, which had never played an away game at Notre Dame. Army and ND tied

T (0-0) at Yankee Stadium. Paul Lillis was captain of Notre Dame's team in 1941.

The Irish were ranked # 3 after the season because of the tie with Army. Otherwise, Notre Dame would have had its first national championship in the Frank Leahy era.

Ironically, it was also Earl "Red Blaik's" first season at Army and the two would be tangling for National Championships throughout the decade of the 1940's. Frank Leah and Red Blaik are immortal legends in American football and both could win football games with any teams. Army and Notre Dame were fortunate to have such great coaches to play football in the 1940's. Army was 5-3-1 in 1941.

When the teams played to a scoreless tie in the fifth Army game of the season, Army's record was 4-0. After the tie with ND, the Cadets would come up short against Harvard, Penn, and Navy, finishing with a 5-3-1 season.

This summary from Scholastic tells the story of the game:

Army 0; ND 0; writeup—Scholastic Magazine

With student spirit on the upsurge as a result of the Illinois rout, the Fighting Irish scrambled through the cheering students at the Circle to make their way to a special train to New York. Speeding eastward, they carried the appeal for revenge on a Cadet eleven that in 1940, with the exception of Steve Juzwik's brilliant touchdown run from a pass interception, had drubbed all the fight out of a high-riding Irish eleven.

A hard rain that began falling in New York on Friday night virtually washed out all these appeals and dampened the spirits of both Cadet and Irish elevens. Saturday afternoon the rain was still falling as seventy-six thousand onlookers huddled under umbrellas and newspapers, and watched the two teams wade up and down the field for two hours.

It was a fierce, hard-hitting" game in which both teams were forced to the monotonous procedure of two or three attempts for muddy gains on the line and then a punt. It was Army's Mazur who kept the Irish sliding in the mud with his seemingly-impossible end runs and amazing cutbacks over the line and his booming punts. Early in the first quarter, Mazur slid around left end behind an army of blockers to the Irish 25. From there Maupin and Hatch moved the ball to the Notre Dame 10 where, despite the mud, the Irish line braced and threw the Cadets back, Harry Wright tried to shake Evans or Juzwik loose around the ends, but Army's ends could not be taken out of play.

Evans' kicks were long but Mazur's were longer, and the Irish were forced to do most of their mudding in their own back yard. Late in the second quarter the slimy pigskin rolled off the side of Mazur's foot on the Army 45. Notre Dame took it up there and with Juzwik sweeping the ends and Evans ploughing for short gains at center, moved to the Cadet 17 where the Army line closed in and the Cadets took the ball on downs.

With Evans and Mazur dueling with third down punts the two teams fought through the third quarter. The Irish went down to the Army 28 on the strength of Creighton Miller's smashing gains at tackle and Bill Earley's slashes inside the right end. There the Notre Dame backs lost their footing and Army took over the ball. The Cadets sent Ralph Hill inside the Irish right end and Hatch over guard to bring the ball down to the Irish 25; there the holes at end and guard closed and the Cadets made big ripples as the Irish forwards cut them down.

With less than two minutes left in the fourth quarter the Irish machine churned over the Army line but the ticking seconds sped by while the Army line gave ground slowly. On the Cadet 20-yard line with seven seconds of play remaining, Harry Wright, moved out on the right wing along with Steve Juzwik and Angelo Bertelli for another try at the Boston College famous triple-flanker, the last chance for the Irish to come out of the Cadet clutch untied and undefeated. The muddy ball came up from center with a wobbling spin, and sailed through Evans' arms. He chased it, picked it up, evaded two tacklers only to be tackled and splashed out of bounds as the game

The 1944 Army ND Game

All Army fans had been counting and were in fact, angry that the Cadets were not beating Notre Dame regularly as the team had been doing in the 1920's. It had been thirteen years since Army had beaten Notre Dame. In fact, the last time Army had scored against the Irish was in 1938. In 1944, the Irish again were the defending national champions, but ND had lost many key players to graduation and enlistment in the armed services. The Irish even lost head coach Frank Leahy and other assistants to military service, and were now being led by Ed McKeever.

1944 Army ND Game

Notre Dame went into the Army game at 5–1 and ranked #5, coming off a 32–13 loss to Navy. The Army squad was being led by the greats -- Glenn Davis and Doc Blanchard. The Cadets also had a quarterback named Doug Kenna, and a transfer from the University of Texas, sprinter Max Minor.

Army simply overwhelmed the Irish. Kenna opened the scoring with a run for touchdown. He wasn't done, as he played defense as well, intercepting an Irish pass, which led to a scoring run by Minor. Kenna then pulled a trifecta of sorts, when he passed for a third score. Davis, a late scratch as a starter, also intercepted a pass, and had two offensive runs for scores. By halftime, Army had a commanding 33–0 lead. Notre Dame had no idea what had hit them.

Kenna added another scoring pass, and Davis another run for a score. Even Army's back-ups got into the act. Harold Tavzel, a second-string tackle, intercepted a poorly thrown pass from the Irish quarterback Frank Dancewicz, and jogged a few yards for another score. When the game was over, Army had whooped Notre Dame 59–0, handing the Irish its worst loss in the program's history. The Irish would recover its season, winning the last three games to finish 8–2 and ranked No. 9 in the nation. That is how good Army was in 1944.

When asked by a reporter about the score, Army halfback Doc Blanchard said, "If there was anyone to blame for the size of the margin, it was Notre Dame, which fired our desire to win with its long humiliation of Army teams."

"Talking to players who actually competed in those games, they were bitter, bitter rivals," said Army executive athletic director Bob Beretta, who's worked at West Point for three decades. "They were challenging for the place of the most elite program in the country.

Many wondered just why there was so much intensity in the Army-ND Game. Everybody wanted to know which team was the best and which team was better than another. The Associated Press college football poll was devised in 1936 to try to answer this simple, yet most divisive question in sports: Who's better? By having a national poll, it also helped give a regional sport more of a national scope. In many ways because of this one factor, it helped define the Army-Notre Dame rivalry as being about the whole country.

"It (the poll) absolutely was a factor. I think it was a happening," AD Beretta said. "All the eyes of the college football world were on New York City and Yankee Stadium for Army-Notre Dame. That was probably going to be the game to determine the national champion. It wasn't a game. It was an event. It was must-see football."

Notre Dame was ranked #1 without dispute three times from 1936-39 and another 30 times in the 1940s, when the Irish won four of their eight national championships. Frank Leahy was able to get every last drop out of ND players and Red Blaik did the same for Army. Though Army was not ranked from 1936-39 it earned the top ranking 22 times in its special decade under Blaik, which included five unbeaten seasons.

1945 Army v Notre Dame

Army overwhelmed war-depleted Notre Dame in 1944 (59–0) and 1945 (48–0), when ND had interim coaches.

1945 Army-ND Game

Again, 1945 wasn't as bad as it had been the year before. Reeling from a loss to Navy a week earlier in 1944, Notre Dame came to Yankee Stadium and got destroyed, 59-0. In 1945, having held Navy to a scoreless tie, the Fighting Irish came in more confident, and it made a difference … for a few minutes.

It was just 7-0 after one quarter before Army began to pour it on. The Cadets scored twice in the second quarter, then Barney Poole blocked a punt, setting up a 21-yard Davis score. For the day, Davis had three touchdowns, Blanchard two.

Notre Dame gained 184 yards and threatened a couple of times. But against the second-best team in the country, Army gained a cool 441 yards and cruised. Again.

This game derives most of its greatness by the fact that it was the first No. 1 versus No. 2 matchup between the Irish and the Cadets. But there was never much question about the actual result.

Army rode tailback Doc Blanchard, who would go on to win the Heisman that year, to follow its 59-0 drubbing of the Irish the previous year with a 48-0 uncontested shutout. Army was truly dominant for the second consecutive year, winning back-to-back national championships.

The 1946 Army vs. Notre Dame football game was another like the 1945 game. It was played on November 9, 1946. This game is regarded as one of the 20th century Games of the Century.

This contest received massive national attention. Before the service academies ceased to be the major football powers, as they were in the 1940's, the game was usually played at a neutral site, where there was a huge field available such as in New York City or Chicago.

Both Army and ND were undefeated going into the 1946 game at Yankee Stadium. Both teams were averaging over 30 points per game. Army came in under the strength of a 25-game winning streak, last losing to Notre Dame in 1943 (26–0), but the Cadets had won the last two contests between the schools by scores of 59–0 and 48–0 respectively.

Army had the defending Heisman Trophy winner, Doc Blanchard, also known as "Mr. Inside," the man who would win it that year, Glenn Davis, also known as "Mr. Outside," and one of the nation's top quarterbacks in Arnold Tucker.

Notre Dame had the quarterback who would win the Heisman the next year, Johnny Lujack, and end Leon Hart of Notre Dame won the Heisman in 1949 (the only time ever that a college football game had four Heisman Trophy winners).

Both Tucker and Lujack were also outstanding defensive backs at a time when football players, college as well as professional, usually played both offense and defense. Notre Dame had defeated eventual 1947 Rose Bowl participant Illinois in Champaign, 26–6, to open the season. On October 26, they won at #17 Iowa, 41–6. The game leading up to this one was a 28–0 Irish defeat of Navy at Baltimore.

Despite the high-scoring and much-hyped offenses of both squads, the game ended in a scoreless tie. Each team's best chance at scoring came in back-to-back drives. Army's Tucker intercepted Lujack, and Lujack then made a touchdown-saving tackle on Blanchard a few plays later.

Notre Dame's defense did something no other team had ever done — it held the famous "Touchdown Twins," Blanchard and Davis, to a total of 79 yards. Both defenses played career-best games. To show just how great the defenses were in that game, and for the season, seven linemen who were in that game were nominated for Lineman of the Week honors in the weekly Associated Press poll.

Joe Steffy, an All-American Army guard who helped shut down the Notre Dame running game, won the honor, followed closely by Notre Dame right tackle George Sullivan and freshman lineman Jim Martin, who helped stifle Army's running attack and who dropped Davis on consecutive plays for losses totaling 17 yards. Both Notre Dame coach Leahy and Army coach Blaik called the game "a terrific battle of defenses."

Both teams would finish the season undefeated with this one tie, but the pundits gave Notre Dame the national championship. It was the weight of the Associated Press that had Army coming in second. Neither team were accepted bowl bids at this time, and so neither could improve or make things worse with a late season loss.

In 1947, the Pacific Coast Conference and the Big Nine Conference, the forerunners of the Pac-12 and Big Ten, signed an agreement to begin with the 1947 Rose Bowl of matching their conference champions. The national sports press wanted either Notre Dame or Army to play against #4 and undefeated UCLA. Instead, #5 Illinois was the first Midwestern team to go by the terms of the agreement, and routed UCLA in the Rose Bowl, 45–14.

With Blanchard, Davis and Tucker having graduated, Army's unbeaten streak would be broken the following year, by Columbia University. Notre Dame would not lose until early in the 1950 season. Sporting News named the 1944-45 Army Cadets and the 1946 Fighting Irish the second and fifth greatest teams of the Twentieth Century respectively.

This was only the sixth time that the number one ranked team faced the number two ranked team since the inception of the Associated Press Football Poll in 1936. This would not happen again until the 1963 Rose Bowl.

Considering that the last two Army encounters at Yankee Stadium in 1944 and 1945 resulted in Army wins of (0-59) and (0-48), one would expect there would be drama in the Army-ND game, and there was exactly that. Both the Irish and the battle-hardened Army team came to win; yet the defenses were so good that neither could score.

Coach Red Blaik's squad would have to be beaten to lose its status as the No.1 team in the nation.

Well, not exactly!

Frank Leahy had coached Notre Dame to a national championship in 1943, then left South Bend for the Navy and spent his duty time in the South Pacific. He returned to Notre Dame in '46 and he had a great bunch of lettermen-turned soldiers who still had playing eligibility remaining. The Irish were loaded and determined to win. Leahy's Irish not only wanted to get back their No.1 ranking, but they were none too happy about the trouncing the team received in the prior two years. They were ready to avenge the 0-59 and 0-48 losses to Army in 1944 and '45. Despite all that, they could not score a point on Army in 1946.

For years of matchups from 1913 to 1946, no games had ever been played at Notre Dame Stadium. So, it was a given that the game would be at Army, which played its home games against Notre Dame at Yankee Stadium.

The wartime gravy train of talent was over for Army, and no significant new players contributed in 1946. After two national championships, the Army team was still great at 7–0 and Notre Dame was 5–0 when the two met on November 9. The #1 Cadets came in averaging 30 points a game while the No.2 Irish averaged 35. Final score: T (0–0).

> **By the way:** The 1941 army / ND game in Frank Leahy's first year at ND, was also a 0-0 tie. The Irish finished 1941 at 8-0-1. It was the only blemish on the record and it prevented Notre Dame from winning a mythical national championship (MNC).

Army's 25–game winning streak was over but the Cadets were still unbeaten. They won their last two games, but had to struggle past Navy. Meanwhile, Notre Dame shut out Northwestern and Tulane and beat Southern Cal by 20.

A week later, the final AP poll gave the championship to the Irish. Nonetheless the end-of-season polling was not always 100% accepted and there was no BCS. Army still claims what is called an MNC for 1946, giving them a trifecta. The MNC stands for Mythical National Championship.

As several other games over the years, the Army-ND game of 1946 was labeled "Game of the Century." Never before was the hype so pervasive as much as this meeting of #1 Army and #2 Notre Dame. Before the ND players and coaches went to fight the war, Notre Dame had won the 1943 mythical national championship (MNC). Army won in 1944 and 1945 when Notre Dame was absent without leave. This 1946 special game featured some outstanding statistics:

> *4 Heisman Trophy winners, 3 Outland Trophy winners, and 10 Hall of Famers, not counting the Hall of Fame coaches on each side. Notre Dame claims MNCs for 1943, 1946, 1947, and 1949, and Army claims MNCs for 1944, 1945, and 1946. This was a true clash of the titans, an*

intersection of 2 of the greatest runs in college football history: Army going 27-0-1 1944-1946 and Notre Dame going 36-0-2 1946-1949.

Army remained #1 after the scoreless tie, but when they struggled to beat 1-8 Navy 21-18 in their finale, as noted, Notre Dame passed them up for #1 in the final AP poll. To make matters murkier in 1946, (11-0) Georgia also claimed an MNC for 1946, based on finishing #1 in the Williamson math formula rating. That's a lame basis for the claim, but Georgia won all their games by more than a TD, and they were thus a worthy contender for the MNC.

Pictured above is the defining play of 1946's "Game of the Century:" Notre Dame's Bill Gompers turning the corner on 4th down and heading for Army's goal line. But alas, he didn't make it. He didn't even reach the 2-yard line for a first down, and this game saw no other serious scoring threats, ending in a 0-0 stalemate. I do not have the link for the required cite below.

Fullback Doc Blanchard and halfback Glenn Davis were still consensus All Americans (AA), for the third year in a row, and Davis also took home the Heisman Trophy this year, Blanchard having won it in 1945. End Hank Foldberg joined them as a consensus AA, and quarterback Arnold Tucker was a non-consensus AA. Guard Joe Steffy was another.

1958 Amy V ND

From ND Student Scholastic Football Review with adjustments:

DAWKINS GETS LOOSE for 14 yards in the second quarter. He gained consistently through Notre Dame's line as did his fellow halfback, Bob Anderson.

DAWKINS (24) DRIVES for goal line from six yards out in final minute of the game. He had put' Army in scoring position by catching pass for 23 yards.

Oct. 11—The Notre Dame dream that had been fondly nurtured ever since the closing games in the 1957 season— an undefeated Notre Dame football team in 1958—^was rudely shattered this afternoon by Army as the Cadets plummeted the Irish from the unbeaten ranks, 14-2.

The game was played in an electrified atmosphere provided by a new Notre Dame Stadium record crowd of 60,564.

Army, bent on avenging last year's spectacular defeat by the Irish and whipping a team that had beaten them with humiliating consistency in many of the two schools' 35 previous gridiron meetings, scored touchdowns in the first and fourth quarters for their third straight victory of the year. The Cadets, carrying a # 3 national ranking into the game, displayed a sound, balanced attack, and capitalized on an exasperating rash of Irish fumbles to give them their eighth win in the series between the two schools.

After quarterback Bob Williams moved the opening kickoff to the Notre Dame 19-yard line, a determined Irish ground offensive advanced the ball to Army's 32 where the drive was stopped by Nick

Pietrosante's fumble. Now in possession of the football. Army impressively demonstrated their vaunted halfback duo of Pete Dawkins and Bob Anderson, who together spearheaded a march that was thwarted on the ND four-yard line where Williams intercepted Cadet quarterback Joe Caldwell's pass.

With Pietrosante bulling into the visitors' line on three straight plays, the Irish netted their fourth first down on the 15. Williams and Jim Just, right halfback, miscued on the next handoff, and an alert Army defenseman. Bob Novogratz, the game's outstanding lineman, pounced on the ball on the ND 21. Thrusts by Dawkins and Anderson drove the ball to the 16-yard line where Caldwell fired to end Jack Morrison who grabbed the pass on the goal line and stepped over for the first touchdown of the game. Jim Kennedy's try for the placement was wide.

Irish left halfback Pat Doyle took the ensuing kickoff in the end zone and sped up the middle for 31 yards as the first quarter ended. With Notre Dame's second unit in the game, Ron Toth, fullback, smashed off-tackle for six yards, and sophomore halfback Ked Mack added two. First-string Irish signal caller, Williams, kept the next handoff himself and pushed up the middle for seven yards. Army was charged guilty of a personal foul and the 15-yarder advanced the ball to the Cadets' 38. Three consecutive line bucks by Toth were contained by Army, and on fourth and six Williams' pass to Mack dropped incomplete.

A clipping penalty marred Dawkins' pitchback around left end, but Caldwell called the very same play on the next down and the Cadets' fleet captain picked up eleven yards. Then Anderson made the first down. With a third and six situation, Caldwell passed to "Lonesome End" Bill Carpenter for a 15- yard gain. Two plays moved the Cadets to the Notre Dame 28, and on third Army called on Carpenter again. This time he fumbled after receiving the pass, but fullback Harry Walters recovered for a one-yard pickup. With fourth and three, Dawkins scampered up the middle for seven yards and a first down on the enemy's 21.

Dawkins again led the assault for the Cadets and put them within striking distance of the Irish goal with a first down on the ND nine. The Notre Dame line buckled itself together and three plays could only advance the ball five more yards. On last down, Caldwell's pass, intended for Anderson in the end zone, was batted down by Norm Odyniec, reserve Irish fullback, and Notre Dame regained possession.

To open the second half, Dawkins fielded Monty Stickles' kickoff, and Pietrosante drove him out of bounds on the 17. Two penalties pushed the Cadets back to their one-yard stripe where on third down, Caldwell stepped back into the end zone to punt. An inspired rush by Stickles, charging in from his left end post, caught Caldwell behind the goal line, and the officials ruled a safety although the Army quarterback vainly tried to throw the ball to a receiver.

Trailing now by only a scant four points, the Irish seemed, determined to break into the lead. 'Displaying an imaginative offense for the first time in the game, ND took the kickoff following the safety and marched swiftly to the Army 34 where they were stopped.

2:53 remained in the quarter as the Irish made another scoring bid. Just broke loose for 15 yards; Odyniec and Pietrosante banged away, driving the ball to the ND 40 as play moved into the final quarter. The march was climaxed as Odyniec streaked around end for 16 yards and a first down on the Army 21. Two incomplete passes after Pietrosante was finally stopped on a line plunge relegated the Irish to a fourth and eleven situation, when George Izo, reserve quarterback, entered the game, obviously to pass. Izo, however, dropped the handoff, giving Army possession on the 23.

After halting another Cadet offensive series in three plays, Notre Dame took a punt on their 45 and started their third drive of the half. This, too, however, was thwarted as Williams' screen pass to Toth failed to gain on fourth down and three, and Army regained the ball on their 35. A combination of Dawkins-Anderson cross bucks and Caldwell's accurate passing steadily moved the visitors down toward the Notre Dame goal as time fleeted by. With seven seconds remaining, Dawkins circled left end and punched into the end zone, placing the Cadets in an impregnable 12-2 lead. Dawkins' pass found Anderson for the two-points. Army picked up a fine win W (14-2).

1995 Army v ND courtesy of NY Times

EAST RUTHERFORD, N.J., Oct. 14— Notre Dame football has elevated itself from sport to myth at the expense of Army. The rivalry produced the "Four Horsemen" nickname in 1924 and the "Win One for the Gipper" speech before the 1928 game. Today, Army came within 2 feet of establishing an unlikely legend of its own, only to see the third-smallest player on the Irish roster make the afternoon's biggest play in rescuing a 28-27 victory over the unyielding Cadets.

With 39 seconds remaining, Army's clever wishbone offense had threatened a magnificent upset as quarterback Ronnie McAda tossed a 7-yard touchdown pass to split end Leon Gantt. Notre Dame, a three-touchdown favorite, had seen its 28-7 lead crumble to a slim point; its last three possessions had ended with two fumbles and an interception. Coach Bob Sutton unhesitatingly called for Army to attempt a two-point conversion. He had no choice, really. Army had won only eight of the first 46 games in this series, none since 1958.

Our players deserved to go for two," Sutton said. "I think they would have been damn disappointed if we didn't."
The ball was placed on the 2-yard line, as a nervous crowd of 74,218 watched at Giants Stadium. Army decided on a "slam-release" pass, in which tight end Ron Leshinski makes a block at the line of scrimmage then slides into the right flat along the goal line. But Leshinski was jostled at the line of scrimmage, and he caught the pass at the 1-yard line.

"He lost his bearings; he didn't know where he was," Sutton said.

Ivory Covington, a 5-foot-10-inch, 163-pound sophomore cornerback from Decatur, Ga., rushed up from Notre Dame's zone coverage and slammed into the 6-3, 240-pound Leshinski, using the tight end's momentum against him. Covington was moving forward, while Leshinski was running sideways. Despite giving up 77 pounds to the tight end, Covington expertly shoved Leshinski out of bounds 2 feet short of the goal line.

"I've got to get in on that play," Leshinski said.

Except that he didn't.

Covington, who is smaller even than Notre Dame's kicker, said that he tried to keep low on the tackle, because he had been taught that "low man wins."

"He probably should have driven me into the end zone with his weight advantage," Covington said. "I'm not as strong as he is. I definitely don't weigh as much. I just wanted to make the play; I just wanted to take him down, and I did."

With the tackle, Notre Dame (5-2) had earned another storied victory in this rivalry, while Army (1-3-1) had lost twice and been tied once in the final minute this season.

"This is a crushing defeat," Army safety Jim Cantelupe said. "This is a game of inches, and they won that inch."
Army, it seemed, won everything else. The Cadets ran wild with a flexed wishbone attack, also called a "wingbone," because both halfbacks are lined up on the wings. With deft ball-handling and committed downfield blocking, the Cadets rushed for 365 yards -- a career-high 159 by halfback Ron Thomas and 104 by John Conroy, the fullback who grew up in Chicago idolizing Notre Dame.

Notre Dame had a considerable size advantage along the offensive line, and the freshman tailback Autry Denson ran confidently for 119 yards and two short touchdowns. Two minutes into the third quarter, quarterback Ron Powlus flipped a screen pass to fullback Marc Edwards, who lumbered untouched for a 46-yard touchdown and a 28-7 Notre Dame lead. Still, Army would not concede.

A 5-yard touchdown run by Conroy pulled Army within 28-14 with 7 minutes 40 seconds left in the third quarter. Notre Dame began to fall apart. Edwards lost a fumble at the Army 4-yard line. Then, with 6:10 remaining in the game, Powlus was intercepted by Army safety Tay Tomasites. Five plays later, Conroy muscled his way to a 3-yard touchdown. The Cadets were within 28-21.

Notre Dame continued to falter. With 2:33 left, the Irish faced fourth-and-inches from their 42-yard line. Coach Lou Holtz, in the press box recovering from neck surgery, tried to call for a timeout through his headset, but the lines got mixed, and he ended up speaking to Notre

Dame's defensive coaches. Holtz wanted a timeout to decide whether to punt or attempt the first down, but his message never got through.

"Much confusion," is how Powlus described the situation.
No play was sent in, Powlus said, so he attempted a quarterback sneak. But he fumbled the snap and linebacker Brian Tucker recovered for Army at the Irish 42.

"When the ball got snapped, I was the most surprised person in the world," Holtz said.

Now Army had a chance to win. McAda, the quarterback, said he had pictured this situation "1,000 times in the last two weeks, us getting the ball with three minutes to go and driving for the winning score."

"It was like I was living my dream," he said.
Except that Covington turned Army's dream into a nightmare.

"The players are tremendously disappointed," Sutton said.

"They have given a lot and they haven't received yet what they deserve. We just have to have the toughness, commitment and conviction that what we're doing is going to pay off. I'm not going to waver on that, and I don't think our team will waver on that."

The Army ND Summation

Notre Dame's ability to gain its unique position among the nation's college football programs was undeniably uniquely fueled by the beginning of its rivalry with Army. It all began with the 1913 aerial-driven upset, through Grantland Rice's description of the Four Horsemen during the 1924 national championship season, to the "win one for the Gipper" victory in 1928, through the epic battles of the 1940s with national championships on the lines--all against the backdrop of the national media and sold-out games with huge numbers of fans in New York City, Chicago, and Philadelphia--only Army was a worthy opponent and the catalyst for Notre Dame's ascension.

We discussed Army's most recent victory in the series in 1958, when the #3 ranked buoyed with the talent of Pete Dawkins defeated the fourth-ranked Irish 14-2 in Notre Dame Stadium. There were a couple of near misses for Army in the 1990s such as the 28-27 thriller, which we discussed, played in the Meadowlands in East Rutherford, New Jersey, in 1995.

The next Army game whenever it gets played may not carry the same stakes as some of those games in the early days of the rivalry. But when you look upon the landscape of college football in 2016 before the game, it's undeniable that these two schools and their epic battles of the 20th century did more to establish college football within the fabric of American society than any other schools to be found.

As of August 2017, Army is not on ND's future schedule and vice versa. I suspect the scheduling will happen soon and the series will continue. Check out the solution below which gives Army an edge in college football.

Solving the recruiting problem for good

I would recommend a return to the days in the past when Army did not have to pay as much attention to NCAA rules. It would make Army, and all the service Academies first choices for the finest athletes in the nation and strengthen the Armed Services to book. What am I talking about?

How about eight years eligibility for any service academy student either before or after their graduation from let's say, USMA West Point. I would suggest up to six years of eligibility for a player at the Academy and additional two at any other school such as Notre Dame. Army had a number of these in their day such as Elmer Oliphant (Degree from Purdue) Christian Cagle (degree from Louisiana Tech) who played college ball for eight years Why not again.

Considering the disadvantages Army has in recruiting this would certainly give the service academies an advantage. For what they do for the citizens of our country, I say that Congress and the President should override the NCAA on this one. Any seconds? I bet Army would be on ND's schedule every year if this rule change were made.

Chapter 22 History of the Army-Navy Game by Mandy Howard etc.

Army-Navy Game Is a Great Tradition

On a cold November afternoon in 1890, two branches of the U.S. armed forces turned to face one another on the field of battle.
The *New York Sun* warned of freezing temperatures that Nov. 24 and reported in a blurb on page 2: "About 180 New Yorkers will go up to West Point at 11 o'clock this morning on a special train. The game will be called at 2 o'clock and will be followed by a hop."
A century and a quarter later, the college football rivalry between the Army Black Knights of the U.S. Military Academy at West Point, N.Y., and the Navy Midshipmen of the U.S. Naval Academy in Annapolis, Md., has become one of the greatest of all time.

Thank you Mandy Howard:
http://www.moaa.org/Content/Publications-and-Media/Features-and-Columns/MOAA-Features/History-of-the-Army-Navy-Football-Game.aspx

Sometimes called the Gray Phantom of West Point, Glenn Davis (41) picks up yardage in Army Navy Game

An impressive history

In 1961, a Plebe named Roger Staubach sat in the stands at the Army-Navy game. "There were 100,000 people there, and [President] John Kennedy was there," Staubach recalls. "I was thinking, What's going to happen next year? I don't think I can play in this thing. It's too big of a deal."

But in 1962, Staubach thrilled audiences nationwide. "My first Army-Navy game and when I played Super Bowl VI against the Dolphins [were] by far the most nervous I've ever been," he says.

"We beat Army that year, and that was as big a thrill as I've ever had winning a football game, when we beat Army in 1962."

After that, the stage was set for the 1963 epic battle between Staubach, who had just won the Heisman Trophy, and Army star quarterback Rollie Stichweh.

That game, however, unexpectedly was postponed, following the tragic assassination of Kennedy, who hadn't missed an Army-Navy game during his presidency.

After a week's postponement, first lady Jacqueline Kennedy asked that the game still be played. So Dec. 7, 1963, the nation turned its eyes to Municipal Stadium in Philadelphia (later renamed John F. Kennedy Stadium). "We played the game on behalf of the Kennedy family," Staubach says.

The 1963 matchup also was the first time college football fans witnessed instant replay. The instant replay machine was equipped with videotapes that had episodes of *I Love Lucy* on them, so if the tapes did not record correctly, there was a distinct possibility the biggest game in the country would be interrupted by a Lucy rerun. CBS Sports Director Tony Verna said in a CBS News interview, "If you foul with the Army-Navy game and mess that up, that was the end of your career." They tempted fate only once, replaying a Stichweh touchdown, which prompted commentator Lindsey Nelson to advise viewers, "Ladies and gentlemen, Army has not scored again."

Unmatched rivalry and tradition

The 1963 game and the rivalry between the two academies have been the subject of numerous articles, documentaries, and books. In 1995, both academies allowed unfettered access to bestselling sports author John Feinstein, who chronicled the college football year for the book *A Civil War: Army vs. Navy*.

The book takes an inside look at the locker rooms, classes, and minds of the young men who have chosen a path that combines intense football and selfless service and opens the door to understanding the unique difficulties that come with playing Division I football at a service academy today. The book proves that though this game is unshakably woven into college football history, the passion and desperate drive to win are what continue to make this rivalry great.

"There's nothing like Army-Navy," Feinstein says, "not just because of the tradition but because of who plays the game."

Lee Fitting, senior coordinating producer with *ESPN College GameDay*, which visited the Army-Navy game for the first time in 2014, agrees. "I'd argue that it may be the greatest rivalry out there," he says. "A lot of these other rivalries, it's only football, football, football, and that's the end goal. That's not the end goal for the cadets and midshipmen. There's a bigger picture and a bigger perspective, and when you bottle that all together, it's unbelievable."

West Point graduate and Duke University basketball coach Mike Krzyzewski says, "The very nature of collegiate sport is to get our student-athletes to put into practice what they learn in the classroom: loyalty, teamwork, trust, competitiveness, all of these important values. You watch the [Army-Navy] game, and you realize they are going to take it even further. They are going to take it to a real battlefield to protect America and to protect our freedoms."

The desire to win might be greater than in any other rivalry, argues the Naval Academy's first Heisman Trophy winner, Joe Bellino, who won the award in 1960. "They are not only playing for themselves or for their schools but for the millions of veterans who are watching the game."

With such great rivalry comes great tradition, and the Army-Navy game does not disappoint.

Krzyzewski remembers marching onto the field as a cadet: "We all want that feeling of being part of something bigger than you," he says. "You're out there on the field and you think, *Wow, I'm a lucky guy*. You get chills."

Staubach's favorite tradition comes at the end of the game, when the two teams stand together and sing both academy alma maters.

"When the game is over, despite this fierce competitiveness that we have, this history, this rivalry, we become one. Midshipmen going over to the Army side, and Army going over to the Navy side. I just think that is really special. I still get emotional," Staubach says.

Bellino agrees the singing of the alma maters still brings tears to his eyes but shares, with a grin, a lesser-known tradition.

"If you could find a plebe cadet that'd bet you, you'd bet his West Point bathrobe that you'd win the game," Bellino says.

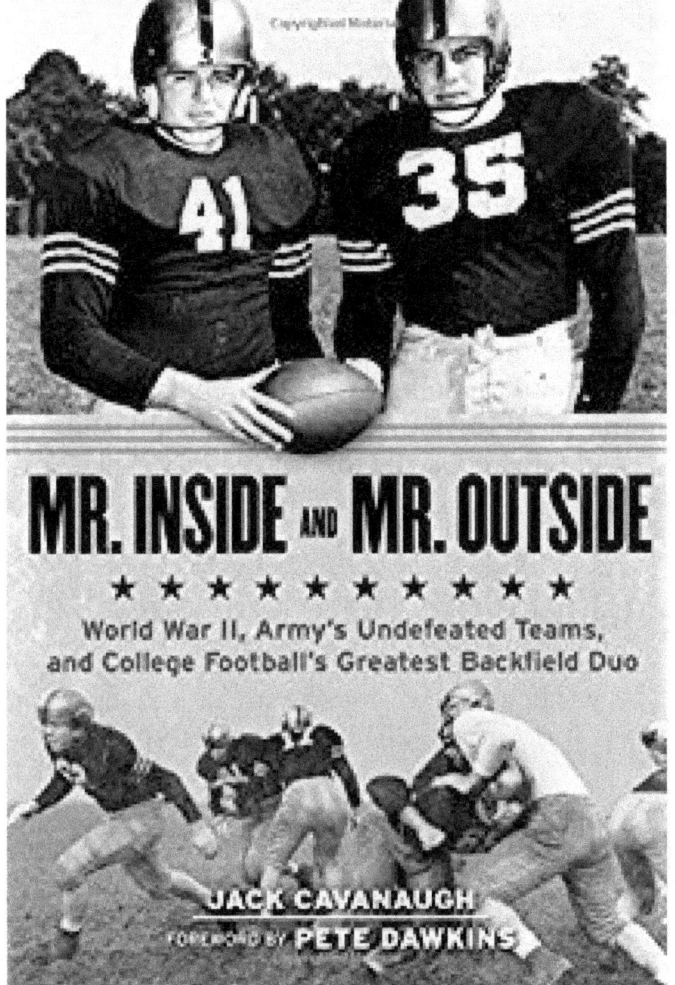

Glenn Davis & Doc Blanchard Never Lost an Army-Navy Game

n

The idea of this surprises Army Maj. Jim Nemec, a former officer representative for the Army football team: "I never heard of plebes betting their bathrobes, at least not in the company I was responsible for. They love their bathrobes. Douglas MacArthur famously wore his in three wars!"

"It gets better," promises Bellino. "If you're lucky enough to win a robe, and you are a varsity athlete, you have the option of putting your varsity letter 'N' on your West Point bathrobe. If you beat Army as an athlete, you receive a star to add to it. It's one of the most beautiful things I own," says Bellino of his West Point bathrobe, covered in six varsity letter N's (three for baseball and three for football) and five stars.

On the 2014 *College GameDay* telecast, ESPN analyst Lee Corso famously showed off the bathrobe he won while he was a Navy assistant.

Add to all of that the feeling of being at the game itself, which, by all accounts, is something you have to experience to understand. "You have to be in the stadium and feel the emotion when the teams come on the field and feel the emotion when they play the national anthem and 8,000 hands snap to attention and understand that every one of the cadets in that stadium and every one of the midshipmen in that stadium have volunteered to die for our country if need be," Feinstein says.

Closing the gap

Currently, Navy is boasting a 14-game streak, the longest in this rivalry's history. [prior to the 2016 Army victory]

Bellino says sooner or later, Army is going to break Navy's winning streak. "But," he continues, "Navy's going to be tough for a number of years, believe me."

In the realm of college football, region to region, fans will claim their rivalry is the greatest. But Army-Navy belongs to the entire nation. The players are future U.S. military officers.

"What replaces Army-Navy?" Krzyzewski asks. "There's nothing," The only question left to ask is: "Go Army, beat Navy, or go Navy, beat Army?"

--- End of Mandy Howard's Fine Piece with pictures added---

Words from Pete Dawkins-- recollections of the Army-Navy Game – from Historynet:

DAWKINS: "I had an unusual run in that we lost one, tied one, and won the one my senior year. So I've had the full kaleidoscope of emotions, from deep despair at a loss to the joy of a victory. My senior year was terribly cold and the turf was frozen, and just before I went out for the coin flip as captain of that team, Coach Blaik said to me, "Now listen, don't try to run back for a touchdown, just make sure you don't fumble." So with those words echoing in my ear, they kicked off to me and an opening appeared, so I cut sharply to my left and my elbow got hit by one of my own players, and the ball went about 20 feet in the air. Navy recovered and scored two plays later. So much for the beginning of my final game of football at Army. But we got the lead and won that game, which is a joyous moment in any Army ballplayer's life."

Notes from 1944 SI Article on Blanchard & Davis
With acknowledgment to Sports Illustrated

"The barometer of Army and Navy's dominance over the rest of college football was another highly regarded team that year: Notre Dame. The Midshipmen managed to best the Fighting Irish 32-13 the first week of November, but the Cadets completely destroyed the squad from South Bend 59-0 a week later in Yankee Stadium. It remains the worst loss in Notre Dame history.

"By that point, the 1944 Army vs. Navy matchup was being touted as the "game of the century" in newspaper accounts, and no less than Grantland Rice predicted it would be "one of the best and most important football games ever played." The big question was where it would be played.
...
"Blaik's pregame speech to his Army team consisted of reading a telegram sent from General Robert Eichelberger, who had been superintendent of West Point two years prior but was then serving in the South Pacific. It concluded, "Win for all the soldiers scattered throughout the world."
...

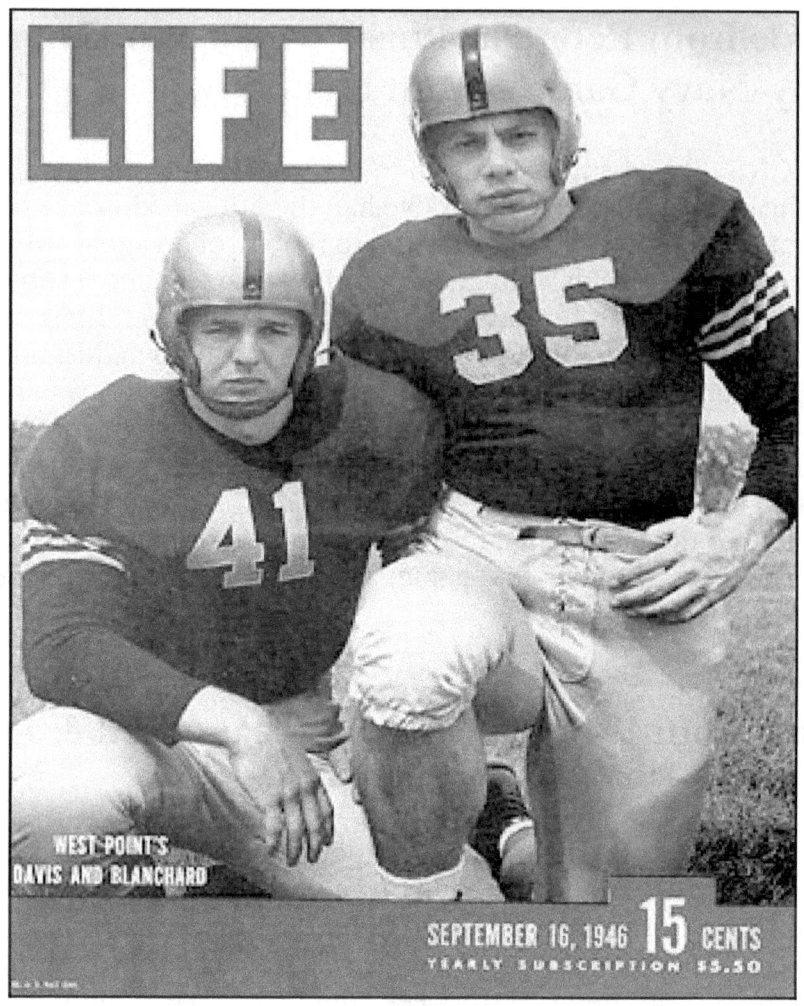

"Army led 7-0 – the first time the Cadets had done so in six years – and that was where the score stood at the intermission.

"The first half proved costly to Navy. The Midshipmen's standout former Crimson Tide players, Whitmire and Jenkins, were forced out of the game due to injuries. The depletion to the defense would prove critical in the final 30 minutes of play.

"In the third quarter, Army blocked a Navy punt and scored a safety when kicker Jack Hansen was downed in the end zone after recovering the ball. The Midshipmen defense stiffened after the kickoff, and a string of tackles for loss and penalties quickly had the Cadets facing third and 47.

"Navy's offense picked up where the defense had left off and went on a 73-yard touchdown drive. Army stopped the Midshipmen once on the goal line but Clyde "Smackover" Scott then smashed it across for the score on the second attempt. As the third period ended it was Army 9, Navy 7, and it remained anybody's ball game.

"The Midshipmen started the fourth quarter driving for the score that would give them the lead, but Army's Davis intercepted a pass and took it to midfield. The Cadets turned to Blanchard, giving him the ball eight consecutive times on a scoring drive that covered 52 yards. Army 16, Navy 7.

"The Midshipmen were forced to punt their next possession, and the Cadets got the ball back on their own 32-yard line. Four plays later, Glen Davis dashed 50 yards for the final touchdown of the game. A few minutes later, the final whistle sounded, and Army had finally beaten its archrival, 23-7.

"Despite throwing five interceptions and fumbling the ball three times, Army kept control of the contest from start to finish. The Cadets outgained the Midshipmen 181-71 on the ground, and Navy was only able to complete 14 of 24 passes for 98 yards."

"Our offense just couldn't get going," explained Comdr. Hagberg. "They whipped us, and that's just about all there is to it."

That's All Folks!

We hope to bring out another version of Great Moments in Army Football in about five years. It will have a nice section on Army West Point Football that offers a commentary on what's new Thank you for choosing this book among the many that are in your options list. I sincerely appreciate it! We plan to offer two new Army titles over the next six months highlighting great players and great coaches of the Black Knights from over the years.

The best to you all – Go Army West Point Black Knights!

LETS GO PUBLISH! Books by Brian Kelly
(Sold at www.bookhawkers.com; Amazon.com, and Kindle.).

Great Moments in Clemson Football CU Football at its best. This is the book.
Great Moments in Florida Gators Football Gators Football from the start. This is the book.
The Constitution Companion. A Guide to Reading and Comprehending the Constitution
The Constitution by Hamilton, Jefferson, & Madison – Big type and in English
PATERNO: The Dark Days After Win # 409. Sky began to fall within days of win # 409 .
JoePa 409 Victories: Say No More!: Winningest Division I-A football coach ever
American College Football: The Beginning From before day one football was played.
Great Coaches in Alabama Football Challenging the coaches of every other program!
Great Coaches in Penn State Football the Best Coaches in PSU's football program
Great Players in Penn State Football The best players in PSU's football program
Great Players in Notre Dame Football The best players in ND's football program
Great Coaches in Notre Dame Football The best coaches in any football program
President Donald J. Trump, Master Builder: Solving the Student Debt Crisis!
President Donald J. Trump, Master Builder: It's Time for Seniors to Get a Break!
President Donald J. Trump, Master Builder: Healthcare & Welfare Accountability
President Donald J. Trump, Master Builder: "Make America Great Again"
President Donald J. Trump, Master Builder: The Annual Guest Plan
Great Players in Alabama Football from Quarterbacks to offensive Linemen Greats!
Great Moments in Alabama Football AU Football from the start. This is the book.
Great Moments in Penn State Football PSU Football, start--games, coaches, players,
Great Moments in Notre Dame Football ND Football, start, games, coaches, players
Four Dollars & Sixty-Two Cents—A Christmas Story That Will Warm Your Heart!
My Red Hat Keeps Me on The Ground. Darraggh's Red Hat is magical
Seniors, Social Security & the Minimum Wage. Things seniors need to know.
How to Write Your First Book and Publish It with CreateSpace
The US Immigration Fix--It's all in here. Finally, an answer.
I had a Dream IBM Could be #1 Again The title is self-explanatory
WineDiets.Com Presents The Wine Diet Learn how to lose weight while having fun.
Wilkes-Barre, PA; Return to Glory Wilkes-Barre City's return to glory
Geoffrey Parsons' Epoch... The Land of Fair Play Better than the original.
The Bill of Rights 4 Dummmies! This is the best book to learn about your rights.
Sol Bloom's Epoch ...Story of the Constitution The best book to learn the Constitution
America 4 Dummmies! All Americans should read to learn about this great country.
The Electoral Colllege 4 Dummmies! How does it really work?
The All-Everything Machine Story about IBM's finest computer server.

Brian has written 122 books. Others can be found at amazon.com/author/brianwkelly

www.ingramcontent.com/pod-product-compliance
Lightning Source LLC
Chambersburg PA
CBHW060448170426
43199CB00011B/1130